PRINCETON ILLUS

BIRDS

OF SOUTH AMERICA
NON-PASSERINES: RHEAS TO
WOODPECKERS

PRINCETON ILLUSTRATED CHECKLISTS

BIRDS
OF SOUTH AMERICA
NON-PASSERINES: RHEAS TO
WOODPECKERS

JORGE R. RODRIGUEZ MATA,
FRANCISCO ERIZE
AND
MAURICE RUMBOLL

Princeton University Press
Princeton and Oxford

PRINCETON ILLUSTRATED CHECKLISTS

Birds of Eastern Africa, by Ber van Perlo
Birds of Southern Africa, by Ber van Perlo
Birds of Southern South America and Antarctica, by Martín R. de la Peña and Maurice Rumboll
Birds of Western and Central Africa, by Ber van Perlo
Birds of Mexico and Central America, by Ber van Perlo
Birds of South America: Non-Passerines: Rheas to Woodpeckers, by Francisco Erize, Jorge R. Rodriguez Mata, and Maurice Rumboll

We dedicate this book to the memory of Claes Olrog and Eugene Eisenman, and to our families, all of whom supported us in our task.

Published in the United States, Canada, and the Philippine Islands by
Princeton University Press
41 William Street, Princeton, New Jersey 08540

Originally published in English by HarperCollins Publishers Ltd under the title:

COLLINS FIELD GUIDE: BIRDS OF SOUTH AMERICA
Text © Jorge R. Rodriguez Mata, Francisco Erize and Maurice Rumboll, 2006
Illustrations © Jorge R. Rodriguez Mata

Library of Congress Control Number 2005936747

ISBN-13: 978-0-691-12688-3
ISBN-10: 0-691-12688-7

This book has been composed in Goudy

nathist.princeton.edu

Edited and designed by D & N Publishing, Hungerford, Berkshire
Color reproduction by Colourscan, Singapore
Printed and bound by Printing Express, Hong Kong

5 7 9 10 8 6 4

CONTENTS

ACKNOWLEDGEMENTS

Over the decades that this work has been in the making very many people have been consulted, have offered information, have given access to collections, or put facilities at our disposal, and to all of them go our most sincere thanks. Without their unstinted support things would have been much more difficult and almost certainly the work would never have seen the light of day. As time dragged by, perhaps they never believed it would get off the ground, but here it is, a monument to their kindness and generosity and unselfishness.

Many have unwittingly aided in putting this all together through their published illustrations, photographs or scientific findings found in innumerable journals, papers or articles, to say nothing of books. To these too, who might just recognise their efforts reflected in the attitude of one of the birds on one of the plates, hearty thanks indeed.
It is inevitable that many who contributed to this work are no longer with us; they are especially remembered, their memory treasured, and we are very sad that they never saw its completion.

As well as those who get special mention in the Preface, and those to whom the book is dedicated, we specially wish to thank for their contributions, support, encouragement and generosity: Peter Alden, María Julia Alsogaray, Dean Amadon, Nelly Bo, Werner Bokermann, Helen Brocklehurst, José Bronfman, John Bull, Marcelo Canevari, Pablo Canevari, Gustavo Carrizo, Aldo Chiappe, Julio Contreras, William Conway, Giovanna Crispo, Martín de la Peña, David Ewert, John Farrand, John Fitzpatrick, Fundaçao Parque Zoologico do Sao Paolo, José María Gallardo, Mike Gochfeld, Rick Hansen, Graham Harris, Helen Hayes, Andrew Johnson, Stuart Keith, Ben King, Michel and Suzanne Kleinbaum, Carlos Kovacs, Wesley Lanyon, Mary Le Croy, George Lowery Jr, Alfredo Manzino, Xavier Martini, Rodolfo Miatello, John Moroni, Norberto Müller, Tito Narosky, Jorge Navas, Allan O'Connel, Gunilla Olrog, John O'Neill, Ted Parker, Kenneth Parkes, Roger Tory Peterson, Pieter Prall, José Priore, Ivy Quspit, José Reich de Magalhaes, Bob Ridgely, Darío Rossi, Lester Short, Helmut Sick, Roberto Siri and Mrs Siri, Roberto Straneck, Arturo Tarak, Guy Tudor, Esperanza Varela, Guillermo Vasina, François Villeumier, George Watson, Yoshika Willis and Dario Yzurieta.

AUTHORS' PREFACE

This book was begun in 1970, when the British naturalist James Fisher suggested to his young Argentine friend Francisco Erize (one of us) to William (Billy) Collins as the person to undertake his dream of adding a South American bird guide to the Collins Field Guide series.

Approached by Michael Walters, of Collins Publishers, Francisco felt confident that he could get together a local team capable of carrying out such a project – provided it was limited to the non-passerine birds, since fitting all 3100 species of the South American birds in just one volume would be quite impossible. To achieve this he could count on his friend Jorge Rodriguez Mata, a talented, young, and little known bird artist, using his own extensive library and photographic archive as reference materials for the illustrations, and also on the participation of Argentina's foremost ornithologist, hero of all local bird-fans, Dr Claes Christian Olrog. Though a Swede by birth, he had immigrated to Argentina some 25 years previously and his determination to encourage people to take an interest in birds had already moved him to produce the first field guide to the birds of Argentina; later he also published a field guide to the non-passerine birds of South America. These were illustrated with his own paintings, rather crude yet not devoid of a certain charm, a sort of Douanier Rousseau among bird artists.

Despite Olrog's valuable and authoritative information and guidance, it was soon realized that the young friends were facing a much more complex task than they ever imagined. The museum specimens needed for the illustrations were scattered throughout museums of all the Americas so Jorge had to perform a lengthy pilgrimage visiting many scientific collections in Argentina and other South American countries, even burying himself in the USA for a year and a half during which time he saw very little but the collections of the American Museum of Natural History (New York) and of the National Museum (Smithsonian, Washington). In those days the information on South American birds was quite scanty, and often confusing or contradictory. South American ornithology was well behind that of other continents.

The death of Dr Olrog and the need to attend other commitments that life imposed on us, forced both of us to put this already very slow project on hold. Renewed interest by Harper Collins in this work, this time through Myles Archibald, stimulated us to revive the work and an intensive production phase ensued. For this we invited Maurice Rumboll to join us in the project. He would have the difficult task of synthesizing the enormous amount of notes gathered during Jorge's pilgrimage, into brief telegraphic texts. As a very experienced field-naturalist, teacher, nature interpreter and writer of English he was better qualified than anybody to complete, edit and put into proper English the other authors' contributions.

However, in recent years a lot more information has become available through the work of a growing legion of ornithologists focusing on the Neotropical Region. Furthermore, since the project's original start, photography took off in a big way, and good photographs of many birds which were not available before, now illustrate an enormous number of magazines and other publications. This has allowed us to clear up many doubts and facilitated the redrawing of many outlines to correct the natural postures; it has also allowed for correction of many eye, beak and leg colours. The increase in ornithological knowledge during this long gestation period forced a complex reformulation of a good deal of this work as it was nearing completion: new species had been discovered, some forms had been downgraded while others promoted to species level, all causing the early plates to be rectified, some even almost redone. Eventually, after 35 years, the ambitious goal has been reached: a book that will allow the general public to understand the rich diversity of non-passerine birds of South America. It will enable the bird-watcher or the specialist already armed with a local guide (many bird guides covering a country or a region have been produced lately) to see which are the bird's relatives over the national border and get a broader picture of this continent's feathered biodiversity.

INTRODUCTION

Because of the incredible variety of birds that live in South America and the as yet unspoilt stretches of habitat in much of the territory, there is a proliferation of observers in the many local enthusiasts and the thousands of bird-watchers who arrive each year to travel the length and breadth of the continent searching out 'hot-spots'. They are usually led by eminent field ornithologists on 'busmans holidays' or very keen and capable guides.

Bird-watching has been a free-time activity of interest to many people for centuries because birds are perhaps the most attractive life forms offered by nature. They are visible, many are colourful, they are audible in their calls and songs, they behave in interesting ways, and furthermore, they are everywhere. Some bird-watchers collect the names of species seen in a never-ending competition, with themselves as much as against others, to see the greatest number. Others simply enjoy watching activities and behaviour and are happy to spend a day by a pond, a patch of forest, a beach... Yet others are content to use the excuse of birding to spend time in a natural environment; their interest goes far beyond the feathered, to plants, mammals, insects... All interest in things natural can only lead to an appreciation of the marvels of creation and a deep and genuine concern for the conservation of nature as a whole. This last has special importance for mankind, not only for deriving pleasure from the experience, but because of the resources and services nature offers us, often not associated in our minds with our very survival. The presence or absence of certain species in nature, their growing or diminishing numbers, and this especially in birds, are indicators of alterations to habitats, climate change and global warming, rising seas, foul air, polluted waters. We must identify the susceptible species to have some gauge of the seriousness of the problem or danger, be it potential or real. The destruction of rainforests or toxic emissions from industrial plants are all reflected in the reduction of indicator species, be they animals, birds or plants, and birds, because of their visibility, are very noticeable in this respect and excellent indicators of the health of the environment, and indeed, of the planet itself.

Birds are also helpful to man in many other ways – reduction of rodent pests, control of insect plagues, pollinators of many plants and disseminators of seeds or even as watchmen against intruders; lapwings and screamers holler at any interloper; all these are aspects as important to nature as they are to us helpful.

Knowing birds, then, is a tool for environmental evaluation and guides for their identification, such as this is, are aimed at a greater and more widespread diffusion of knowledge which can be useful as well as a pleasure to all.

THE BIRDS IN THIS BOOK

It is hard not to brag when introducing the birds of this continent. Nearly one third of the 9,500 species of birds in the world are here. When Gondwana broke up some 120 million years ago and its component continents drifted away from each other, South America was a huge island. Its birds, enjoying their exclusivity, radiated to occupy all the possible niches. Further, the length of the continent, nearly 8,000km (5,000 miles), and the differences in elevation of its land made for an enormous variety of habitats. This came to an end with the connection with North America over a chain of islands (later the isthmus of Panama), but by then the continent boasted double the number of endemic families of its nearest competitor, Australia. The north-west corner of the continent is still a 'hot-spot' for speciation as populations become isolated in valleys, oases, or on mountain tops, and go their own way along the evolutionary road. Some exotics still shoulder their way in and establish themselves, but the vast majority of South American birds are exclusive to this continent.

A brief scanning of the plates herein will surely suffice to convince the reader that there are a lot of 'specials' in South America: plate after plate of gorgeous hummingbirds (there are 24 plates of these alone), the four species of seedsnipe (a peculiar endemic family), brilliant trogons, motmots, jacamars, puffbirds, six plates to illustrate the 44 species of tinamous; all families endemic to the region. Even in the families shared with other regions, the whole gamut of species is impressive. Where else could one imagine eight species of coots, many woodpeckers with the piculets taking centre stage in their variety. And many differences between the sexes, all illustrated – what a world of birds this continent really is!

Because of the geography and humankind's habit of occupying first the 'easy' lands or concentrating in towns, many areas have barely been visited and are yet to be explored, which will surely lead to further discoveries of new species of bird. A new grebe was found as recently as 1974, showy and easily seen on the open water where it lives, and not more than 200m from a much-frequented main summer tourist highway through desert steppe. More recently a new genus of peculiar owlet turned up in dense cane in the upper reaches of the cloud-forest/paramo fringe. All very exciting!

With the variety of habitats and the almost pristine nature of many of the less welcoming and hospitable habitats on the continent, discoveries of new areas and previously unknown species are likely to be mostly in forested areas where birds are heard more often than seen (hence the importance of knowing bird calls), or in isolated pockets of habitat surrounded by another and different type – an unexplored copse in a desert, for example. At the same time many new laboratory research techniques are being devised and are being applied to sorting out taxonomical conundrums with startling results. For example, the New World vultures seem not to be birds of prey at all but related to the storks. The Hoatzin, for years considered a gallinaceous-type bird, was discovered to be an aberrant cuckoo. Some families have been invalidated, some genera are recognised as families, species are lumped, others split up… one wonders where it will all end, but of course it never will as evolution (as much of birds as of our research techniques) keeps the winning post just out of sight, around the corner.

The area covered by this book is strictly South America, and not the entire Neotropics which extend up through Panama to Mexico, but includes those offshore islands which have obvious zoogeographical connections with the mainland: Trinidad, Galapagos, Falklands, Juan Fernandez, and those of the Scotia Arc which are the stepping stones to the Antarctic mainland – again ornithologically connected. Descriptions of all the 3,100 species of South American birds could never fit in a single pocket-sized volume, so here we deal only with the first 1,300 or so – the non-passerines or all orders except the passerines (perching or 'dicky' birds to some). So in the other pocket one will have to carry a regional, country or local guidebook as well to complete the information regarding the other 1,800 or so species.

When planning this book the taxonomy was based on the classic guides to the birds of South America by C. C. Olrog (1968) and Meyer de Schauensee (1966 and 1970). Because of the gestation period of this book (three and a half decades or so), revisions, validations, reorganisations and reordering of families, genera etc. have dictated reformulation of many parts as it was nearing completion. Further, the more recent availability of good photographs and the volume of field research have induced the revision of the early plates; whole genera had to be reworked. In the lack of any official check-list of the birds of South America, the complex and rather confusing panorama emerging from the wealth of new scientific papers was clarified by the *Handbook of Birds of the World* (del Hoyo *et al.*, 1992 to 2004), which was of course a basic and inordinately useful text to follow for the latest opinion on species.

Even so, on occasions we have retained what may be considered by some to be 'antiquated' names, often giving them in brackets, in deference to long-established usage and for the simple reason that in the explosion of material produced and published to satisfy demands by many research institutions for their scientists to 'publish or perish', we are distrustful of some of the changes and findings – they have a habit of changing back over time. This accounts for our not necessarily agreeing with all the lumping and splitting of species in which the latter has resulted. We hope this is understandable to most users of this guide.

While the traditional taxonomic order followed in the Handbook (del Hoyo *et al.*, 1992 to 2004) has been basically respected, we have taken the liberty to rearrange the sequence of families within the orders for practical reasons. For a final up-dating to the most recent adjustments in the scientific names we have followed *The Howard & Moore Complete Check-list of the Birds of the World* (Dickinson, ed., 2003).

The texts for each species facing the plates has been kept to a minimum for reasons of space; however, the salient details for identification are present: a brief description (though the colour plates should suffice), some indication of calls where helpful, differences between males, females, juveniles and immatures as well as morphs, habitat type, size (always tricky but comparatively useful), a small distribution map except where this is so localised (a valley, a slope etc.) that it is best detailed in the text. There is much difficulty in setting bird calls down in human terms and language, but somehow an indication of the voice should be given in any field-guide, especially where it aids in recognition of a species. Only clear and distinct calls are given, subtle variations and alarms are avoided.

The information in the distribution maps is as yet very incomplete, but the distribution shown is as known to date from available information. However, birds have wings, and the green areas marked on the maps are not cages, so birds can (and do) move out of the ranges portrayed. The measurement given for each species is from the tip of the bill to the longest tail feathers when the bird is laid out flat. This may vary markedly between sexes. Wingspan is given for certain oceanic species, but is hard to estimate in flight as there are no nearby references from which to gauge.

One section is devoted to texts on the families, with more detail given for the endemic South American families, which are perhaps generally less well known. The text includes comments on behaviour and other characteristics of each group, and also gives the number of species the family contains worldwide and in South America.

The birds are illustrated to scale in the plates, though there are vignettes of birds performing characteristic actions, or illustrating different forms or various plumages. The illustration of any species is of a typical plumage chosen from a series of museum specimens for the race concerned. Great care has been taken to show the birds in typical postures.

A small proportion of the birds herein are not residents, but migrate from northern climes. Others are accidentals, reported once or twice only; seabirds are notorious wanderers and several merely reach our waters when driven by storms and wind. Some species are thought to be extinct, others known to be so, but hope springs eternal.

No book on birds is ever final. As such, this guide will, we hope, be a sort of challenge to be supplanted over time by others who will do it better, as surely will be the case with this as with every other guide. Till then, let it stand.

ABBREVIATIONS

For reasons of space abbreviations are unavoidable but have been kept to a minimum. Nevertheless they are as obvious as they can be:

Ad – adult
br – breeding plumage
C – central
cm – centimetres
Imm – immature
Is – Island or Islands
Juv – juvenile
N, S, E, W – north, south, east and west
non-br – non-breeding plumage
R – race or subspecies
R[1] – additional race or subspecies
Sec – second
WS – wing-span
♂ – male
♀ – female

Barranquilla
Maracaibo
Caracas
VENEZUELA
Orinoco
Georgetown
Paramaribo
GUYANA
Cayenne
SURINAME
French
Guiana
Medellín
Bogotá
Puerto
Ayacucho
Cali
COLOMBIA
Galapagos
Islands
Quito
ECUADOR
Guayaquil
Japurá
Amazon
Basin
Manaus
Negro
Amazon
Belém
Fortaleza
Iquitos
Purus
Xingu
PERU
Ucayali
Trujillo
Porto
Velho
Araguaia
Tocantins
São Francisco
Recife
BRAZIL
Lima
Cusco
Lake
Titicaca
La Paz
BOLIVIA
Santa Cruz
Cuiabá
Brasília
Goiânia
Salvador
Arequipa
Sucre
Arica
Belo
Horizonte
PACIFIC
OCEAN
Antofagasta
PARAGUAY
Asunción
Curitiba
São
Paulo
Rio de
Janeiro
Salado
Islas de los
Desventurados
CHILE
ARGENTINA
Paraná
Córdoba
Uruguay
Concordia
URUGUAY
Porto Alegre
Archipiélago
Juan Fernández
Santiago
Mendoza
Buenos
Aires
Montevideo
Concepción
Neuquén
Mar del Plata
ATLANTIC
Puerto Montt
Viedma
OCEAN
Comodoro Rivadavia
Falklands-Malvinas
Stanley
Punta Arenas
Ushuaia
Isla Grande
de Tierra del Fuego
South Georgia
South Shetland
Islands
South
Sandwich
Islands
Antarctic Peninsula
South Orkney
Islands

CONSERVATION

Vast areas of the South American continent are as yet unexplored ornithologically and also retain much of their pristine qualities. But pressure from the ever-advancing "agricultural frontier" and invading livestock husbandry are having detrimental effects on the areas and the species of wildlife that live there.

It is not hunting (either commercial, or for sport or subsistence) and pesticides that most threaten the survival of species of birds, though commerce is detrimental in certain target species such as parrots. The most serious threat to all species of wildlife is the destruction or alteration of the habitat. Rainforests are felled for cattle and crops, deserts are turned green for production by irrigation, wetlands are drained, winding rivers straightened in canals, or dammed, flooding enormous areas – these are real threats. Making local residents aware of this is half the battle – henceforth they can weigh the consequences before acting to alter the natural habitat in which they live. Laying down land-use policies may help in this respect.

While the rate of destruction of the rainforests and cloud forests of South America – the most extensive in the world and home to the highest number of bird species – has been causing international concern, they are not the only biomes that are under threat. In fact, some of the most critically endangered birds in South America are the Junin Flightless Grebe of the high Andes, the Ruddy-headed Goose of Patagonia or Spix's Macaw of arid regions of Brazil, now extinct in the wild.

Most countries have systems of national parks and areas set aside for conservation, but as yet there are gaps in a comprehensive coverage to which present administrators aspire. Over time the systems may be completed , or perhaps not. Further, the commitment to running national parks as they should be managed varies from country to country, concepts change under pressure (social as well as economic), or merely by the whims and ignorance of politicians.

Political decisions are often not the wisest in terms of facing the future and complying with the Biodiversity Convention (Rio '92). The quality of management of any one of these systems has often dropped suddenly by changes in the political leadership, or by ill-advised projects of decentralization which do not take into account the lack of resources, expertise or conservation interest or understanding in the lower levels of administration. One can only hope that things will improve.

Even if this were bettered, government protected areas would not be sufficient to conserve a reasonable proportion of the continent's wildlife. It will be essential to develop schemes and a generalized conscience to encourage conservation on private lands. Such ideas are only in their infancy in most countries in South America, or do not exist at all yet. The attitude of the landowner who is willing to set aside some of his land for protection of wildlife, or the mere tolerance of nature on the part of others, may be threatened by heritage partition between generations, or the need for maximum production demanded by globalization, and by ever-increasing taxation.

Laying down land-use policies which take the environment into account might help in this direction, but they are not implemented as yet. It must not be left to National Park authorities and those of similar reserves alone to protect wildlife. This is everyone's responsibility, locals, visitors, industrialists and businessmen, politicians and officials of every branch of government. Fortunately, in every country on the continent, there are a growing number of conservation-minded people and non-governmental organizations which they join to give weight to their efforts, doing their best to raise public awareness of the value of biodiversity and the need to conserve it, through environmental education, amongst other tools. This is of crucial importance when directed at land-users and locals, as well as their children. These then can evaluate the consequences of any action that may alter the natural habitat where they live.

There are at present a number of international agreements and conventions which influence the course of events, such as the ones on trade in endangered species, world heritage sites, wetlands protection, migratory species, etc. These may be helpful in making politicians aware of the importance of these subjects in the eyes of the international community and that it may be worth considering them. It remains to be seen whether the drawing up of wise land-use plans and their implementation by the corresponding government entities will be effected soon enough to balance habitat destruction before too much of the South American wealth of wildlife is lost.

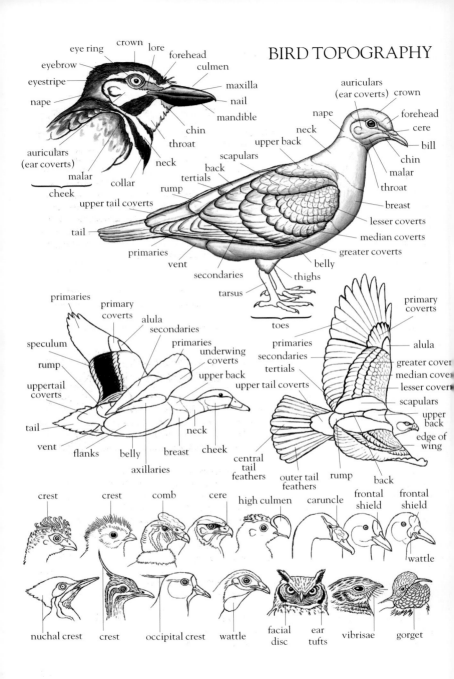

BIRD TOPOGRAPHY

eye ring
crown
lore
forehead
eyebrow
culmen
eyestripe
maxilla
nape
nail
mandible
chin
throat
auriculars
(ear coverts)
neck
malar
collar
cheek

auriculars
(ear coverts) crown
forehead
cere
nape
bill
neck
chin
upper back
malar
scapulars
throat
back
breast
tertials
rump
lesser coverts
upper tail coverts
median coverts
greater coverts
tail
belly
primaries
vent
thighs
secondaries
tarsus
toes

primaries
primary
coverts
alula
secondaries
speculum
primaries
underwing
coverts
rump
upper back
uppertail
coverts
upper tail coverts
tail
neck
vent
flanks
belly
breast
cheek
axillaries

primary
coverts
primaries
alula
secondaries
greater cover
tertials
median cove
lesser cover
scapulars
upper
back
edge of
wing
central
tail
feathers
outer tail
feathers
rump
back

crest
crest
comb
cere
high culmen
caruncle
frontal
shield
frontal
shield
wattle

nuchal crest
crest
occipital crest
wattle
facial
disc
ear
tufts
vibrisae
gorget

16

FAMILY DESCRIPTIONS

RHEIDAE – RHEAS
Order Struthioniformes

Rheas are large, social, flightless birds of the open steppe, grassland and upland plains, or thin brushland. They are the ostrich-like birds of S America, and are able to run at great speed – up to 60kph – to outdistance danger. They can weigh 20kg and more. Their huge floppy wings are simply a case for the body and are also used in escaping, being thrown to one side as the bird jinks the other way.

Males are saddled with incubation and rearing the chicks while the females are simply the egg-layers; each hen in the flock gathered and sired by the dominant territorial male lays in or near the nest he has prepared before proceeding to the territory of the next male in order of hierarchy where the same happens, thus providing clutches for each of the males in turn. After incubating the clutch of from 12 to over 30 eggs for 35–40 days, it is the male who jealously cares for the vulnerable chicks as they roam over the plains in a flock.

Mainly vegetarian, but they also take a certain quantity of insects and small vertebrates as opportunity arises.

Persecuted for their feathers to make dusters, they have been extirpated over large regions where agriculture is king. Fortunately, today both species are being farmed in a more sustainable way – herded, corralled and plucked.

The race in the high Andean plateaus may be a separate species – the Puna Rhea.

TINAMIDAE – TINAMOUS
Order Tinamiformes

An exclusively neotropical family of ground birds. Tinamous have dumpy, compact bodies, short rounded wings, small heads on a long neck (extended when alarmed) and virtually lack any tail. Bills are slightly down-curved and the strong legs generally shortish with 3 or 4 toes. Superficially they look like the partridges of the Old World but are anatomically and behaviourally very different and are related to the rheas.

Their plumage is designed to blend in with background and the vegetation, being a beautifully camouflaged mix of browns, chestnut, cinnamon, grey, buff, all with darker and lighter spotting, streaking and barring. For this reason they are much more often heard than seen. Woodland and forest species have more uniform coloration though some are barred and speckled on the lower belly and undertail. This they use to advantage while hiding: they squat and raise their rear end high to continually present a camouflaged underside to the passing potential predator, turning slowly all the while. Grassland and open country species tend to be more mottled and speckled and simply squat in the presence of danger. There are no notable differences between the sexes though females are slightly larger than males. Only in a few forest species of *Crypturellus* do females and males differ in tone and pattern of plumage. Juveniles can only be told by size as the plumages are identical to the adults'.

Tinamous are timid and shy; great walkers, they only take wing as a last resort, and that for relatively short distances. Flight is rowdy, whirring and low, wings stiffly angled downwards, like quail. They alternate this with stretches of gliding.

Their fine flesh is much sought by game-shooters; their natural predators include foxes, cats, grisons, opossums, armadillos, monkeys, peccaries, hawks, harriers, falcons, storks, larger lizards and snakes.

Their reproductive potential is great and many species bring off several broods in favourable seasons. The nest is a simple scrape lined with plant material and the occasional feather. Groups of two or three females lay for one male at a time and when his clutch is complete, lay for male number two, then three… In only very few species is reproduction achieved in pairs. Eggs are of solid colours with a high gloss finish in open country species while those of woodland and forest generally have a half-mat finish. The colours range through pale blue, lavender, cinnamon, milk chocolate, bitter chocolate, olive, reddish brown and so on. Eggs of both *Tinamotis* species have fine white speckling over the whole surface. Clutches vary between two–15 eggs. Incubation is undertaken by the male and takes between 17–22 days. The male also rears the chicks which are precocial and can fly short distances at just a few days of age.

Though terrestrial, the genus *Tinamus* sleeps perched on thickish boughs well off the ground while the rest simply scratch a small depression in the earth, sand or leaf litter for their roost.

Their food includes seeds, sprouts, buds, leaves, bulbs, fruit, insects and their grubs, snails, and some small vertebrates such as field mice, nestlings, reptiles. *Rhynchotus* species use their longish curved bills to dig for grubs and bulbs. Forest species turn over leaf litter with their bills, in search for food; they do not use their feet to scrape as do gallinaceous birds. Tinamous take dust baths and bathe during light showers.

Vocalisations are varied and consist of trilled, sharp, fluty, loud whistles, sometimes deeper and melancholy in forest species, or high-pitched in open country species. Some are short and repeated often, others long with longer intervals between calls. A knowledge of these can help in identification of the species.

These birds are found in the most varied habitats from sea-level upwards: in grassland, steppe, scrub, savannahs, woodland, forest, to high mountainsides, gorges and plateaus up to 4,500m elevation.

Tinamous are broadly divided into two groups – woodland and open country species. The first includes *Tinamus*, *Nothocercus* and *Crypturellus* while the more open country species include the genera *Rhynchotus*, *Nothura*, *Nothoprocta*, *Eudromia*, *Tinamotis* and *Taoniscus*. There are 46 species, 44 of which are found in S America.

SPHENISCIDAE – PENGUINS
Order Sphenisciformes

Perhaps the least bird-like birds, penguins are unmistakably seabirds; they are exclusively of the S hemisphere though one species is found on the Equator. Though usually thought of as being from frigid regions, a number of species are from warm temperate and even tropical climates, many are from cool temperate regions and the subantarctic, only three are strictly from the Antarctic proper.

Penguins are flightless in air but propel themselves by 'flying' through water on wings which have evolved into paddles. They are totally feathered with scale-like plumage, which is well oiled for impermeability. They also possess a thick layer of subcutaneous fat for insulation in cooler waters where they spend most of their lives. Perfectly adapted to life at sea and in the water, penguins are uncomfortable on land and walk with a waddle as they stand on short legs at the lower end of the body, which is a perfect position for their job as rudders. In a hurry to escape danger they go down onto their bellies and toboggan, using flippers and feet for propulsion.

In some species migrations are over long distances and follow the movements of their fish food. To breathe while travelling, they 'porpoise', leaping clear of the water to snatch a breath as they advance.

Both sexes incubate and rear the chicks. Rituals of courtship and pair recognition take place at the nest site. There seems to be a likelihood of pairs reforming in successive years as they meet at the previous nest-site. Penguin colonies are often noisy and smelly places.

Penguins can be divided into groups in order of size. The largest are the *Aptenodytes* (King and Emperor), large and with yellow around the head. These make no nest but carry the single egg on their feet during incubation, covering it with a fold of belly skin where the temporarily featherless and highly blood-irrigated brood-patch is located. Their diet seems to be mainly squid for which they dive to great depths.

The 'ringed' or collared penguins (*Spheniscus*) are mostly tropical though one species extends as far south as Tierra del Fuego. Because of the heat where they reproduce, nests are usually burrows which both members of the pair excavate. Small fish are their chief source of food. In this group only the Magellanic is expanding its range N and increasing in numbers.

The three long-tailed species (*Pygoscellis*) are from colder climates and one is strictly Antarctic. In the races of Gentoo, the Antarctic populations have shorter bills, an adaptation to the severity of their S breeding-grounds, as opposed to the longer bills of birds in cool temperate areas where the N populations live. These seem not to migrate and thereby provide, in their all year coming and going from the traditional sandy beaches, a sort of 'predation cushion' for the year-round breeding Kings.

Only two crested penguins (*Eudyptes*) are found on this side of the world. Both use clifftops for their huge colonies and reach these places along long-established ladder-like cuts and paths. Both species lay two eggs, but generally manage to rear only one chick.

There are 17 species, ten of which are in this region.

PODICIPEDIDAE – GREBES
Order Podicipediformes

Grebes are so well adapted to their life in and on the water that they are very clumsy in any attempt at walking. Legs are positioned far back on the body, fine for propulsion in water, like propellers on ships, but inconvenient on land where they mostly push themselves forward on their bellies. Toes are almost rigid, with stiff lobes for propelling the bird when swimming. They dive for their prey, mostly arthropods, molluscs and fish of different sizes according to seasonal abundance and the bird's own size.

Grebes only emerge from water to climb onto the floating nest or to migrate, which they do on the denser air of night. Courtship consists of some of the most spectacular 'dances' among waterbirds and ritual offering of 'presents' such as bits of waterweed. They lay up to seven eggs which they cover with the rotting vegetation on leaving the nest to feed or in the face of danger – the result is that the once pure white eggs become stained and dirty. Both sexes incubate and care for the young. Chicks leave the nest soon after hatching and accompany the parents who dive to find food for them during the first weeks of life. Chicks are conspicuously striped at first. They are carried on the parents' backs, covered for brooding by the wings. Being tied to the water, some two species on larger lakes are flightless and as a consequence severely endangered.

There are 22 species in the world, nine in S America of which one is recently extinct, one threatened, one endangered and one discovered as recently as 1974.

DIOMEDEIDAE – ALBATROSSES
Order Procellariiformes

These huge oceanic birds are mostly denizens of the S seas, nesting on oceanic islands and the subantarctic. Many have distinct juvenile and sub-adult plumages which they sport for varying periods, according to the group to which they belong. They can be divided into three basic groups: the giants, Wandering and Royal Albatrosses; the 'Mollymawks', all black-backed with varying head colours and patterns; and the Sooty Albatrosses, two species which are somewhat different from the rest in shape, having long, very narrow and angular wings and long graded tails.

Albatrosses are dynamic soarers and use the slight up-currents of air displaced by advancing waves for loft. When they gather speed, an upward loop is performed to move on or back to another wave. In still air they sit disconcertedly on the water waiting for another blow, which in these S waters is not long in coming.

All S species nest on truncated 'cones' with a scoop in the top where the single egg is laid. Both sexes take turns in incubation which lasts over 60 days. When the chick is half-grown, both parents absent themselves from the nest in search of food, when the unattended chick sits atop the nest and protects itself by squirting vomited oily mush at intruders, not without first warning by showing an extended 'grin' across the lower face.

The Sooty Albatrosses are cliff nesters while the rest prefer the flat ground on the tops. These last can walk better than petrels but must take a run to get airborne, while those near or on cliffs just jump off into the wind and are away. Sooties perform a wonderful courtship 'ballet' on the wing, perfectly mirrored movements adding grace to their spectacular flight.

Several years are spent at sea subsequent to fledging and thereafter several more in establishing a pair-bond before attempting to nest.

Food consists mainly of squid which is taken at the surface and probably during the hours of darkness, as also fish and carrion, but the Black-browed has been seen to dive for over 10 seconds after fish. Following fishing-vessels is a further form of obtaining food, sometimes in thousands as they wait for gash and offal to be thrown overboard as well as taking injured fish from the nets being hauled aboard.

There has been an alarming decline in the numbers of the Wandering Albatross as females and males split up for different feeding-grounds and the females get taken on the long-lines of tuna and other fishermen and drown. A preponderance of males does nothing for the success of pair-bonding.

There are some 14 species in the world, ten in waters adjacent to S America.

PROCELLARIIDAE –
PETRELS AND SHEARWATERS
Order Procellariiformes

A family of oceanic birds related to the albatrosses and those families that follow – all called 'tubenoses' for having their nostrils in pipes along the top of the bill either joined or paired. In the Giant Petrels the birds' size reaches something in the range of the albatrosses, and so on down the scale to the size of a dove (Prions). Sailors knew them by such names as Stinkers or Nelly, Muttonbirds, Whale-birds, Shoemaker, etc.

Gregarious nesters, they gather on islands where all but the largest species burrow into peat, scree, sand or even use cracks in cliff-faces; generally the smaller the species, the longer the burrow. Only one egg is laid and both adults do the incubating, relief at the nest taking place at dusk when avian predators such as skuas are inactive. At such times swarms of flutter-ing birds arrive from the sea and drop out of the air; a cacophonous din starts up as pairs meet in the burrows. Chicks accumulate enormous amounts of fat and by their 4th to 6th week of age are considerably larger than their parents. At this stage both parents go to sea to find food and the chick is left unguarded in the nest. For the last week before fledging the fat is convert-ed into plumage and young birds leave the colony. The exceptions are the Giant Petrels which, because of their size and powerful bills, are perfectly capable of defending the nest which is on the shingle of beaches or islets.

The inadvertent introduction of rats to many islands, usually from wrecked ships, has caused great reduction of numbers in species nesting on rat-infested islands. To combat the rat menace cats or mongooses have been released on certain islands, aggravating the effect of predation; even pigs and rabbits are destructive on these fragile sites, the first rooting out the nestlings, the latter competing for the burrows. Because of this several species are on the verge of extinction and others believed extinct.

Various groups are recognisable more by their flight patterns than by shape, size or col-oration. Shearwaters fly close to the water on their long migrations around the oceans, usually in huge loose flocks. Pterodromes or Gadfly Petrels make high loops alternating with the near-surface flight. Pintado Petrels are followers of ships; prions suddenly appear in large numbers and pass on; they are hard to tell apart but all are dove-grey with black tips to the tail.

There are 70 species in this family, 42 in the S American seas.

HYDROBATIDAE – STORM-PETRELS
Order Procellariiformes

Swallow-like in size (the largest is only 25cm) and somewhat so in appear-ance, these delicate birds are the thistledown of the oceans, blown about at the whim of the wind, appearing in numbers often at the onset of a storm (hence the name) but present in all conditions. They are even reluctant to settle on the water where they float high, so find patches of floating kelp to rest on. Their long, slender and deli-cate legs with webbed feet are of little use for propulsion on land or in the water but are used to paddle and stir up the plankton in the upper layers of the surface without alighting, in hovering flight. They feed on tiny crustaceans and other invertebrates, including squid, and small fish, though they do not disdain galley refuse from ships or even whale faeces.

Truly pelagic, they are familiar to sailors as the fluttery, tiny, dark birds which often follow their vessels. Generically mariners referred to them as Mother Carey's Chickens.

They nest in tunnels, burrows and clefts in rock which they enter and leave in darkness (with the exception of a Galapagos race) by flying skilfully in and out, to avoid predators, and where the single egg is laid which is inordinately large for the size of the bird. Both sexes take turns at incubation which, at six or seven weeks, is unusually long for such a small bird.

Of the 20 world species, 15 come within the area covered by this book.

PELECANOIDIDAE – DIVING-PETRELS
Order Procellariiformes

Three of the four species of this family are birds of the cold S seas, the exception being the Peruvian Diving-petrel in the Humboldt current up the W coast of S America. The four species are all in the same genus and are very similar and hard to tell apart though the Magellanic has a diagnostic gill-line. They tend to hang around coastal waters though some individuals or small flocks may be found at sea, far from land.

Diving petrels are dumpy and solid. Their wings must serve them for flying in air as well as propulsion under water so are shortish and broad, beaten fast in flight. In daylight hours they spend only one or two seconds at the surface to catch a breath as here they are very vulnerable to predation by the larger petrels and albatrosses. To take to the air they emerge from the sea like a little Polaris missile, flying in water and immediately converting to aerial mode.

They nest in tunnels in peat on islands or above the tree line in the scree where this exists. At the nest sites they are nocturnal to avoid predation. It is said that after abandoning the chick in the nest, at about eight weeks of age, parents moult all their flight-feathers at once and so remain flightless for a period, unique among petrels.

PHAETHONTIDAE – TROPICBIRDS
Order Pelecaniformes

Medium-sized birds with the appearance and behaviour somewhere between boobies and terns; when flying gracefully along, their main differentiating characteristic becomes evident – the two extraordinarily long central tail feathers. Tropicbirds are rarely out of tropical seas and often far from land. They are seldom found in flocks but gather at nesting sites on cliffs or flats on oceanic islands where they build no nest but lay their single egg on the rock or sand, nearly always under some protection from elements and predators. They seldom come down to the surface of the sea except to plunge after their prey – fish or squid. Weak swimmers, they float buoyantly. Occasionally they fly over to inspect passing shipping, circle once or twice and head off again. Their main enemy appears to be humans, who gather their eggs for consumption. Tail feathers are harvested by some islanders for adornments in certain regions, but these are plucked from the incubating bird which seems not to harm it.

There are three species in the world, all in S America.

PELECANIDAE – PELICANS
Order Pelecaniformes

Pelicans are enormous birds of coastal regions. They have extraordinary beaks with an elastic gular pouch used as a scoop for catching fish. Only the Brown Pelican dives to catch its food, plummeting into the sea from a height. Nesting is in large colonies, the larger species nests on the ground, lesser species nest on bushes. Usually two or three eggs are laid and both sexes incubate. Young of the ground-nesters gather in pods. When small they are fed by both parents on regurgitated liquid food dribbled into the chick's bill; later, chicks reach into the parent's throat to get their ration.

There are seven or eight species in the family, depending on the authority consulted, since some give the S American race full specific status.

SULIDAE – BOOBIES
Order Pelecaniformes

This family is only represented by boobies in S America.

Boobies (Genus *Sula*) are the more tropical versions of the gannets (Genus

Morus) of the N Atlantic, the Cape of Good Hope area and the Tasman Sea. Unlike gannets, which migrate, they are sedentary. All have conical bills and bare faces and fully webbed feet (between all four toes). The feet and bare faces are highly coloured or simply black and made great show of in courtship and pair-bonding. On long, narrow, somewhat angular wings they fly high over the sea and plunge-dive onto schools of fish which they chase underwater, sometimes to depths of up to 27m, propelled by feet and partly open wings.

They nest on inaccessible islands or cliffs or flat tops where they are out of reach of humans, of whom they seem unafraid. Their very name derives from their landing on ships and being taken by hand by hungry sailors, who credited their lack of fear as idiocy.

All but one species (from the Indian Ocean) are colonial nesters. The Peruvian is recorded in a colony of over a million pairs on an island in the Humboldt Current. The nests are built in bushes or on the ground. It seems that the frequency of nesting depends on the availability of their fish food stocks and fish displacement. Usually one egg is laid, but some species lay up to four and rear most of the chicks. In single-egg clutches the egg is incubated wrapped in the large feet, a characteristic of this and only one other family of birds – the anhingas.

There are nine species in the world of which five nest on S American offshore islands.

PHALACROCORACIDAE – CORMORANTS
Order Pelecaniformes

S America, especially in its S reaches, is generously endowed with cormorants. According to the divergent opinions of specialists there are between six and nine species involved here because of the upgrading of some of the different races of the Imperial Cormorant, but much work must be done on the systematics before a clear picture emerges. For the same reason the number of species in the world may vary from 33 to 40.

Cormorants (or shags as some would call them) are from both inland freshwater habitats and sea-coasts. All feed on fish and dive from the surface for their food. Some species often fish coordinatedly, driving schools before them and all diving at once; others fish singly. For propulsion underwater they use their totally webbed feet which are placed far back on the body and gives them an upright posture on land. Cormorants fly strongly with outstretched necks.

They nest colonially on cliffs, trees, low and/or flat-topped islands. Three or more chalky whitish eggs are laid in a nest built up of weeds and other materials – sticks, stiff moulted feathers, bones.

Plumages are the same in both sexes. Adult cormorants lack nostrils and breathe through the corners of the slightly open bill. They have bare faces and gular regions and when uncomfortably hot flutter the gular sac with beaks slightly open. Some species commonly spread their wings to dry after a period of fishing.

Nuptial plumage differs slightly from non-breeding and in some species involves a crest which is soon worn away. Also in some species a caruncle in the place of the nostrils enlarges and colours-up, this being in fact a desalination gland which eliminates much of the salt ingested with their food.

Vocalisations are piglike grunts or squeaky notes.

ANHINGIDAE – ANHINGAS
Order Pelecaniformes

Evidently related to cormorants, these share the general shape and many habits. Anhingas are but two species in the world though some specialists would have them split into more. The American species is the least salt-water of all these totipalmate families and very seldom seen even on brackish, back-of-the-beach lagoons. Overall more slender than cormorants (the Guarani indians call them the 'snake cormorant', *Mbiguá Mboí*), while fishing they often only show neck and head above the water as they swim along. Their bill is sharp and with it they spear their catch; at the surface they juggle it into position for swallowing head first. The tail is large and fan-shaped. There is a difference in plumage between the sexes.

Anhingas are usually colonial nesters but fish singly. Like cormorants, anhingas spread their wings to dry. They are often seen soaring on thermals, their long neck and tail giving them a cross-like appearance.

FREGATIDAE – FRIGATEBIRDS
Order Pelecaniformes

Pirates if ever there were, frigatebirds have perfected the art and to a certain extent live by robbing other birds of their catch in aerial persecution till, in desperation, birds with distended crops (cormorants, boobies, pelicans or gulls) or a beak full of fish, regurgitate or drop it, whereupon the frigatebird goes after the falling morsels and catches them in the air or at the water's surface, snapped up in passing flight. They can and do also catch their own food, especially flying-fish, though any floating object is tried; they also prey on nestlings in colonies of social birds and snap up baby turtles as they struggle across the beach from the nest to the safety of the sea.

They soar on coastal updrafts awaiting the return of those food-laden birds, or at sea, flying at great height to watch other species locating prey. Very long angular wings give them great manoeuvrability in the air. Tiny legs, however, are inadequate for walking on land, though they perch on slender twigs with certain ease.

Basically black and white, although the white varies with species, sex and age. Males have inflatable scarlet balloons (gular pouches) wobbled with accompanying vocalisations and trembling of their outstretched wings in their spectacular courtship. The tail is huge and deeply forked.

Nesting is on the tops of bushes or trees. A single egg is laid in a nest built by the female at a site chosen by the male, of twigs taken from the vegetation on the wing, or again, filched from other more industrious birds.

There are five species in the world, three in South America.

ARDEIDAE – HERONS AND BITTERNS
Order Ciconiiformes

All members of this family are long-necked, long-legged wading birds though some have adapted to dry uplands. They include the herons, egrets, bitterns, tiger-herons, the Boat-billed Heron and night-herons. In flight they carry their necks in a folded 'S'. The bill is straight, long and pointed. They stand on all 4 toes, the hallux being at the same level on the leg as the rest.

They have 'powder-down' patches on breast, rump and flanks which continually provide a greasy talcum with which they clean their feathers in preening.

Food items include just about anything that moves – batrachians, reptiles, insects, fish, small mammals and birds, etc. They stand or crouch motionless waiting for prey to approach (sometimes stirring it up from the bottom by motions of the feet) and strike with lightning speed, stretching out their necks like uncoiling springs to spear or snap up the victim.

Nesting is in heronries, in trees or reed-beds – sometimes huge colonies with many thousands of birds, an exciting spectacle; usually egrets compose the majority, but these colonies often include other families such as ibis and storks. Clutches are usually of three or more blue eggs.

Typical herons vary in size from the tiny Striated and Green Herons to the gigantic 1.5m (5ft) Goliath Heron of Africa. The Ardeidae are diurnal and found in temperate and tropical zones, hardly ever in cooler climates which they seem to reach only after fledging, in explosive scattering dispersions.

Egrets are all white (or have a white phase). Most sport fine plumes which decorate them in nuptial plumage, growing on the upper back. The aberrant Cattle Egret in its recently expanded distribution, lacks plumes and associates with large grazing animals which stir up the insects upon which it feeds.

Bitterns are the most cryptically coloured in browns and stripes as they blend in with the reed-beds where they live. Unlike the rest of the family some lay green eggs. Species active at night are the night-herons and the Boat-billed Heron (once in a separate family) which feed on fish and frogs.

There are 61 species in the world, 24 in S America.

CICONIIDAE – STORKS
Order Ciconiiformes

Only three of the 19 species of storks in the world are found in S America and all are white with some black. Storks are long-necked and long-legged birds of marshy areas and grasslands, though the Wood Stork prefers swamps with trees in much of its range, and the Jabiru needs isolated tall trees for nesting. The Maguari Stork is the most typical stork of the three. Its fledged juveniles are black for a few weeks after leaving the nest.

They all have large bills, huge in the Jabiru (appearing slightly upturned) and down-curved at the tip in the Wood Stork. Two species have featherless heads. Storks have no vocal chords and express themselves by castanetting the bill and throwing the head around. They also defecate on their legs to control body heat. Sometimes they are seen soaring on thermals. They tend to be solitary hunters though the Wood Stork is active in small flocks and the Jabiru often in pairs. Storks fly with neck out-stretched, legs trailing well beyond the tail. Though the Jabiru nests singly, the others are more or less colonial, the Maguari Stork using reed-beds to this purpose. All stalk through damp grassy areas and the edges of water to find their prey – virtually anything that moves, reptiles, batrachians, insects and small mammals or bird chicks.

THRESKIORNITHIDAE – IBIS AND SPOONBILLS
Order Ciconiiformes

This family of long-necked, long-legged birds includes two distinct groups – the ibis with their characteristic long, slender and down-curved bill, many species with bare faces or throats, and the unmistakable spoonbills.

Typically of wetland habitats, preferably with standing or slow-flowing water, ibis search for their food by tactile foraging, probing rapidly and repeatedly into the mud for aquatic insects, larvae, crustaceans, molluscs, small fish, tadpoles and amphibians. They also supplement their diet with a certain amount of vegetable matter and some species frequent dry grasslands as well as the preferred shallow waters.

Usually found in pairs or small flocks – some species in huge flocks – they fly to and from their roosts often a long way from feeding-grounds, in long irregular strings or V-formations, thus benefiting from aerodynamic uplift from the bird in front of them.

Both ibis and spoonbills nest in colonies in reed-beds, woods, swamps, low islands or cliff-faces. Clutch contains 3–5 eggs in the stick or reed nest.

The Roseate Spoonbill, the only spoonbill in S America, is a stunning pink bird with an inordinately shaped bill – a flat appendage which looks too large for the face – with which it scythes through the water, bill partly open to snap onto anything edible.

Of the 32 species in the world, 12 are found in S America.

PHOENICOPTERIDAE – FLAMINGOS
Order Phoenicopteriformes

Flamingos are impossible to confuse with any other bird. They are pink (grey in juveniles) and sport extremely long necks and heads which they hold extended in flight. The peculiar bill is adapted to filtering minute organisms, often from the surface cm or so of the water – usually saline. This specialised bill is worked upside down, with the maxilla immersed, the tongue doing the pumping. All along the edge are fine platelets to catch and retain the algae, diatoms and crustaceans which constitute most of the diet. They are known to stir up the mud with their webbed feet to circulate organisms buried there.

Flamingos are gregarious and social birds, always in flocks; at nesting colonies they congregate in huge numbers. Here they build up a cylindrical mud nest to about 30cm or more above the water level and there lay the one egg. Young stay in the nest for a short time, then form crèches or nurseries and keep together. Unlike other birds, flamingos are unique in that the chicks attain full plumage before completing their growth, so amongst the grey youngsters some small individuals can often be seen.

There are six species in the world, four in S America, of which two are virtually restricted to the Andean lakes.

ANHIMIDAE – SCREAMERS
Order Anseriformes

Only three species constitute this peculiarly S American family, which seems to be related to the waterfowl though there are notable differences. Like geese, they are birds of the wetlands and even of upland grasslands where they graze. However, here the similarity ends. They often perch in trees, lack webs between the three forward toes and are completely feathered, lacking featherless tracts. Under the skin of the breast they have a layer of bubbles – like bubble-wrap.

Screamers build large platform nests of floating reeds and rushes where the (usually) five creamy white eggs are laid. Chicks are covered with golden down for the first weeks of life, then turn grey. They can all swim, but jerkily and slowly.

Screamers are well named as their voices, higher pitched in males than females, are very loud and carry far. Usually they duet their calls.

Pairs seem to stick to territories year-round and unmated birds and immatures form flocks, often huge, where mate selection and battles take place. In these the carpal spurs on the leading edge of the wing come into play. The horny sheaths of these often break free and remain imbedded in the breast muscles.

On calm autumn days the Southern Screamer soars on thermals and could be mistaken for a large bird of prey but for the very audible calls.

ANATIDAE – DUCKS, GEESE AND SWANS
Order Anseriformes

These are waterbirds of varying sizes and coloration with long or longish necks, compact bodies and short legs. The three forward toes are webbed for swimming, the hind toe is short and higher up the tarsus. Bills in this family are uniquely characteristic – flat and broad, with a rounded tip terminating in a 'nail'; the sides have lamellae for filtering out their food from the water or mud. Eyes are small and tails usually graduated, often terminating in a point. Feathering is compact and waterproof. They moult all flight feathers at once which renders them flightless till they grow again, escaping danger by scooting over the water and diving. During this time males of the more colourful species assume an 'eclipse' plumage somewhat similar to females. This state can last up to 1 month. Sexes can be very similar or totally different, with colourful males. The males sometimes have protuberances or caruncles, and crests (this last present in some females). Many species have contrasting wing patterns, especially those with specula of glossy or metallic colours. Juveniles are generally like adults but duller.

Nearly all species are good flyers with rapid, strong wing-beats which are audible in some species. They move around in answer to availability of food and water conditions, arriving suddenly in large flocks, or moving away in times of drought. Many are seasonal migrants, and some arrive in S America from N America.

Food is very varied, most anatids being omnivorous, while some are basically vegetarians. Some 'bibble' at the surface or, submerging neck and head, up-end or even dive to reach their food on the bottom; others simply graze or find spilled grain in stubble fields or in the droppings of grain-fed cattle. Many species are the means of dispersal of aquatic plants by feeding on their seeds. Ducklings often chase and catch insects at the surface.

Voices are very varied: males usually have high-pitched or whistling calls while females emit rough, deeper, gruffer calls. Whistling-duck calls are particularly striking.

Most species are gregarious and only split into pairs during the nesting season. Males of some species (swans, geese, steamer-ducks) are strongly territorial. They nest midst the emergent aquatic vegetation, in grasslands or amongst rocks at varying distances from water. A few use hollow trees or holes in banks, Monk Parakeet nests or similar large stick nests (Black-bellied Tree-duck, Ashy-headed Goose, Speckled Teal, Ringed Teal, Torrent Duck, Comb Duck, Muscovy Duck and Brazilian Merganser). Nests are lined with down (except stiff-tailed diving ducks) taken from the breast of incubating birds; eggs are usually whitish to cream-coloured. Stiff-tails lay proportionately huge, rough-surfaced eggs. The clutch is of up to 17 eggs though 6–10 is more usual. The females of some species dump eggs all in one nest. In most species it is the female which incubates but in swans and whistling ducks, males share this duty. Incubation varies between 25 (Black-headed Duck) and 40 days (swans), but the Torrent Duck takes 43 days. Ducklings are precocial and covered with dense, waterproof down. They swim, dive, feed and fend for themselves within hours of hatching. Both sexes, or only the female, are in charge of raising the brood, according to the species. Adults often play the 'broken-wing' act to draw intruding or potential predators away from the brood or nest. Some of the larger species, such as the swans, pair for life. The Black-headed Duck is a parasitic breeder, laying its eggs in the nests of many other species of birds nesting in marshes.

There are 147 species in the family, 43 in S America.

CATHARTIDAE –
NEW WORLD VULTURES
Order Falconiformes

The New World vultures are placed with the birds of prey, as are the Old World vultures, but this may only be because of their apparent similarities in form and diet. Some believe that they are more closely related to the storks, and there are reasons to believe this may be so. They have no voice and express themselves corporally and with hissing, they control their temperature with defecations onto the legs. Unlike either, they have a keen sense of smell which stands them in good stead to discover the dead animals on which they feed. All but the King Vulture are basically black, all with featherless heads as befits carrion-eaters. Some are migratory, others sedentary, but all can cover great distances in displacement looking for food.

The California Condor of N America is severely endangered in the wild. Captive breeding has replaced some birds in their habitat from which they had all but vanished.

Larger species are solitary except at carcasses, while the smaller are almost gregarious and use communal roosts.

One of the largest flying birds, the Andean Condor, is of this family, with its 3m wingspan and 12kg weight. The smaller Black and Turkey Vultures are well adapted to urban settings and rubbish dumps.

Cliffs with crannies, caves, hollow trees and abandoned buildings are all nesting sites for the various species. No nest is attempted, the egg or eggs are lad directly on the ground. Both parents incubate and feed regurgitated carrion to the young. The single chick of the Condor remains in the nest for six months or more, the parents nesting every other year or so.

There are seven species in the world, six in S America.

ACCIPITRIDAE – EAGLES AND HAWKS
Order Falconiformes

This is one of the most diverse families of birds with some 217 species. In size, for example, there are some which weigh as little as 120g while others reach 8kg. It is divided into several 'groups' such as the kites, harriers, goshawks, buzzards (*Buteo* species) with the Harpy Eagle, and the booted eagles. Its members are found on all continents except the Antarctic and many show a remarkable degree of specialisation.

The larger species are mostly birds of open spaces with a wide field of view, though forest species are of necessity reduced in their field of vision.

Food is as varied as the species themselves and they obtain sustenance from just about everything between termites and carrion (insects, crustaceans, reptiles, fish, birds and mammals) but take it on the ground or from taller vegetation such as treetops. Some are indeed opportunists and do not shun anything in the animal line that is offered them. They have very keen eyesight to detect their prey, and powerful talons to snatch and hold it.

Both sexes build the stick nests in elevated positions on trees and cliffs, though the harriers nest on the ground and lay many more eggs than others of the family; indeed, some of the largest eagles lay only one egg and take so long to rear the chick that reproduction is not an annual event for them. The nests of the larger species are used year after year. Incubation takes anything between 30–60 days according to species.

Those of more temperate or tropical climates tend to be sedentary but some species migrate long distances, as is the case of Swainson's Hawk which comes to S America from N America to follow the swarms of locusts (today just grasshoppers, since locusts were eliminated in the middle of the 20th century, thereby providing a service to agriculturalists).

All species have broad or rounded wings and long tails (this with one exception – the adult Black-chested Buzzard-eagle) for soaring or for manoeuvrability in woods and thickets. Territories are not much disputed, the resident birds simply showing themselves by perching in exposed positions, sometimes calling, though this is probably for pair-bonding, certainly the case in duets.

There are 235 species worldwide, 59 in S America.

FALCONIDAE – FALCONS AND CARACARAS
Order Falconiformes

Typical species (*Falco*) in this family are diurnal predators with sharp pointed wings for aerial pursuit of their prey, but there are exceptions such as the caracaras and forest-falcons. They are usually birds of open country, sight playing a major role in finding prey. The long-tailed, round-winged forest falcons are the exception, living, as their name implies, in forests and even hunting at dusk and in the dark, finding their bird or mammal prey by sound.

The family is cosmopolitan, found on all continents except the Antarctic. Birds from cold climates migrate, some over long distances, others are sedentary. Prey varies with species, larger falcons specialising in birds, lesser species such as kestrels taking insects, reptiles and small rodents on the ground, while caracaras feed mostly on rubbish and carrion though they can on occasions catch smaller prey; *Daptrius* feeds on wasps.

Caracaras build stick nests but most of the other species use holes in trees, ledges and crannies or ledges on cliffs, woodpecker holes and even nest-boxes. Some even use other birds' nests as a platform or to enter – the Spot-winged Falconet mostly uses the enormous stick nests of Monk Parakeets. All lay 2–6 eggs, except the Laughing Falcon which lays one. Incubation takes 28–30 days and during this time the male feeds the female as she attends the eggs; after hatching, though the male does the greater part of finding food for the brood, the female helps.

There is some evidence that the caracaras, the Crested especially, are pest species where sheep-farming on extensive range is practised. They harasses the ewe in labour and attack the new-born weakling by first going for the eyes.

There are 60 species in the world, 22 in S America.

CRACIDAE – GUANS AND CHACHALACAS
Order Galliformes

An exclusively neotropical family of gallinaceous bird of sizes between a bantam and a small turkey, the curassows, chachalacas and guans are some

44 species of forests and woods. They have short and rounded wings for getting from tree to tree, though some species are not adverse to descending to the ground, as they do to gather grit or to bathe, for example. Their legs and feet are longish and strong for agile clambering through the branches of trees.

The curassows are the largest and most terrestrial of the cracids, often feeding on the ground on fallen fruit, but quickly take to the trees when startled. Their plumages are black with white or chestnut underparts, their heads ornamented with curly crests, bare skin, wattles and knobs all of bright colours which vary according to species. Most display sexual dimorphism.

More arboreal in habits and denizens of dense forests are the guans, of dark brown coloration, with bare faces and red wattles. Both sexes are the same. The outer three or four primaries on each wing are adapted for showing off and 'drumming' out their messages of love and territory. The vocalisations are quiet and merely to maintain contact with other members of the flock or the mate.

Piping-guans are the size of guans but are black with broad white patches on the wing coverts, bare faces and hanging wattles. They inhabit open woodland as well as dense forest.

Chachalacas are the smallest of the family and are feathered in different shades of browns; they are generally found in smallish flocks and are locally abundant in open woods and savannah. One cannot miss the vocalisations in the case of the chachalacas as they create a tremendous shindig at dawn, in chorus, just as the sun tops the horizon; during the day they keep silent, and repeat the performance at dusk.

All are vegetarians and feed on fruit and seeds though some animal food is taken – insects and small vertebrates – when opportunity arises. Nesting is in trees where stick nests are built by both sexes. The chicks leave the nest and follow the parents through the treetops.

Many species form flocks of up to a dozen individuals but separate out into pairs for breeding. Being excellent table-birds, they are all much hunted for food.

There are 50 species in the family, 43 in S America.

ODONTOPHORIDAE – NEW WORLD QUAILS
Order Galliformes

An exclusively New World family, Odontophoridae has only recently been separated from Phasianidae, the wide-ranging family grouping of pheasants, peacocks, partridges, Old World quails, grouse and turkeys, none of which are present in South America. Of the 32 species of New World quails, 15 inhabit this continent and all but three are of one genus. Wood-quail (*Odontophorus*) are pigeon-sized, terrestrial, gallinaceous birds of the tropical forests, unspectacular and very hard to see in such dense habitat. They are silent most of the day but vocal at dusk, emitting amazingly loud calls – one of the special evening sounds of these forests as they go to roost. They live in small flocks or family groups, scratching up the leaf litter with their feet in search of seed and fruit, probably also arthropods. Of the three other and smaller species present on the continent, the California Quail was introduced

ARAMIDAE – LIMPKIN
Order Gruiformes

The one and only member of this family is tied to aquatic habitats – it frequents marshes, swamps, roadside ditches, rice-paddies and temporary puddles, reed-beds, flooded woods and tall grass on their fringes.

The Limpkin bears a certain similarity to ibis with its dark colours, long legs and down-curved bill, broad wings, but its wing-beat is above the horizontal with a rapid up-beat (crane-like). It is found singly, in pairs or flocks (on migratory displacements), and on occasions they concentrate around abundant food.

It is a good walker and wader in open areas, though often can be seen perched on trees. When nervous it flicks its tail and throws its head forward and backwards. It takes a short run to take to the air. Loud calls are mostly at dusk and dawn, even at night, a crazy rolling cackle. Food consists of snails, bivalves, crabs, reptiles, frogs, insects, grubs and other small prey. Under their regular feeding-posts there are often piles of snail-shells.

Nests are in emergent water plants, in bushes or trees near the water, made of reeds or twigs where 5–7 violaceous brown lightly spotted eggs are laid. Incubation takes 26–28 days. Chicks soon leave the nest to follow their parents who care for them and provide food. Juveniles are duller than adults.

The Limpkin is exclusively from the New World's tropical and temperate regions.

PSOPHIIDAE – TRUMPETERS
Order Gruiformes

An endemic S American family with only three species. These are round-backed chicken-like birds of the rainforest floor that live in loose groups and roost in trees. The name is well earned as they trumpet loud deep calls, even louder when aggression between individuals is expressed. Displays involve dancing and leaping in the manner of cranes. Nesting is in hollow trees; the 6–10 round eggs are white and chicks leave the nest to be cared for by one (or both?) parents. They are patterned with stripes and spots on a black ground colour.

Trumpeters are vegetarians and eat fruit and berries, but also take insects as opportunity arises.

RALLIDAE – RAILS, COOTS, CRAKES AND GALLINULES
Order Gruiformes

Nearly all members of the Rallidae are, to a greater or lesser extent, connected with aquatic habitat, be it open water or edge of marsh. Their size varies enormously from the large wood-rails, through the more aquatic coots, to tiny crakes of the genus *Laterallus*.

Bills range from long to short, some with a frontal shield. The wings of all are rounded, heads small and necks longish. As might be expected the legs and toes are long. Most species have shortish tails which they raise to the vertical when nervous. Most are shy denizens of taller grasses, reeds and emergent waterside vegetation in which they are hard to see, though some very few species are found in dry grassland or forest. They are reluctant fliers and mostly run from danger or intruders, taking to the air only as a last resort and for short distances. The larger species are less timorous and may be seen crossing open spaces, while the smaller species are almost impossible to see or flush.

Long or migratory flights are undertaken only at night. During dry periods other aerial displacements of this nature 'follow the rain' to colonise newly or temporarily flooded areas.

The exception to the general rule are the coots which are true waterbirds and live on lakes and in open water of marshes, and are visible and often rowdy. Coots are the only members of the family with lobed toes as befits birds which spend most of their time swimming.

Gallinules are an intermediate form in the floating vegetation and edges. Coots and some gallinules have frontal shields which help in identification, and are all visibly territorial during the nesting season and chase off and battle with neighbours and intruders, scooting over the water, engaging with bill and feet which have sharp claws. At other times of the year they congregate in rafts of hundreds. Within the range of the Black-headed Duck, coot nests are very often parasitised by this duck, but only for incubation.

Though coots are basically vegetarian and feed on water plants, grass and seeds, other members of the family are truly omnivorous: adding insects and their larvae, snails, small clams, crustaceans and fish, the larger species taking frogs, small rodents, reptiles, eggs and young of other birds.

Voices vary from the crazy cackles of the wood-rails, the quieter calls of the coots and the tiny, tinny trills of small crakes. It is helpful to know the calls of the hard-to-see species as it is the best way to know of their presence. Many species duet, some are vociferous only at dawn and dusk, or even at night.

Both members of the pair are involved in construction of the nest, incubation and rearing of the precocial young. Nests are either cup-shaped, simple platforms or rafts of floating vegetation according to the group to which the species belongs. Clutches vary from 2–15 eggs though they are usually between 3–6. Egg colour varies from olive through browns to lilac, buff, cream or white, all with specking in brown, purple, blackish or rust. Incubation takes from 17–27 days, again, depending on the species. Chicks usually leave the nest within 2–4 days and henceforth follow their parents which care for them and bring them food in their bills. Practically all young are covered in black down when they hatch and have colourful designs on bill, forehead and face. When feathered the colours are duller (browns, black and grey) than those of adults, with darker bills and legs.

The family is found worldwide, there being 133 species, 47 in S America.

HELIORNITHIDAE – SUNGREBE
Order Gruiformes

The finfoots of the Old World and the Sungrebe of the New.

There are three members of this family of worldwide, disjunct distribution; the smallest species is found in S America. They are extremely shy and retiring waterbirds of tropical forest streams and lakes where they are not common, confining themselves to unmolested areas.

Sungrebes have lobed toes for swimming and a stiff tail for a rudder, and dives readily to escape. The diet is thought to include fish and other waterlife including snails, frogs, insects and their larvae. Both sexes attend the nest which is often on debris left by floods, on branches over the water or floating trunks. From 2–5 speckled eggs are laid but the rest of the breeding cycle is yet unknown.

The call of the Sungrebe is four long, low-pitched whistles.

EURYPIGIDAE – SUNBITTERN
Order Gruiformes

This distinctively patterned bird is a denizen of the waterside in forest where it stalks its prey, consisting of small riparian life, crustaceans and minnows. It occurs singly or in pairs and flies up into trees for refuge.

Birds display by opening the large rounded wings and fan tail to show a remarkable design in browns, greys, black and whitish, a position it holds for longish periods.

Nesting is in trees, a pile of decaying plant material with a scoop on the top where the two speckled eggs are laid. Both parents take turns in incubation. There is only one species in the family, exclusively S and C American.

CARIAMIDAE – SERIEMAS
Order Gruiformes

Only two species compose this exclusively S American family. They are large, long-legged ground birds that are reluctant to fly except when hotly pursued. Shy because hunted for food through the ages, they run swiftly along trails and openings in the brushland undergrowth.

Their diet is varied: they feed on anything that moves, including snakes, and a certain amount of plant material. Usually in company, either pairs or small family groups, they wander through the open woodland where they live out their lives. The larger species (Red-legged) is found in the more humid habitats while the smaller Black-legged prefers more arid and scrubby woods.

They nest off the ground, in the larger trees, where two eggs are laid, and the chicks are kept in the nest and fed by both parents. Vocalisations are like mad laughter, loud and cacophonous, often in chorus or duets.

JACANIDAE – JACANAS
Order Charadriiformes

There are eight species of this unmistakable family of birds, with enormously long toes and nails to spread their weight over an area of floating surface weed or leaves on which they live. On, under and amongst the floating vegetation they find their seed, snail, insect and crustacean diet, often lifting the edge of leaves to discover items of food.

Nests are built of floating weed in which four darkly scribbled eggs are laid. Chicks leave the nest shortly after hatching. They are tiny and helpless at hatching, as they have to learn to manage the inordinately long toes which, in the advanced stages of development of the embryo, form a sort of open basket lining the inside of the shell. If the young are too small to step across a gap in the vegetation, the adult, usually the male who undertakes the lion's share of nesting responsibilities, carries them firmly held under the wing against his flank and thus gets them across. In this situation the chicks' feet are seen dangling and exposed.

Rowdy and quarrelsome, probably polyandrous (unusual amongst birds), there is much activity, chasing, threats with contrastingly coloured wings held high and carpal spurs exposed, at places where several birds are present.

Of the 8 species that exist in the world only one is S American.

ROSTRATULIDAE – PAINTED SNIPE
Order Charadriiformes

Only two species belong to this family, one in Africa, Asia and Australia and one S of central S America. Somewhat snipe-like in general appearance, they are more brightly coloured than snipe and the bill is down-curved at the tip. They frequent the edge of marshes.

Crepuscular and nocturnal in habits, they are reclusive and hard to find during the day. Females are larger and more brightly coloured than males. When flushed they fly a short distance, legs dangling, in a wobbly and erratic way, somewhat bat-like.

Food consists mainly of earthworms and other invertebrates. The Old World species is polyandrous and males incubate and rear the young, but it appears that in the S American species incubation is the duty of the female.

HAEMATOPODIDAE –
OYSTERCATCHERS
Order Charadriiformes

Black or black and white birds of the seashore, oystercatchers have long red, knife-like laterally compressed bills for dealing with mussels and other bivalves or gastropod limpets which constitute their diet. They are paired up during the nesting season, and often in large flocks at other times. They are particularly vocal while breeding, with loud whistled peeping, piping calls in courtship, in territorial aggression and threats.

The various species have different preferences as to breeding habitat: sandy beaches, rocky coasts or even wet short grass of inland valleys where worms are the staple diet. The nest is a scrape on the sand, shingle or ground, or in a depression in rock, slightly lined with plant material in which usually three eggs are laid. Both parents incubate and rear the young.

There are 11 species worldwide, three of which are found in S America.

CHARADRIIDAE –
PLOVERS AND LAPWINGS
Order Charadriiformes

All the family except the Diademed Sandpiper-plover are birds with shortish, straight bills and longish legs. They are classed as shorebirds though several species do not know what a shore is. Wings of the lapwings are rounded and broad while those of the plovers are sharply pointed. Bills are for pecking at the surface rather than probing as in the Scolopacids, the closest related family.

These birds frequent sea and lake shores, mudflats, meadows, steppe, high mountain plateaus and even desert. They are strictly eaters of animal food: insects, worms and crustaceans.

The plovers come in two forms: from the N hemisphere and on migration the Golden and Black-bellied which return to their nesting areas sporting their colourful breeding plumages; local plovers, those resident and breeding in S America, are grey above and white beneath. All however have a noticeable bar in the wing, certain contrasts in colour of the tail (both these characteristics seen in flight) and most also have a variable breast-band or two. Colours on the head appear in nuptial plumages. Lapwings are much larger than the others and are usually pied black, white and grey, in startling patterns.

Certain S American species are the exceptions to the general rules; the Magellanic Plover scratches like a chicken to find its food, courts rather like an oystercatcher, has a crop to bring food and feed its chick at the nest site – all evidence enough for some experts that it is in fact in a family of its own. The lovely Rufous-chested Dotterel is a bird of arid steppe, and the Diademed Sandpiper-plover, as mentioned above, is exceptional in the length of its bill as also in the habitat it occupies – high Andean bogs.

34

Some of the typical plovers (*Chardrius*) paddle with one foot at a time to stir up the mud and displace little creatures it feeds on.

Nesting is on the ground, nearly all lay four eggs (three in harsher habitats) and play the 'broken wing' trick to lead intruders away from the nest or chicks which are incredibly hard to find when they squat. Highly protective of nest and chicks, lapwings are aggressive and dive-bomb intruders, screaming all the while. Incubation is from 24–30 days and both parents attend the chicks. Many species gather in great flocks for migration (their winter).

There are 67 species in the world, 16 in S America.

SCOLOPACIDAE –
SNIPE, SANDPIPERS AND RELATIVES
Order Charadriiformes

Apart from snipe and sandpipers, this family also includes godwits, curlews and such. All species have more or less long bills, in some cases very long, which also can be down-curved, slightly upturned or straight, used for probing mud and soft substrate in search of worms, crustaceans, insects and their larvae, or pecking small prey such as sand-hoppers from beaches in the case of sandpipers. They are birds of seashores, mudflats, beaches, meadows, the edge of marshes. There are aberrant members of the family, the turnstones perhaps being the most so in their gaudy pied plumage and having a shortish bill.

Most species nest above the 50°N parallel and several migrate S as far as Tierra del Fuego, covering over 16,000km each way.

They are all cryptically coloured, patterned brownish or grey above, paler or white below. Many show flashes of dark and pale bars in the wings, and the tails are often diagnostic.

Snipe perform aerial displays to claim territory and for courtship, emitting a strange drumming sound with rhythms varying with species, a sound produced not vocally but with the outer tail feathers, in shallow dives. Smaller species are collectively known as 'peeps' for their call. They are difficult to tell apart though with practice this becomes easier as one becomes familiar with calls, habitats and behaviour. The snipe and dowitchers, of which seven species are to be found in this continent, demand particular attention for identification.

They flock up for migration, though they are aggressively territorial on the nesting-grounds.

One branch of the family is the phalaropes, three species of strange, swimming waders with sufficient differences to merit, perhaps, their status as a family, which they held until recently. In the phalaropes, the female attains a colourful breeding plumage; she initiates courtship and has nothing to do with the nesting or raising of the chicks, all these chores being left to the male. They migrate at sea, in huge flocks, seldom coming to land, on a great swing which they perform over the oceans. They feed by swimming on the surface and paddling with the feet which are partly lobed for better effect, stirring up tiny plankton.

There are 86 species in the world, 36 found in S America, nearly all migratory from N America.

RECURVIROSTRIDAE –
STILTS AND AVOCETS
Order Charadriiformes

Elegant, usually gregarious, long-legged waterside birds, in S America black and white. Avocets have upcurved bills with which they sweep the surface of the water or near the bottom. Stilts have slender, straight and pointed bills for probing and picking. All feed on small aquatic or riparian organisms.

The nest is a waterside platform of vegetation, often in boggy situations to discourage access by predators. Usually four eggs are laid and incubated by both sexes. Nesting is occasionally in colonies.

Voices are sharp squeaky and high-pitched yelps.

There are four species of avocets and three stilts in the world, one of each resident in S America.

BURHINIDAE – THICK-KNEES
Order Charadriiformes

Though classed with the waders and shorebirds of damp places, S American thick-knees (also known as stone-curlews) are birds of arid country (sandy and stony plains) and active mostly at night but alert in daylight. Looking somewhat like enormous plovers, they are fast runners that feed on animal food from lizards to small invertebrates. They are scattered in pairs or flock in groups of up to 30.

The nest is an unlined scrape, usually in the shade, in which two eggs are laid. The female does most of the incubation, the male standing sentinel in the shade at a short distance. During the hours of darkness these birds are highly vocal with loud, wailing, sonorous calls dropping off at the end.

There are nine species in the world, two in S America.

THINOCORIDAE – SEEDSNIPE
Order Charadriiformes

The four species of seedsnipe are exclusively S American inhabitants of steppe and high mountain terrain. They migrate in winter, mountain species simply descending to nearby plains while the smaller species of the steppe move N.

Seedsnipe are unlike any other shorebirds in their diet which is totally vegetarian, to which end the bills are short and sparrow-like. The short legs give them a dovelike appearance in their movements.

They are usually found in small flocks or family groups, or in pairs when nesting.

The nest is a scrape on the ground with scarcely any lining; three or four eggs are laid and these are almost totally buried in the substrate which keeps them warm when the bird is off feeding. It seems to be only the female that incubates.

Voices are sonorous and deep, rhythmical two- or three-syllabled, rolling variations on 'cor' or 'caw'.

CHIONIDIDAE – SHEATHBILLS
Order Charadriiformes

Giving the lie to their peaceful, unblemished, totally innocent appearance, sheathbills are in fact bold scavengers, hanging around the periphery of colonial sea-mammals and birds where they filch unattended eggs and small chicks as well as performing the undertaker's and dustman's jobs. They also become beachcombers out of the breeding season. In the presence of humans they are unafraid and curious.

Though nesting only in the Antarctic and subantarctic regions, there are non-breeding populations on the S shores of continental and island S America. They nest in protected nooks and crannies (behind the seat in an abandoned lavatory in a former scientific station was an apt site) and two or three whitish eggs marked brown are laid.

There are two species worldwide, one of which is found in southern S America.

STERCORARIIDAE – SKUAS AND JAEGERS
Order Charadriiformes

Skuas are like big brown gulls with a white patch near the tip of each wing and smaller but stronger bills for predation on other and colonial seabirds such as terns, penguins, gulls and cormorants. During the nesting season they are found on the periphery of colonies of such and feed on stolen eggs and chicks.

Their nest is a lined scrape where two or three large olive eggs with black and brown markings are laid. In defence of the nest skuas dive at intruders to drive them off, even coming into contact by striking with the leading edge of the wing.

There is confusion and lack of agreement as to the species, some authorities believing them to be but one or two, others splitting them up into many species. Out of the nesting season they cover vast distances over the oceans, and birds ringed in S populations (or species) are often found off NE N America.

Jaegers are more slender and vary in their plumage from having white underparts, to very dark or even barred in juveniles. Mostly they can be identified by the differing central tail feathers but these are moulted on migration and so are missing for a time. They nest in Arctic regions and migrate at sea or in coastal waters, following the migrations of terns. From these they obtain their food by piracy, harassing them; to escape, the terns give up their catch which the jaegers then feed on.

All species of this family are found in S America, some merely as migrants.

LARIDAE – GULLS
Order Charadriiformes

Gulls are coastal or inland birds. Mostly black, white and grey, (though the young of many species show varying degreed of browns), and web-footed. They are often associated with man and have become scavengers in all harbours and around shipping near coasts but not far out at sea. Dumps are especially attractive to many species where they feed on garbage. Some species live by this alone, though others do in fact take live prey of smaller crustaceans, fish and other organisms, even eggs of other species. Mostly they wait on shores for the sea to offer up morsels. In the last 30 years Kelp Gulls in S areas have learned to take mussels, fly up to a height and drop them on hard surfaces such as the pavement of coast-hugging roads to get at the tender insides. This was first reported in the Falklands in the 1960s but is now done by birds all along the Patagonian coast.

Gulls are gregarious and colonial nesters, forming their colonies on coastal headlands and islands, both on flat ground and, in some species, cliffs. In the case of freshwater species, colonies are in reed-beds or on lake shores. The Grey Gull nests well inland in the high Andean desert, singly. Eggs are typically speckled dark on a greenish, brown or grey base colour.

Many gulls have three or four juvenile and immature plumages between fledging and the adult plumage. They migrate up and down the coasts but are seldom pelagic. They fly with constant wing-beats which differentiates them from the albatrosses that may be found with them in S regions, when relative size is hard to gauge.

This family used to include the terns. There are 51 species in the world, 14 in S America.

STERNIDAE – TERNS
Order Charadriiformes

Once included in the family of gulls, terns now are thought to be a separate taxon. Slender birds with narrow wings and often long tails, sharp bills and weak legs, terns are fishers that catch their food by diving on fish when these are near the surface. There are some species from freshwater habitats but most are sea and coastal birds.

They are gregarious and nest colonially. These nesting aggregations are on unmolested headlands and flat-topped islands and are particularly prone to being abandoned in the early stages of egg-laying and incubation by any molestation. The nest is a scrape with a plant material lining. The normal clutch is three or four eggs. Around colonies, terns are vociferous at any intrusion and the screaming calls emitted by thousands of birds, together with their dive-bombing, are enough to drive away the less determined visitors.

Most terns have breeding and non-breeding plumages as well as juvenile and immature. Many species are very similar which makes identification difficult, but the breeding or non-breeding plumages in their respective summers and winters will facilitate this recognition.

The Arctic Tern performs one of the most remarkable migrations: a huge figure-of-eight through the whole of the Atlantic, reaching Antarctic regions at the height of S summer. This migration is attended by piratical jaegers all the way.

There are 44 species of terns in the world, 24 found within the scope of this book.

RHYNCHOPIDAE – SKIMMERS
Order Charadriiformes

Somewhat resembling terns and probably closely related, to the point that some consider it an aberrant tern, the skimmers' main characteristic is the protruding mandible which is knife-like and used in fishing. To feed, the skimmer flies low at the surface of the water with the tip of its mandible immersed, slicing the water. When contact is made with a fish at the surface the bill clamps shut, the fish is immediately lifted out of the water and swallowed.

Of the three species in the world, only one is found in S America.

COLUMBIDAE – PIGEONS AND DOVES
Order Columbiformes

Pigeons and doves have thin, short bills with a fleshy base and prominent cere which extends to include the nostrils. They are small headed, robust, and have well-developed wings for fast flight on strong wing-beats. On taking flight they make a clatter with the wings. Tails are rounded or square, some pointed. They are densely feathered but feathers drop out easily as a defence against predators. Colours are mostly greys and browns, chestnut or vinaceous, sometimes with a sheen on the hind-neck. Species from arid regions are more modestly coloured and somewhat cryptically so, while forest species have more colour and contrasts. Sexes are the same in most species; male are a little bigger and slightly brighter in coloration. In *Claravis*, some *Geotrygon*, some *Columbina* and the Scaled Pigeon there is a notable difference between the sexes.

When nervous they throw their head forward. Generally they are good walkers taking short steps in search of their food – seed, grain and small fruit. They drink in a characteristic way by submerging the bill and sucking up water. Many species are gregarious, some forming flocks of thousands of birds. During the nesting season they form isolated pairs though some species seem almost colonial. The 'dove of peace' is a misnomer as they are aggressive and querulous and fight fiercely with the bill and with wing-slapping. Males perform showy courtships: following the female, they inflate their neck and partly open their wings and tail while they bow and coo. There is mutual preening and what might be described as kissing. Males of some species make territorial flights with clapping wings on the ascent, followed by a gliding descent on wings held stiffly at different angles according to species.

Nests are rudimentary platforms of twigs through which the eggs may usually be seen from below. Some species (*Metriopelia* ground-doves and the Eared Dove) can nest on the ground. Clutches are one or two white, creamy or buff oval eggs, incubated by both sexes. Incubation takes 16–19 (*Columba*), 14 (*Zenaida* and *Leptotila*), 12–13 for Ground-doves and 11 days for the Ruddy Quail-dove, followed by 11 days to fledging, though this is uncommonly short, most requiring about 15. The nestlings are fed by regurgitation of a 'milk' secreted by the adults' crop. When food is abundant several clutches may be brought off in a year, even into winter.

Some open-country species are benefited by the advance of the agricultural 'frontier' as forest and woodland are cleared. The availability of food from agriculture and in stubble fields has allowed species like the Picazuro and the Spot-winged Pigeons to become very abundant and extend their range. An extreme case is that of the Eared Dove which in certain areas has populations of several million birds. Their mass movements in NE Brazil are famous. Some species have daily flight-patterns between roosts and feeding areas.

The Rock Dove is perhaps the best known species of bird in the world. From time immemorial it has been bred and domesticated, but is also free-living and associated with man in urban situations practically all over the world.

The family is cosmopolitan with 309 species, 48 of which are in S America.

PSITTACIDAE – PARROTS, MACAWS, PARAKEETS AND PARROTLETS
Order Psittaciformes

Noisy arboreal birds which are mostly green. They vary in size from the enormous macaws of over 1m in length to the sparrow-sized parrotlets. Their bills are characteristically strong and hooked, designed to cut and crush nuts, seeds and other fruit, flowers, buds and sprouts. Legs are very short, two toes forwards and two backward which are handy to hold food while they feed, or to climb through the vegetation, when they also use the bill as a 3rd hold. They can even hang for periods in acrobatic movements.

The plumage is compact and attractive, combining green with other colours such as red, orange, yellow, blue or black. Few species show sexual dimorphism. With a few exceptions juveniles are like adults but duller in colour and design. Wings vary from long and pointed to short and rounded as also do tails, according to the genus. They fly fast, continually beating their wings which are at an angle below the horizontal.

Gregarious, they are often found in noisy flocks or pairs flying over the canopy of forest or woods. Daily flights are between roosts and feeding areas. They follow flowering, seeding and fruiting cycles and visit plantations and crops. Pairs are stable and keep to the area near the nest during the breeding season. Though rowdy in flight, when feeding or resting in trees they are silent and are camouflaged in the foliage.

Courtship consists of mutual preening, billing and tendernesses, with varied vocalisations. They nest in hollows in trees, in palms, banks, arboreal termite nests, woodpecker holes, with little or no material to line the nest chamber. Only the Monk Parakeets build a nest with sticks, which is communal with several entrances, 1 per pair. This nest is used throughout the year and, as more pairs join, it grows over time into a huge somewhat cylindrical or spherical edifice, high in tall trees, on electricity pylons and other man-made towers. Eggs are white and somewhat rounded. Chicks are altricial and fed on regurgitated food and a secretion from the adults' crop.

Many species in this family are able to imitate human language and are easy to keep in captivity. This, together with their attractive plumage and personalities, make them popular pets generating an uncontrolled illegal trade, the prime reason for the extinction of some species, endangering others; this threat is added to yet another – the destruction of their habitat. At least nine species and eight races have become extinct since 1600.

There are 332 species in the family, distributed in forests and woods throughout the world's tropical and temperate zones, though some species are denizens of open areas and mountains; 121 species are present in S America.

CUCULIDAE – CUCKOOS
Order Cuculiformes

Typical cuckoos have strong bills which are somewhat curved; they have elongated bodies and long, graduated tails, short legs (except ground-cuckoos – *Neomorphus* – which are terrestrial) with two toes forward and two back. They are mostly modestly coloured with browns, greys, black, cream, cinnamon and white predominating. Sexes are similar and juveniles resemble adults but are duller.

Cuckoos of the genus *Coccyzus* are usually arboreal and solitary, jumping with agility from branch to branch, without using their wings. They are shy and hide in the more dense vegetation. Their flight is erratic and fairly fast, especially those species which migrate. They are champion eaters of caterpillars and grubs.

The Striped Cuckoo and both the *Dromococcyx* species are very hard to see as they live in the densest foliage, as also are the ground-cuckoos which live on the forest floor. Usually they are first detected by their calls.

Anis and the Guira Cuckoo are sociable and are found in small flocks. They are visible as they perch in open situations on the edge of woods and forest. Their flight is slow, alternating flapping with gliding in irregular follow-the-leader formation, calling as they go. When cold they often bunch up on a single branch for warmth to soak up the sun on their sparsely-feathered backs. They are often seen searching for their food on the ground: fruit, insects, small vertebrates such as rodents, lizards, frogs, nestlings of other birds and their eggs, grubs, while some forest species are known to follow the marches of army ants to catch what is flushed. They also frequent grassland fires for a similar reason.

The cuckoo of Europe is famous as a parasitic nester but this is not the case with nearly all the New World species – only the Striped Cuckoo and the two *Dromococcyx* species practise this method. Most nests are low in dense vegetation, a simple platform of twigs lined with lichens and leaves. Anis and the Guira Cuckoo are disorderly and build big, deep communal nests low in the foliage. Several females lay in it and there can be over 20 eggs in the nest. Chicks can leave the nest at seven days, unable to fly. The parasitic species lay dull white eggs with dark brown or rusty spotting, mainly in nests of Furnariids and tyrants. The parasitic Striped Cuckoo's egg has a very short incubation and hatches before or together with the hosts' eggs. The chick kills its adoptive nestmates and throws them out of the nest. Thus, alone, it gets all the attention and food from its unwitting smaller foster-parents. It leaves the nest at the tender age of about 18 days, before it can fly, scrambling agilely after its deluded 'parents'.

Species of open country are benefited by increasing deforestation while those of forests and woods are thus ever more restricted in their habitat.

The family is found worldwide and there are 136 species, 23 in S America.

OPISTHOCOMIDAE – HOATZIN
Order Opisthocomiformes

The only species of this family and order is exclusively neotropical and has, over the years, been difficult to classify because of its peculiarities. Some studies would relate it to the Galliform birds (by its inmunological and feather structure) but others (on proteins in egg-white) would have it close to the Anis and the Guira Cuckoo, this last being somewhat similar in outward appearance to the Hoatzin. However, it also bears a certain resemblance to what we imagine *Archaeopteryx* to have looked like, even to the presence of a claw on the leading edge of the wing which young Hoatzins possess.

The sexes are the same, with short bill and long untidy crest. Plumage is lax, wings large and often droop, hanging from the gaunt body. It moves clumsily from branch to branch, wings half open as if losing its balance. It is even awkward in flight and only takes wing over short distances.

Its voice is strange and does not seem to belong to any bird. They live in sedentary groups in trees and bushes at the edge of water. Food consists of leaves, sprouts, flowers and fruit. To cope with this diet it has a peculiar and very large double crop to digest the hard and caustic leaves, most of which have an unpleasant odour; the Hoatzin itself exudes a disagreeable smell. Perhaps for this reason it has few predators and is extremely abundant.

Nests, which are placed in the branches near or over the water, are a platform of twigs. Breeding is possibly polygamous, mating indiscriminate: all group members incubate and attend the nestlings. The unique claw which the young possess is for climbing through the branches; sometimes they hang there by this alone. In extreme danger they drop into the water, swim and even dive to escape (though sometimes piranhas take them). Panic over, they climb back to the nest. This behaviour of leaving the nest in the face of danger is shared by the Anis and the Guira Cuckoo. On moulting into the definitive plumage their claws disappear.

TYTONIDAE – BARN OWLS
Order Strigiformes

Barn Owls differ from typical owls (Strigidae) so slightly that many believe they are one family. The facial disk is heart-shaped – somewhat like a monkey, with blackish eyes. They also have unusually long legs for an owl, longer than the tail, and feathered down to the toes. A comb-like serration on the claw of the middle toe is a characteristic shared with some nightjars and herons.

The Barn Owl is cosmopolitan and often associated with humans by its habit of occupying barn lofts, belfries and other quiet buildings for nesting. The others of the family are grassland, woodland or forest birds, nesting on the ground, but the typical and cosmopolitan species may once have nested in hollow trees, crannies in cliffs and even used old hawk nests. From 3–6 round white eggs are laid on the floor, the number answering to the availability of rodents. Hatching is staggered as the female begins incubation with the 1st egg. Only the female incubates, the male providing her with food. Owlets hatch at intervals of days, so the first has an advantage and is the most likely to survive.

Mouser supreme, it is seldom seen before late dusk, preferring darkness, though voices are often heard coming from the roost earlier. It hunts by sound and can capture a moving vole in total darkness, using the face-disk as a parabola to funnel sound to its ears.

Calls of the S American form include a long shushing, a long clickety call and very occasionally a scream.

There are 16 species in the world, but only one in S America.

STRIGIDAE – TYPICAL OWLS
Order Strigiformes

Much the larger of the two families of owl, this contains some 171 species in 24 genera, 33 species in S America. Like the above, typical owls have frontal eyes, a facial disk of fine feathers, the ability to turn the head 180° and soft plumage for soundless flight. Most are variously streaked, speckled and barred in cryptic brown, buff and pale coloration to resemble lichens or bark, which makes them hard to find in tree roosts.

Should they be active in daylight, small birds will certainly mob any owl on the move and drive it away.

Owls come in a enormous variety of sizes from the huge Eagle Owl to the tiny Elf Owl. They hunt in various ways, from pouncing from a perch to dropping onto prey from the air.

Widely distributed from the Arctic to cold S climes, they occupy a great variety of habitats from tundra to high mountains, grasslands, deserts, woods and forest. Their habitual roosts and nesting sites can be located by the presence of 'pellets', compact capsules of regurgitated indigestible materials such as hair, feathers, bones and the harder parts of the exoskeleton of insects. There are even two species that feed mainly on fish. A few owls are diurnal as well as nocturnal, especially the Burrowing Owl of grasslands and arid habitats. The tiny *Glaucidium* are all found active during daylight hours, mostly detected by the attention-calling mobbing passerines.

Nests are mostly in hollow trees and such places though several species nest on the ground or in trees. Eggs of all species are white and very spherical; the clutch size simply reflects the abundance of food resources at the time. Staggered hatching usually occurs which means that the last of the brood may not make it to fledging should resources diminish.

Voices include the 'hooting' calls always associated with owls, but also whistles, screeches, wails, trills and 'chatter'.

STEATORNITHIDAE – OILBIRD
Order Caprimulgiformes

The only species in this family is behaviourally and ecologically very different from the nightjars which are also in the order. The bill is strong and hooked; it lives in caves and uses echolocation (audible to the human ear) for flying and navigating in the total darkness of these caves; the legs are extremely weak, and no use for perching. It can cling to rock walls and squats on its nest. The diet is fruit (especially of palms), for which Oilbirds travel far over the forest. This they do by sight and smell. They pluck the fruit from the trees while flying. The pulp is digested, the hard kernel and seed regurgitated.

Oilbird calls consist of wails, croaks and screams, over and above the clicks used for echolocation.

Nests are in the caves and serve as roosts year-round for the pair which is permanent. Up to four white eggs are laid at long intervals between each, but incubation starts with the first. Chicks develop slowly and before fledging become extremely fat (hence the name), weighing almost twice as much as the parents. They slim down while redirecting the resources into adult plumage, possibly six months after the 1st egg was laid.

NYCTIBIIDAE – POTOOS
Order Caprimulgiformes

A family of five species which are exclusively from warmer climes of C and S America. They are all forest birds though some species, notably the Common Potoo, prefer the less dense areas and even frequent plantations. They differ from the Caprimulgidae in being totally arboreal and perching upright during daylight hours on some snag to look like the continuation of that broken branch, to which purpose their superbly camouflaged plumage serves them well. They do not have rictal bristles and the bill is notably down-curved at the tip.

Potoos are insectivorous and sally from perches to snap up passing insects.

They do not build nests, but carefully lay the single egg on the irregularities of a broken-off branch or bark where it is incubated by both sexes. Chicks are white at first, during which period they are carefully brooded and hidden by the attending adult, but when camouflaged plumage is attained they sit alone on their bough and, like the adults, simulate being the end of a snag.

CAPRIMULGIDAE –
NIGHTJARS AND NIGHTHAWKS
Order Caprimulgiformes

Cosmopolitan but for in New Zealand and on oceanic islands, some 89 species compose this family of nocturnal insectivorous birds that catch their prey on the wing in swallow-like flight. Their legs are weak and tiny. They sit on the ground or on branches – even cables – during daylight hours and flush only as a last resort. Their camouflaged plumage makes them very hard to detect among the leaf-litter where they are wont to roost and nest. They have comb-like serrations on the middle toe which is perhaps used in preening the feathers of the head and neck.

Clutch size is one or two eggs, usually wonderfully camouflaged in the leaf-litter. Nighthawks tend to nest on horizontal branches. No nest is built and species that nest on the ground in effect roll the eggs slightly each time they land to incubate, so the site moves appreciably over the incubation period. They are also known to deliberately move the egg, held in the bill, when frequently disturbed. Females incubate during daylight but males relieve them at the peak feeding times of dawn and dusk.

They are hard to see well and often one depends more on the calls for identification than on the fleeting glimpses; even in the beam of a torch where they are dazzled into immobility, they show few of the field marks essential for this. Many species have white bands on the primaries which are shown only in flight, but these are often lacking or brownish in the female, and some sport long to enormously long tails or peculiar pennant flight feathers. Nightjars call while perched but nighthawks call on the wing.

Of this family it is known that one species hibernates in the strict sense of the word; with lowered metabolism it sleeps over winter in some nook or cranny. Others from more temperate climes migrate, while the tropical species are thought to be sedentary.

While nighthawks are swift-like and spend long periods on the wing hawking flying insects, nightjars are wont to sally from lookouts, usually on the ground, with a fine field of view, such as a roadside. Here their eyes shine red in the beam of cars' headlights, and there are many road-kill victims.

There are 29 species in S America, and these include some spectacularly plumed females.

APODIDAE – SWIFTS
Order Apodiformes

Swifts are the birds most adapted to a life on the wing and spend the greater part of their life flying. They have short and dense feathering and an aerodynamic body-shape that has evolved for fast and erratic flight. This consists mostly of rapid wing-beats with brief darting glides. A member of this family is, according to some, the fastest being on earth, challenging the Peregrine Falcon. They do nearly everything on the wing: feed, drink, copulate and snooze. They use thermals to rise to great heights, right out of sight. They are gregarious and often form great flocks, and only come to earth to roost or attend the nest. In flight they call shrilly, with high-pitched screeches and gurgles. Swifts are modestly dark coloured, most being sooty blackish or blackish brown, sometimes with white. Sexes are alike. Some species are very difficult or impossible to identify in the field because of their close similarities; behaviour and calls can be of great help here.

Swifts are superficially like swallows but their wings are narrower, longer, and swept backwards, and normally they fly much faster and with more flapping than swallows. Unlike swallows, swifts are incapable of perching on twigs, wires and such, or even on the ground. Their extremely short legs (a-podidae means legless) and feet have four weak toes pointing forward with strong curved claws adapted for hanging from vertical surfaces. Tail feathers are stiff and the shafts jut beyond the vanes to serve as a support. They are often found around rock-faces or cliffs, waterfalls, big caves, hollow trees, palm trees, wells, chimneys, and other similar structures built by humans. If they ever end up on the ground it is extremely difficult and often impossible for them to get back into the air. To drink they swoop over the surface of water.

They have large dark eyes set somewhat forward-looking and the bill is minute but the gape is huge, a sort of 'funnel' to scoop up insects in flight. They consume enormous numbers of insects and are therefore our benefactors.

The nest is small and cup-shaped and stuck to or on ledges, or closed with an entrance from below, adhering to a palm frond (*Tachornis*). It is made of twigs, mosses and feathers, all pasted together with mud and saliva. To feed the young, parents collect insects and cache them in a gular pouch under the tongue. Breeding occurs during the rainy season when insects abound.

Swifts are principally from tropical and subtropical regions where they can obtain their food throughout the year; those populations from more temperate climes fly tropicwards as winter approaches. Swifts from the mountains perform altitudinal migrations in due season. Out of the breeding season they sometimes abandon the area and travel long distances. Some N American species reach S America. The more gregarious genera such as *Sterptoprogne* often roost in big caves, hundreds or even thousands of individuals at a time. The accumulation of their dropping is so great that in some places it is used as fertiliser. The famous Birds' Nest Soup of oriental cuisine is in fact that of a species of swift which makes the nest almost exclusively of its saliva.

In S America there are four main groups: large swifts (*Streptoprocne*), medium-sized swifts (*Cypseloides*), small swifts (*Chaetura*) and swifts with long, forked tails (*Aeronautes*, *Panyptila*, *Micropanyptila* and *Reinarda*). The family is practically world-wide. Of the 92 species, 31 live in S America.

TROCHILIDAE – HUMMINGBIRDS
Order Apodiformes

This family is exclusive to the New World but the great majority are S American birds – the jewels of the forests and woods, of shimmering colours and strange life-styles. Theirs, and theirs only, is the capacity for flying 'on the spot', reversing and shooting away at up to 70kph. This acrobatic flight has evolved for sipping nectar – their main food – from flowers. To this end they are provided with long slender bills for probing into the depths of flowers, and a 'hollow' tongue for sucking up the juices. Some species are tied by the shape of their bill to specific plants – a sicklebill to turn some 'impossible' corner, a swordbill to reach the depths of very long corollas of tube-like flowers, even one with a sharp upturned bill. As flower visitors they are important pollinators. In hovering before a flower they perform a peculiar figure-of-eight wing-beat.

Hummingbirds are generally tiny though one, the Giant, is the size of a thrush. They perform aerial displays for courtship. Males establish a feeding territory to which females come for food and mating. That is the only effort males put into the process of reproduction; females build the eggcup-shaped nest, lay two white eggs and raise the chicks.

Though mostly green, hummingbirds show a great variety of brightly contrasting patches of reds and orange, yellow, blues, pinks, with tufts on throat, double crests, strange tails, ruffs and much more.

Though mainly birds of forest habitats, they are also found in woods, in high mountains, marshes, oases in deserts and elsewhere.

There are some 323 species in the world, 246 in S America.

TROGONIDAE –
TROGONS AND QUETZALS
Order Trogoniformes

This is a family unique in its order and distributed in Africa (three species) and Asia (12 species), while the rest are from the New World, a good proportion of the 39 worldwide species being found in S America. They are birds of forests in the tropics and subtropics, some living up to 4,300m-high in the Andes.

The family includes the quetzals which are candidates for the most gorgeous birds in the world, but trogons proper are lovely also in a quieter way. They are splendidly attired in deep shining colours on the upperparts and breast, brilliantly contrasting with yellows, pinks and scarlet on the lower underparts; females are duller. They hold themselves almost erect and somewhat hunched with tail held vertically, showing different amounts of white pattern on the underside. Though they perch in clearings and are vociferous, they are hard to see in the vegetation because they keep still for minutes at a time and their calls are somewhat ventriloqual. Perched thus, trogons only move their head slowly to search for insects which constitute part of their diet in the neotropics; the Asian species are totally insectivorous. They snap up insects on the wing or pick them off the vegetation in flight. Berries constitute the rest of their intake which they pick off fruiting trees, again in flight. It seems that to this end they have serrations on the cutting edge of the bill, absent in Asian species.

The legs of trogons are of little help except for perching – small and weak, with their own particular arrangement of toes one and two backwards, three and four forwards (in other families of birds this arrangement is achieved with one and four reversed, two and three forward).

Trogons are hole-nesters but, with bills unsuitable for hollowing tree trunks, they select rotten stumps especially of the tree-nettle type. Some species favour termite or paper-wasp nests, eating all the wasps first, then gorging on the larvae. Both adults incubate the 2–4 whitish or pale eggs.

ALCEDINIDAE – KINGFISHERS
Order Coraciiformes

This is certainly not the kingfisher continent. Of the 92 species in the world only six are found in S America. These six are all true kingfishers in that they would disdain food of any but aquatic origin – others in Africa, Australia and Asia are predominantly insectivorous.

All are large-headed with proportionately long, pointed bills, tiny legs and feet, these with the three forward-pointing toes joined for a third of their length. Several of the S American species have erectile crests which add to the size of the head.

The species covered here are mostly denizens of fresh water though they are sometimes on fjordland sea-coast and saline lagoons where they surely take other prey than fish – crustaceans, tadpoles and insect larvae have been recorded in their diets. They usually fish from a perch by, or over the water, from which they spot their prey and dart straight at it to catch it firmly in the bill, 'fly' to the surface using their wings and straight back to the perch where the minnow is processed – stunned by whacking it against the branch, juggled till the head is pointing towards the gape, and swallowed.

Nests are in holes in earth banks, 1–3m in length, at the end of which there is a chamber where the 5–10 roundish white eggs are laid. No lining is provided but when the young are being fed, a carpet of fish bones and scales accumulates. Sheaths covering the feathers sprouting on the nestlings remain till just before fledging, giving the young a 'hedgehog' appearance.

Calls in the larger species are rattled, or squeaky screams in the smaller versions and almost clicking noises in the tiny ones.

They fly straight and fast just above the surface of the water, though the larger species fly high, calling all the time as they follow the course of the river.

MOMOTIDAE – MOTMOTS
Order Coraciiformes

Forest birds with long tails, often ending in 'racquets' at the tip of the central tail feathers (except one species), the naked part of the barb often being purposefully stripped of vanes by the bird itself. Some populations or individuals do not perform this 'beautification', having a completely vaned tail. Bills are strong and somewhat down-curved with a serrate cutting edge. Motmots are large-headed, short-necked and somewhat long-bodied, with very short legs and small feet, three toes forward, one back;

the two outer fore-toes are joined. Their short, rounded wings are an adaptation to flight through forest vegetation. Sexes are similar, with attractive colours, green dominating in combination with rufous, bright blue and black.

They are shy and very hard to see. They perch amidst foliage at low or medium height and remain immobile for long periods. When alarmed or attentive they move the tail from side to side like a pendulum. Motmots fly only short distances, and are solitary or in pairs. Often the call is the only indication of their presence.

Food consists of beetles, dragonflies, butterflies and other arthropods, and small vertebrates such as frogs, lizards, eggs and nestlings. They can take their prey from the floor by stirring up leaf-litter, off the vegetation, or capture it in flight, in this case returning to the same perch where they bang it on the branch to kill or soften it before swallowing. They also feed on a variety of fruits and, like toucans, disperse the seed through the forest in their faeces. They are known to follow columns of army ants to snap up anything that flees.

Calls are deep, hollow notes, mostly heard at dawn and dusk. They duet during courtship or upon meeting up as a way of reaffirming territorial rights or the pair bond. Pairs stay together year-round. Usually they hunt separately though keep contact through vocalisations.

Nests are burrows in the ground or into banks, up to 2m long, in the former with two exits. Both sexes dig, chipping away with bills and shooting loose material out with the feet. Nests are seldom reused and the construction takes several weeks. This is done long before the nesting season, the rainy seasons being preferred because of the soft earth. Clutch size is 3–5 (rarely two or six) white, almost round eggs. Both members of the pair incubate for 17–21 days, and both feed the chicks in the nest, bringing food in their bills; it is softened up for them when they are small. At first food consists only of insects which are later alternated with fruit. They fledge at about 30 days, wearing similar plumage to the adults.

This is an exclusively neotropical family with nine species, five in S America.

GALBULIDAE – JACAMARS
Order Galbuliformes

Jacamars are exclusively a S American family, comprising small birds with very long, sharp bills, short wings and proportionately longish tails. They have very short legs and feet with two toes forward and two back. Most species have brilliant metallic hues especially on the upperparts, though some are more modest and dull in this respect. Only in certain species do the sexes have different plumages

They perch on the outer exposed branches at low or middle levels of trees, though a few prefer the crowns of trees; all perch with the bill pointing slightly upwards. Here they wait for some insect to fly by, and dart out acrobatically, snap it up and return to the same lookout.

The nest is a deep burrow dug into a river bank, a roadside cutting or in a termites' nest in a tree, where 2–4 four round white eggs are laid. Several birds may cooperate in digging the tunnel which is also used for roosting. Incubation (in the Rufous-tailed Jacamar) is by both parents and lasts 19–23 days. Chicks fledge at 19–26 days.

Vocalisations are high-pitched, sometimes melodious.

They are found throughout the tropics and subtropics where they are to be seen on the edge of clearings in forests, woods, savannahs, forestry plantations, secondary growth, scrubby and bushy vegetation, most often along rivers and streams or by water.

The 16 species divide up into two groups: brilliant-coloured jacamars including *Galbula* (nine species, the exception in this genus is a blackish species with a very long tail) and *Jacamerops* (one) with its thick, decurved bill; and smaller, dull-coloured *Brachygalba* (four) and *Jacamaralcyon* (one), and the robust-billed *Galbalcyrhynchus* (one).

BUCCONIDAE – PUFFBIRDS
Order Galbuliformes

The puffbird family is exclusively neotropical and found in forests and woods, savannahs, scrubby terrain and open country with scattered trees, tropical, subtropical or temperate. They have dumpy, rounded bodies, very short necks and large heads, a heavy hook-tipped bill, less so in some species. Feathering is soft and puffy, wings rounded and short; tail length varies from moderately long to long, and is usually narrow. The legs are very short and the small feet have two toes forward and two back. There are vibrissae at the base of the bill.

Coloration is limited mostly to browns, buff, white and black and there is no sexual difference in plumage (one exception). They seem lethargic and passive for which they earn uncomplimentary names in the vernacular such as *Juan Bobo* – 'John the Dunce'.

They are generally unflappable, perch on some horizontal branch or liana and infrequently sally from these exposed perches to snap up some passing insect, often returning to the same spot. They change their lookout suddenly, in short, silent flights. Their food consists mainly of insects and other arthropods: they take large beetles and grubs from foliage or by descending to the ground; small vertebrates such as lizards, frogs and some fruit complete their diet.

Solitary, in pairs or small groups (families perhaps), the genera *Nystalus*, *Bucco* and *Micromonacha* frequent the lower and middle branches of trees. *Notharchus* prefers the exposed branches of the crowns of trees or in the crown itself, *Nonnula* hides in thick foliage of the dark lower levels of forest. *Monasa* species perch on exposed or semi-exposed branches at all levels below the crowns; these are more active than other genera and frequently fly from branch to branch, sometimes following troops of monkeys to snap up the flushed insects. *Malacoptila* are particularly passive and frequent the dark interior of the forest or some shady edge. They are occasionally seen in mixed foraging flocks or with antbirds (Formicariidae).

Chelidoptera is the exception in the family, being active and versatile. It looks like a swallow and has a peculiar undulant flight, sometimes even acrobatic in pursuing insect prey which it snaps up on the wing after a rapid chase. It perches on the ground, on exposed sandbanks in rivers, on roots poking out of a bank or on bare twigs at all levels of the forest up to the crown of trees.

Some *Nystalus* such as the White-eared Puffbird are frequently seen perched on posts or telephone wires by the roadside.

All members of the family are mostly silent and can perch for long periods without uttering a sound. They vocalise with the beak pointing above the horizontal and wagging their tail, which they also do when nervous, holding themselves more upright. Some species call in duet. Calls are very varied according to the group or the species.

They nest in deep burrows which they dig into banks or mounds of earth, in level ground, in termite mounds in trees, in hollows in tree trunks or the abandoned nest of horneros (Furnariidae). They generally lay 2–4 round white eggs; both parent birds incubate for 15–18 (White-faced Nunbird) or 15 days (Swallow-winged Puffbird) and tend the chicks in the nest till they fledge at 37 or 38 days.

The Bucconidae can be divided into several groups according to size, proportions, coloration and design.

Puffbirds, 22 species in the genera *Notharchus* (four), *Bucco* (four), *Hypnelus* (two), *Malacoptila* (seven), *Nystalus* (four) and *Micromonacha* (one);
Nunlets, five species in the genus *Nonnula*;
Nunbirds, *Monasa* (four) and *Hapaloptila* (one);
The Swallow-wing, one species in the genus *Chelidoptera*.
There are 32 species in the family, all of them found in S America.

CAPITONIDAE – BARBETS
Order Piciformes

Though varied and numerous in Asia and Africa, barbets are few in S America.

They are highly coloured arboreal birds of the forest, and are chunky, short-necked, with a heavy bill and rictal bristles, large heads, short-legs, two toes forward, two back. Most species show sexual dimorphism, a few with sexes alike. They live in pairs or small groups and feed primarily on fruit, berries and buds, yet include insects in their diet. Indigestible parts such as pips and insect wing-cases are regurgitated as pellets.

Nests are in holes in trees with soft wood, mostly excavated by themselves, where 2–5 white eggs are laid. Incubation takes about 15 days and the nestlings keep to the nest for 31–42 days. Both sexes incubate and feed chicks in the nest.

Calls are usually unimaginative series all of the same note, often the only sounds to be heard in the heat of the day, but some duet, while other species are almost silent.

There are 82 species in this family, 14 in S America, mostly in NW tropical habitats.

RAMPHASTIDAE – TOUCANS
Order Piciformes

The toucans are a characteristic neotropical family. They are known for their huge, disproportionate, gaudily coloured bills which in spite of the size are remarkably lightweight, being structured internally with struts and hollow cells divided by very thin bony walls.

The plumages and bare rings around the eye are contrastingly coloured, with scarlet, yellow, bright green, pale blue, white, black and chestnut being the dominant hues. The body is long, wings short and rounded, tail squarish or long and graduated. The feet are four-toed, two forward and two back. Other than having a longer bill, males and females are the same except in *Selenidera* toucanets where there is a notable difference in the coloration of the sexes. Juveniles have toned-down and smaller bills and paler face coloration.

Toucans are sociable though never in big flocks, usually solitary or in pairs and small groups; energetic, jumping around from branch to branch or quiet and watchful, sometimes perching in one place for considerable periods. They fly from tree to tree in search of fruit, their main food, though they also take insects, small reptiles and frogs, even bats and certainly eggs and nestlings of other birds. In flight they flap and glide alternately and are often seen playing follow-the-leader.

They nest in hollows in trees or abandoned woodpecker holes where they lay 1–5 almost round white eggs which both sexes incubate for 15–18 days. Chicks hatch naked and are attended by both parents till they fledge at 42–52 days of age. Parents continue to feed chicks for a further three weeks.

The smaller species also use hollows in trees as communal roosts. Their sleeping position is strange as they lay the bill along their back and cover it with the tail which is brought forward.

Curious and noisy, when alarmed they perch in a very horizontal posture while they produce their alarm calls. Their voices are varied: croaks, deep 'caws', yelps, shrill creaking and high-pitched like scraping glass, according to species.

There are several groups within the family: small toucanets (*Baillonius*, *Selenidera*, *Aulacorynchus*), araçaries (*Pteroglossus*), Andean toucans (*Andigena*) and the larger toucans (*Ramphastos*).

Of the 40 species in the family, 39 are S American.

PICIDAE – WOODPECKERS
Order Piciformes

The family includes all woodpeckers in their various sizes down to the tiny piculets. They are nearly all arboreal and are adapted to spending their lives on tree trunks and branches. They have short, strong legs with two toes forward, two back, with long sharp claws to hold firmly to bark and other irregularities of the places where they perch. Their tail-shafts are stiff and the feathers pointed, serving as a 3rd support. An exception to this last are the tiny piculets which have a 'soft' tail which is not used for support; these are even able to hang from the twigs over which they are working.

Their flight is undulant as a result of alternating flapping with brief periods of holding their wings to their bodies.

The bill is strong, pointed and used as a chisel to access the galleries of insects, or their eggs and larvae living under the bark or in the wood and on which they feed. To extract them they use their specially long tongue which has barbs on the tip to stab and withdraw their prey. Bills are also used for tapping to locate the tunnels by the hollow response. They can also detect the larvae by ear as these chew their way through the wood. There are special adaptations of bone and muscle between the bill and cranium and also in the neck for absorbing the shocks of hammering, thus protecting soft tissues. Some species such as the flickers feed mainly on ants on the ground; they have a sticky secretion on the tongue with which to collect them. There are species which make rings of perforations on tree trunks and feed on the sap that leaks out. Lastly, some other species even turn to fruit and seeds.

Because of these specialisations several species of woodpeckers can all use one area without competing for the food resources. Large species usually occupy the thicker trunks and branches, and so on down to the piculets which glean over twigs.

Plumage is varied with colourful heads and necks. Usually there is a difference between the sexes with males sporting red crests and malar stripes while in the female these are reduced or absent. Several species have notable crests. Dark and light colours combined is a frequent pattern, forming bars, patches and other designs.

All members of the family have territorial calls and several other vocalisations. They also produce mechanical sounds termed 'drumming', which serve territorial purposes and as communication between male and female; these are produced by fast, rhythmic hammering on hollow or resonant wood. This is very different from the irregular sounds made while chipping away to reach their prey.

Woodpeckers nest in holes dug out by themselves in tree trunks and branches. A few species dispense with trees (Andean Flicker, and Field Flicker on occasions) and dig their nest into banks and tall termite mounds. They lay 2–5 shiny, round white eggs. Incubation takes 12 –14 days. The fledglings are in the nest for 21–36 days and are fed for a further month by both parents. The family keeps together till the next breeding season. Some species have 'helpers' (non-parent birds) at the nest. When nests are abandoned they are used by many other species of hole-nesting birds. Dry trees and fallen logs of climax vegetation are fundamental for the larger members of this family as the greater abundance of wood-boring larvae and insects is essential to their diet. Deforestation and selective logging are affecting certain species. Forestry plantations are of little use, trees being all of one species, healthy and of the same age.

One species, though not in S America (the Imperial Woodpecker of Mexico), has not been recorded since 1958 and another (the Ivory-bill) only survives in a tiny population in Cuba having vanished from SE USA, probably because of the destruction, reduction or alteration of habitat.

There are 217 species worldwide (except in Australia and Oceania where, unaccountably, they do not exist), of which 83 are found in S America.

SPECIES DESCRIPTIONS
AND COLOUR PLATES

RHEAS (RHEIDAE)

A primitive S American family of ratites, unable to fly, powerful runners, live in flocks. Social. Several ♀s contribute to a nest. ♂ incubates and rears chicks. Omnivorous, feed on plant material and small animals. Voice a deep and ventriloquial boom.

1 GREATER RHEA *Rhea americana*   170cm
Huge and hefty. Iris pale. Grey. Base of neck and sides of breast blackish. Huge wings with long floppy feathers covering body, tipped blackish. Short body feathers and thighs dirty white. No tail. Powerful legs greyish. No feathering onto tarsus. ♀ usually less hefty, base of neck paler. Juv paler and more uniform, no black on neck. Open plains, grassland, sparse woods, savannah, steppe, cultivated land.

2 LESSER RHEA *Pterocnemia pennata*   140cm
Smaller than Greater Rhea. Bill short. Dark iris. Body more rounded. No black on neck. Floppy wing feathers hang lower on thighs. Generally somewhat browner. White tips of feathers very visible in fresh plumage, wearing off with time. Body and thighs brownish white. Feathering onto tarsi. Juv duller and more uniform. Puna or high Andean race (Puna Rhea, *P. p. garleppi*) is somewhat browner. Some think this a separate species. Open terrain, steppe, arid and stony areas, brushland, plains to mountains and Puna. This species replaces 1 in arid regions.

1♂

1

1♀

1♀

1♀

1♂

2 juv

2

RODRIGUEZ MATA

TINAMOUS (TINAMIDAE)

Tinamus tinamous are typical of rainforests, in deep shade and dense vegetation, on the forest floor; seldom if ever fly. The eyes are noticeably large; strong legs pale blue-grey, though horn-white in one species. There is a notable hump on the rump where the tail drops almost vertically. They roost on lower limbs of trees. Calls are mournful, hollow, low-pitched whistles.

1   GREAT TINAMOU *Tinamus major*   42cm
Variable. Three races. Upperparts brownish olive barred blackish, below brownish buff, finely barred darker. Forehead, crown and nape (or whole head) chestnut. Dark race (*T. m. latifrons*): upperparts blackish brown barred black, crown and nape blackish brown. Tropical rainforest and cloud-forest up to 1,500m in mountains.

2   SOLITARY TINAMOU *Tinamus solitarius*   50cm
Above dark brown barred blackish, with lighter speckling. Brownish-grey breast, rest of underparts greyish buff and cinnamon-buff with fine blackish barring. Line down the side of the neck ochreous buff. Dark floor of tropical and subtropical rainforest. At dusk emits 3 slow and mournful whistled notes, the last half a tone lower.

3   BLACK TINAMOU *Tinamus osgoodi*   46cm
Overall very dark. Upperparts brownish black, underparts blackish brown, undertail chestnut. Head and neck blackish slate, feathers edged black giving a scaly effect. Upland tropical and subtropical rainforest between 1,500 and 2,500m.

4   GREY TINAMOU *Tinamus tao*   52cm
Overall bluish grey, upperparts with alternating thicker and finer black barring, less so on paler underside. Throat and line down the side of the neck white. Mountains up to 2,000m in tropical, subtropical and cloud-forests.

5   WHITE-THROATED TINAMOU *Tinamus guttatus*   38cm
Small. Noticeable white dots between the dark barring on the upperparts; below buffy brown, darker on upper breast. Barred dark brownish on belly and undertail. Forehead and crown grey, rest of head and neck ochreous buff with black scaling. Horn-white legs. Tropical rainforest at low elevation (100–200m).

Nothocercus tinamous are smaller, and found in rainforests in the Andes. They are hard to see but their calls can be heard at a considerable distance.

6   TAWNY-BREASTED TINAMOU *Nothocercus julius*   38cm
Reddish-chestnut head, white throat. Upperparts dark brown barred blackish; underparts rufous cinnamon. Buffy white spots on the sides. Subtropical and temperate rainforests in foothills, low open woodlands up to 3,000m.

7   HOODED TINAMOU *Nothocercus nigrocapillus*   38cm
Grey head, browner on forehead and cheeks; whitish throat. Dark brown, finely barred darker above; cinnamon-brown below. Buffy-white spots on the sides and belly. Flight feathers dark brown barred black. Subtropical rainforest in the foothills and mountains.

8   HIGHLAND TINAMOU *Nothocercus bonapartei*   36cm
Slaty black head, cinnamon throat. Upperparts and neck chocolate-brown, below reddish cinnamon, all barred black. Buffy-white spots on sides, belly and lower upperparts. Subtropical and temperate forests in the foothills and mountains, cloud-forest, humid grasslands, 500–2,500m.

ODRIGUEZ MATA

TINAMOUS (TINAMIDAE)

Crypturellus tinamous are dumpy, dark and dull coloured. Bills and feet are variable in colour. Sexes are alike. Whistles and trills are loud, helping in identification and in locating them, but they are hard to see.

1 CINEREOUS TINAMOU *Crypturellus cinereus*   30cm
Very dark and uniform brown. Cap cinnamon-rufous faintly streaked white on sides of neck. Legs dirty pinkish brown. Calls are like a tremulous police-whistle. Lowland floodable tropical forest, brush, thickets and secondary growth near rivers and swamps, varzea, savannah, regrowth and plantations.

2 BERLEPSCH'S TINAMOU *Crypturellus berlepschi*   30cm
Very dark and uniform brownish black. Faint white streaking on sides of neck. Legs dirty pinkish brown. Wet forest, older secondary forest, hills, coastal lowlands. Some consider this a race of 1.

3 UNDULATED TINAMOU *Crypturellus undulatus*   30cm
Head, neck and upperparts dark chestnut-brown, underparts pale brownish grey. All but breast and belly faintly vermiculated blackish. Whitish throat. Another race has more buffy underparts, upperparts notably finely barred blackish; and all gradations in between. Bill and legs pale grey. Call is a mournful 4-note whistle rising on slurred last note. Humid tropical forest, gallery forest, varzea, woods, scrub, thickets, secondary growth, edges and clearings, transition woods, patches of woods, savannah and regrowth.

4 BROWN TINAMOU *Crypturellus obsoletus*   30cm
Greyish head. Upperparts uniform chestnutty brown, underparts buffy cinnamon, scaled black below. Legs yellowish. Eye orange. One form has the head grey but is deep chestnut overall. There are all gradations in between. Call is a succession of strident, accelerating whistles rising in pitch until almost inaudible. Lowland and mountain tropical and subtropical forest.

5 TEPUI TINAMOU *Crypturellus ptaritepui*   28cm
Like darker races of 4 but differs in having only the face greyish; forehead, crown, nape and hind-neck dark chestnut. Underparts dark brown without black scaling on belly and undertail. Dense subtropical cloud-forest. Local in SE Bolívar, Venezuela.

6 TATAUPA TINAMOU *Crypturellus tataupa*   24cm
Head, neck and breast lead-grey, darker on head. Dark chocolate-brown upperparts. Lower belly and undertail coverts black, feathers edged whitish giving effect of scaling. Bill pinkish red. Eye dark brown, legs vinaceous red. Call is a series of loud whistled *preeeps* rising then descending in pitch and volume, accelerating towards the end. Tropical and subtropical forests, open woods, transition woods, dry woods, scrubland and thickets, wooded valleys, savannah and regrowth.

7 SMALL-BILLED TINAMOU *Crypturellus parvirostris*   20–24cm
Like 6 but smaller bill, red with greyish tip. Eye pale orange. Legs coral-red. Head, neck and breast browner. Call starts with a single *pip* – longish silence – then another *pip*, these accelerating until they fuse into *churrs* that descend to nothing. Open areas with bush and scattered trees, tall grassland, open woods, edge of forest.

RODRIGUEZ MATA

TINAMOUS (TINAMIDAE)

1 BLACK-CAPPED TINAMOU *Crypturellus atrocapillus* 30cm
Head brownish black, throat cinnamon. Neck and upper breast slaty grey.
Lower breast cinnamon-chestnut grading to buffy on undertail coverts. Barring
on flanks. Rest of upperparts dark brown vermiculated blackish in ♂, barred
buffy and blackish in ♀. Legs reddish pink. Humid tropical forests, secondary
growth, bush and thickets, deciduous tropical forest. This species once
included the Red-legged Tinamou (3 below).

2 CHOCO TINAMOU *Cryptarellus kerriae* 28cm
Head slaty black, throat white. Neck and breast blackish brown. Upper belly
and flanks brownish cinnamon. ♀: blackish and buff barring on upperparts,
almost absent in the plain dark brown ♂: Feet reddish pink. Call is a low-
pitched, tremulous, resonant whistle about 1 sec long. Montane tropical forest.
Rare and local. This may be a race of the Slaty-breasted Tinamou (C.
boucardi), from C America.

3 RED-LEGGED TINAMOU *Crypturellus erythropus* 30cm
Head, hind-neck and upperparts brownish chestnut. Throat whitish. Foreneck
and breast brownish grey. Rest of underparts tawny cinnamon turning buff and
barred blackish on flanks and undertail coverts. ♀ differs by strongly barred
black and buff on lower upperparts and wings. Legs reddish pink. Call is a clear,
trisyllabic whistle, mostly at dusk. Dry and open woods, low deciduous woods,
brushland, thickets, copses. The race C. *e. idoneus* differs in being browner on
upperparts and more browny grey on underparts. Some place it with the
Thicket Tinamou (C. *cinnamomeus*) of C America.

4 BRAZILIAN TINAMOU *Crypturellus strigulosus* 30cm
Virtually the same as 3. Differs only in brownish-grey breast and whitish belly.
Legs pale greyish. Humid forest, woods, brushland and thickets.

5 YELLOW-LEGGED TINAMOU *Crypturellus noctivagus* 35cm
The largest of the genus. Striking whitish brow and throat. Head, neck and
back brownish chestnut, in part finely barred black. Rest of upperparts barred
buff and black. Breast tawny buff, paler on lower underparts, barred black on
flanks and undertail coverts. Yellow legs. ♂: brownish-grey neck. A brighter
race with rufous wash on brow, throat and breast, also lacks white on central
belly. Yellow legs have olive wash. Call is a low-pitched 3- or 4-syllable whistle,
1st note accented and descending in pitch, the rest evenly pitched. Transition
dry woods, humid forest, brushland and thickets, gallery forest, savannah, edge
and clearings in forest.

1♂

1♀

2♂

2♀

3R♂

3♀

3♂

5♂

4♂

5♀

4♀

5R♂

RODRIGUEZ MATA

TINAMOUS (TINAMIDAE)

1 BARRED TINAMOU *Crypturellus casiquiare* 26cm
Rufous-chestnut head, very white throat. Neck, breast and flanks lead-grey, paling to whitish belly. Lower belly and undertail coverts buffy, barred black. Back and rest of upperparts barred dark ochre and black. Legs pale greyish olive. Call is a whistle, followed by up to 30 shorter notes, rising at first, slowing at end. Dense lowland, sandy-belt tropical forest near rivers.

2 PALE-BROWED TINAMOU *Crypturellus transfasciatus* 29cm
Whitish brow and throat. Upperparts brown-barred and slightly scaled buff and black on lower back. Breast pale greyish brown, rest of underparts greyish cream, partly barred black. Reddish-pink legs. ♂: barring on lower back less evident. Open woods, transition woods, scattered trees, brushland and thickets in dry tropical areas.

3 LITTLE TINAMOU *Crypturellus soui* 22cm
Small. Almost uniform coloration, no black markings. Many races. Typical form ♀: greyish head, whitish throat, upperparts browny chestnut, underparts tawny brown. Other races varying to generally more chestnut or to dark chocolate with tawny throat. Legs of ♀ are dirty cream or olive-washed cream. ♂ browner on neck and upperparts. Underparts tawny brown. Pale olive-grey legs. Call is a series of tremulous, penetrating whistles rising in pitch and volume. Humid or dry brushland and thickets, secondary growth, edge of transition woods and forests, cloud-forest, clearings, regrowth, plantations.

4 BARTLETT'S TINAMOU *Crypturellus bartletti* 24cm
Small. Short bill. Blackish-brown head, white throat. Neck and breast dark brown. Upperparts barred black and brown. Underparts tawny rufous grading to buff, somewhat barred lower. Legs greyish cream. Humid tropical forest. Once considered a race of 5.

5 RUSTY TINAMOU *Crypturellus brevirostris* 24cm
Small. Short bill. Chestnut head, white throat. Neck and breast rufous. Upperparts barred chestnut and black. Underparts tawny rufous grading to buff, somewhat barred black under belly. Legs greyish cream. Tropical forest and varzea.

6 VARIEGATED TINAMOU *Crypturellus variegatus* 28cm
Long, straight bill. Head lead-grey to blackish. Throat white washed rufous. Neck and breast rufous. Upperparts barred rufous and black. Underparts tawny rufous grading to buff, barred black below. Legs pale grey. Call is a long, plaintive, descending whistle (pause) followed by 3–5 short, rising notes. Tropical and subtropical forest in mountains, woods, open areas with scattered trees, from humid to relatively dry areas.

7 GREY-LEGGED TINAMOU *Crypturellus duidae* 30cm
Large and hefty. Head, neck, breast and upper back rufous. Throat white. Rest of upperparts barred and scaled black and chestnut to black and buff on lower back and upper tail coverts. Underparts tawny rufous grading to buff, barred black below. Legs dirty cream, pale grey, or creamy grey. ♂: dorsally uniform chestnutty brown. Humid forest, brushland, thickets, open woods.

1

2♂

2♀

3R♀

4

3R♀

3♂

3♀

5

7♂

6

7♀

RODRIGUEZ MATA

TINAMOUS (TINAMIDAE)

Nothoprocta tinamous are brushland and semi-open-country species.

1 ANDEAN TINAMOU *Nothoprocta pentlandii*   26cm
Greyish brown. Upperparts generally dark with few contrasting markings.
Breast greyer, washed lavender and partly dotted whitish. Flanks barred and
spotted whitish and brownish. Legs yellowish. Call is a sharp, ascending,
piercing *wheeet*. Ravines, slopes with brush, grass with scattered trees,
vegetation along streams, cultivated land.

2 CHILEAN TINAMOU *Nothoprocta perdicaria*   30cm
Brownish grey with contrasting black and whitish designs on back. Dark
crown. Foreneck and breast greyish dotted and streaked whitish. Flight
feathers barred black on cinnamon-rufous. Another form generally more buffy
cinnamon. Grassland, scrub and cultivated land.

3 CURVE-BILLED TINAMOU *Nothoprocta curvirostris*   28cm
Upperparts brownish grey with contrasting black and whitish design. Neck
whitish buff streaked and dotted black. Breast and rest of underparts tawny
with black and white markings on flanks and upper breast. Flight feathers
barred cinnamon-rufous and blackish. Humid to semiarid areas in Puna and
Páramos, cultivated areas.

4 ORNATE TINAMOU *Nothoprocta ornata*   35cm
Robust. Upperparts brownish with contrasting designs in black, whitish and
ochre. Head and neck with notable black spotting. Breast pale grey washed
lavender. Underparts light buffy grey with faint cinnamon barring on flanks. Call
is a short, sharp whistle rising in pitch. Puna, high mountain steppe, grass with
patchy scrub, often near water. A race that some consider a species, Kalinowski's
Tinamou (*N. o. kalinovskii*), differs in smaller bill; darker and more rufous
cinnamon on breast and neck, spotted only on throat and face, more uniform on
back. Probably extinct.

5 TACZANOWSKI'S TINAMOU *Nothoprocta taczanowskii*   36cm
Like 4. Long, heavy down-curved bill. Face and neck dark greyish brown,
crown and ear coverts blacker. Neck and breast greyish brown barred and
dotted blackish and whitish. Rest of underparts barred cinnamon and blackish.
Puna, semiarid scrub, bunch grass, open woods, cultivated fields.

6 BRUSHLAND TINAMOU *Nothoprocta cinerascens*   32cm
Slender. Upperparts brownish grey with whitish, buff and black design. Black
topknot raised when alarmed. Face and neck greyish white speckled and streaked
blackish. Breast grey dotted white, faintly barred black. Rest of underparts barred
greyish brown and whitish. Call is a series of mournful, rising whistled *wheeews* at
1 per sec, the last 4 evenly pitched. Open woods and brushland in dry areas.

Red-winged tinamous are large with long bills for digging up grubs and bulbs, and
prying for insects. Long-legged; rufous wings and whirring sound startle in flight.

7 RED-WINGED TINAMOU *Rhynchotus rufescens*   42cm
Head and neck ochreous. Crown streaked with black. Upperparts and flanks
scaled ochreous brown, black and white. Breast plain ochreous brown. Call is a
whistled *tooweeoo – who-who-who*, last notes falling in pitch and volume. Open
country with tall grass, often damp bottom-lands, sometimes with scattered
trees.

8 HUAYCO TINAMOU *Rhynchotus maculicollis*   42cm
Like 7 but head speckled and neck streaked black. Breast entirely barred. Tall
grass in high Andean valleys with brush and scattered small trees, cultivated
land. Some consider this the same as 7.

RODRIGUEZ MATA

TINAMOUS (TINAMIDAE)

1 SPOTTED NOTHURA *Nothura maculosa*   23cm
Ochreous, black, buff and whitish design on upperparts. Neck spotted black, irregular barring on flanks. Brightness varies with race. Flight feathers all barred. Calls are a long, even trill, and a long series of *peep* whistles at 2 per sec, ending in a rapid, descending *tiddle-toddle-too*. Short grass in open country, or with scattered trees, cultivated fields. The race *N. m. chacoensis* (*Chaco nothura*) may be a separate species.

2 DARWIN'S NOTHURA *Nothura darwinii*   21cm
Pale, buffy version of 1, less contrasting design on upperparts, breast and flanks. Flight feathers with inner vane all dark brown (wings seem darker). Call is a long series of *peeps* as in 1, but no coda at the end. Dry, sandy grassland, rolling hills with short grass, sometimes with bushes and small trees; grassy clearings in open woods, cultivated land. Replaces 1 in drier country.

3 LESSER NOTHURA *Nothura minor*   18cm
Small version of 1 with upperparts and flanks more rufous. Inner vane of flight feathers dark brown. Open short-grass savannah, with scrub and trees, even tall grass, flooded areas, cultivated land.

4 WHITE-BELLIED NOTHURA *Nothura boraquira*   27cm
Like 1 but whiter below. Crown notably black when raised in alarm. Sides of breast and flanks more finely spotted and barred respectively. Inner web of flight feathers all blackish. Legs strong yellow. Long high-pitched whistle dropping in pitch at the end. Open country, short-grass savannah, scrubby grassland with scattered trees, cultivated fields.

5 DWARF TINAMOU *Taoniscus nanus*   15cm
Tiny. Like a miniature *Nothura*. Dumpier. Upperparts rufous ochreous, barred and scaled black-and-whitish. Breast and flanks barred black, spotted white. Insect-like call. Open country with tall grass, sometimes with bushes and trees, cerrado, savannah.

6 PATAGONIAN TINAMOU *Tinamotis ingoufi*   37cm
Striking. White lines across face and down neck. Upperparts and flanks scaled ochreous, chestnut, grey and whitish. Undertail coverts ochreous. Rufous flight feathers. Call is lovely, melodious *twee-oos* with variations. Stony steppe with short sparse grasses and low scrub.

7 PUNA TINAMOU *Tinamotis pentlandii*   40cm
Striking white lines across face and down neck. Upperparts brown with olive wash, stronger on upper tail coverts, all edged, dotted and streaked buffy white. Breast, belly and flanks barred whitish buff and brownish grey. Undertail deep rufous. Flight feathers barred, inner web dark brown. Calls *kay-oo* with last syllable stressed. Above 3,500m in Andean steppe with bunch grass and scattered low scrub, sandy or stony country.

8 ELEGANT CRESTED TINAMOU *Eudromia elegans*   39cm
Long pointed crest. White lines on face and upper neck. Upperparts brownish grey with varying creamy white and black spotting. Blackish streaking on creamy fore-neck and breast. Other races are darker with more contrasting designs, or paler and more buffy generally. Calls include a whistled rhythmic 3-syllable *we? we do*, descending a tone on last note. Scrub, open country, steppe, open woods, dry grassland, cultivated land.

9 QUEBRACHO CRESTED TINAMOU *Eudromia formosa*   41cm
Like 8 but lines on neck reach base of neck. Upperparts brownish cinnamon. Blackish design on upperparts has bars, streaks and irregular patterns. Shyer and more easily flushed than 8. Dry chaco woods, grasslands, scrub with scattered trees.

RODRIGUEZ MATA

PENGUINS (SPHENISCIDAE)

1 **GALAPAGOS PENGUIN** *Spheniscus mendiculus*   50cm
Small. Black head and upperparts. Narrow white line from eye, down around
cheeks and lower throat. 2 pectoral collars, the upper less defined, the lower
extending down flanks. Underparts white. Juv: head and breast grey. Beaches
and rocky coasts, nearby sea. Endemic to Galapagos Is, Ecuador.

2 **HUMBOLDT PENGUIN** *Spheniscus humboldti*   68cm
Robust blackish bill with base, lores and eye-ring pinkish. Head and upperparts
black. White brow extends to circle cheeks and lower throat. One broad black
pectoral band extends down flanks. Underparts white. Juv: head, neck,
upperparts and breast greyish. Beaches, rocky shores, neighbouring sea.

3 **MAGELLANIC PENGUIN** *Spheniscus magellanicus*   70cm
Blackish bill. Black lores. Eye-ring and bare fore-part of brow pinkish. Narrow
white line at base of bill. Head and upperparts black. Broad white brow
extends down round cheeks and lower throat. 2 black pectoral collars, the
lower extending down flanks. Underparts white. Juv: head, upperparts and
neck greyish. Beaches, coasts, nearby areas for nesting, sea.

4 **ROCKHOPPER PENGUIN** *Eudyptes chrysocome (crestatus)*   60cm
Bill sealing-wax red. Head and upperparts black. Thin brow and dangling rigid
tufts yellow. Slight occipital crest. Underparts white. Juv lacks tufts. Whitish-
grey throat and chin. Rocky shores to cliff-tops, sea.

5 **MACARONI PENGUIN** *Eudyptes chrysolophus*   65cm
Heavy bill sealing-wax red. Gape salmon-pink. Head and upperparts black.
Golden-yellow brow from mid-forehead ends in floppy tufts. Underparts white.
Juv lacks tufts. Whitish up to chin. Rocky shores to cliff-tops and sea.

6 **GENTOO PENGUIN** *Pygoscelis papua*   75cm
Bill reddish orange, tip and culmen black. Head and upperparts dull black.
White band from eye to eye over crown. Underparts white. Juv white up to
chin. Sandy beaches and areas of grass inland where it nests (subantarctic
islands), rocky shores (Antarctic), sea.

7 **ADELIE PENGUIN** *Pygoscelis adeliae*   65cm
Bill short, dull red and black. Head and upperparts black. Slight occipital crest.
White eye-ring. Underparts white. Juv: white extends up to chin. Rocky
coasts, stony beaches, ice floes, sea.

8 **CHINSTRAP PENGUIN** *Pygoscelis antarcticus*   70cm
Bill black. Cap and upperparts black. Underparts white. Thin black line across
cheeks and under chin. Juv: black mottling on face. Stony beaches, rocky
shores and adjacent areas, ice floes, sea.

9 **KING PENGUIN** *Aptenodytes patagonicus*   95cm
Bill black with orangy-pink patch at base of lower mandible. Head black.
Longish golden-orange patch from side of nape down sides of neck to upper
breast. Rest of upperparts bluish grey. Underparts white. Juv patch yellowish
white. Sandy and pebbly beaches, of subantarctic islands, nearby seas.

10 **EMPEROR PENGUIN** *Aptenodytes forsteri*   110cm
Huge and robust. Bill black with pink line on lower mandible. Black head. Big
roundish yellow patches on back and side of neck, upper breast or neck washed
yellow. Upperparts bluish grey. Underparts white. Juv duller. Ice pack and sea
ice to snowfields inland, seas.

RODRIGUEZ MATA

GREBES (PODICIPEDIDAE)

1 PIED-BILLED GREBE *Podilymbus podiceps*   30cm
Brownish grey. Black throat. Thick ivory bill crossed by black band. Pale eye-ring. Non-br plumage duller. Throat whitish, no black on bill. Juv: blackish streaks and markings on cheeks and neck. Lakes, rivers, streams, roadside ditches, marshes, dams and other fresh water, often with floating or emergent vegetation.

2 HOODED GREBE *Podiceps gallardoi*   28cm
White. Black head and back. Forehead and brow white, crest rufous. Red eye, bare yellow eye-ring. Juv: blackish and white, lacks crest. Smallish open upland lakes in arid Patagonian steppe. Marine estuaries in winter.

3 WHITE-TUFTED GREBE *Rollandia (Podiceps) rolland*   25–32cm
Head, neck and upperparts black. Large ear tufts white. Flanks chestnut, faintly streaked blackish. Non-br plumage overall greyish brown. Ear tuft less conspicuous. Juv: paler neck, incipient ear tuft. Lakes, marshes, roadside ditches, rivers, streams, more or less vegetation. Also sea coast in winter. The Falkland Is race is much larger and darker. Some believe it to be a valid species.

4 SILVERY GREBE *Podiceps occipitalis*   26cm
Silvery white. Head lead-grey. Slight crest and hind-neck black. Ear tuft golden yellow (or blackish in Andean race). Eye golden yellow or orange. Upperparts blackish grey. Flanks somewhat streaked blackish. Non-br plumage duller. Ear tufts less conspicuous. Juv lacks ear-tufts and is duller. Patagonian and high Andean lakes with submerged or emergent vegetation.

5 JUNIN FLIGHTLESS GREBE *Podiceps taczanowskii*   33cm
Large version of Andean form of 4. Differs in proportionately longer bill, more elegantly slender head and neck. Endemic to Lake Junin in central Peruvian Andes. Endangered.

6 LEAST GREBE *Tachybaptus (Podiceps) dominicus*   21cm
Smallest. Orangy-yellow eye. Head and neck grey, crown and throat black. Rest brownish grey. Non-br plumage duller, with whitish throat. Juv is like non-br but has stripes on cheek. Small lakes and marshes with dense vegetation, swamps, roadside ditches.

7 COLOMBIAN GREBE *Podiceps andinus*   30cm
Black hood. Short crest. Ear tufts golden rufous. Neck chestnut. Back blackish. Flanks slightly streaked blackish. Reddish-orange eye. Non-br plumage with white throat and chin. No ear tuft. Andean lakes with emergent vegetation. Apparently extinct since 1977. Some believe it to have been a race of the Black-necked Grebe (*P. nigricollis*).

8 SHORT-WINGED GREBE *Rollandia (Centropelma) microptera*   40cm
Bill chestnut and yellow. Tufts on forehead and nape chestnut streaked black. Sparse ear tufts black. Throat, cheeks, fore-neck and breast white. Hind-neck chestnutty rufous. Upperparts and flanks blackish brown. Non-br plumage duller. Juv: duller, rufous stripes on cheeks. Lakes in high Andes with emergent vegetation. Lakes Umayo, Titicaca and Poopo between Peru and Bolivia.

9 GREAT GREBE *Podiceps major*   60cm
Long black bill. Notable erectile crest and line down hind-neck black. Rest of head dark grey, rest of neck chestnutty rufous. Upperparts and flanks blackish grey. Non-br plumage duller. Horn-coloured bill. Juv: cheeks slightly marked greyish. S race darker and brighter. Lakes, marshes, rivers, edge of the sea.

1 non-br

1 br

2

3 br

3 non-br

3R

4R

4

5

6 br

7

8

9 non-br

9 br

RODRIGUEZ MATA

ALBATROSSES (DIOMEDEIDAE)

1 WAVED ALBATROSS *Phoebastria (Diomedea) irrorata*   90cm, WS 225cm
Unmistakable. Long bill yellowish ochre. Head whitish, washed yellow on nape and hind-neck. Body, upperwings and tail greyish brown, finely vermiculated on breast. Underwing whitish bordered greyish brown, axillaries blackish brown. Juv: duller bill, whiter head. Oceanic islands and tropical sea. Galapagos and La Plata islands (Ecuador). Does not follow ships.

2 YELLOW-NOSED ALBATROSS *Thalassarche (Diomedea) chlororhynchos*
75cm, WS 230cm
Bill black, yellow along culmen, slightly more orange at nail. Head, neck and underparts white. Dark brow. Upperwings and tail blackish. Underwing white bordered blackish, broader so on leading edge. Juv: bill all black. Oceanic islands and sea. Sometimes follows ships.

3 SHY ALBATROSS *Thalassarche (Diomedea) cauta*   95cm, WS 240cm
Nominal race has white head with grey wash on cheek. Bill uniform pale greyish yellow, tip of mandible and maxilla yellow. Dark brow. Body white. Upperwing and tail black. Underwing white, narrowly bordered black. *D. c. salvini*: bill pale olive-grey, culmen and tip yellow; dark brown tip of mandible. Pale grey hood, cap white. Darker brow. Juv bill pale grey, whitish band before black tip. Incomplete greyish collar. Oceanic islands and sea. Follows ships. The race *T. c. eremita*, with lead-grey head and neck and brilliant yellow bill, tipped black on its maxilla, may be a separate species: Chatham's Albatross.

4 BLACK-BROWED ALBATROSS *Thalassarche (Diomedea) melanophrys*
85cm, WS 240cm
Yellow bill, orange tip. Notable black brow. All-white body. Tail, back and upperwing black. Underwing narrowly white down the centre, broadly bordered black under leading edge. Juv: bill blackish brown. Darker underwing. Incomplete greyish-brown collar. At sea, oceanic islands. Follows ships.

5 GREY-HEADED ALBATROSS *Thalassarche (Diomedea) chrysostoma*
82cm, WS 200cm
Bill black, culmen and line along lower mandible yellow, orange at nail. Grey head. Back, upperwings and tail black. Underwing with narrow white central stripe bordered black, more so under leading edge. Juv: underwing almost all black, pattern of adult's underwing barely insinuated. Blackish bill. Head grey, throat and cheeks paler. Immature birds with worn plumage have whiter head and incomplete brownish-grey collar and brow. Oceanic islands and sea. Rarely follows ships.

6 BULLER'S ALBATROSS *Thalassarche (Diomedea) bulleri* 80cm, WS 210cm
Black bill with yellow culmen and line below mandible. Head grey, cap white. Body white. Upperwings, back and tail black. Underwing white, narrowly bordered black. Juv: bill blackish brown with black tip. Face, neck and throat darker and browner. Oceanic islands and sea. Follows ships.

RODRÍGUEZ MATA

ALBATROSSES (DIOMEDEIDAE) **AND PETRELS** (PROCELLARIIDAE)

1 ROYAL ALBATROSS *Diomedea epomophora*   120cm, WS 350cm
Huge. Pale pink bill, black line along cutting edge. Old birds are white with black primaries and following edge of wing. Juv tail black. Lower back and rump vermiculated blackish brown. In intermediate plumages top of wing blackish (*D. e. sanfordi* keeps this plumage through life), white invading with age from forward base of wing. Head, body and tail always white. Oceanic islands and ocean. Seldom follows ships.

2 WANDERING ALBATROSS *Diomedea exulans*   120cm, WS 350cm
Huge. Pink bill (no black line). White. Upperwings blackish, variably mottled white and with round white spot near base. White increases with age. Underwing white, following edge and tip bordered black. Tail tipped black, turning white with age. Juv chocolate-brown. Face, throat and underwing white. Intermediate forms are greyish brown, increasingly white. Oceanic islands and oceans. Follows ships.

3 DARK-MANTLED SOOTY ALBATROSS
Phoebetria fusca   85cm, WS 210cm
Bill black with yellow-orange line along mandible. White crescent behind eye. All blackish brown, blacker hood. Long, narrow, pointed wings. Graded tail ends in point. Juv: nuchal collar and upper back paler. Oceanic islands and oceans. Sometimes follows ships.

4 LIGHT-MANTLED SOOTY ALBATROSS
Phoebetria palpebrata   85cm, WS 210cm
Like 3 but body lighter, buffy greyish brown. Blue line along mandible. Juv: less marked and with whitish line on bill, less noticeable white behind eye. Oceanic islands and oceans.

5 SOUTHERN GIANT PETREL *Macronectes giganteus*   88cm, WS 190cm
Bill ochreous yellow, tip washed olive. Brownish grey. Head lighter, to white with age. Juv blackish brown. Intermediate plumages according to age. There is an all-white form, usually with occasional scattered dark feathers. Oceanic islands, seas and coastal areas. Follows ships.

6 NORTHERN GIANT PETREL *Macronectes halli*   88cm, WS 190cm
Differs from 5 in bill having chestnutty tip. No white morph. Never has white head; always has some blackish-grey mottling on crown and hind-neck. Juv all glossy black. Oceanic islands and seas. Does not follow ships.

1 ad

1 juv

2 ad

5 ad
white
form

2 ad

2 ad

2 im

2 juv

5 juv

5 ad
dark
form

3

4

4

5

2

1

4

RODRÍGUEZ MATA

PETRELS AND PRIONS (PROCELLARIIDAE)

1 **CAPE PETREL** *Daption capense*   40cm, WS 90cm
Unmistakable. Black hood. Upperparts almost chequered black and white. Underparts white. Underwing edged blackish. Tail black. Oceanic islands and seas. Follows ships.

2 **ANTARCTIC PETREL** *Thalassoica antarctica*   43cm, WS 104cm
Chocolate-brown. Flight feathers mostly white. White upper tail coverts, base of tail and underparts. Subantarctic islands and seas.

3 **SOUTHERN FULMAR** *Fulmarus glacialoides*   46cm, WS 110cm
Upperparts silvery grey. White underparts. Trailing edge and broad tip of wing black, white at base of inner primaries. Pink bill, black tip. Subantarctic islands, sea.

4 **SNOW PETREL** *Pagodroma nivea*   32cm, WS 80cm
All white, black bill. Inland Antarctic cliffs for nesting, sea ice, nearby sea.

5 **GREY PETREL** *Procellaria cinerea*   48cm, WS 120cm
Bill dark ivory and black. Upperparts grey. Underparts white. Underwing blackish grey paling towards tip, flight feathers grey. Subantarctic islands and southern oceans.

6 **WHITE-CHINNED PETREL** *Procellaria aequinoctialis*   56cm, WS 140cm
Bill ivory, black lines along culmen and on mandible. Brownish black. Variable white spot on chin. A northern race (*P. a. conspicillata*) has white circling face. Oceanic islands, southern seas.

WESTLAND PETREL
Procellaria westlandica   52cm, WS 135cm (not illustrated)
Like 6 but bill tipped black and no white chin: a large version of 7. Seas. Accidentally off Chile. May be a race of 6.

7 **BLACK PETREL** *Procellaria parkinsoni*   48cm, WS 115cm
Like 6 but smaller. Bill ivory, tip blackish. All brownish black (no white chin). Oceanic islands and ocean. Galapagos seas.

8 **BLUE PETREL** *Halobaena caerulea*   30cm, WS 60cm
Like a prion but tail-tip white and square. Bill black. Forehead scaled blackish and white. Crown, nape and half-collar blackish. Face white with blackish mask. Upperparts bluish grey with blackish 'W'. Underparts white. Oceanic islands and southern seas.

9 **SLENDER-BILLED PRION** *Pachyptila belcheri*   26cm, WS 56cm
Bill slender, blue, black culmen. Broad white brow accented by blackish eye-stripe. Bluish-grey half-collar. Upperparts bluish grey with blackish 'W'. Tail slightly wedged, black tip. Oceanic islands and sea. Very gregarious.

10 **FAIRY PRION** *Pachyptila turtur*   24cm, WS 55cm
Differs from 9 in shorter, heavier and all-blue bill. Forehead, crown and face mask less contrasted. Tail-tip broadly black. Oceanic islands and adjacent seas.

11 **BROAD-BILLED PRION** *Pachyptila vittata*   28cm, WS 60cm
Like 9 but large-headed. Very wide and thick bill black. Mask, forehead and crown blackish. Narrow white brow. Oceanic islands, seas. Accidental S Atlantic.

12 **ANTARCTIC or DOVE PRION** *Pachyptila desolata*   27cm, WS 60cm
Like 11 but bill smaller and blue with black along culmen and line on mandible. Forehead and crown paler, less mask. White at base of bill. Oceanic islands and sea.

13 **SALVIN'S PRION** *Pachyptila salvini*   27cm, WS 60cm (only bill illustrated)
Virtually identical to 12 but bill broader towards tip. Oceanic islands and sea. Some believe this to be a race of 12. Accidental in Chile and Peru.

RODRIGUEZ MATA

SHEARWATERS (PROCELLARIIDAE)

1 KIRITIMATI SHEARWATER *Puffinus nativitatis*   36cm, WS 75cm
Small. All sooty brown. Dark underwing. Blackish bill and feet. Easter Island and sea.

2 GREATER SHEARWATER *Puffinus gravis*   50cm, WS 108cm
Brownish-black cap. Incomplete white collar. Upperparts blackish brown. Upper tail coverts white, tail blackish. Underparts white. Greyish-brown patch on belly. Underwing white with two blackish diagonal lines. Oceanic islands and sea.

3 PINK-FOOTED SHEARWATER *Puffinus creatopus*   48cm, WS 108cm
Bill pink, tip dark. Feet pale pink. Dark greyish-brown upperparts. Underparts dirty white. Flanks brownish grey. Oceanic islands and sea.

4 SHORT-TAILED SHEARWATER *Puffinus tenuirostris*   36cm, WS 75cm
Uniform sooty brown. Slightly darker head. Very short, slender dark bill. Feet pale pinkish. Easter Island, doubtfully in S American Pacific waters.

5 SOOTY SHEARWATER *Puffinus griseus*   43cm, WS 105cm
Bill and feet blackish pink. All sooty brown. Underwing silvery white. Axillaries and proximal underwing coverts dark. Oceanic islands and sea.

6 WEDGE-TAILED SHEARWATER *Puffinus pacificus*   46cm, WS 100cm
Bill blackish grey, basally pinkish. Feet pink. All sooty brown. Longish wedge-shaped tail. Pale form has throat, underparts and underwing white. Oceanic islands and sea. Doubtfully in S American Pacific waters.

7 FLESH-FOOTED SHEARWATER *Puffinus carneipes*   48cm, WS 108cm
Hefty. Bill pale pinkish, blackish tip. All sooty brown. Tail less wedged than other shearwaters, somewhat rounded. Oceanic islands and sea. Doubtfully in S American waters.

RODRIGUEZ MATA

SHEARWATERS AND PETRELS (PROCELLARIIDAE)

1 BULLER'S SHEARWATER *Puffinus bulleri*   45cm, WS 95cm
Unmistakable. Bill pale blue and black. Feet pale pinkish. Upperparts grey and patterned with 2 contrasting diagonals (one blackish, one pale) across proximal part of wing. Cap and wing-tip blackish. Tail black. Underparts white. Oceanic islands and sea.

2 AUDUBON'S SHEARWATER *Puffinus lherminieri*   28cm, WS 66cm
Small. Bill blackish grey. Feet pinkish. White eye-ring. Upperparts dark brown. Underparts white. Undertail and tail blackish brown. Broad margin of underwing blackish. Oceanic islands and sea.

3 LITTLE SHEARWATER *Puffinus assimilis*   27cm, WS 65cm
Short, slender bill black. Feet pale blue. Upperparts greyish, wing coverts edged whitish. Face and sides of neck greyish, slightly scaled white. Underparts white. Undertail coverts white. Underwing narrowly edged blackish. Oceanic islands and sea.

4 MANX SHEARWATER *Puffinus puffinus*   35cm, WS 85cm
Longish bill blackish. Pink feet. Face and sides of neck blackish. Upperparts blackish contrasting with white underparts. Edge of underwing, tail and wing-tips blackish. Oceanic islands and sea.

5 CORY'S SHEARWATER *Calonectris diomedea*   52cm, WS 110cm
Bill yellow, black band across tip. Feet pink. Upperparts brownish grey. Wings and tail blackish brown. Upper tail coverts edged whitish. Border of greater and medial wing coverts pale. Black tail. Underparts white. Oceanic islands and sea.

6 KERGUELEN PETREL *Aphodroma (Pterodroma) brevirostris*   35cm, WS 80cm
All slate-grey. Cap slightly darker. Underwings pale with dark diagonal band. Oceanic islands and sea.

7 GREAT-WINGED PETREL *Pterodroma macroptera*   40cm, WS 100cm
Heavy black bill. All sooty brown. Fore-face whitish. Black feet. Oceanic islands and sea.

8 KERMADEC PETREL *Pterodroma neglecta*   39cm, WS 90cm
Short, thick, black bill. Feet dirty pink, webs blackish. Dark form like a skua: blackish brown, base of primaries whitish. Light form: upperparts dark brown; underparts dirty white, vermiculated greyish brown. There are intermediate forms. Oceanic islands and sea.

9 HERALD PETREL *Pterodroma arminjoniana*   38cm, WS 90cm
Like dark form of 8 but base of primaries brownish grey. Light form differs from 8 in more marked cap and darker pectoral collar. Underwing dark, base of primaries whitish. Oceanic islands and sea.

RODRIGUEZ MATA

PETRELS (PROCELLARIIDAE)

1 **ATLANTIC or HOODED PETREL** *Pterodroma incerta*   43cm, WS 105cm
Head and collar dark brown. White throat in worn plumage. Upperparts
blackish brown. Underparts and flanks white. Underwing, vent and tail
blackish brown. Oceanic islands and sea.

2 **JUAN FERNANDEZ PETREL** *Pterodroma externa*   43cm, WS 98cm
Bill black, feet pale pinkish. White forehead. Crown, nape and around eye
blackish. Faint whitish collar on hind-neck. Upperparts, sides of neck and back
grey. Topside of wing has blackish 'W'. White band on rump. Tail blackish grey.
Upper tail coverts whitish. Underwing white, black spot at bend. Oceanic
islands and sea.

3 **WHITE-HEADED PETREL** *Pterodroma lessonii*   43cm, WS 100cm
Bill black, feet pale pinkish. White face, blackish mask, grey half-collar.
Washed pale grey on crown and neck. Upperparts grey. Tail white, centrally
grey. Topside of wings and rump blackish grey with indistinct 'W'. Underparts
white. Underwing blackish grey. Oceanic islands and sea.

4 **SOFT-PLUMAGED PETREL** *Pterodroma mollis*   33cm, WS 88cm
Bill black, feet pale pinkish. Face and throat white. Small blackish mask.
Crown, back and tail grey. Upperwings grey with indistinct 'W'. Pectoral collar
grey. Underparts white. Underwing whitish with black edge, tip and diagonal
band. Oceanic islands and sea.

5 **BLACK-CAPPED PETREL** *Pterodroma hasitata*   40cm, WS 95cm
Bill black, feet pale pinkish Upperparts blackish brown with contrasting
whitish collar. Rump and tail coverts white. Forehead scaled black and white.
Underparts white. Underwing white, broadly edged black and with black
diagonal band. Oceanic islands and sea.

6 **MOTTLED PETREL** *Pterodroma inexpectata*   35cm, WS 75cm
Bill black, feet pale pinkish. Upperparts, mask, lower underparts and flanks
dark grey. Upperwing grey with black 'W'. Face, throat, upper breast,
underwing, vent and sides of rump white. Striking black diagonal band on
underwing. Oceanic islands and sea.

7 **DARK-RUMPED PETREL** *Pterodroma phaeopygia*   42cm, WS 93cm
Bill black, feet pale pinkish. Crown, upperparts and half-collar blackish brown.
Forehead white. Underparts white to sides of rump. Black diagonal line under
wing. Variable black patch on axillaries. Long wedge-shaped tail. Oceanic
islands and sea.

8 **MAS A TIERRA PETREL** *Pterodroma defilippiana*   26cm, WS 66cm
Bill black, feet sky-blue. Blackish mask. Crown, back, upper tail coverts and
tail grey, outers white. Wings grey with black 'W'. Inner web of primaries
white. Forehead, underparts and sides of rump white. Half-collar grey. Oceanic
islands and sea. Some believe this to be a race of Cook's Petrel (*P. cookii*).

9 **GOULD'S PETREL** *Pterodroma leucoptera*   28cm, WS 68cm
Bill black, feet sky-blue. Crown and mask black. Hind-neck, back and upper
tail coverts grey. Upperwing grey with black 'W', white on inner web of
primaries. Forehead and underparts white, invading side of rump. Underwing
white with black along distal leading edge slanting diagonally towards body.
A darker race (*P. l. brevipes*) has a complete collar, greyish belly and flanks.
Oceanic islands and sea.

10 **STEJNEGER'S PETREL** *Pterodroma longirostris*   26cm, WS 66cm
Like 9 but smaller. Bill more slender. Tail slightly longer and more wedge-
shaped. Black on head reaches upper back. Leading edge of wing has 2 white
spots in black margin when seen from below. Oceanic islands and sea.

RODRIGUEZ MATA

STORM-PETRELS (HYDROBATIDAE)

1 WILSON'S STORM-PETREL *Oceanites oceanicus* 18cm, WS 40cm
Sooty black. Upper tail coverts and sides of rump white, extending onto vent.
Greater secondary wing coverts brownish grey. Square tail. Long legs black,
webs yellow. Oceanic islands and sea.

2 WHITE-VENTED STORM-PETREL *Oceanites gracilis* 16cm, WS 35cm
Like 1 but smaller. Lower belly white. Oceanic islands and sea.

3 WEDGE-RUMPED STORM-PETREL *Oceanodroma tethys* 18cm, WS 41cm
Like 1 and 2 but white rump and upper tail coverts, extending onto vent. Legs
shorter, more slender, all black. Tail barely forked. Oceanic islands and sea.

4 HORNBY'S STORM-PETREL *Oceanodroma hornbyi* 22cm, WS 43cm
Blackish crown, nape, hind-neck and around eye. Forehead and underparts to
sides of rump white. Pectoral collar blackish. Back to mid-rump grey. Whitish-
grey diagonal band across upperwing. Underwing blackish. Tail deeply forked.
Oceanic islands and sea.

5 POLYNESIAN or WHITE-THROATED STORM-PETREL
Nesofregetta fuliginosa 25cm, WS 51cm
White underparts. White band across rump. Blackish pectoral collar. Tail
barely forked. Underwing coverts white. There is an all-blackish form and
variable intermediate forms mottled blackish on underparts. Oceanic islands
and sea.

6 LEACH'S STORM-PETREL *Oceanodroma leucorhoa* 20cm, WS 46cm
All sooty black. Diagonal line across upperwing whitish grey. Broad white
rump with mid-line grey, though this is hard to see or incomplete. Long forked
tail. One race (*O. l. socorroensis*) has a faintly blackish-grey rump. Oceanic
islands and sea.

7 BAND-RUMPED STORM-PETREL *Oceanodroma castro* 20cm, WS 43cm
Sooty black. Diagonal band on upperwing greyish. Band on rump and part of
vent white. Tail barely forked. Oceanic islands and sea.

8 MARKHAM'S STORM-PETREL *Oceanodroma markhami* 23cm, WS 47cm
Sooty black. Diagonal band on upperwing whitish grey. Long, deeply forked
tail. Oceanic islands and sea.

9 BLACK STORM-PETREL *Oceanodroma melania* 24cm, WS 49cm
Very like 8 but heftier. Tail shorter and less forked. Diagonal band on
upperwing less marked. Oceanic islands and sea.

RODRÍGUEZ MATA

PETREL (PROCELLARIIDAE)
STORM-PETRELS (HYDROBATIDAE)
AND DIVING-PETRELS (PELECANOIDIDAE)

1 BULWER'S PETREL *Bulweria bulwerii*   26cm, WS 65cm
Sooty black. Whitish-brown diagonal band on upperwing. Long wedge-shaped
tail looks pointed in flight. Oceanic islands and sea.

2 LEAST STORM-PETREL
Oceanodroma (Halocyptena) microsoma   13cm, WS 30cm
Very small. Sooty black. Pale brownish diagonal band on upperwing. Long
wedge-shaped tail looks pointed in flight. Oceanic islands and sea.

3 BLACK-BELLIED STORM-PETREL *Fregetta tropica*   20cm, WS 47cm
Sooty black. Rump, underwing, flanks and sides of belly white. Broad black
band down mid-belly. Square tail. Oceanic islands and sea.

4 WHITE-FACED STORM-PETREL *Pelagodroma marina*   20cm, WS 43cm
White face with black mask. Back, rump, greater wing coverts and half-collar
pale grey. Blacker on crown, flight feathers and slightly forked tail. Forehead
and brow white. Underparts all white. Oceanic islands and sea.

5 GREY-BACKED STORM-PETREL *Garrodia nereis*   17cm, WS 38cm
Black hood. Upperparts dark grey, darker on flight feathers and tail-tip.
Greater wing coverts tipped white. Underparts and underwing white. Square
tail. Oceanic islands and sea.

6 WHITE-BELLIED STORM-PETREL *Fregetta grallaria*   20cm, WS 45cm
Like 3 but lacks black down central belly. Oceanic islands and sea.

Diving-petrels are tiny and dumpy, with short wings and tail. They are in their
element underwater and fly fast on whirring wings. They spend no time on the surface.

7 MAGELLANIC DIVING-PETREL *Pelecanoides magellani* 20cm, WS 33cm
Upperparts black, border of scapulars and greater coverts white; underparts
white. Flanks flecked grey. White from throat extends to form a gill-line.
Islands, adjacent fjordland waters and seas.

8 SOUTH GEORGIA DIVING-PETREL *Pelecanoides georgicus* 20cm, WS 33cm
Like 7 but dark grey face, notable white scapular line and grey flanks. Oceanic
islands and adjacent seas.

9 COMMON DIVING-PETREL *Pelecanoides urinatrix*   23cm, WS 35cm
Face dark grey. Upperparts plain blackish, scapulars barely tipped white.
Underparts white. Flanks faintly mottled grey, most birds with an insinuated pale
collar. Oceanic islands and seas. Some consider the S Atlantic races (*P. u. exsul*
and *P. u. berard*) as composing a separate species, the Falkland Diving-petrel.

10 PERUVIAN DIVING-PETREL *Pelecanoides garnotii*   22cm, WS 35cm
Heavy bill. Black face. Upperparts black. White line on scapulars. Underparts
white. Faint gill-line. Faintly mottled on flanks. Offshore islands and sea.

RODRIGUEZ MATA

BOOBIES (SULIDAE)
AND PELICANS (PELECANIDAE)

1 PERUVIAN BOOBY *Sula variegata*   75cm
Head, neck and underparts white. Back and tail dark brown, back feathers
edged white. Upper tail coverts whitish. Underwing dark, axillaries white. Feet
blackish blue. Juv: head, neck and underparts brown, all flecked whitish.
Coastal waters, offshore islands, coasts.

2 BROWN BOOBY *Sula leucogaster*   70cm
Head, breast and upperparts chocolate-brown. Lower underparts white. Part of
underwing white. Yellow bill and feet. Juv as adult but underparts lightly
mottled brown. Sea and oceanic islands, coasts.

3 BLUE-FOOTED BOOBY *Sula nebouxii*   80cm
Head and neck whitish flecked dark brown. White patch on upper back. Back
dark brown, feathers edged white. Wings dark brown. Rump and upper tail
coverts white. Tail dark brown, central pair of feathers lighter. Underparts
white. Underwing dark brown, axillaries white. Blue feet. Bill and bare face
bluish grey. Juv: head dark brown, throat and neck pale brown flecked darker.
Feet brownish grey. Oceanic islands and sea, coasts.

4 MASKED BOOBY *Sula dactylatra*   85cm
White. Black flight feathers, tail and bare face. Bill yellow. Feet brownish grey.
Juv: head, back, wings and tail dark brown. Back feathers edged whitish. Bluish
mask, yellowish bill. Oceanic islands, sea and cliffs. E. Pacific race considered
by some a separate species: Nazca Booby (*Sula granti*).

5 RED-FOOTED BOOBY *Sula sula*   70cm
White. Flight feathers black. Pink and blue face, bill pale greyish blue. Feet
bright red. Some specimens have black tail (like 4). Dark form pale brown.
Wings and tail blackish brown. Juv: greyish brown, paler below. Feet yellowish.
Bill blackish-brown. Sea and coast, oceanic islands.

6 BROWN PELICAN *Pelecanus occidentalis*   110–150cm
Enormous and hefty. Breeding plumage: part of head and throat white. Neck
chocolate-brown. Rest blackish grey flecked ashy grey. Non-br plumage paler,
head and neck white. Juv: generally duller and browner. Underparts white.
The S race from C Peru southward is far larger; some consider it a separate
species (Peruvian Pelican *P. thagus*). Coast, adjacent waters, oceanic islands.

4

5

2

3

1

1

2

3

4 juv

4

5 white form

5 brown form

6 non-br

RODRÍGUEZ MATA

6 br

CORMORANTS (PHALACROCORACIDAE) AND ANHINGA (ANHINGIDAE)

1 IMPERIAL CORMORANT *Phalacrocorax atriceps* 72cm
In breeding plumage upperparts black with bluish-violet sheen. Underparts and line on lesser wing coverts white. Forward-curling crest and (in one form) patch on back white. Blue eye-ring and yellow caruncles. Non-br plumage has blackish-brown upperparts, crest absent. Juv duller. King Cormorant (*P. a. albiventer*) has more of the cheeks and neck black and never has the white patch on back (it is considered a separate species by some). Headlands, coasts and coastal waters, oceanic islands.

2 ROCK CORMORANT *Phalacrocorax magellanicus* 65cm
Head, neck and upperparts black, glossy in breeding plumage. Bare red face. Variably white ear-patch, sometimes onto throat and fore-neck. Lower breast and belly white. Variable iris. Juv: all black for 1–2 months, becoming white in patches. Rocky coasts and cliffs, coastal waters.

3 GUANAY CORMORANT *Phalacrocorax bougainvillii* 76cm
Head, neck and upperparts black. Oval throat-patch and underparts white. Red face, green eye. Short crest briefly in breeding plumage. Juv: brownish black above, dirty white below. Coastal waters, coasts, offshore islands.

4 RED-LEGGED CORMORANT *Phalacrocorax gaimardi* 60cm
Elegant. Grey, slightly paler below. White patch on side of neck. Wing and scapular coverts tipped whitish. Flight feathers and tail blackish. Bill yellow, fore-face and feet bright red. Juv duller, lacks white on sides of neck. Throat whitish. Fore-face and feet pink. Rias, tide-rips and cliffs.

5 NEOTROPICAL CORMORANT *Phalacrocorax brasilianus (olivaceus)* 73cm
In breeding plumage black. White line at gape. White auricular tuft. Bare gape blackish. Green iris. Non-brs are duller brownish black, gape yellowish. Juv: brownish above, whitish-brown below. Inland waters of every kind, sea coasts, nearby islands.

6 FLIGHTLESS CORMORANT *Phalacrocorax (Nannopterum) harrisi* 100cm
Huge and hefty. Rudimentary wings. Blackish brown, lighter below. Green iris. Juv blacker and more uniform. Iris brown. Galapagos seashores. Ecuador.

7 ANHINGA *Anhinga anhinga* 80cm
Long, sharp bill. Snakelike head and neck. Large wings. Huge fantail. ♂: black with silvery white on wing coverts and scapulars. ♀: head, neck and breast brownish buff. Juv like ♀, browner above, buff down to belly and flanks. Swamps, marshes, lakes, rivers, always with trees on fringes.

1

1R

1 br

1R br

1R

2

2

2

3

2

3

3 br

4

2

2

4

5 br

5 non-br

4

5

7♀

7♂

6

7♂

7♂

6

RODRÍGUEZ MATA

TROPICBIRDS (PHAETHONTIDAE)
AND FRIGATEBIRDS (FREGATIDAE)

1   RED-BILLED TROPICBIRD *Phaethon aethereus*   60cm, tail 40cm
White. Red bill. Black line through eye onto nape. Upperparts barred black.
Wing-tips black. Juv similar; yellow bill with blackish tip. Eye-line forms
nuchal collar. Short tail, feathers tipped blackish. Oceanic islands and sea.

2   WHITE-TAILED TROPICBIRD *Phaethon lepturus*   41cm, tail 40cm
White. Yellow to orange bill. Black line through eye. Black diagonal along
greater secondary coverts and scapulars. Outer primaries black. White central
tail feathers very long and slender. Juv: bill yellow tipped blackish. No nuchal
collar. Upperparts barred. Primaries black. Short tail. Oceanic islands and sea.

3   RED-TAILED TROPICBIRD *Phaethon rubricauda*   43cm, tail 40cm
White. Red bill. Black line through eye. Some scapulars and tertials edged
black. Long and slender central tail feathers red. Juv: like that of 2 but less
black on wing-tips. Oceanic islands and sea.

4   GREAT FRIGATEBIRD *Fregata minor*   95cm, WS 215cm
♂ glossy black. Green sheen on back. Lighter bar along greater and median
wing coverts. Brilliant red gular pouch inflated in display. ♀ black. Throat,
fore-neck and breast dirty white. Upper wing coverts whitish brown. Red eye-
ring. Juv like ♀ but brownish black. Head and neck tawny turning whitish.
Breast brownish black turning whitish in 2nd plumage, appearing like juv 5.
White on belly. Coastal sea and oceanic islands.

5   MAGNIFICENT FRIGATEBIRD *Fregata magnificens*   100cm, WS 240cm
♂ glossy black. Purply and violaceous sheen on back. Red gular pouch. ♀:
black hood, white breast and upper-belly. Upper wing coverts whitish brown.
Pale blue eye-ring. Juv brownish black. Head, neck, central breast and part of
belly white. Coastal seas, bays, over beaches and oceanic islands.

6   LESSER FRIGATEBIRD *Fregata ariel*   75cm, WS 185cm
♂ glossy black. Back feathers with green, blue or purple sheen. Red gular
pouch. White band across flanks and through axillaries. ♀ has black hood, and
white breast, upper belly and some axillaries. Reddish-pink eye-ring. Juv like
♀ but head, neck tawny becoming like juv 5 in next plumage. Breast blackish
brown. Belly, flanks and axillaries white. Coastal sea, oceanic islands.

RODRÍGUEZ MATA

HERONS (ARDEIDAE)

1 BOAT-BILLED HERON *Cochlearius cochlearius* 50cm
Nocturnal. Very wide, heavy bill blackish. Black cap. Tuft of long feathers from occipital (longer in nuptial plumage). Forehead, face, neck and breast white. Upperparts grey. Underparts cinnamon, flanks black. Juv upperparts cinnamon-brown. Brownish buff below. Rivers and swamps in dense forest, gallery forest, mangroves.

2 ZIG-ZAG HERON *Zebrilus undulatus* 32cm
Short, thick neck. Bill black, mandible pinkish. Dense occipital crest. Upperparts blackish, irregularly and finely barred whitish buff. Buffy brown below finely barred black. Juv: head and neck cinnamon. Crest blackish. Fore-neck buffy faintly streaked blackish. Underparts buffy sparsely streaked blackish. Forest streams, swamps with dense vegetation, waterholes.

3 STRIATED HERON *Butorides striatus* 40cm
Black cap. Legs greenish yellow. Neck, upperparts, lower underparts bluish grey. Fore-neck with tawny and white lines. Wings darker bluish-green, feathers edged white. In nuptial plumage long back feathers. Legs orange. Juv mostly brownish streaked whitish, paler below. Legs greenish yellow. Intermediate forms between this species and 4 and 5 have been found. Fresh and salt water, mangroves, coasts, lagoons.

4 GREEN HERON *Butorides virescens* 40cm
Similar to 3 but with chestnut neck-sides. Mangroves, salt- and freshwater marshes and mud-flats, and coral beaches of Northern (Caribbean) strip of South America. Considered by some a race of 3.

5 LAVA or PLUMBEOUS HERON *Butorides sundevalli* 40cm
All lead-grey. Chin-spot white. In nuptial plumage has long pale grey feathers on back. Legs yellowish orange. Juv: head and neck whitish streaked blackish. Upperparts blackish grey streaked whitish. Wing feathers edged white. Rocky seashore, inland waters. Endemic to Galapagos Is, Ecuador. Some believe this to be a race of 3.

6 YELLOW-CROWNED NIGHT HERON
Nycticorax (Nyctanassa) violacea 60cm
Crepuscular but also active by day. Heavy black bill. Head black, forehead, central crown and occipital crest white, washed yellow. White stripe on cheek. Rest bluish grey, feathers on upperparts and wings darker and edged whitish. Juv: greyish brown streaked white. Underparts more whitish streaked blackish. Mangroves, shores, estuaries, small lagoons, less in freshwater habitat with trees.

7 BLACK-CROWNED NIGHT HERON *Nycticorax nycticorax* 58cm
Crepuscular and nocturnal. Crown and upperparts blackish. Fine white nuchal plumes. Wings and tail grey. Underparts white, varying through grey to blackish according to forms. Juv: mostly brown streaked whitish. Whitish throat. Underparts whitish streaked brown. Tree-lined lakes, marshes, rivers and streams, seashores, coasts, oceanic islands, roadside ditches, waterholes, mangroves, swamps.

RODRIGUEZ MATA

EGRETS AND HERONS (ARDEIDAE)

1 CATTLE EGRET *Bubulcus ibis*   50cm
White. Short neck. Shortish yellow bill. Legs brownish yellow. In br plumage
cap, back and breast cinnamon-buff; orange legs. Juv: bill, bare face and legs
greyish. Fields, open spaces, rural areas, mostly short grass, around cattle.

2 SNOWY EGRET *Egretta thula*   57cm
White. Black bill. Legs blackish, feet yellow. In br plumage has an occipital
tuft, long breast feathers, recurved aigrets on back. Juv: greenish-yellow legs
and feet. Bill and bare face duller. Edge of marshes, lagoons, estuaries, coastal
areas, fields.

3 REDDISH EGRET *Egretta rufescens*   75cm
Erectile bushy crest. Bill pinkish, tipped black. Legs blackish grey. Dark form
with chestnut head and neck. Rest slate-grey. Pale form all white. In br
plumage has long aigrets on back, long feathers on breast. Juv white form has
blackish bill; dark form mostly greyish brown. Coastal lagoons, salt water, sea
coasts, beaches, reefs, mangroves.

4 LITTLE BLUE HERON *Egretta (Florida) caerulea*   60cm
Bare face and slightly decurved bill greyish blue, this tipped black. Legs
greenish. Head and neck chocolate-brown with lilac tint. Rest slate-grey. In br
plumage nuchal tuft and long feathers on back. Juv all white. Bill yellowish
grey tipped black. Legs greenish grey. Marshes, lakes, rivers, streams, estuaries,
beaches, mangroves, other coastal areas.

5 GREAT EGRET *Ardea (Egretta) alba*   95cm
Large. White. Yellow bill. Legs black. In br plumage has long aigrets on back.
Juv like non-br adult. Lakes, marshes, other fresh waters, nearby grassland and
open areas, seashore.

6 TRICOLOURED HERON *Egretta tricolor*   70cm
Slender with long neck and bill. Bill yellow and blue, blackish tip. Legs yellow.
Head, neck and upperparts dark slaty blue, more chestnut on breast. Fore-neck
white with lines of chestnut and black streaks. Underparts white. In br plumage
has white occipital tuft, and long buffy aigrets on back. Juv: upperparts browner.
Coastal lagoons, beaches, mangroves, temporary ponds, streams and other
bodies of fresh water.

7 AGAMI or CHESTNUT-BELLIED HERON *Agamia agami*   70cm
Very long, slender yellow and black bill. Yellow legs. Black head, white throat.
Neck and underparts chestnut. White and chestnut lines down fore-neck. Base
of neck and breast bluish grey finely streaked white. Upper back, wings and tail
bottle-green. In br plumage face creamy-white. Long whitish-blue feathers
from occipital and on back. Juv: dull brown upperparts, blacker on crown and
back. Whitish underparts streaked dark on lower breast. Shady bogs, swamps,
streams, ponds in dense pristine forest, mangroves.

8 WHISTLING HERON *Syrigma sibilatrix*   58cm
Bill pink, tip black. Crown and occipital crest slaty grey. Buff neck. Upperparts
grey. Wing coverts ochreous, edged black. Underparts whitish. Juv: dull, neck
streaked grey. Fields, short grass, islands of trees, scattered trees, near woods,
always near fresh water.

9 CAPPED HERON *Pilherodius pileatus*   60cm
Bill pale blue with pink at mid-mandible. White forehead. Black cap. Long
white occipital crest. Head and neck washed cream, rest white. Juv duller.
Black cap streaked whitish. Lakes, swamps, temporary puddles, rivers and
streams, in forest.

1 non-br

1 br

2 br

2 non-br

3 pale form

3 dark form

4 juv

4

9

8

7

6

5 non-br

5 br

RODRIGUEZ MATA

TIGER-HERONS AND BITTERNS (ARDEIDAE)

1 BARE-THROATED TIGER-HERON *Tigrisoma mexicanum* 78cm
Black cap. Grey from behind eye down neck. Bare yellow throat. Neck and
breast barred blackish and buff. Two lines down fore-neck. Upperparts finely
barred blackish brown and buff. Belly brownish rufous. Juv: like all tiger-
herons but throat bare and yellow. Watercourses in forest, swamps,
mangroves, estuaries.

2 FASCIATED TIGER-HERON *Tigrisoma fasciatum* 68cm
Bill and legs proportionately shorter than other tiger-herons. Cap black. Dark
brownish grey from behind eye down side of upper neck. Neck, breast and
upperparts blackish brown finely barred buff. White lines down fore-neck.
Belly vinaceous cinnamon. Juv: like 3 but legs and bill shorter. Forest streams
and rivers in mountains and hills.

3 RUFESCENT TIGER-HERON *Tigrisoma lineatum* 72cm
Bare face striking yellow. Head, neck and breast rufous chestnut. Two white
lines down fore-neck. Upperparts brown, finely vermiculated black. Belly
vinaceous cinnamon. Juv like others, irregularly barred blackish brown and
ochreous cinnamon. Underparts whiter. Swamps, marshes, rivers, streams,
temporary puddles, all with trees on banks in forest or woods, mangroves,
dense reed-beds in savannah and open areas.

4 PINNATED BITTERN *Botaurus pinnatus* 70cm
Like a young tiger-heron. More streaked on upperparts. Bill and legs yellowish,
big feet. Neck barred dark brown and ochreous. Fore-neck
ochreous buff with tawny streaks forming lines. Underparts buffy white with
irregular brown streaking. Juv like adult but duller. Lakes and marshes,
riverside reed-beds, tall and dense emergent vegetation, flooded grassland,
rice-paddies.

5 STRIPE-BACKED BITTERN *Ixobrychus involucris* 32cm
Tiny. Buff with black, cinnamon and white streaking on back. Fore-neck white
with lines of buff streaks. Underparts buffy white. Juv more streaked on neck
and upperparts. Lakes and marshes with dense reed-beds and other tall
emergent vegetation.

6 LEAST BITTERN *Ixobrychus exilis* 30cm
Cap and back black. Neck tawny rufous to buff, fore-neck white with tawny
buff lines. Upperwings tawny buff, primaries blackish. Underparts whiter. ♀
has blackish-brown cap and back. Juv like ♀ but has streaks on neck and
upperwing. Swamps, lakes, with very dense tall emergent vegetation.

RODRÍGUEZ MATA

HERONS (ARDEIDAE) **AND STORKS** (CICONIIDAE)

1 GREAT BLUE HERON *Ardea herodias*   130cm
Bill black and yellow. Centre of forehead and crown white, sides of both and
nape and occipital crest black. Whitish face. Neck and upperparts light grey
washed vinaceous. Fore-neck white with line of black streaks. Flanks and lower
belly black. Bend of wing and leggings pale chestnut. In nuptial plumage crest,
breast and back feathers are longer. Juv duller. Neck paler and streaked
blackish. Underparts whitish streaked blackish. Lacks occipital crest.
Estuaries, coasts, mangroves, swamps, lakes, fresh and salt water.

2 COCOI HERON *Ardea cocoi*   125cm
Cap and occipital crest black. Neck and back greyish white. Line of black
streaks on fore-neck. Wings and tail darker grey. Belly and fore-part of flanks
black. Leggings and undertail coverts white. In breeding plumage crest, breast
and back feathers are very long. Juv duller, fore-neck more streaked. Flanks and
underparts whitish streaked greyish. No occipital crest. Marshes, lakes,
streams, swamps, rivers, roadside ditches, other freshwater bodies, estuaries,
mangroves, seashores.

3 WOOD STORK *Mycteria americana*   100cm
Bare head and neck blackish grey. Bill slightly down-curved. White; flight
feathers and tail black. Blackish legs, feet pinkish. Juv: bill ivory, head and
neck feathered grey. Lakes, marshes, temporary puddles, roadside ditches,
swamps, other freshwater bodies, mangroves.

4 JABIRU *Jabiru mycteria*   140cm
White. Huge slightly upturned bill, head bare and neck black. Bare red collar.
Juv washed pale brown in parts. Swamps, marshes, lakes, rivers, flooded grass,
savannah and open areas with scattered trees.

5 MAGUARI STORK *Ciconia maguari*   120cm
Bill horn-coloured, black tip. Bare face and red legs. White; scapulars, flight
feathers and tail black. Juv: black for a short time after fledging, then
increasingly white. Marshes, flooded grass, fields, roadside ditches, streams,
temporary water.

1

2

1 juv

2 juv

2

2

3

3

4

4

3 juv

5

3

4

5

RODRÍGUEZ MATA

IBISES AND SPOONBILL (THRESKIORNITHIDAE)

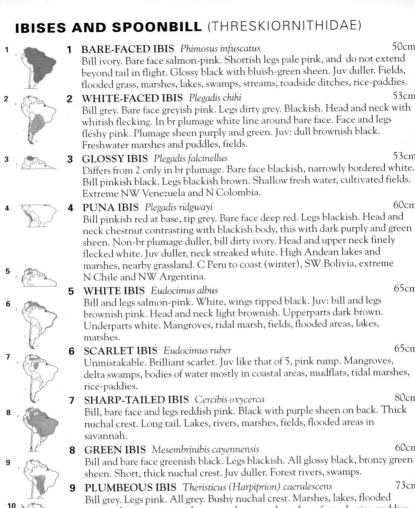

1 BARE-FACED IBIS *Phimosus infuscatus*   50cm
Bill ivory. Bare face salmon-pink. Shortish legs pale pink, and do not extend
beyond tail in flight. Glossy black with bluish-green sheen. Juv duller. Fields,
flooded grass, marshes, lakes, swamps, streams, roadside ditches, rice-paddies.

2 WHITE-FACED IBIS *Plegadis chihi*   53cm
Bill grey. Bare face greyish pink. Legs dirty grey. Blackish. Head and neck with
whitish flecking. In br plumage white line around bare face. Face and legs
fleshy pink. Plumage sheen purply and green. Juv: dull brownish black.
Freshwater marshes and puddles, fields.

3 GLOSSY IBIS *Plegadis falcinellus*   53cm
Differs from 2 only in br plumage. Bare face blackish, narrowly bordered white.
Bill pinkish black. Legs blackish brown. Shallow fresh water, cultivated fields.
Extreme NW Venezuela and N Colombia.

4 PUNA IBIS *Plegadis ridgwayi*   60cm
Bill pinkish red at base, tip grey. Bare face deep red. Legs blackish. Head and
neck chestnut contrasting with blackish body, this with dark purply and green
sheen. Non-br plumage duller, bill dirty ivory. Head and upper neck finely
flecked white. Juv duller, neck streaked white. High Andean lakes and
marshes, nearby grassland. C Peru to coast (winter), SW Bolivia, extreme
N Chile and NW Argentina.

5 WHITE IBIS *Eudocimus albus*   65cm
Bill and legs salmon-pink. White, wings tipped black. Juv: bill and legs
brownish pink. Head and neck light brownish. Upperparts dark brown.
Underparts white. Mangroves, tidal marsh, fields, flooded areas, lakes,
marshes.

6 SCARLET IBIS *Eudocimus ruber*   65cm
Unmistakable. Brilliant scarlet. Juv like that of 5, pink rump. Mangroves,
delta swamps, bodies of water mostly in coastal areas, mudflats, tidal marshes,
rice-paddies.

7 SHARP-TAILED IBIS *Cercibis oxycerca*   80cm
Bill, bare face and legs reddish pink. Black with purple sheen on back. Thick
nuchal crest. Long tail. Lakes, rivers, marshes, fields, flooded areas in
savannah.

8 GREEN IBIS *Mesembrinibis cayennensis*   60cm
Bill and bare face greenish black. Legs blackish. All glossy black, bronzy green
sheen. Short, thick nuchal crest. Juv duller. Forest rivers, swamps.

9 PLUMBEOUS IBIS *Theristicus (Harpiprion) caerulescens*   73cm
Bill grey. Legs pink. All grey. Bushy nuchal crest. Marshes, lakes, flooded
savannah, open areas with scattered trees and patches of woods, rice-paddies.

10 BLACK-FACED IBIS *Theristicus melanopis*   73cm
Bare face and wattles black. Legs pink. Head and neck buffy cinnamon.
Upperparts grey. Pectoral collar grey. Underparts and tail black. Nominal race
in short grass in damp bottom-lands, flooded areas, open woods. Ploughed fields
and short grass on wintering grounds. N race (*T. m. branickii*) paler. Highlands.

11 BUFF-NECKED IBIS *Theristicus caudatus*   73cm
Like 10, but silvery-white greater wing coverts and no pectoral collar. S race
has grey upper belly. Open woods and forest, savannah, open country, fields,
small marshes, flooded areas, lakes, ponds, rivers, streams, also hill country.

12 ROSEATE SPOONBILL *Ajaia ajaja*   85cm
Unmistakable. Spatulate bill. Mostly pink, carmine on wing coverts and
breast. Wings all pink. Juv dull pinkish white. Edge of lakes, marshes, swamps,
mangroves, in lowlands.

ODRÍGUEZ MATA

FLAMINGOS (PHOENICOPTERIDAE)
AND SCREAMERS (ANHIMIDAE)

1 GREATER FLAMINGO *Phoenicopterus ruber*   120cm
Flamingo with the proportionately longest neck and legs. Distal third of bill black, rest ivory with pink patch on mandible. Legs whitish pink, 'knee' and foot pink. Head and neck scarlet-pink. Rest pink faintly streaked brighter. Tertials scarlet-pink. Rest of flight feathers black. Non-br plumage paler and duller. Juv: dirty browny grey, whiter below, all faintly tinted pink. Shallow coastal lagoons and salt ponds, no emergent vegetation, estuaries, bays, sheltered coasts, flats between mangroves.

2 CHILEAN FLAMINGO *Phoenicopterus chilensis*   100cm
Distal half of bill black, proximal ivory. Legs greyish blue, red at 'knee' and foot. Overall pink. Breast and upper back streaked scarlet-pink. Wing coverts and tertials scarlet. Rest of flight feathers black. Non-br plumage paler and more uniform. Juv: pale greyish brown tinged pink, whitish below. Coverts and back streaked darker. Shallow and saline lakes, on plains and in highlands, seashore, lagoons, estuaries, bays and sheltered waters; freshwater marshes temporarily or on migration.

3 ANDEAN FLAMINGO *Phoenicoparrus andinus*   115cm
Heftiest flamingo. Heavy bill; distal half black, proximal cream, red at base of mandible and spot before eye. Legs yellowish ivory. Head and neck bright pink slightly tinged vinaceous. Rest pale pink somewhat streaked darker pink. Flight feathers form a conspicuous black triangle over rump and tail. Non-br plumage paler and duller. Juv like that of 2 but blackish triangle covering rump and tail. High Andean saline lakes. Descends to the plains in winter.

4 JAMES'S or PUNA FLAMINGO *Phoenicoparrus jamesi*   90cm
The smallest flamingo. Bill short and thick, tip black, rest bright yellow. Lores sealing-wax red. Legs red. Head and upper neck pink, lower neck whitish pink. Base of neck, breast and upper back streaked scarlet. Long dorsal plumes scarlet covering most of black triangle of flight feathers. Non-br plumage paler and duller – no scarlet. Legs yellowish. Juv like that of 3 but smaller. High Andean saline lakes; descends in winter.

5 NORTHERN SCREAMER *Chauna chavaria*   85cm
Cap and nuchal crest grey. Throat and cheeks whitish. Upper neck blackish. Rest grey, darker on upperparts. Reddish-pink legs. Edge of swamps, lakes, marshes and rivers, open or wooded areas, bodies of fresh water with abundant emergent and floating vegetation.

6 SOUTHERN SCREAMER *Chauna torquata*   85cm
Head and nuchal crest grey. Face paler. White ring-collar. Black velvety choker. Rest grey, upperparts darker. Legs pinkish red. Edge of lakes, marshes, temporary water, rivers and streams, roadside ditches, all preferably with emergent and floating vegetation, fields near water, open or wooded areas.

7 HORNED SCREAMER *Anhima cornuta*   85cm
Long, slender 'horn' angles forwards from forehead. Greenish-black crown, lower neck and breast scaled white. Head and upper neck black. Belly white. Legs grey. Underwing coverts white. Shores of rivers, lakes and swamps, oxbows, in forest or grassland.

RODRIGUEZ MATA

GEESE, SWANS AND COSCOROBA (ANATIDAE)

Sheld-geese are reminiscent of true geese, colourful, with small bills, and with boldly patterned wings in flight. They are migratory and frequent short grass near water or seashore (1 species). Males whistle, females honk.

1 ASHY-HEADED GOOSE *Chloephaga poliocephala*   55cm
Sexes alike. Head and upper neck grey. Lower neck, upper back and breast reddish chestnut. Flanks barred black and white. Belly white. Tail black. Wings striking black and white with dark metallic-green speculum. Edge of Patagonian woods, short grass by water. Often nests in trees. Agricultural land in winter, steppe on migration.

2 UPLAND or MAGELLAN GOOSE *Chloephaga picta*   65cm
♂: white head and upper neck, underparts all barred black and white, or these all white (1 form). Upper back barred black and white, lower upperparts dark grey. Tail black, some with varying white on outer feathers. ♀: head and neck vary from buffy to rufous. Barred parts black and buff. Back brownish grey. Wings of both striking black and white with dark metallic-green speculum. Short grass in valley bottoms near water; croplands in winter, steppe on migration.

3 RUDDY-HEADED GOOSE *Chloephaga rubidiceps*   52cm
Like a small ♀ 2. Head more rufous, barring finer, lower belly and undertail cinnamon. Upperparts browner. Wings striking black and white with dark metallic-green speculum. On short grass in valleys in open country, steppe, near water, agricultural land in winter. The continental population is endangered.

4 KELP GOOSE *Chloephaga hybrida*   60cm
♂: all white. Legs yellow in both sexes. ♀: bill pale pink. White eye-ring. Head, neck and back blackish brown. Breast, flanks and upper belly barred black and white. Hind-parts all white. In flight, striking black and white wings with metallic-green speculum. Young ♂: white with irregular brownish patches. Rocky seashore. Feed on seaweeds at low tide.

5 ANDEAN GOOSE *Chloephaga melanoptera*   75cm
Sexes the same. Thick neck. Bill and legs pink. Mostly white with upper back streaked black, lower back and tail black. Conspicuous wing white with black primaries and dark purply-green speculum. Call: ♂ whistles, ♀ gruff *prayer, prayer*. High Andean lakes and streams, short grass. Lower in winter.

6 ORINOCO GOOSE *Neochen jubata*   55cm
Upright stance. Thick neck. Head, neck and breast buffy cream. Rest tawny rufous, black and white. Legs reddish pink. Black wings with metallic-green coverts and a white triangle on secondaries. ♂ whistling *sheweeps* and guttural honks; deep, growled *howgs* from ♀. River banks, muddy beaches and islands in rivers in forest.

7 BLACK-NECKED SWAN *Cygnus melancoryphus*   120cm
Unmistakable. Bill greyish blue; reddish-pink knob. Head and neck black, white post-ocular line. Rest all white. Pale pink feet. Juv: dull neck and hardly any caruncle. Call quiet and whistled *whews*. Lakes and lagoons, open water, dense reed-beds with clearings, estuaries, edge of the sea, saline lakes.

8 COSCOROBA SWAN *Coscoroba coscoroba*   110cm
Bill bright red. All white, black wing-tips. Pinkish-red feet. Juv: brownish patches, especially at nape. Call an onomatopoeic trumpeted 3-syllable *cón currah*. Often ashore. Open saline lagoons, freshwater lakes and marshes with reed-beds, estuaries, sheltered seashore. Though swanlike, perhaps more closely related to whistling-ducks.

1

2♂

2♀

2♀

1

2♂
barred
form

2♂
white
form

3

3

4♂

4♂

4♀

5

5

6

6

RODRIGUEZ MATA

7

7

8

8

DUCKS (ANATIDAE)

Whistling-ducks (also known as tree-ducks) are upright and long-legged, slow in flight on shorter and rounded wings. They are more terrestrial than other ducks and 1 species very often perches on trees. All have high-pitched whistled calls heard both day and night.

1   BLACK-BELLIED WHISTLING-DUCK *Dendrocygna autumnalis*   49cm
Red bill, pink feet. Crown and neck tawny chestnut. Face and breast brownish grey. Upperparts chestnut. Belly black. Black wings with contrasting white band, coverts greyish buff and ochreous. 4-syllable *hay-heeheehee*. Marshes and lakes, preferably with trees, flooded woods, mangroves, rice-paddies. Frequently perched in trees.

2   FULVOUS WHISTLING-DUCK *Dendrocygna bicolor*   49cm
Mostly tawny fulvous with streaking on upper neck, scalloped barring on dark brown upper back, flanks with black and white streaking along edge of feathers. White undertail and rump, black tail. Wings mostly blackish brown. Bi-syllabic whistled *teweeew*. Lakes, marshes, temporary ponds, flooded areas, roadside ditches, rice-paddies.

3   WHITE-FACED WHISTLING-DUCK *Dendrocygna viduata*   47cm
White face and throat-patch. Rest of head and upper neck black. Lower neck and breast rufous chestnut. Underparts and tail black. Flanks finely barred black, tawny and white. Upperparts dark brown, feathers edged tawny buff. Wings blackish brown. 3-syllable *see-wee-wee*. Lakes, marshes, temporary ponds, flooded areas, roadside ditches, rice-paddies.

4   MUSCOVY DUCK *Cairina moschata*   ♂ 85cm, ♀ 65cm
Unmistakable. Huge and heavy. All black with green, purple and blue gloss. All wing coverts white. Juv duller and lacks white in wings. Flooded woods, lakes, marshes and rivers in forest and woods. Often perches.

5   COMB DUCK *Sarkidiornis melanotos*   ♂ 76cm, ♀ 55cm
Black and white. Upperparts black with purplish, green and blue sheen. Bill black with prominent caruncle (♂ only). Black flecking on white face and neck. Blackish flanks. Wings black with bright gloss on secondaries and coverts. Female flanks scalloped grey. Swamps and marshes, lakes, flooded grass, rivers in woody areas and savannah, rice-paddies. Perches in trees.

6   CRESTED DUCK *Lophonetta specularioides*   55cm
Somewhat conspicuous nuchal crest. Dark mask. Mostly brownish buff with dark brown scaling. Lower upperparts dark. Conspicuous black and white wing with purply-copper wing speculum seen in flight. Primaries and tail blackish. ♂ calls *djeeeew*, ♀ quacks. Inlets and sea. High mountain lakes and rivers, lagoons.

7   SPECTACLED DUCK *Speculanas* (*Anas*) *specularis*   52cm
White 'spectacles' and 'choker'. Rest of the head and upper neck dark chocolate. Flanks and upper back blackish brown, scaled buffy. Breast and rest of underparts buffy brown. Black wings with greenish-blue gloss on coverts, bright purply-copper speculum with black and white trailing edge. Female 'barks'. Mountain tarns above tree line, lakes, fast-flowing rivers near woods.

1

1

4♂

4 juv

4♂

4♀

2

2

5♀

5♂

5♂

5♀

RODRIGUEZ HATA

3

3

6

6

7

7

DUCKS (ANATIDAE)

1 NORTHERN PINTAIL *Anas acuta*   56cm
Head and upper neck dark chocolate contrasting with white rest of neck,
breast and underparts. Upper back and flanks vermiculated grey. Long black
plumes edged white on back. Long, sharp black tail. ♀: buffy brown speckled
and scalloped buff and blackish. Bill bluish grey. Lakes, other fresh water.
Migrant from N America.

2 YELLOW-BILLED or BROWN PINTAIL *Anas georgica*   48cm
Bill yellow with black culmen. Brownish buff and dark brown, scaled
especially on breast and flanks. Long pointed tail. Call is a quiet, fast *piriweep*
whistle. Marshes, lakes, flooded grassland, stubble fields, roadside ditches,
rice-paddies, seashore. 2R is a small dark race (*A. g. georgica*) in S Georgia.
2R¹ is Niceforo's Pintail (*A. g. niceforoi*), now extinct, which may have been a
distinct species.

3 WHITE-CHEEKED PINTAIL *Anas bahamensis*   48cm
White cheeks and throat. Overall tawny cinnamon spotted black on neck,
breast and flanks. Tail creamy white. Bill blue and red. Open brackish lakes with
little or no vegetation, marshes, lakes with reeds, mangroves, tidal areas, ponds.

4 SPECKLED TEAL *Anas flavirostris*   38cm
Bill yellow with black culmen. Short neck. Brownish grey, darker head. Slight
occipital crest on male. Breast spotted black, flanks and undertail plain
brownish grey. ♂'s call is a high-pitched, fast *piriweep* whistle, ♀'s a quiet *jziiiu.*
Lakes, temporary puddles, roadside ditches, streams, flooded grasslands,
sometimes near trees for nesting, high Andean lakes and sea coasts. An
Andean race (Sharp-winged Teal *A. f. oxyptera*) has pale buffy-grey breast,
flanks and underparts. Another race (*A. f. andium*) has dark grey bill.

5 PUNA TEAL *Anas puna*   48cm
Like 6 but larger, bill heavier, blue with black culmen. Cap black, cheeks and
neck creamy, flanks and tail vermiculated. High Andean lakes. Some consider
this a race of 6.

6 SILVER TEAL *Anas versicolor*   41cm
Bill blue and yellow with black culmen. Brownish-black cap. Rest of head and
neck buffy cream, breast dotted black. Flanks barred black and whitish, more
finely so on rump and tail. Marshes, ponds and lakes, streams with reeds and
floating vegetation, flooded grasslands.

7 RINGED TEAL *Callonetta (Anas) leucophrys*   36cm
Showy. Bill light blue, legs pale pink. Crown, line down hind-neck and half-
collar black framing buffy-cream face. Breast pinkish dotted black. Flanks
vermiculated grey. Back reddish chestnut. Rump, tail and undertail black with
large white patch on sides. Black wings, metallic-green speculum, white oval
on greater coverts. ♀: grey bill, pink feet. Head and neck brown with white
brow and line from ear coverts; throat and fore-neck white. Upperparts brown,
breast and flanks irregularly barred brown and whitish. Marshes with floating
vegetation and nearby trees, flooded woods and savannah, roadside ditches
and temporary ponds. Perches; nests in hollow trees and Monk Parakeet nests.

8 BRAZILIAN TEAL *Amazonetta (Anas) brasiliensis*   41cm
Bill and legs bright red. Brown and buffy brown, tawnier on breast. Black spots
on flanks. Cheeks and part of neck whitish. Crown and tail blackish. Wings
black with startling green and blue sheen on upper side and contrasting white
triangle on secondaries. ♀: bill lead-grey, legs red. White markings before eye
and at base of bill. Cheek and throat whitish. Water with floating vegetation,
streams, flooded savannah, rice-paddies.

RODRIGUEZ MATA

DUCKS (ANATIDAE)

1 RED SHOVELER *Anas platalea*   48cm
Big black bill, slightly spoon-shaped. Eyes white. Head and neck creamy
flecked blackish. Breast, flanks, belly and upper back tawny orange dotted
black. Lower body and long, sharp tail black and white. Wings show pale blue
coverts separated by a white line from a dark green speculum. ♀: dark brown
and buff, spotted and scaled. Head and neck paler. Long, pointed tail. Wings
like ♂ but duller. Lakes, marshes, temporary ponds, flooded grassland, streams,
roadside ditches, fresh or brackish.

2 NORTHERN SHOVELER *Anas clypeata*   48cm
Large 'shovelling' black bill. Head and neck bottle-green. Breast white. Flanks
and belly chestnut. Back and tail black and white. Wing coverts pale blue,
speculum dark green with white borders. Female blackish brown and buff, all
spotted, scaled and marked. Lakes and marshes, fresh and brackish. Migratory
from N America.

3 BLUE-WINGED TEAL *Anas discors*   38cm
Head lead-blue, crown black. Notable white half-moon on fore-face. Neck,
breast and flanks ochreous buff spotted and barred black. Lower back blackish,
feathers edged ochreous. Tail and undertail black. White patch on side of
lower body. Wings with pale blue coverts divided by white line from dark
metallic-green speculum. ♀ almost indistinguishable from that of Cinnamon
Teal (4, below) but white area on face at the base of bill more notable, and
scaling on flanks smaller. Lakes, marshes, fresh or salt water, estuaries,
mangrove swamps. Migratory from N America.

4 CINNAMON TEAL *Anas cyanoptera*   42cm
Bill black. All deep reddish chestnut. Wings with pale-blue coverts separated
from dark metallic-green speculum by white line. ♀: browny buff and dark brown
combine to make a scaly effect. Head and neck flecked, crown dark brown. Wing
like ♂ but duller. ♂'s eclipse and juv plumages: intermediate between ♂ and ♀
plumages. Marshes, lakes with emergent vegetation, roadside ditches, temporary
ponds, flooded fields.

5 GREEN-WINGED TEAL *Anas crecca*   35cm
Small and smart. Chestnut head, metallic-green mask. Female scaled greyish
brown and buff. Accidental from N America, reported only once, in Colombia.

6 AMERICAN WIGEON *Anas americana*   47cm
Forehead and crown white. Dark metallic-green mask. Rest of head and neck
whitish flecked black. Breast and flanks browny cinnamon. Tail black, white
patch on side of lower body. White wing-patch on coverts, speculum metallic
green, black and white. ♀: head buffy cream heavily flecked blackish.
Migratory from N America, in N Colombia and NW Venezuela.

7 CHILOE or SOUTHERN WIGEON *Anas sibilatrix*   50cm
Bill pale blue. Fore-face white, rest black with green sheen behind eye.
Whitish ear-spot. Breast and upper back black and white, scaled. Rest of
upperparts with black feathers edged white. Cinnamon on flanks. Underparts
white. Black tail. Notable white patch on wing coverts, speculum metallic
blackish green. ♀: dull version of ♂. Call a longish, *whoooweeeeteeooo*,
whistled and fairly high-pitched. Lakes, marshes, temporary ponds, roadside
ditches, flooded fields, short grass on dryland.

RODRIGUEZ MATA

DUCKS (ANATIDAE)

1 LESSER SCAUP *Aythya affinis*   41cm
Dumpy and large-headed. Bill pale blue. Head, neck and breast shiny black, slight crest on hind-crown. Upperparts vermiculated black and white. Flanks and underparts white. Undertail, rump and tail black. Wings with white flight feathers, black lesser coverts and scapulars. ♀: dark brown and greyish brown with white on fore-face. Lakes and sea coasts. Migratory from N America.

2 RING-NECKED SCAUP or DUCK *Aythya collaris*   42cm
Dumpy and large-headed. Bill pale blue, black and white at the tip and white line at the base. Slight crest on hind-crown. Head, neck, breast, back and tail black with blue and purple sheen. White flanks barely vermiculated with grey. Flight feathers pale grey, primaries tipped black. ♀: dark brown, cheeks paler. White on fore-face and throat, white eye-ring and line back from eye. Lakes, saline coastal lagoons, bays. Migratory from N America. Occasional in N Venezuela.

3 ROSY-BILLED POCHARD *Netta peposaca*   55cm
Big. Pinkish-red bill and caruncle. Head, neck, breast and upperparts black, the first two with purply gloss. Flanks vermiculated grey. Undertail white. Wings with striking white bar. ♀: bill pale blue-grey. Brown, darker above. Whitish eye-ring, and at throat and base of bill. Undertail white. Call is a deep *aaark*. Lakes with reeds, marshes, temporary ponds, streams, roadside ditches, flooded grasslands, open water, stubble fields and rice-paddies.

4 SOUTHERN POCHARD *Netta erythrophthalma*   50cm
Bill pale greyish blue. Mostly black with purply sheen. Flanks chestnut. Striking white band in wing. ♀: brown, darker upperparts. Head with white post-ocular line down to fore-neck, white throat and at base of bill. Undertail white. Lakes and marshes, temporary ponds, often with reed-beds, Andean lakes.

5 BRAZILIAN MERGANSER *Mergus octosetaceus*   53cm
Black bill long and slender with 'teeth'. Head, upper neck and drooping crest black with green sheen. Upperparts black. Lower neck, breast, flanks and underparts vermiculated grey and black. Legs pinkish red. Wings with double white patch on secondaries. Rivers and streams in dense forest and gallery forest. In flight looks like a cormorant but white in wing is diagnostic. Dives for fish and invertebrates in forest rivers with rapids, waterfalls and clean, clear water. Endangered. Probably now only in Brazil (Serra do Canastra and Chapada dos Veadeiros National Parks and 4 other locations) though formerly also in E Paraguay and NE Argentina.

6 TORRENT DUCK *Merganetta armata*   38cm
Unmistakable. Slender. Long, rigid tail. Narrow red bill. Red legs. Head and neck white with black lines along crown and down hind-neck, from eye down neck (S form) and across cheek to throat and fore-neck. Breast and upper flanks black. Rest of underparts cinnamon streaked black. Dorsal feathers black edged white. Other forms all lack line from eye to throat; N race (Colombia, Venezuela) has white underparts. ♀ head and hind-neck grey. Throat, lower cheeks, neck, breast, flanks and rest of underparts tawny rufous. Dorsal feathers blackish grey edged white. Incredibly agile on the surface and diving in white-water rivers and streams in the Andes, where it feeds on insect larvae, some molluscs and perhaps small fishes.

1♂

1♀

1♂

1♂

1♀

3♀

3♂

2♀

2♂

3♀

2♀

2♂

♂

4♀

4♀

4♂

4♂

5♀

5♂

5♂

5♀

6♀

6♂

6♂

6R♂

6R♂

6♀

RODRIGUEZ MATA

DUCKS (ANATIDAE)

1 BLACK-HEADED DUCK *Heteronetta atricapilla* 40cm
Floats low. Bill dull pale blue with pink at the base. Head and upper neck black.
Upperparts dark brown. Wings brownish black. ♀: bill brownish grey. Head, neck
and upperparts dirty brown, faint buffy-white brow. Silent. Dense vegetation in
lakes, roadside ditches, marshes, open water, flooded areas. Parasitic nester.

Stiff-tails dive for food. Reluctant to fly. 3 and 4 often hold their tails erect.

2 MASKED DUCK *Nomonyx (Oxyura) dominicus* 32cm
Low flotation. Never raises tail. Very secretive. Bright blue bill. Black face.
White eye-ring. Nape, neck, breast and flanks tawny rufous, these streaked
black. Upperparts rufous, streaked black. ♀: grey bill. Head dark brown with 2
buff stripes across face. Dense floating vegetation in marshes, roadside ditches,
rice-paddies, oxbows.

3 LAKE DUCK *Oxyura vittata* 37cm
Blue bill. Black head and upper neck. Rest reddish chestnut. Cut-off between
black and chestnut almost horizontal. Eclipse plumage intermediate between
this and that of ♀. ♀: brownish-grey bill. Upper head dark brownish with 1
white stripe. Lower cheeks, throat and upper neck whitish. Body brown, darker
above, breast and flanks barred buff. Open water of marshes, lakes, roadside
ditches, temporary ponds, with dense reed-beds.

4 ANDEAN DUCK *Oxyura ferruginea* 42cm
Broad bill pale blue. Head and upper neck black. Body deep chestnut. Tail
shorter than in 3. Undertail dirty white. Cut-off between black and chestnut
slanted backwards. ♀: brownish-grey bill. Dark blackish brown, scaled and
barred on breast and flanks. 1 faint stripe through face. A N race has varying
white on the face (*O. f. andina*). Open mountain lakes, marshes, some reed-
beds, dams, lakes on Patagonian steppe. Perhaps a race of the Ruddy Duck
(*O. jamaicensis*) from N America.

Steamer-ducks are huge and hefty, with large heads. They dive for their food – of
fish, mussels, crab and insect larvae – using wings for propulsion and 'steam' like old
paddle boats to escape danger (1 species flies).

5 FLYING STEAMER-DUCK *Tachyeres patachonicus* 68cm
Least hefty. Wings reach base of longish tail. ♂: head greyish white with post-
ocular streak and eye-ring white. Rusty wash on breast and throat. ♀ darker.
Bill olive with a touch of yellow at the base. Head dark brownish grey, white
post-ocular line. Juv: darker than ♀, blue-grey bill, no post-ocular stripe.
Inland fresh and brackish ponds and lakes, rivers, sea coasts mostly in winter.

6 FALKLAND STEAMER-DUCK *Tachyeres brachypterus* 70cm
Flightless. Like 5 but very much larger and heftier. Heavy bill. Wings barely
reach rump. ♂: head grey, white eye-ring and post-ocular streak. Rusty wash on
throat and breast, head paling with age to white. ♀ like 5's. Sea coasts,
protected waters of inlets, bays and coves. The birds on continental S America
(Chubut, Argentina) are considered by some to be a separate species, White-
headed Steamer-duck *T. leucocephalus*.

7 MAGELLANIC STEAMER-DUCK *Tachyeres pteneres* 80cm
Flightless. The heaviest and heftiest. Wings barely reach base of rump.
Generally paler and more uniform between the sexes. ♀: slightly darker face.
Bill of both ♂ and ♀ very thick at the base, orangy yellow. Juv: dark head and
olive-grey bill. Sheltered waters of channels and fjords.

2♂

2♂ eclipse

3♀

3♂

3♂ eclipse

3♀

2♀

1♂

1♀

1♀

1♂

4♂

4♂

4♀

5♂ worn plumage

5 juv

5♀

5♂

5♂ fresh plumage

6♂ worn plumage

6♂ fresh plumage

6♀

7♂

7♀

6♂

7♂

RODRIGUEZ MATA

NEW WORLD VULTURES (CATHARTIDAE)

Though vulturine in appearance and habits these birds may be related to storks.

1 GREATER YELLOW-HEADED VULTURE *Cathartes melambrotos* 78cm
Like 2 but bulkier. Deep black. In flight, wings held horizontal; from below, inner primaries notably dark, forming an area contrasting with the rest of flight feathers. Shafts of outer primaries white when seen from above. Tail proportionately longer and wings broader. Perches upright. Less wobbly flight. Only primary lowland tropical forests.

2 LESSER YELLOW-HEADED VULTURE *Cathartes burrovianus* 64cm
Slender. Dull brownish black. Folded wings extend well beyond tail. Bare head yellowish to orangy red with blue on crown. From below, pale flight feathers contrast with dark underwing coverts. From above, white shafts of outer primaries visible, giving the impression of a pale area at a distance. Tail shortish. Juv: browner, head greyish brown. Perches somewhat horizontally. In flight, wings above the horizontal, wobbly flight low and usually over grass. Savannah, wet grassland with scattered trees.

3 TURKEY VULTURE *Cathartes aura* 70cm
Brownish black. Bare head reddish (whitish nape in some races). In flight, long, fairly broad wings; from below, pale flight feathers contrast with coverts. Flies higher than 2 with wings in shallow 'V'. Shafts of outer primaries dark. Folded wings as long as tail. Perches fairly horizontal. Juv: head greyish brown. Desert coasts, grassland, savannah, edge, lowland tropical forest, woods, mountains, urban settings.

4 BLACK VULTURE *Coragyps atratus* 60cm
All black. Bare head blackish grey. Broad wings. Base of primaries whitish, forming an area seen in flight. Short, broad tail. Alternates flapping with gliding. Forest, open country, scrubby or desert areas, urban settings, rubbish tips.

5 KING VULTURE *Sarcoramphus papa* 80cm
White, washed cream on upper back. Flight feathers and tail black. Head orange, black, grey and cream. Iris white. Grey muffler on neck. Juv: all blackish, may be taken for a Black Vulture. Forest, woods, savannah, forested areas.

6 ANDEAN CONDOR *Vultur gryphus* 120cm
Huge and imposing. Bare head, ♂ with comb on forehead, absent in ♀. White ruff on neck. Long, broad wings, primaries splayed. Upperwing coverts white. Juv: all blackish brown. Mountains, Andes and others, to sea coasts in some areas.

HAWKS (ACCIPITRIDAE)

1   WHITE-NECKED HAWK *Leucopternis lacernulatus*   ♂ 40cm, ♀ 43cm
Head and underparts white. Black back and wings. Black flecking on hind-neck.
Short tail black with very broad white subterminal band. Coastal mountainous
Atlantic forest.

2   WHITE HAWK *Leucopternis albicollis*   ♂ 48cm, ♀ 58cm
Variable races. Head, neck and underparts white, or with streaked crown and
neck; another with white back and wing coverts. Back and wings black, feather
tips variably edged white. Tail black, white at base and tip (or white with narrow
black subterminal band). Streaks on crown, hind-neck and back vary from faint
to heavy, according to race. Rainforest, edge, open woods, lowlands, mountains.

3   GREY-BACKED HAWK *Leucopternis occidentalis*   ♂ 49cm, ♀ 57cm
Upperparts blackish lead. Underparts white. Crown, cheeks and sides of the
neck densely streaked. Tail white with broad subterminal black band.
Deciduous and evergreen forest, and cloud-forest.

4   MANTLED HAWK *Leucopternis polionotus*   ♂ 47cm, ♀ 56cm
Head, neck and underparts white, upperparts black, flight feathers tipped
white. Upper tail coverts edged white. Tail white, basal half black. Tropical
forest in mountains.

5   BARRED HAWK *Leucopternis princeps*   ♂ 53cm, ♀ 59cm
Head, neck, upper breast and upperparts blackish slate. Rest of underparts
white barred dark slate. Tail blackish slate, 3 narrowish white bars on basal
half. In flight, underwing all barred. Montane forest to subtropical uplands,
clearings, edge.

6   BLACK-FACED HAWK *Leucopternis melanops*   ♂ 38cm, ♀ 43cm
Small. Cere and legs orange. Lores and around eye black. Crown, hind-neck
and upper back white streaked black. Upperparts black with white markings.
Underparts white. Tail black with white medial band and narrow tip. Lowland
rainforest, gallery forest, mangroves.

7   SEMI-PLUMBEOUS HAWK *Leucopternis semiplumbeus*   ♂ 33cm, ♀ 38cm
Smallest. Dumpy with short rounded wings. Cere and legs orange. Head and
upperparts lead-grey. Throat and rest of underparts white, faintly streaked grey
on sides of breast. Tail blackish slate with narrowish white medial band.
Humid forest, patches, edge, tall secondary growth.

8   WHITE-BROWED HAWK *Leucopternis kuhli*   ♂ 37cm, ♀ 45cm
Small. Crown and face-mask black. White brow. Back of cheek, sides of neck and
of breast white streaked black. Upperparts dark slate-grey. Underparts white. Tail
black with white band and tip. Cere and legs orange. Lowland tropical rainforest.

9   SLATE-COLOURED HAWK *Leucopternis schistaceus*   ♂ 43cm, ♀ 47cm
Hefty. All dark slate-grey, including underwing. Cere, bare face, and longish
legs bright orange. Iris yellow. Tail with mid-band and fine tip white. Juv:
barred black and white on lower belly and underwing. Sometimes 2 white
bands on tail. Lowland tropical and varzea forest, usually near water,
mangroves, gallery forest.

10   PLUMBEOUS HAWK *Leucopternis plumbeus*   ♂ 35cm, ♀ 39cm
Small and dumpy. Rounded wings. All dark slate-grey. Underwing with base of
flight feathers whitish. Cere and legs bright orange. Face all feathered. Red iris.
Tail with white mid-band. Juv: barred blackish and white as 9. Tail with 2
white bands. Lowland and foothill tropical rainforest.

RODRIGUEZ MATA

HAWKS (ACCIPITRIDAE)

Accipiters are efficient sylvan hunters, with broad, rounded wings and long tails that allow them to steer amazingly well through the vegetation. Smallish head, slender tarsi and long toes used especially for capturing birds in flight. Hard to see.

1   TINY HAWK *Accipiter superciliosus*   ♂ 22cm, ♀ 27cm
Smallest. Red eye. Upperparts dark grey, paler on cheeks. Underparts white barred dark grey. Underwing and flight feathers barred. Tail proportionately shorter than the rest of the genus, barred blackish and grey. Juv: upperparts dark brown. Underparts buff barred rufous. Tail more narrowly barred. Humid rainforest, varzea, gallery, cloud-forest, edge and clearings, deforested areas, woods.

2   SEMICOLLARED HAWK *Accipiter collaris*   ♂ 25cm, ♀ 30cm
Like 1 but larger. Longer tail. Crown and nape blackish, cheeks and collar on hind-neck white barred black. Underparts white broadly barred blackish. Juv: upperparts and cheeks dark chestnut-brown. Rufous hind-collar. Underparts tawny buff barred rufous. Tail with 6 narrow black bands. Subtropical rainforest, cloud-forest, edge and clearings in montane rainforest, generally at higher elevations than 1.

3   GREY-BELLIED GOSHAWK *Accipiter poliogaster*   ♂ 42cm, ♀ 52cm
Largest. Upperparts blackish. Cheeks to hind-neck grey or blackish. Underparts white or washed grey. Tail blackish with 3 bands and tip grey. Juv: very like adult Ornate Hawk-eagle without a crest and unfeathered tarsi. Black cap and malar streak. Cheeks, neck and sides of breast rufous. Throat and mid-breast white with lines of black streaks down centre and on edges. Upperpart feathers edged whitish. Lower underparts white barred black. Tropical and subtropical rainforest, edge and clearings, riverine forest, woods.

4   RUFOUS-THIGHED HAWK *Accipiter erythronemius*   ♂ 24cm, ♀ 33cm
Variable. Crown and upperparts dark grey. Face and underparts buffy white barred cinnamon. Thighs cinnamon. Vent white. Underwing buffy white and greyish white barred blackish. Tail grey with 4 broad black bands. Other phases have rufous, buffy white and rufous, or white underparts, and there is also a black form and intermediates. Juv: upperparts brown, feathers edged buff. Underparts buffy white, streaked cinnamon. Tropical, subtropical and temperate forest, edge and clearings, savannah, dry woods. Some consider the Andean race a separate species: the Plain-breasted Hawk *Accipiter ventralis*; while the N species (Sharp-shinned Hawk *Accipiter striatus*) may include the two above.

5   BICOLOURED HAWK *Accipiter bicolor*   ♂ 35cm, ♀ 43cm
Crown and upperparts dark grey. Cheeks and underparts grey. Vent white, thighs rufous. Axillaries and underwing rufous or buffy white according to race. Flight feathers barred. Tail dark grey with 3 bands and blackish tip. Juv: underparts and nuchal collar buffy cream, or cinnamon underparts, according to race. The S Andean form adult has whitish cheeks, somewhat streaked blackish grey. Underparts barred rusty, each bar edged blackish. Juv: upperparts browner, feathers edged buffy cinnamon. Underparts and neck buffy white streaked blackish brown. Thighs cinnamon-buff. Woods and forest, gallery forest, savannah with palms, Cerrado, rainforest, *Araucaria* woods. The S race (Chilean Hawk *A. b. chilensis*) is often believed to be a separate species.

1

1

3

3 juv

1 juv

3

2

2 juv

5 juv

5
juv

ean
us
n

4R
ndean
juv

4
4R
Andean
intermediate
form

an
e
n

4
juv

5

5R S
race

4

5

4R
Andean
lack form

5R juv
S race

5

RODRIGUEZ MATA

OSPREY, HAWKS AND HARRIERS (ACCIPITRIDAE)

1 OSPREY *Pandion haliaetus* ♂ 50cm, ♀ 57cm
Dark brown and white. Brown mask that continues down neck. Short nuchal
crest. Breast streaked brown. Long, angular wings. Powerful tarsae and toes.
Flies like a huge gull over water to catch fish in spectacular dives. Perches on
snags and rocks near water. Usually solitary. Migrates from N America. Inland
and coastal waters.

2 CRANE HAWK *Geranospiza caerulescens* ♂ 45cm, ♀ 53cm
Nearly all grey or variably barred white on underparts according to race. Long
black tail with two broad white bands and white tip. Broad wings; black
primaries with white median band. Very long orange legs. Red eye. There is a
black form. Juv: underparts creamy white streaked grey, face creamy. Often
hunts clambering agilely in trees searching for small vertebrates and insects.
Call is a hollow *how*. Edge of forest, gallery forest, mangroves, swamps, chaco
woods, savannah, patches of woods and scattered trees.

3 LONG-WINGED HARRIER *Circus buffoni* ♂ 46cm, ♀ 57cm
Long broad wings and tail. ♂ black hood, whitish face and gill-line. Upperparts
blackish, rump white. Flight feathers pale grey barred blackish. Underparts
white or slightly creamy. Underwing barred. Tail broadly banded blackish and
pale grey. ♀ dark brown hood, cream face and gill-line. Upperparts dark
brown, rump white. Underparts creamy with fine brown streaking. Tail buffy
grey with three visible dark-brown bands. Underwing creamy streaked brown.
Juv: head and neck dark brown streaked creamy. Underparts and underwing
coverts buffy cream densely streaked brown. Vent and thighs chestnut streaked
brown. Tail buffy grey with five blackish bands. There are black forms and
intermediate immatures. Low, wobbly glider that drops on its small prey –
reptiles, rodents and small birds; seldom seen perched. Damp grasslands, reeds,
marshes, rice paddies, cereal crops and stubble.

4 CINEREOUS HARRIER *Circus cinereus* ♂ 40cm, ♀ 50cm
♂ head, neck, upper breast and upperparts ash grey. Rump white. Underparts
white finely barred rusty. Tail whitish grey with central feathers and
subterminal band blackish. Flight feathers mostly white tipped black. ♀ head
and upperparts brown faintly streaked buff. Facial pattern little marked.
Upperparts dark brown, feathers edged cinnamon buff; rump white. Flight
feathers grey barred black. Underparts barred white and rust. Underwing white
finely barred rusty, flight feathers whitish grey barred blackish. Trailing edge of
wing blackish. Tail whitish grey with three visible blackish bands. Both sexes
have yellow eye. Juv: head and neck densely streaked buff. Upperparts brown,
feathers notably edged cinnamon buff. Underparts creamy buff streaked
brown. Underwing whitish, finely barred rusty. Tail greyish buff with five
visible blackish bands. Wing-beat faster than 3; flies low, wings in shallow 'V',
perches in grass or on fences. Preys on rodents and birds, sometimes takes these
on the wing. Open grassland and low scrub.

5 NORTHERN HARRIER *Circus cyaneus* ♂ 53cm, ♀ 53cm
Like 4. ♂ differs in underparts streaked rusty. Tail grey with 5 blackish bars. ♀
very like juv 4 but underwing coverts buffy, streaked dark brown. Juv lower ·
underparts and vent cinnamon. Breast and underwing cinnamon streaked
blackish. Damp lowland grass, freshwater marshes, reed-beds, tall grasses.
Migrates from NAmerica. Accidental in Colombia and Venezuela.

1

1

1

2 juv

2

1

2R

2

4 juv

4♀

3 black form

4♂

4♂

3 imm
dark form

4♀

3 juv

3♀

3♂

5 juv

3♀

3♂

4♂

3♂

4♂

3♀

HAWKS (ACCIPITRIDAE)

1 BROAD-WINGED HAWK *Buteo platypterus* ♂ 35cm, ♀ 44cm
Small and compact. Upperparts brown, feathers edged buffy cinnamon. Throat white. Underparts irregularly barred white and rufous. Vent white. Tail black with 2 wide bands and tip white. Broad wings, flight feathers barred and following edge black. Juv: underparts creamy streaked dark brown. Malar stripe and mid-throat dark brown. Tip and following edge of wing blackish. Tail with 5 blackish bars. Trusting, perches in the open, by roads. Hunts rodents, frogs, reptiles, crabs and small vertebrates from a perch. Partly wooded areas, edge of forest, woods, cleared areas, cultivated land, plantations from plains to above tree line in mountains. Migratory from N America.

2 SHORT-TAILED HAWK *Buteo brachyurus* ♂ 35cm, ♀ 40cm
Long, broad wings and short tail notable in flight, wing-tips bent upwards. Upperparts blackish. Forehead and underparts white. Underwing coverts white, flight feathers barred. Wing-tips and following edge blackish. Tail with 3 black bars and broad subterminal band. There is an all black form with flight feathers and tail as in the typical form. Juv: head and sides of neck brown, streaked creamy. Forehead creamy. Upperparts dark brown, feathers edged buff. Underparts creamy. Broad dark brown streaks on sides of breast, finer and sparse on rest of underparts, denser on flanks. Underwing creamy. Tail with 6 blackish bars. Trusting, perches in open. Hunts on the wing. Forest and woods, mountains to plains, open land, scattered trees, thorny woods, often near water.

3 WHITE-THROATED HAWK *Buteo albigula* ♂ 38cm, ♀ 47cm
Tail longer and wings narrower than 2. Cheeks streaked. Upperparts brown, feathers edged cinnamon. Underparts white. Sides of throat, of breast and flanks rusty, feathers edged whitish. Lower breast and mid belly sparsely streaked, thighs finely barred rusty. Underwing white, barred and streaked rusty and blackish brown. Tail with faint grey bars and subterminal band. Juv: underparts streaked blackish brown. Thighs creamy, streaked. Underwing whitish streaked blackish brown. Tail with 10 grey bars. Within woods. Flies with agility through the vegetation. Andean woods from sea level to alpine, stunted vegetation. Hunts birds and rodents. Rises on thermals. Southern birds move N in winter.

4 RUFOUS-TAILED HAWK *Buteo ventralis* ♂ 55cm, ♀ 60cm
Hefty. Short legs, powerful feet with long toes. Upperparts dark brown. Throat and mid breast white. Rest of underparts densely streaked and barred rusty and blackish. Thighs barred rufous. Tail from above rich rufous, barred black. Underwing whitish streaked brown and rusty. Dark brown patch under leading edge. Tip and following edge of flight feathers blackish. There is a black form. Juv: upperparts blackish brown with irregular whitish markings. Underparts creamy white streaked blackish brown. From below tail whitish with 8 grey bars. Blackish patch under leading edge of wing. Wing-tips black. Within woods, rare and hard to see. Hunts birds up to duck-size. S Andean woods.

5 GALAPAGOS HAWK *Buteo galapagoensis* ♂ 50cm, ♀ 55cm
Sooty black. Juv: upperparts dark brown, feathers edged buffy cinnamon or whitish. Underparts cinnamon buff streaked dark brown. Tail greyish finely barred blackish grey. Imm variably creamy on head and underparts. Very trusting, perches in open. Feeds on small vertebrates and insects. Seashores to woods in mountains. Endemic to Galapagos Is (Ecuador).

HAWKS (ACCIPITRIDAE)

1 WHITE-TAILED HAWK *Buteo albicaudatus* ♂ 52cm, ♀ 60cm
Upperparts and hood blackish grey. 'Shoulders' rufous. Underparts white, finely barred blackish grey on flanks. Thighs finely barred blackish grey or rust. Short tail white with black subterminal band, rest finely barred grey. Another race differs in all underparts and throat being white. In flight long wings, broader at the base. Underwing coverts white or with variable barring blackish or rusty. Wing-tips and trailing edge black. When perched, wings are much longer than tail. There is a black form. Juv: very like 2's but longer-winged, upperparts darker and more uniform. 'Shoulder' feathers edged rufous. Brow, mid-cheek and underparts creamy white. Contrasting blackish malar stripe extending to sides of breast. Variable blackish on chin or throat. Lower underparts creamy with blackish streaking; barring on vent and thighs. Tail whitish finely barred grey. In flight differs from 3 in whitish flanks and underwing densely streaked blackish. Imm blacker; mid breast, cheeks and brow whitish. Perches very exposed, often by roads. Open grasslands, with trees, bushy steppe, savannah, open woods, plantations.

2 RED-BACKED HAWK *Buteo polyosoma* ♂ 45cm, ♀ 55cm
♂ upperparts grey, underparts white. Black subterminal band on white tail. In flight underwing white, flight feathers faintly barred greyish; wing-tip and trailing edge blackish. ♀ back rufous. Wings shorter than 1, do not pass tail when perched. Very variable with black, rufous, grey and intermediate forms, with more or less barring on wings and underparts. Juv like that of 1 but more cinnamon buff generally. Dark markings brown and less contrasting. Feather edges more evident, cinnamon buff. In flight flanks and underwing very buff, streaked brown. Wing-tip blackish. Tail whitish grey finely barred darker grey. The large high mountain form of C Colombia to NW Argentina was once considered the Puna Hawk (*B. poecilochrous*), with broader wings, longer than tail when perched. Visible on exposed perches, often by roads. Sea level to high mountains in steppe and brushland, upland grass, temperate forest, gallery forest, paramo.

3 SWAINSON'S HAWK *Buteo swainsoni* ♂ 48cm, ♀ 55cm
A great soarer, often in flocks, sometimes hundreds. Characteristic flight with wings in a shallow 'V'. Shorter legs than other Buteos. White throat and around base of bill, rest of head and upperparts brown. Chestnutty breast. Rest of underparts white, somewhat barred and streaked chestnut. Tail whitish grey with 7 black bars. In flight, underwing white contrasting with grey flight feathers barred black. Intermediate form with darker breast, underparts cinnamon, barred chestnut. There is a blackish brown phase. Juv like that of 2 but face paler and cream. Underparts buffy cream with blackish patches on sides of breast. In flight, underwings buffy, barred and streaked blackish brown. Flight feathers greyish, barred blackish. Tail whitish grey with 8 blackish bars. Unafraid. Perches on posts or on ground. Feeds mostly on grasshoppers and locusts. Open fields, scattered trees and bushes. Migratory from N America.

4 ZONE-TAILED HAWK *Buteo albonotatus* ♂ 45cm, ♀ 55cm
Very long and broad wings. Tail long. In flight like a Turkey Vulture. All black but for two visible white bands on the tail. Flight feathers seen from below grey with blackish barring. Juv: like ad but white markings on breast and belly. Tail with 8 greyish white bars. Savannah, woods, cultivated fields, damp or dry deciduous forests, bushy areas, caatinga.

1 juv

1 black form

3 juv

3 black form

3 intermediate form

3

juv

1

1R

3 juv

3

3 juv

3 pale form

1

2 black form

4

2♀

2 juv

4

2R♀

♂

2♂

2 juv

2R♂

2 rufous form

HAWKS (ACCIPITRIDAE)

1 BLACK-COLLARED HAWK *Busarellus nigricollis*　♂ 46cm, ♀ 50cm
Head and neck cream-coloured. Fore-neck black. Rest cinnamon-rufous.
Flight-feathers blackish. Tail barred with broad subterminal black band, tip
whitish. Juv: head streaked blackish. Black collar. Back blackish brown, wings
cinnamon-rufous barred and mottled blackish brown. Underparts buffy white
to tawny streaked and barred blackish brown. Always near water in open
country to tropical forest, savannah, mangroves.

2 SAVANNA HAWK *Buteogallus (Heterospizias) meridionalis*　♂ 48cm, ♀ 58cm
Overall cinnamon, back and part of wing dark brown. Underparts finely barred
blackish. Bold cinnamon-rufous and black wing-pattern in flight. Tail black
with white mid-band and tip. Juv browner. Breast creamy white, streaked, sides
dark. Tail barred. Open grassland and savannah, with scattered trees or palms,
marshes in woods, edge of forest, riverine forest, mangroves.

③ BLACK-CHESTED BUZZARD-EAGLE
Geranoaetus melanoleucus　　　　　　　　　♂ 62cm, ♀ 78cm
Huge. Broad wings and very short tail giving delta-wing effect. Upperparts and
breast grey, paler on throat and wing coverts, darker on breast, barred on wings.
Lower underparts whitish, faintly barred (or pure white). Tail grey. Juv: brown,
underparts buffy white and densely streaked. Long tail barred. Mountains with
trees and bushes, chaco, savannah, steppe, lowlands, Páramos.

4 BAY-WINGED or HARRIS'S HAWK *Parabuteo unicinctus* ♂ 47cm, ♀ 55cm
Brownish black with rufous wing coverts and leggings. Rump and vent white.
Base and tip of tail white, rest blackish. In flight, wings broad and rounded, tail
long; underwing rufous, flight feathers black. Juv: upperparts browner, more
streaked and barred. Shoulders washed rufous. Underparts buffy white heavily
streaked blackish brown. Thighs barred cinnamon and buffy white. Tail finely
barred grey and blackish. Open woods, chaco, savannah, swamps, often near
water in arid habitats.

5 RUFOUS CRAB-HAWK *Buteogallus aequinoctialis*　　♂ 42cm, ♀ 47cm
Hood and upperparts blackish brown. Coverts, scapulars and tertials edged
cinnamon-rufous. Secondaries rufous tipped black. Underparts and underwing
cinnamon-rufous finely barred blackish. Primaries black, secondaries tipped
black. Short tail black with narrow white mid-bar and tip. Long orange legs.
Juv like that of 6 but upperparts paler. Underparts flecked rufous brown and
more sparsely. Leggings paler barred. Mangroves, saline coastal marshes, wet
savannah, river shores.

6 GREAT BLACK HAWK *Buteogallus urubitinga*　　　　♂ 50cm, ♀ 65cm
All black, base and tip of tail white. Yellow cere and bare before eye. Long
yellow legs. Juv: post-ocular, upperparts and sides of breast blackish brown,
barred cinnamon on coverts and flight feathers. Brow, cheeks and underparts
dirty white streaked blackish brown. Thighs and tail barred rich buff and
blackish brown. Always near water, gallery forest, savannah, wet grassland
with scattered trees, edge, deltas, chaco woods, forest edge, clearings.

7 COMMON BLACK HAWK *Buteogallus anthracinus*　　♂ 42cm, ♀ 53cm
Very like 6 but smaller. Legs and tail proportionately shorter. More and brighter
bare area on face. Tail black with white mid-band and tip. Juv: very like 6 but tail
with 7 blackish-brown bars on tail, much broader than 6's. Always near water, sea
coasts, mangroves, swamps, tidal flats, beaches. *B. a. subtilis* is considered by some
a separate species: Mangrove Black Hawk.

juv

juv

1

1

3

3

2

3

3 juv

4 juv

4

5

6

7

6 juv

RODRIGUEZ MATA

EAGLES (ACCIPITRIDAE)

1 CRESTED EAGLE *Morphnus guianensis* ♂ 80cm, ♀ 90cm
Like 2 but less massive. Bill and legs more slender. Head and breast grey. Single crest. Upperparts blackish, marbled and irregularly barred greyish. Underparts white, faintly and finely barred tawny. Dark form densely barred black, extending onto underwing. Head and breast blackish. Tail proportionately longer. In flight, very broad rounded wings. White axillaries. Juv: starts whiter above than that of 2. Imm very like 2 but back and shoulders paler, marbled grey and white. Tail with many narrow black bands. Lowland tropical and subtropical forest, gallery forest.

2 HARPY EAGLE *Harpia harpyja* ♂ 90cm, ♀ 105cm
Huge and powerful. Very thick tarsus and bill. Head grey with blackish double crest. Upperparts and pectoral collar blackish. Faintly barred dark grey on flight feathers. Underparts white barred black on thighs. In flight, very large rounded wings. Axillaries black. Juv: head and neck white. Upperparts grey. Tail with many narrow black bands. The collar starts to appear at an early age, grey. No black axillaries. Preferably lowland primary tropical and subtropical forest and woods.

3 SOLITARY EAGLE *Harpyhaliaetus solitarius* ♂ 70cm, ♀ 78cm
All slaty black. Tail with wide white band and white tip. Slight nuchal crest. Short tail and huge wings noted in flight. Juv: upperparts dark brown. Head and underparts buffy white with blackish-brown streaks. Sides of neck, and line around hind-cheek dark brown. Tail marbled pale grey. Montane forest and cloud-forest.

4 CROWNED EAGLE *Harpyhaliaetus coronatus* ♂ 70cm, ♀ 80cm
Long visible crest. All pale slate-grey. Outer flight feathers and tail blackish, this with wide white band and white tip. Juv: upperparts greyish brown. Head and underparts whitish, finely streaked blackish. Dark patches on sides of upper breast. Thighs dark greyish-brown. Tail whitish marbled grey, dark subterminal band. Dry open woods, savannah, chaco woods, bushy areas, caatinga, grassland with palms.

1

1 juv

3 juv

3

1

3

1 dark
form

1 juv

2 juv

3

3 juv

2

4

4 juv

2

2 juv

4

4 juv

RODRIGUEZ MATA

EAGLES (ACCIPITRIDAE)

1 ORNATE HAWK-EAGLE *Spizaetus ornatus* ♂ 65cm, ♀ 70cm
Crown and long slender erectile crest black. Face and neck cinnamon-rufous.
White from chin to breast, edged with long black moustache-like malar streak.
Upperparts black and greyish brown. Lower underparts white, heavily barred
black. Tail and underwing barred black and whitish. Thick feathered tarsi and
powerful talons. In flight, short, broad, rounded wings and long tail show broad
barring. Juv: head and underparts white, barred black on lower flanks and
leggings. Tail more narrowly barred. Primary humid tropical and subtropical
and gallery forest, edge.

2 BLACK HAWK-EAGLE *Spizaetus tyrannus* ♂ 65cm, ♀ 75cm
Black, short, thick occipital crest with white markings. Belly, vent, thighs and
feathered tarsi barred black and white. Long tail with wide black and dappled-
grey bands. In flight, wings broad and rounded, underwing dark with
concentric pale barring. Juv: crested as adult. Upperparts dark brown, feathers
edged paler. Pale brow, dark cheeks. Underparts buffy white, streaked on breast
and barred below dark brown. Tail more narrowly barred. Tropical and
subtropical humid forest and edges, gallery forest, secondary growth, woods.

3 BLACK-AND-CHESTNUT EAGLE *Oroaetus isidori* ♂ 70cm, ♀ 85cm
Very large. Visible crest. Head and upperparts brownish black. Underparts to
feathered tarsi all chestnut, finely streaked black. Lower flanks and leggings
brushed blackish. Long tail whitish with wide black subterminal band. Huge
wing: in flight underwing coverts chestnut, flight feathers whitish faintly
barred and notably tipped black. Juv: upperparts greyish brown, feathers edged
pale. Flight feathers faintly barred darker. Head and underparts buffy white
streaked brown on crest, sides of neck and breast, flanks and tarsi, these washed
pale brown. Tail dappled whitish with 3 narrow blackish bands and broad
subterminal band. Underwing coverts buffy white streaked dark, flight feathers
whitish with blackish bars and tips. Humid, undisturbed montane forest.

4 BLACK-AND-WHITE HAWK-EAGLE
Spizastur melanoleucus ♂ 55cm, ♀ 60cm
Slightly crested black crown-patch. Head, underparts and feathered tarsi
white. Back and wings blackish. Tail pale brownish grey narrowly barred black.
Black bill, lores and around eye contrast with yellow cere and iris. In flight,
broad, somewhat rounded wings, tail long. Underwing coverts white, flight
feathers pale greyish barred blackish grey. Juv like adult. Humid forest near
edge, clearings and gallery forest.

RODRIGUEZ MATA

KITES AND HAWKS (ACCIPITRIDAE)

1 **SNAIL KITE** *Rosthramus sociabilis* 40–44cm
♂ slate black; rump, upper tail coverts, vent and base of tail white. Slender hooked bill. Pinky red cere and legs, red eye. ♀ blackish brown. Head and underparts somewhat streaked whitish buff. Juv upperparts brown, feathers edged buffy cinnamon. Underparts buffy cream streaked brown. Solitary or loose flocks. Flies slowly over bodies of water. Feeds exclusively on water snails. Nasal *ke-ke-ke-ke* call. Any freshwater body, mangroves.

2 **SLENDER-BILLED KITE** *Rosthramus hamatus* 35–39cm
All slate black. Wings and tail proportionately shorter than 1. Bill thicker. Eye yellow. Juv like ad but tail with 2 narrow white bars and white tip. Faint barring on primaries and vent. Solitary, pairs or small flocks. Feeds on snails, rarely crabs. Repeated noisy cat-like call. Bodies of fresh water, edge of flooded forest, rainforest ponds, varzea, swamps.

3 **HOOK-BILLED KITE** *Chondrohierax uncinatus* 40–45cm
Heavy hooked bill. Eye white. Notable bare skin before eye yellow and greyish green. Cere yellow. In flight primaries spread like fingers. Long tail, very short legs and toes. ♂ upperparts grey. Underparts barred grey and white. Tail black with 2 broad bands and tip whitish grey. Underwing barred grey and white. Flight feathers greyish white notably barred black. ♀ upperparts brown. Face grey, crown blackish. Cinnamon half-collar. Underparts and underwing barred rusty and white. Juv: upperparts blackish brown. Underparts creamy somewhat marked blackish brown. Cream half-collar. Tail with 4 blackish bars. Brown eye. Solitary or pairs. Mostly feeds in trees or ground on snails. Whistled *hee-teeteeteetee*. Gallery, cloud, deciduous and rainforest, savannah, edge, woods, cleared areas and scattered trees.

4 **WHITE-RUMPED HAWK** *Buteo (Rupornis) leucorrhous* ♂ 33cm, ♀ 37cm
Mostly black but rump, upper tail coverts, vent and 2 bands on tail white. Thighs cinnamon faintly barred brown. Eye yellow. Juv upperparts brown, feathers edged buff. Underparts buffy, streaked brown. Thighs cinnamon, barred brown. Tail with 3 blackish bands. Rare. Feeds on small vertebrates and insects. Dense vegetation of cloud-forest, rainforest, chaco woods.

5 **ROADSIDE HAWK** *Buteo (Rupornis) magnirostris* ♂ 34cm, ♀ 41cm
Hood and upperparts brown. Underparts barred whitish and cinnamon. In flight notable rufous tail and flight feathers. Wing-tip and trailing edge blackish. Eye pale yellow. Juv: forehead and brow buffy white. Hood brown, streaked buffy. Back feathers edged buff. Breast streaked cinnamon. Abundant; perches on poles and wires beside roads. Flaps then glides in straight flight, soars in circles on high, calling *cheecheechee….* Opportunist. Edge of woods and forests, open woods, gallery forests, patches of woods, savannah, plantations, parks and gardens, even cities.

6 **GREY HAWK** *Asturina (Buteo) nitida* ♂ 39cm, ♀ 45cm
Mostly grey. Barred grey and white on underparts. Tail black with broad band and tip white. Wings broad, narrower at body. Underwing barred grey and white. Flight feathers whitish grey, barred dark grey. Juv: upperparts brown, feathers edged buffy cream. Brow and cheek pale, malar stripe blackish brown. Underparts and underwing buffy cream streaked dark brown. Tail with 7 blackish bars. Perches high in the foliage. Woods, savannah, open woods, grassland, edge of rainforest to dry open country with trees.

134

KITES (ACCIPITRIDAE)

1 SWALLOW-TAILED KITE *Elanoides forficatus*   ♂ 55cm, ♀ 65cm
Black and white. Long forked tail. Great flyer in small flocks or pairs. Forest edge, woods, gallery forest, open woods, swampy areas.

2 PEARL KITE *Gampsonyx swainsonii*   ♂ 20cm, ♀ 25cm
Like a tiny falcon. Black and white with forehead and cheeks cinnamon buff. Half-collar. Cinnamon thighs. Flanks white or cinnamon according to race. Open woods, savannah, palm groves, open land with trees, edge, dry woods.

3 WHITE-TAILED KITE *Elanus leucurus*   34–36cm
Upperparts grey. Head and underparts white. Wing coverts black. Juv: streaked on crown and breast. Often hovers. Falls on its rodent prey. Open woods, savannah, copses, open fields with scattered trees, parks, gardens, even cities.

4 PLUMBEOUS KITE *Ictinia plumbea*   34–37cm
Long, sharp wings. Head and underparts grey. Upperparts blackish grey. Primaries mostly rufous. Black tail with two narrow white bars. Juv: head and underparts buffy cream streaked blackish grey. Primaries basally cinnamon. Tail with 3 white bars. Underwing buffy cream. Perches on bare emergent branches; sometimes in small flocks. Forest, savannah, gallery forest, woods.

5 MISSISSIPPI KITE *Ictinia mississippiensis*   35–38cm
Like 4 but primaries with very little rufous. Secondaries tipped whitish. Tail black. Juv differs from 4 by chestnut streaking on underparts. Underwing cinnamon streaked dark chestnut. Primaries all blackish. Migratory. Behaves like 4. Savannah, woods, forest edge.

6 RUFOUS-THIGHED KITE *Harpagus diodon*   ♂ 30cm, ♀ 36cm
Blackish head. Throat white with blackish mid-line. Upperparts greyish black. Underparts pale grey. Tail underside whitish grey with 4 blackish bars. Underwing and thighs chestnutty rufous. Juv: upperparts blackish brown, underparts cream streaked and barred. Thighs chestnutty rufous. Tail with 5 blackish bars. In topmost foliage. Tropical and subtropical forests and woods.

7 DOUBLE-TOOTHED KITE *Harpagus bidentatus*   ♂ 31cm, ♀ 37cm
Head grey. Throat white with black mid-line. Upperparts blackish brown. Rufous breast. Rest of underparts and thighs barred rufous and white. ♀ underparts more uniform. Tail from below whitish grey with 3 blackish bars. Underwing buffy cream. Juv: upperparts brown. Brownish mid-line down throat. Underparts buffy cream, streaked. Tail with 4 blackish bars. Perches among foliage. Edge, cleared areas, rainforest, cloud-forest, woods.

8 GREY-HEADED KITE *Leptodon cayanensis*   ♂ 47cm, ♀ 53cm
Hood grey. Upperparts black, underparts white. Very long tail black with 2 broad whitish bands. Broad, rounded wings. Underwing coverts black. Flight feathers concentrically barred. Juv: crown and upperparts blackish brown. Cheeks and sides of neck rufous. Malar and mid-line on throat blackish, rest of throat white. Underparts white finely streaked black. Tail buff with 3 black bars. Underwing white, streaked brown. Dark juv hood and upperparts blackish. Underparts buffy, with broad blackish stripes. Light juv crown and back blackish. Head and underparts creamy white. Rare. Near water. Humid forest, woods, savannah, gallery forest.

9 WHITE-COLLARED KITE *Leptodon forbesi*   ♂ 49cm, ♀ 53cm
Pale grey crown. Head, neck and underparts white. Upperparts blackish. Tail black with very broad whitish band. Underwing white, flight feathers as in 8. Scarcely known. Atlantic rainforest. Very rare and endangered.

WOODLAND FALCONS (FALCONIDAE)

Small-headed, long-legged, slender raptors, forest-falcons are hard to see in the forest, which they do not leave. They have broad, rounded wings and a long, rounded tail – and are thus adapted to flight in dense stands of trees.

1 COLLARED FOREST-FALCON *Micrastur semitorquatus* ♂ 45cm, ♀ 58cm
Cap, hind-cheek, upperparts and wings black. Rest of cheek, collar and underparts white. Tail with 3 narrow white bands and white tip. Underwing coverts white. There are buffy to pale cinnamon and black forms. Juv: more cinnamon, barred blackish brown. Call a lengthening series of loud *cows* after a stuttering start. Lowland tropical and subtropical rainforest, dense secondary growth, mangroves, gallery forest and cloud-forest.

2 BUCKLEY'S FOREST-FALCON *Micrastur buckleyi* ♂ 40cm, ♀ 50cm
Small version of 1. Juv differs in having white on cheeks and barring only on flanks. Forest in lowlands and to 1,800m. E Ecuador, NE Peru, SW Colombia and adjacent Brazil. Sometimes considered a race or morph of 1.

3 SLATY-BACKED FOREST-FALCON *Micrastur mirandollei* ♂ 40cm, ♀ 45cm
Upperparts slate-grey, underparts white. Blackish tail with 2 narrow pale-grey bands and tip. Underwing white. Juv: breast with broad brownish-grey streaks. Tropical lowland rainforest, gallery forest, secondary growth.

4 BARRED FOREST-FALCON *Micrastur ruficollis* ♂ 35cm, ♀ 40cm
Small. Variable. Upperparts brown. Face, neck and breast cinnamon. Rest of underparts white barred blackish brown. Tail blackish brown with 4 narrow white bands. Cere and bare around eye dirty yellow. Iris brownish yellow. Grey phase with barring up to the throat and 3 bands on tail. Juv: less or no barring on underparts and underwing, white to buff or cinnamon-buff. Throat and line above and below cheeks white. Dark half-collar. Upperparts darker brown. Call at dawn and dusk a loud *ka-oo ka-oo....* Tropical and subtropical montane, humid, swampy, gallery, rain- and semi-deciduous forests, edge and clearings, tall secondary growth.

5 LINED FOREST-FALCON *Micrastur gilvicollis* ♂ 32cm, ♀ 38cm
Like grey form of 4 but cere and bare around eye orange, iris white, tail proportionately shorter with 1 or 2 very narrow white bands. Underparts less densely barred on breast and upper belly, white below, or all barred. Juv: upperparts dark brown, feathers edged whitish. White patch on nape. White gill-line to throat. Underparts white with heavy blackish-brown barring. Primary lowland humid tropical forest, terra firme forest. A race in SW Colombia and NW Ecuador, with only one narrow band on the tail, may be a separate species: Plumbeous Forest-falcon, *Micrastur plumbeus*.

6 SPOT-WINGED FALCONET *Spiziapteryx circumcincta* ♂ 28cm, ♀ 31cm
Upperparts brownish grey streaked blackish. White dots on wing coverts. White rump seen in flight. Underparts pale greyish streaked blackish. Brow, moustachial streak, throat and vent white. Flight feathers and outer tail feathers blackish with white lines of dots forming bars. Rounded broad wings, longish rounded tail. Perches on outer branches. Dry and chaco woods, dry savannah, plains and hills.

7 LAUGHING FALCON *Herpetotheres cachinans* ♂ 45cm, ♀ 55cm
Unmistakable; large-headed and hefty. Mask to nape black. Rest of head and underparts buffy cream. Upperparts dark brown. Barred tail. Passive, perches on outer branches. Calls in duetted laughing *wha wha wha...*, even after dark. Edge of forest, savannah with palm, near water, woods, cerrado, gallery forest.

1 ck m

1 juv

1

1 juv

2 juv

1 buffy form

1

2

4 juv

4 juv

4 juv

4 juv

3

3

3 juv

3

uv

4

4

7

4

5

4 grey form

5 juv

6

6

7

7

RODRIGUEZ MATA

CARACARAS (FALCONIDAE)

Caracaras are aberrant falcons with crow-like scavenging habits though they do also take small prey. The larger species come into conflict with sheep farmers.

1 CRESTED CARACARA *Caracara (Polyborus) plancus* ♂ 48cm, ♀ 56cm
Bare face yellowish or pink. Cap blackish brown with slight occipital crest. Cheeks, neck and breast buffy white barred dark brown. Rest of body dark brown. Base of primaries whitish, finely barred. Tail whitish faintly barred with dark brown terminal band. Juv: generally paler and streaked on neck and breast. Open land, pastures, savannah, woods, steppe, mountains, farms. The Northern race may be a separate species: *Caracara cheryway* (Crested Caracara, the South becoming Southern Caracara).

2 YELLOW-HEADED CARACARA *Milvago chimachima* ♂ 40cm, ♀ 43cm
Head, neck and underparts buff. Dark brown post-ocular streak and rest of upperparts. Tail barred whitish and with terminal blackish-brown band. Base of primaries whitish. Juv like 3 but broadly barred dark on neck and breast; wings and tail as in adult. Open country with scattered trees, pastures, savannah with palms, farms, agricultural land, edge of forest.

3 CHIMANGO CARACARA *Milvago chimango* ♂ 38cm, ♀ 42cm
Generally brown, paler below to whitish vent. Base of primaries whitish. Tail whitish finely barred blackish, darkening towards tip. Farm and cultivated land, rubbish dumps, low in mountains, steppe, open woods, marshes, coastal regions, towns.

4 CARUNCULATED CARACARA *Phalcoboenus carunculatus* ♂ 49cm, ♀ 55cm
Bare face and legs yellow-orange. Caruncles on sides of throat and behind eye. Slight topknot. Overall black. Fore-neck, breast and upper belly irregularly streaked white. Lower belly, vent, upper tail coverts, thighs and underwing white. Juv: upperparts dark brown; head, rump and underparts mottled lighter. Pale base of primaries. Paramos, grassy pastures, some scattered bushes, 3,000–4,000m.

5 MOUNTAIN CARACARA *Phalcoboenus megalopterus* ♂ 49cm, ♀ 55cm
Bare pinky-orange face. Legs yellow. Upperparts, neck, breast and flanks black. Rest of underparts, underwing coverts and tip of tail white. Juv like a largish 3 but a shade more chestnut, tail more uniform; wing-patch and rump more tawny. Puna, high mountain desert, upland grassland, often near water.

6 WHITE-THROATED CARACARA
Phalcoboenus albogularis ♂ 49cm, ♀ 55cm
Yellow cere and legs. Upperparts black, underparts white, streaked on flanks. Juv extremely like that of 5. Upper mountain slopes to sea level, S Andean woods, rubbish dumps.

7 STRIATED CARACARA *Phalcoboenus australis* ♂ 55cm, ♀ 65cm
Generally black with white streaking on neck and breast. Vent, thighs and underwing cinnamon-rufous. Tip of tail white. Juv: more uniform, browner, duller. Upper back cinnamon. Rocky shores, open lowlands, to low coastal mountains, around colonies of seabirds and mammals.

8 RED-THROATED CARACARA
Ibycter (Daptrius) americanus ♂ 47cm, ♀ 55cm
Bare face red and blue. Bill yellow. Legs orangy red. Shiny black, lower underparts white. Juv: bare fore-face yellowish, sides of face and throat black. Black generally duller. Tropical lowland forest to mountains, deciduous forest, cerrado.

9 BLACK CARACARA *Daptrius ater* ♂ 43cm, ♀ 48cm
Bare face orange to yellow on throat. Bill black. Legs yellow. Glossy black. Broad white band at base of tail. Juv: bare face and legs duller. Underparts faintly barred and dotted buff. Broad base of tail white with 3 or 4 black bars. Woods, savannah, edge, clearings, riverine forest, mangroves.

RODRIGUEZ MATA

FALCONS (FALCONIDAE)

Falcons are open-area birds with sharp wings and longish tails for agile, fast flight. They catch prey on the wing, often acting in pairs.

1 AMERICAN KESTREL *Falco sparverius* ♂ 23cm, ♀ 28cm
Small. Crown bluish grey. Moustache, ear coverts and spot on nape black. Upper back rufous, somewhat barred black. Wing coverts greyish blue spotted black. Seen from above, tail rufous, tip black. Underparts buffy white dotted black on flanks. ♀: upperparts rufous barred blackish. Underparts streaked brown. Hovers. Mountains to the sea, including urban areas.

2 MERLIN *Falco columbarius* ♂ 25cm, ♀ 33cm
Crown and upperparts bluish lead-grey. Face, hind-neck, underparts and thighs buffy streaked dark brown. Vent buffy white. Tail grey with 3 black bands. ♀ like ♂ but upperparts browner. Juv like ♀ but back feathers finely edged buff. Fields, bushy areas, seaside fields, arid terrain, edge of woods and of forest. Migratory from N America.

3 APLOMADO FALCON *Falco femoralis* ♂ 36cm, ♀ 44cm
Crown, post-ocular to nape and hind-neck, moustache streak all lead-grey, as are upperparts. Brow, cheeks, throat and breast whitish or buffy. Flanks and upper belly greyish, finely barred white. Lower underparts tawny. Tail barred blackish and whitish. Juv: upperparts dark brown, feathers edged buff. Buffy-cinnamon throat, cheeks, brow and breast, this densely streaked. Flanks and upper belly blackish brown, feathers finely edged buff. Anywhere except dense forest and mountain tops.

4 BAT FALCON *Falco rufigularis* ♂ 24cm, ♀ 30cm
Small and dark. Upperparts and cheeks black. Throat, lower cheeks and upper breast whitish or washed rufous. Breast, upper belly and flanks black, finely barred white. Lower underparts rufous. Tail black with 4 narrow white bands. Juv like adult. Active at dusk. Lowland tropical and subtropical forest to mountains, edge and clearings, deforested areas with scattered trees.

5 ORANGE-BREASTED FALCON *Falco deiroleucus* ♂ 33cm, ♀ 39cm
A larger and powerful version of 4. Short tarsi with long powerful toes. Upperparts and all cheek black. Upper breast rufous streaked black. Lower breast, flanks black barred rufous. Rest of underparts chestnut-rufous. Short black tail with 2 fine bars. Juv: paler on underparts, all barred buffy white and black. Upperparts blackish, faintly washed brown, feathers finely edged buff. Upper tail coverts with notable buffy-white margin. Forest in mountains and foothills, edge and clearings of tropical and subtropical forest, chaco woods, gallery forest, outcrops as lookouts. Rare throughout its distribution.

6 PEREGRINE FALCON *Falco peregrinus* ♂ 37cm, ♀ 50cm
Upperparts and cheeks blackish (or dark grey, according to race). In some, the cheek is whitish ochre with blackish moustache streak. Throat white. Rest of underparts ochreous (or whitish ochre) streaked and barred black, washed greyer below. Juv: upperparts brownish black, feathers edged cinnamon-buff. Underparts buffy white (or pale cinnamon), heavily streaked. Pale morph: upperparts pale grey, barred. White cheek with blackish moustachial streak. Underparts white, faintly barred on flanks. Juv: upperparts dark brown, feathers edged buffy white. Underparts white, slightly streaked brown. Sea level to mountains, all habitats except forest, but including urban downtowns, towers and skyscrapers.

1 hovering

1 ♂

1 ♀

1

2

2

1

2

4

4

4

3 juv

3

3

5 juv

5

5

3

3

6

6

ad pale form

6

6

6

6 juv pale form

6

6 juv

6 juv

RODRIGUEZ MATA

CURASSOWS (CRACIDAE)

1 **NOCTURNAL CURASSOW** *Nothocrax urumutum* 60cm
Heavy orange bill. Bare face colourful. Cap with black, long, curly feathers
forming an erectile crest. Chestnut, more cinnamon on belly. Upperparts
finely barred black. Outer tail feathers black tipped buff. Dense humid forest,
temporarily or permanently flooded, terra firme forest, usually near rivers.

2 **SALVIN'S CURASSOW** *Mitu salvini* 89cm
Notable red bill with high, arched culmen. Glossy bluish black, feathers edged
black. Lower underparts and tail-tip white. Bushy erectile crest of straight
feathers. Wine-red legs. Humid terra firme forest, forested ravines, hills and
plains.

3 **RAZOR-BILLED CURASSOW** *Mitu tuberosum* 89cm
Notable red bill, culmen highly arched. Glossy bluish black, feathers edged
black. Lower underparts chestnut. Tail tipped white. Bushy erectile crest of
straight feathers. Winy-red legs. Lowland forest.

4 **CRESTLESS CURASSOW** *Mitu tomentosum* 85cm
Red bill. Cap of hairlike bristly feathers. Glossy bluish black, feathers edged
black. Lower underparts and tail-tip chestnut. Wine-red legs. Riverine
rainforest and terra firme forest, gallery forest, dense undergrowth.

5 **NORTHERN HELMETED CURASSOW** *Pauxi pauxi* 90cm
Red bill with pale blue fig-shaped frontal knob. Glossy bluish black, feathers
edged black. Lower underparts and tail-tip white. Legs wine-red. ♀ like ♂, but
one morph has lower underparts cream. Body barred black and brownish,
lower breast tawny. Humid montane and dense cloud-forest, steep slopes.

6 **SOUTHERN HELMETED CURASSOW** *Pauxi unicornis* 90cm
Like 5 but horn-shaped frontal knob. Sexes alike. Montane forest, steep slopes,
ravines, even precipices, usually with small streams. Some believe this to be a
race of 5.

7 **BLACK CURASSOW** *Crax alector* 90cm
Pale grey bill, cere orange or orangy yellow. Bare eye-ring blue, lower edge
yellow. Black crest of dense forward-curling feathers. Glossy blackish blue,
feathers edged black. Lower underparts white. Blue-grey legs. ♀: white spots in
the crest. Cloud-forest, rainforest, gallery forest, terra firme forest, riverine
brush and thickets.

8 **YELLOW-KNOBBED CURASSOW** *Crax daubentoni* 91cm
Bill and eye-ring dark grey. Knobbly cere yellow. Long, forward-curling
feathers form notable crest. Glossy black. Lower underparts white. Legs bluish
grey. ♀: white dots in crest, no cere, fine white scaling on breast. Tip of tail
white. Gallery forest, basal forest, rainforest, deciduous forest, savannah with
scattered trees, semiarid vegetation, often near rivers.

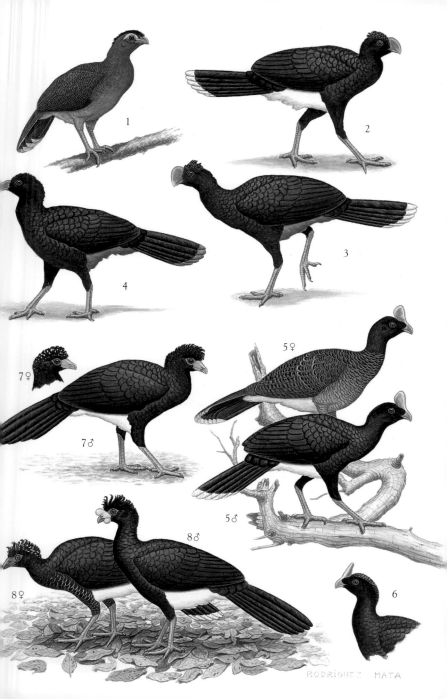

CURASSOWS (CRACIDAE)

1 BARE-FACED CURASSOW *Crax fasciolata*   90cm
Grey bill, yellow cere. Bare eye-ring grey. Glossy black. Forward-curling
feathers form bushy crest. Lower underparts and narrow tip of tail white. Legs
violaceous grey. ♀ crest basally white. Upperparts and tail barred white (varies
with race). No cere. Underparts tawny buff, barred black on breast. Legs
pinkish. Gallery forest and patches, woods, edge.

2 BLUE-BILLED CURASSOW *Crax alberti*   91cm
Pale grey bill, with blue, 2-lobed cere below bill. Bare face around eye blackish.
Long bushy crest of forward-curling feathers. Glossy black with slight blue
sheen. Lower underparts and tail-tip white. Legs vinaceous grey. ♀: blue cere
lacks caruncles. Crest with white spotting. Upperparts, breast and tail finely
barred white. Lower underparts rufous cinnamon. Pinkish legs. Lowland
humid forest and foothills. One morph of the ♀ had basally white crest
feathers, barring and scaling up onto neck, barely barred tail and black-barred
leggings. Unrecorded in the wild since 1978.

3 WATTLED CURASSOW *Crax globulosa*   90cm
Bill and bare skin around eye blackish. Knobbly red cere with 1 round lobe
above, 2 below. Black bushy crest of forward-curling feathers. Glossy black,
slight blue sheen. Lower underparts white. Legs blackish, sometimes washed
violaceous. ♀ lacks lobes on cere. White spotting in crown. Wings, breast and
leggings faintly barred whitish (sometimes plain). Lower underparts
cinnamon. Legs like ♂. Riverine forest, varzea, near water, drier forest.

4 RED-BILLED CURASSOW *Crax blumenbachii*   90cm
Blackish bill and bare skin around eye. Cere and 1 spherical knob below red.
Dense crest of forward-curling feathers, shorter and more curly than others of
the genus. Glossy black, slight blue sheen. Lower underparts white. Legs dark
grey. ♀ lacks cere. Crest with white spotting. Upper belly, leggings and wings
barred rufous. Lower underparts cinnamon. Legs vinaceous pink. Tall humid
rainforest, river islands and spits, dense secondary growth, near water.

5 GREAT CURASSOW *Crax rubra*   91cm
Pale grey bill, yellow cere with 1 round knob above. Bushy crest of long
forward-curling feathers. Bare skin around eye blackish grey. Glossy black with
faint blue sheen. Lower underparts white. Legs grey or blackish grey. ♀: ivory
bill. Crest feathers basally white. Head and upper breast white, scaled black.
Upperparts and breast rufous faintly barred black. Tail barred buff, rufous and
black. Lower underparts tawny. Legs pinkish. A form of ♀ has neck, back and
wings broadly barred black. A dark form of ♀ is blackish chestnut with
blackish tail. Pristine humid lowland forest to foothills.

6 ALAGOAS CURASSOW *Mitu mitu* (not illustrated)   83cm
Like 3 of previous page, but with a more moderate bill, a bare area around the
ear, and tail narrowly tipped pale brown. Lowland rainforest, in Alagoas (NE
Brazil). Probably extinct in the wild.

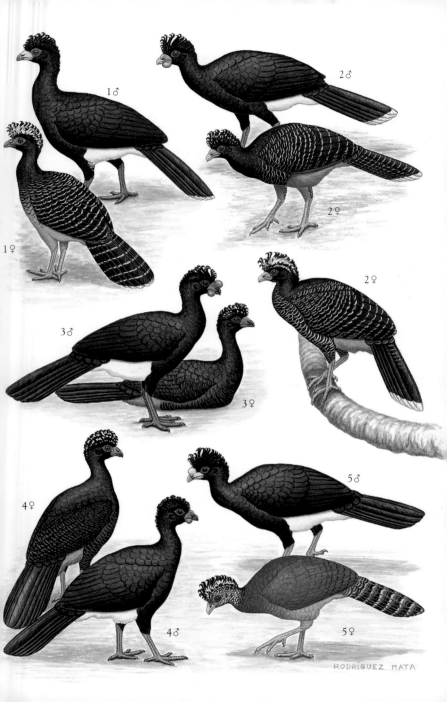

1♂

1♀

2♂

2♀

2♀

3♂

3♀

4♀

4♂

5♂

5♀

RODRIGUEZ MATA

GUANS (CRACIDAE)

1 BLACK-FRONTED PIPING-GUAN *Pipile jacutinga* 74cm
Black. White wing-patch. Forehead black. Crown and nape white. Breast
scaled white. Bill basally blue, tip black. Black face, white eye-ring. Wattle
blue and red. Rainforest near watercourses, mountains and hills.

2 WHITE-THROATED PIPING-GUAN *Pipile grayi* 73cm
Only member of genus with bill basally white, tip black. Crown, nape, throat
and long, slender wattle white. Rainforest, edge, gallery forest, savannah,
copses in palm groves. Some believe this to be a race of 3.

3 BLUE-THROATED PIPING-GUAN *Pipile cumanensis* 72cm
Black. Greater wing coverts white, rest edged white. Bill basally light blue. Face
white. Triangular wattle blackish blue. Cap and nape faintly streaked. Rainforest
near rivers, varzea, terra firme forest, gallery forest, copses in palm groves, edge.

4 TRINIDAD PIPING-GUAN *Pipile pipile* 72cm
Differs from 3 only in cap and nape markedly streaked black, bare face washed
pale blue. Crowns of undisturbed primary forest, montane forest, steep terrain.
Only on Trinidad. Critically endangered.

5 RED-THROATED PIPING-GUAN *Pipile cujubi* 72cm
Differs from 4 in red wattle with small blue area under chin. Breast feathers
bordered white. White face. Rainforest, riverine forest in lowlands. The Red-
throated Piping-guan (*P. c. nattereri*), considered by some to be a separate
species, has whiter cap and nape.

6 WATTLED GUAN *Aburria aburri* 71cm
All black, body with bronzy-olive sheen. Head and neck with blue sheen. Blue
bill tipped black. Long fine wattle orangy salmon-pink. Upper montane
tropical forest, rainforest, cloud-forest, edge, secondary growth, copses.

7 WHITE-BROWED GUAN *Penelope jacucaca* 73cm
Uniformly dark chestnut-brown. Slight olive sheen on upperparts. Breast,
back and wing coverts edged white. Bare face edged black. Long brow white.
Caatinga with stunted trees and shrubs, cactus and thorny thickets.

8 CHESTNUT-BELLIED GUAN *Penelope ochrogaster* 78cm
Crest whitish and chestnut. Face edged black. White brow. Neck and
underparts chestnut, but contrasting dark olive-brown back, wings and tail.
Breast, back and wing coverts scaled white. Lowland tropical forest, gallery
forest, swampy forest, deciduous forest, patches.

9 WHITE-CRESTED GUAN *Penelope pileata* 80cm
White crest, feathers tipped chestnut. Neck and underparts chestnut.
Contrasting blackish-olive back, wings and tail. Bare face edged black. Breast,
back and wing coverts scaled white. Tropical lowland forest.

10 CAUCA GUAN *Penelope perspicax* 76cm
Head and neck blackish grey, becoming browner lower on body and grading to
rufous chestnut on wings, lower body and tail. Neck, breast and upper back
feathers scaled white. Humid forest. W Colombia, upper Cauca valley.
Severely threatened.

11 SPIX'S GUAN *Penelope jacquaçu* 70cm
Upperparts, breast and tail dark olive-brown. Rest of underparts and upper tail
coverts brownish chestnut. Breast and upper back feathers scaled white.
Rainforest and cloud-forest, edge, gallery forest, clearings with scattered trees.
P. j. granti is larger (81cm) and darker – overall greenish black with less scaling.
Some believe this to be a separate species (Guyana and neighbouring
E Venezuela S of the Orinoco).

RODRÍGUEZ MATA

GUANS (CRACIDAE)

1 CRESTED GUAN *Penelope purpurascens* 85cm
Mostly dark brownish olive contrasting with dark chestnut lower belly, tail coverts and tail. Tip of tail blackish. Cap and hind-neck blacker. Fore-neck, breast, wing coverts and upper back scaled white. Lowland rainforest, edge, sometimes in drier forest, hills.

2 WHITE-WINGED GUAN *Penelope albipennis* 80cm
Primary flight feathers white, very visible in flight. Overall dark brownish olive. Fore-neck and breast scaled whitish. Leggings, lower belly and undertail coverts dark chestnut. Bare face pinkish lilac. Bill pale blue tipped black. Dry woods and deciduous forest on mountain slopes, deep valleys and ravines with running streams, gallery forest, forested deltas. Extreme NW Peru, Lambayeque.

3 BAND-TAILED GUAN *Penelope argyrotis* 60cm
Smallish and relatively dumpy. Short legs. Brown with slight chestnut sheen. Underparts brownish chestnut. Scaled white on fore-neck, upper back and underparts. Tail with cinnamon tip. Long brow and ear-coverts white, these streaked black. Montane rainforest, cloud-forest, edge, tall secondary growth, plantations. The race *P .a. barbata* may be a separate species: Bearded Guan.

4 ANDEAN GUAN *Penelope montagni* 58cm
Smallish and dumpy. Short legs. Like 3. Tail all very dark brownish chestnut. Slight brow. Tiny red wattle somewhat feathered. Montane rainforest, edge, secondary growth, slopes with impenetrable humid forest covered with epiphytes, dwarf forest and forest patches at greater elevations.

5 RED-FACED GUAN *Penelope dabbenei* 70cm
Bare face reddish orange. Short legs. Brown with slight olive sheen on neck and upperparts. Blackish-brown tail. Faint scaling on fore-neck, breast and upper back. Alder woods and temperate montane forest.

6 BAUDO GUAN *Penelope ortoni* 65cm
Uniform chestnut-brown, scaled white on fore-neck and breast. Humid rainforest especially at foot of mountains.

7 DUSKY-LEGGED GUAN *Penelope obscura* 73cm
Legs dark violaceous grey. Generally very dark blackish brown. Slight dark chestnut wash on lower underparts. Head and neck blackish. Faint brow in one race. Fore-neck, breast, wing coverts and upper back scaled white, varying according to race. Woods, forest, gallery forest in plains, deltas, lower montane forest and ravines.

8 MARAIL GUAN *Penelope marail* 63cm
Legs pinky grey. Upperparts, breast and tail dark olive. Fore-neck and breast scaled white. Rest of underparts dirty chestnut-brown. Long faint brow. Rainforest, especially near water, secondary growth.

9 RUSTY-MARGINED GUAN *Penelope superciliaris* 63cm
Grey legs. Long notable brow whitish, less so in some specimens. Upperparts and tail dark olive, wing and upper tail coverts edged rufous or tawny cinnamon. Fore-neck and breast scaled whitish. Lower underparts tinted dirty chestnut. Forest in lowlands or valleys, secondary growth, edge of plantations, groves in cerrado, woods, caatinga, gallery forest.

10 SICKLE-WINGED GUAN *Chamaepetes goudotii* 64cm
No wattle. Head, neck, upperparts and tail brownish olive. Contrasting chestnut-rufous breast and rest of underparts, faintly scaled on breast. Bare face and base of bill pale blue, eye red. Montane rainforest, tall secondary growth, woods, coffee plantations.

RODRIGUEZ MATA

CHACHALACAS (CRACIDAE)

1 RUFOUS-VENTED CHACHALACA *Ortalis ruficauda*   53cm
Head and upper neck greyish. Upperparts olive-brown. Tail blackish olive with greenish sheen. All outer tail feathers tipped rufous. Underparts cinnamon-buff. Undertail coverts chestnutty rufous. One race (*O. r. ruficrissa*) has white tips to the tail. Edge of woods and forest, brushland, dry thorny woods, deforested areas with scattered trees, riverine woods, gallery forest.

2 CHACO CHACHALACA *Ortalis canicollis*   53cm
Bare face reddish pink. Bill and feet creamy coloured. Head and neck grey. Upperparts olive-brown. Tail blackish olive with green sheen. Outer tail feathers tipped rufous. Underparts dirty buff grading to cinnamon undertail coverts. Dry woods and transition to forest, brushland with scattered trees, palm groves, savannah with patches of woods.

3 RUFOUS-HEADED CHACHALACA *Ortalis erythroptera*   52cm
Head, neck and primary flight feathers rufous. Upperparts brownish olive. Tail blackish olive with green sheen. Outer tail feathers tipped rufous. Underparts dirty whitish-buff. Undertail coverts cinnamon. Deciduous woods, savannah, brushland with trees, foot of mountains.

4 LITTLE CHACHALACA *Ortalis motmot*   53cm
Legs pinkish red. Head, upper neck and outer tail feathers rufous. Upperparts olive-brown, central tail feathers brownish olive. Underparts brownish buff. Edge of rainforest and cloud-forest, brushland with low trees, cleared areas with scattered trees.

5 BUFF-BROWED CHACHALACA *Ortalis superciliaris*   42cm
Upperparts and tail dark olive-brown. Outer tail fathers tipped rufous. Head and neck dark brown. Faint greyish brow and streaks on fore-neck. Breast faintly scaled greyish, rest of underparts brownish buff. Edge of woods and forest, brushland with small scattered trees, dry woods.

6 SPECKLED CHACHALACA *Ortalis guttata*   47cm
Cap blackish brown. Upperparts and tail dark olive-brown. Outer tail feathers tipped rufous (all rufous when seen from below). Fore-neck and breast spotted and marked whitish. Underparts buffy brown. Brushland with scattered low trees, edge of rainforest, gallery forest, clearings with secondary growth, regrowth and palm groves with bushes and low trees. 6R White-bellied Chachalaca (*O. g. aracuan*) has ochreous-cinnamon cap and hind-neck. Lighter upperparts; lower underparts dirty white, more buffy on undertail coverts. There are intermediate forms. Scaled Chachalaca (*O. g. squamata*) has dark browny-cinnamon cap and hind-neck. Underparts brown, slightly washed greyish. Colombian Chachalaca (*O. g. columbiana*) is larger with paler upperparts. Cap and hind-neck pale slate-grey, scaling on breast very fine. Some consider each of these as separate species.

7 CHESTNUT-WINGED CHACHALACA *Ortalis garrula*   50cm
Head, neck and breast dull cinnamon. Upperparts olive-brown. Tail blackish olive, outer feathers tipped white. Primary flight feathers rufous. Lower underparts white. Deciduous woods with shrubs, edge of humid forest, dry brushland, thickets, secondary growth, mangroves.

8 GREY-HEADED CHACHALACA *Ortalis cinereiceps*   49cm
Like 7 but head and neck grey. Tail-tips and underparts buffy white, these browner towards undertail coverts. Brush and thickets with scattered trees, secondary growth, clearings and edge of forest, riverine vegetation. Some believe this to be a race of 7.

RODRIGUEZ MATA

NEW WORLD QUAILS (ODONTOPHORIDAE)

1 CALIFORNIAN QUAIL *Callipepla (Lophortyx) californicus* 25cm
Black crest curled forwards. Black bib, edged white. Forehead and brow white.
Grey breast. Upperparts olive-grey. Upper belly ochre, feathers edged black.
Flanks olive-grey streaked white. ♀: short crest. Duller. Face and throat
whitish, finely speckled brownish grey. Arid slopes, ravines in lower
mountains, scrub and thickets, brushland steppe, edge, clearings in woods.

2 CRESTED BOBWHITE *Colinus cristatus* 20cm
Crest pale buff. Forehead creamy. Face and throat tawny or creamy (according
to race). Hind-neck, line down side of neck and collar black and white.
Upperparts scalloped black, whitish and brown. Breast vinaceous tinted
cinnamon. Flanks and underparts with big white spots. ♀: duller, with smaller
crest. Open flat land, brush, grassland, thickets, plantations.

Wood-quail have a short, heavy bill, erectile bushy crest and cryptic coloration.
They are shy, live in small family groups and frequent the forest floor.

3 TACARCUNA WOOD-QUAIL *Odontophorus dialeucos* 25cm
Cap and bib blackish brown. White around eye, on chin and malar stripe.
Pectoral collar white. Line from eye to hind-neck ochre to chestnut. Body dark
brown vermiculated blackish. Forest on slopes. Extreme NW Colombia (N
Choco, bordering on Panama).

4 SPOT-WINGED WOOD-QUAIL *Odontophorus capueira* 27cm
Erectile crest brown. Bare face orangy red. All underparts brownish grey.
Upperparts marked, streaked and barred brown, black and buff, dotted white
on wing coverts. ♀: duller, less crest. Dense parts of shady forest, regrowth.

5 GORGETED WOOD-QUAIL *Odontophorus strophium* 26cm
Head and neck black. Post-ocular streak, chin, malar stripe and collar white.
Back and wings dark brown barred, spotted and vermiculated black and buff.
Underparts tawny rufous, breast neatly streaked white. ♀: duller, underparts
dark grey. Temperate and subtropical montane forest and oak woods.

6 VENEZUELAN WOOD-QUAIL *Odontophorus columbianus* 28cm
Cap blackish brown. Post-ocular line to neck cinnamon. Cheek black and
speckled. Pectoral collar black. White throat and half-collar. Upperparts dark
brown, marked, vermiculated and streaked black, cinnamon and ochre.
Underparts ochre-brown, breast with neat white triangular markings, barred
blackish on lower belly. Cloud-forest, edge of clearings at upper elevations.

7 BLACK-FRONTED WOOD-QUAIL *Odontophorus atrifrons* 28cm
Forehead, face and throat black. Crown and nape chestnut. Upperparts dark
brown, spotted, speckled, vermiculated and barred black, buff and rufous.
Breast and belly buffy chestnut, neatly and sparsely spotted white, slight
blackish-brown barring. Another race has buffy-grey breast, spotted white.
Cloud-forest.

8 STRIPE-FACED WOOD-QUAIL *Odontophorus balliviani* 28cm
Black face-mask. Rufous cap. Ochre brow. Chin and malar stripe ochreous and
rufous. Neck and upperparts dark brown, these spotted, vermiculated, streaked
and barred blackish, buff and rufous. Underparts dark chestnut with white
black-bordered arrow-marks. Dense montane forest, thickets, tree-ferns and
cane, humid cloud-forest.

3

1♀   1♂

2♀

2♂

4

5♀   5♂

6

7R

7   8

RODRIGUEZ MATA

WOOD-QUAILS (ODONTOPHORIDAE)

1 MARBLED WOOD-QUAIL *Odontophorus gujanensis* 28cm
Bare skin around eye reddish orange. Generally dark brown. Upperparts
spotted, marked, barred and vermiculated black, buff, rufous and whitish.
Underparts greyish brown (or tawny brown according to race), lightly barred
black. Head more chestnutty. Post-ocular stripe ochreous. Humid forest, tall
secondary growth, rainforest, cloud-forest.

2 DARK-BACKED WOOD-QUAIL *Odontophorus melanonotos* 28cm
Dark brown, faintly vermiculated blackish. Throat, neck and breast chestnutty
rufous. Subtropical montane forest.

3 CHESTNUT WOOD-QUAIL *Odontophorus hyperythrus* 28cm
Head, neck and upper breast chestnutty rufous. White ear-patch. Crown and
nape dark brown. Lower belly and upperparts dark brown, these marked,
spotted, vermiculated and barred black, ochre and whitish. ♀: broad white line
through face. Breast and belly brownish grey. Humid montane forest, dense
edges, secondary growth.

4 RUFOUS-BREASTED WOOD-QUAIL *Odontophorus speciosus* 29cm
Black head. Faint speckled post-ocular streak down neck. Upperparts dark
brown, barred, mottled, streaked, spotted and vermiculated white, ochre and
black. Fore-neck chestnut. Breast and belly chestnutty rufous. ♀: underparts
grey. Tropical and montane forest.

5 STARRED WOOD-QUAIL *Odontophorus stellatus* 29cm
Bare skin around eye orangy red. Cap and long bushy crest chestnut. Cheeks,
throat and neck grey. Upperparts dark brown, barred, mottled, streaked,
spotted and vermiculated black, rufous, buff and white. Underparts chestnutty
rufous with neat white spots on breast. Tropical and riverine forest.

6 RUFOUS-FRONTED WOOD-QUAIL *Odontophorus erythrops* 29cm
Forehead and face rufous chestnut, crown brownish black. Speckled white
malar stripe, black bib, white collar. Upperparts dark brown, vermiculated,
barred and mottled black and buff. Underparts chestnutty rufous. Humid forest
and rainforest, foothills and lower slopes.

7 TAWNY-FACED QUAIL *Rhynchortyx cinctus* 20cm
Small. Like miniature wood-quail. No crest. Head chestnut and rufous, ochre
post-ocular streak. Throat, neck and breast grey. Back and upperparts dark
brown, mottled, vermiculated and barred black, rufous and buff. Lower
underparts buffy ochre. ♀: head, neck and breast chestnut. Post-ocular streak
and throat white flecked black. Underparts scaled black and white. Humid
forest.

1R

1

2

3♀

3♂

4♂

4♀

5

6

7♂

7♀

RODRIGUEZ MATA

TRUMPETERS (PSOPHIIDAE), **SUNBITTERN** (EURIPYGIDAE), **SUNGREBE** (HELIORNITHIDAE) **& SERIEMAS** (CARIAMIDAE)

Trumpeters are terrestrial, gregarious, exclusively Amazonian birds. Omnivorous. Voices, unlike a trumpet, are a resonant *boomm* and *ooomm*.

1 PALE-WINGED TRUMPETER *Psophia leucoptera*   50cm
Black with greenish or blue sheen on breast, fore-neck and some wing coverts. Inner flight feathers white (or ochreous, according to race). Dense, unmodified tropical forest away from human settlement, from lowlands to mountains.

2 GREY-WINGED TRUMPETER *Psophia crepitans*   50cm
As 1 but inner flight feathers grey, with ochre only on mid-back. Humid tropical forest from lowlands to mountains, terra firme forests.

3 DARK-WINGED TRUMPETER *Psophia viridis*   50cm
Unlike other species in having green upper back and inner flight feathers. Sheen on breast and wing coverts purplish blue. One race has ochreous-olive back and inner flight feathers, and a purple sheen on breast and coverts. Humid, lowland tropical forest.

4 SUNBITTERN *Eurypyga helias*   45cm
Unmistakably coloured and patterned. Wings very notable in flight. Black head with 2 white lines. Usually solitary. Wades in shallow water, on stony shores and muddy beaches in dappled shade of forest. Silent and shy. When alarmed, flies to neighbouring lower branches. Gallery forest and water's edge in humid forest in lowlands and mountains.

5 SUNGREBE *Heliornis fulica*   29cm
Head and neck strikingly marked black and white. ♂: white cheeks and eye-ring, blackish maxilla, yellowish mandible. ♀: cheeks cinnamon, red eye-ring, reddish maxilla. Usually solitary and shy. Swims and dives well. Scuttles over surface or flies low to flee. Bodies of quiet water in forest with overhanging vegetation, or densely vegetated.

Terrestrial, long-legged birds, seriemas stalk expectantly in search of prey; rowdy calls carry great distances. Singly, pairs or small flocks. Only fly to escape to nearby trees.

6 RED-LEGGED SERIEMA *Cariama cristata*   90cm
Large. Notable untidy frontal crest. Bill and legs red. Bare blue around eye. Brownish-grey upperparts, slightly vermiculated. Underparts whitish, slightly streaked. Flight feathers barred black and white. Outer tail feathers tipped white. Open thorny woods and brush, chaco, caatinga and cerrado, open areas with trees or bushes.

7 BLACK-LEGGED SERIEMA *Chunga burmeisteri*   70cm
Lacks crest. Bill, eye-ring and legs black. Upperparts and tail grey, slightly vermiculated. Underparts paler. Flight feathers barred black and white. Open dry woods.

RODRÍGUEZ MATA

LIMPKIN (ARAMIDAE) **AND RAILS** (RALLIDAE)

1 LIMPKIN *Aramus guarauna*   66cm
All dark brown, flecked white on head and neck. Long bill horn-coloured. Call
is a very loud series of crazy *krrrrow…kerrow*. Marshes with dense vegetation,
riverside woods, roadside ditches, lakes, flooded grass, rice-paddies, temporary
ponds, bogs, mangroves.

Rails (*Rallus/Pardirallus*) are heard more than seen, and are shy and secretive
denizens of damp places with thick vegetation. Tail held erect when alarmed.

2 BLACKISH RAIL *Pardirallus (Rallus) nigricans*   34cm
Upperparts blackish brown tinged olive. Tail black. Throat whitish. Underparts dark lead-grey. Bill yellowish green, yellower at the base. Bright red legs.
Call is a high-pitched, whistled duet of *dweeeeets* and *chik chuks*. Swamps, tall
grass around marshes, flooded areas, rice-paddies.

3 PLUMBEOUS RAIL *Pardirallus (Rallus) sanguinolentus*   35cm
Upperparts blackish brown, feathers edged dark brown, all washed olive.
Underparts very dark lead-grey. Bill greenish yellow, base of maxilla pale blue,
base of mandible bright red. Red legs. Call is a duetted series of *wheeew rreeets*,
punctuated by *teerreeets* and deep bass *doo doomphs*. Dense vegetation of
marshes, streams, roadside ditches.

4 SPOTTED RAIL *Pardirallus (Rallus) maculatus*   27cm
All spotted black and white, barred on flanks. Bill greenish yellow with red at
the base of mandible, pale blue on maxilla. Red legs. Call is a whistled *wheeee-
dididee*, louder on first note. Dense emergent vegetation of marshes, temporary
ponds, tall grass by wetlands, roadside ditches, flooded areas, rice-paddies.

5 PLAIN-FLANKED RAIL *Rallus wetmorei*   27cm
No barring. Upperparts dark brown, back feathers edged buffy brown.
Underparts buffy greyish brown. Mangroves, fresh and brackish coastal ponds,
estuaries. N coast of Venezuela (E Falcon, N Carabobo and Aragua).
Endangered. Some consider it a race of 6.

6 CLAPPER RAIL *Rallus longirostris*   33cm
Upperparts blackish brown, back feathers bordered buffy brown. Vinaceous
cinnamon on breast. Flanks and rest of underparts barred black and white. Bill
pinkish, culmen blackish. Call is a series of loud, rapid *kak* or *kek* notes,
descending and getting weaker at end. Salt, brackish and freshwater marshes
with tall emergent vegetation, flooded grass, mangroves.

7 BOGOTA RAIL *Rallus semiplumbeus*   27cm
Upperparts blackish brown, feathers edged buffy brown. Wing coverts
chestnut. Face, neck, breast and upper belly grey. Undertail barred. Legs and
bill dirty pink, this with black culmen. Call is a clear, whistled *peeep*. Marshes
and reed-beds around lakes. E Andes of Colombia (Cundinamarca and
Boyaca). Endangered.

8 VIRGINIA RAIL *Rallus limicola*   24cm
Upperparts blackish brown, back feathers edged buffy brown. Wing coverts
chestnut. Face grey. Slight whitish brow. Fore-neck, breast and upper belly
vinaceous cinnamon. Undertail barred. Bill and legs dirty coral-pink, culmen
blackish. Juv darker and duller. Call is a metallic clattering, loud, rapid *kid kid
kirik kirik…*. Swamps and freshwater marshes with tall emergent vegetation,
flooded grass.

9 AUSTRAL RAIL *Rallus antarcticus*   22cm
Differs from 8 in that face, neck, breast, upper belly are very dark lead-grey.
Flanks, lower belly and undertail barred black and white. Small lakes, streams
and bodies of water with reed-beds and other vegetation. Considered by some a
race of 8.

RODRIGUEZ MATA

CRAKES AND WOOD-RAILS (RALLIDAE)

1   CHESTNUT-HEADED CRAKE *Anurolimnas castaneiceps*   20cm
Very short tail. Short greenish-yellow bill. Head, neck, breast and upper belly
reddish chestnut. Rest dark olive-brown. Red legs. Long, loud antiphonal duet
kook tocock, kook tocock…. terra firme rainforest, secondary growth and
thickets along stream banks, lowlands, foot of hills, plantations.

2   UNIFORM CRAKE *Amaurolimnas concolor*   22cm
Short tail. Shortish greenish-yellow bill. Upperparts brown. Cheeks and
underparts tawny rufous. Red legs. Call is a long series of loud *tooees* rising in
volume, then descending. Flooded thickets, secondary growth away from
water, shady swamps near waterholes and streams, tall grass on edge of marshes
and of mangroves and cultivated land, clearings in palm groves.

Wood-rails live around water, although sometimes are seen far from water. They run
from danger with tail raised. Strong bills. They are rowdy, their calls duets or
choruses, but they are shy – mostly heard and not seen.

3   RED-WINGED WOOD-RAIL *Aramides calopterus*   33cm
Sides of neck and band in wing chestnut-red. Primaries black. Breast and belly
bluish grey. Swamps, near streams.

4   BROWN WOOD-RAIL *Aramides wolfi*   36cm
Dark grey head. Rest of body and wings dark chestnut. Call is a loud, repeated
kwee cor mwee. Mangroves, rivers, gallery forest, riverine and woodland swamp.

5   LITTLE WOOD-RAIL *Aramides mangle*   30cm
Grey head. Hind-neck and upper back bluish grey. Fore-neck, breast and flanks
tawny rufous. Coastal swamps, muddy shores, mangroves, thickets and nearby
tall grass.

6   RUFOUS-NECKED WOOD-RAIL *Aramides axilaris*   32cm
Head, neck and breast rufous. Upper back bluish grey. Calls *pick* or *pyok*
repeated. Swamps and bogs, dense thickets, coastal swamps, mangroves,
deciduous woods, thorny woods, edge, rainforest, cloud-forest.

7   SLATY-BREASTED WOOD-RAIL *Aramides saracura*   36cm
Forehead, crown and nape lead-grey. Face brownish grey. Hind-neck and upper
back brownish cinnamon. Fore-neck, breast and flanks bluish lead-grey. Call is a
loud, strident, usually duetted *wok…wahkwahk…wok…wahkwahk….* Often far
from water. Rainforest, dense vegetation near water, swamps and rivers in forest.

8   GREY-NECKED WOOD-RAIL *Aramides cajanea*   39cm
Head, neck and upper back lead-grey, crown washed brownish. Breast and
flanks tawny rufous. Call is a loud *chiri – cot, chiri – cot…* with *coos* thrown in.
Swamps, tall riverine vegetation, mangroves, lakes, marshes, temporary ponds,
rainforest, humid deciduous woods, sometimes far from water, tall grass, scrub,
sugarcane, forestry plantations.

9   GIANT WOOD-RAIL *Aramides ypecaha*   46cm
Forehead, fore-face, fore-neck and breast grey. Back of the head and hind-neck
vinaceous cinnamon. Sides of the breast and flanks pale vinaceous. Call is a
screamed duet of *ha, ha, patterha, wok wok,* deranged and wild. Edge of
marshes, lakes and rivers, all with tall, dense vegetation, tall grass, thickets,
often with trees and shrubs, sometimes far from water on roads and fields.

RODRIGUEZ MATA

CRAKES (RALLIDAE)

1 BLACK CRAKE or RAIL *Laterallus jamaicensis*   14cm
Very small and dark. Upperparts have discontinuous barring. Upper back plain, brownish chestnut. Breast grey. Flight feathers all blackish. Calls insistently *tip trrrr tip trrrr…*. Tall grass near water, flooded grass in brackish areas, reeds with grass, cultivated fields.

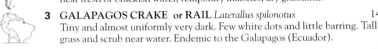

2 DOT-WINGED CRAKE *Porzana (Laterallus) spilopterus*   14cm
Very small and dark. Differs from 1 in crown to upper back with black and dark brown markings. Flight feathers all blackish. Flooded tall grass and vegetation near fresh or brackish water, temporary marshes, dry grassland.

3 GALAPAGOS CRAKE or RAIL *Laterallus spilonotus*   14cm
Tiny and almost uniformly very dark. Few white dots and little barring. Tall grass and scrub near water. Endemic to the Galapagos (Ecuador).

4 GREY-BREASTED CRAKE *Laterallus exilis*   15cm
Head, sides of neck and breast grey. Hind-neck and upper back rufous chestnut. Flanks, belly and undertail barred black and white. Legs buffy olive. Call is a series of *pinks*. Humid or flooded grasses by ditches, bogs, lakes and other bodies of water, rice-paddies.

5 RUFOUS-SIDED CRAKE *Laterallus melanophaius*   17cm
Crown brownish grey. Cheeks, sides of the neck and breast, and undertail tawny rufous. Flanks barred black and white. Throat to mid-belly white. Legs buffy olive. Call is a long, descending trilled *prrrrrrrrrrrr*. Tall grass, reeds, canes, bushes in damp or partly flooded areas near small lakes, marshes, streams and rivers with or without nearby trees.

6 WHITE-THROATED CRAKE *Laterallus albigularis*   15cm
Head, neck and breast rufous and tawny. Flanks, belly and undertail barred black and white. Legs greyish green. Calls like 5, a long, descending *churrrrr* trill. Tall grass, partially flooded areas, bogs, forest clearings, thickets by streams.

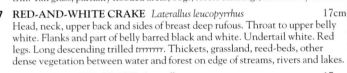

7 RED-AND-WHITE CRAKE *Laterallus leucopyrrhus*   17cm
Head, neck, upper back and sides of breast deep rufous. Throat to upper belly white. Flanks and part of belly barred black and white. Undertail white. Red legs. Long descending trilled *trrrrrrr*. Thickets, grassland, reed-beds, other dense vegetation between water and forest on edge of streams, rivers and lakes.

8 RUFOUS-FACED CRAKE *Laterallus xenopterus*   17cm
Head to upper back deep rufous. Rest of upperparts black barred white. Tail black. Sides of neck and breast tawny. Legs purply chocolate. Tall damp or partially flooded grass, marshes bordered by gallery forest and Cerrado, dense thickets.

9 RUSSET-CROWNED CRAKE *Anurolimnas (Laterallus) viridis*   17cm
No barring anywhere. Cap rufous chestnut. Face dark brownish grey. Breast and flanks dark rufous, more tawny undertail. Pinkish-red legs. Call like other *Laterallus* but more staccato. Damp, partly flooded grass, dry grass with bushes, sometimes far from water.

10 BLACK-BANDED CRAKE *Anurolimnas (Laterallus) fasciatus*   19cm
Head, neck and breast deep rufous chestnut. Flanks, rest of underparts and undertail barred black and pale rust. Pinkish-red legs. Tall damp or slightly flooded grass, bogs, vegetation along stream banks and ponds.

11 RUSTY-FLANKED CRAKE *Laterallus levraudi*   16cm
No barring anywhere. Forehead, cheeks, sides of breast, rest of underparts rusty rufous. Crown, hind-neck brownish grey. Throat, fore-neck and centre of breast white. Pinkish-red legs. Tall grass and vegetation by swamps, marshes, lagoons, flooded or dry grassland.

RODRIGUEZ MATA

CRAKES AND GALLINULES (RALLIDAE)

1 SPOT-FLANKED GALLINULE *Gallinula (Porphyriops) melanops*   26cm
Bill and frontal shield lime-green. Flanks brownish spotted white. Upperparts
chestnut and olive-brown. Lakes, marshes, temporary ponds and roadside
ditches, with much floating and emergent vegetation.

2 SORA CRAKE or RAIL *Porzana carolina*   22cm
Bill yellow. Black fore-face. Upperparts brownish olive, feathers edged white
and streaked black. Flanks barred. Calls *keek* when alarmed. Tall grass on edge
of water, reed-beds and other emergent plants, edge of bogs, flooded grassland,
mangroves, rice-paddies.

3 ASH-THROATED CRAKE *Porzana albicollis*   25cm
Bill greenish yellow. Upperparts blackish, feathers edged olive. Face to belly
grey. Throat whitish. Legs greenish. Calls a series of loud *rrrrow*, *krrrrow* (as in
cow) while ♀ joins in with *piri-piris*. Tall grasses in marshes, flooded areas, edge
of lakes by forest, reed-beds, rice-paddies.

4 YELLOW-BREASTED CRAKE *Porzana (Poliolimnas) flaviventer*   13cm
Tiny. Crown and line through the eye blackish, separated by an interrupted
white brow. Upperparts streaked, barred and spotted cinnamon, blackish and
white. Yellowish cream on cheeks, sides of neck and breast. Flanks, lower belly
and undertail barred. Legs ochreous yellow. Call is a single or repeated *kreer* or
kreee. Tall grass in flooded areas around water and temporary puddles, floating
and emergent vegetation of ditches, streams, bogs, mangroves.

5 OCELLATED CRAKE *Micropygia schomburgkii*   14cm
Very small. Overall rich ochre, cinnamon wash on upperparts, which have
drop-shaped spots with black borders. Light red legs. Voice is an insect-like
prrrssss. Tall damp grass near water and bogs, dry grassland and savannah.

6 SPECKLED CRAKE *Coturnicops notatus*   13cm
Tiny and dark. Mouse-like. Very rare. Brownish-black spotted, barred and
dotted white. White patch on secondaries seen in flight. Call is a quiet *coueee-
cab* and *peep* in alarm. Tall savannah grass, dense marshy vegetation,
rice-paddies and alfalfa fields, wet edge of forest, ditches, flooded fields, tall
grass by temporary puddles.

7 PAINT-BILLED CRAKE *Neocrex erythrops*   15cm
Greenish-yellow bill with bright red base. Upperparts uniform brownish olive.
Face, neck and underparts grey. Lower belly and undertail barred. Red legs.
Call is a series of frog-like, guttural *qurrrk auk qurrrk auk....* Damp grass with
trees or in open country, dense reeds around bodies of water, rice-paddies.

8 COLOMBIAN CRAKE *Neocrex colombiana*   15cm
Like 7 but with plain buffy-white undertail and lower belly. Damp or flooded
grass. Considered by some to be a race of 7.

9 PURPLE GALLINULE *Porphyrio (Porphyrula) martinica*   30cm
Unmistakable. Red bill with yellow tip, frontal shield pale blue. Head, neck
and underparts intense blue with purple gloss. Undertail white. Upperparts
bluish green with bronzy wash. Large yellow legs. Juv: looks like 10 but head,
neck and breast tinted brownish and buff. Tall vegetation and trees on the
shore, dense floating and emergent vegetation at edge of lakes and rivers,
marshes, temporary ponds, flooded grassland, rice-paddies.

10 AZURE GALLINULE *Porphyrio (Porphyrula) flavirostris*   26cm
Unmistakable. Sides of head, neck, flanks and wing pale blue. Underparts
white. Bill and legs yellow. Usually silent. Floating and emergent vegetation in
marshes, lakes and rivers, temporary ponds, rice-paddies.

MOORHEN AND COOTS (RALLIDAE)

1 MOORHEN *Gallinula chloropus*   34cm
Like a slender coot. Wings project above straight back. Swims with head thrown forward and jerking. Blackish slate-grey, darker on head, neck and upperparts. White line along flanks. White undertail. Shield and bill scarlet, bill tipped yellow. Juv duller. Call a long *keh keh…kehro kehro…kehrk kehrk*. Marshes, rivers, pond, roadside ditches, usually with abundant vegetation, floating and emergent.

Coots are predominantly black, the differences mostly seen in the bill and shield. Reluctant fliers, they scoot over water to escape or threaten. They often walk along shores. Juvs are dull, paler versions of adults with darker, blackish-yellow bills.

2 CARIBBEAN COOT *Fulica caribaea*   37cm
Bill and broad shield white with purply-chestnut sub-apical ring. Shield sometimes washed yellow. Lakes, ponds, edge of marshes with emergent and floating vegetation.

3 AMERICAN COOT *Fulica americana*   34cm
Bill and lower shield chalky white with purply-chestnut sub-apical ring and upper shield. Bill washed yellow at the base in breeding condition. Legs yellowish olive. Lakes, ponds with reed-beds and other aquatic vegetation.

4 ANDEAN COOT *Fulica ardesiaca*   46cm
Bill yellowish white. Prominent rounded shield purply chestnut (or white washed yellow in breeding condition in some populations). Greenish-grey legs. High Andean lakes sometimes with reeds and rushes, always with submerged vegetation.

5 RED-GARTERED COOT *Fulica armillata*   43cm
Bill and pointed frontal shield yellow, divided by an irregular reddish-chestnut band. When swimming, the 'knees' breaking the surface show the red 'garter'. Legs yellowish olive. Heftier than the next 2 species, with which it is mostly found. Juv: head and neck whitish grey, body blackish grey. Lakes, marshes, roadside ditches, streams, rivers, reed-beds, temporary ponds and flooded fields, brackish lakes with little or no emergent vegetation.

6 WHITE-WINGED COOT *Fulica leucoptera*   37cm
Yellow bill. Rounded frontal shield varies with seasons from whitish, through yellow to yellowish orange. Tips of flight feathers whitish grey, seen in flight. Legs greyish olive. Lakes, marshes with emergent vegetation, roadside ditches, temporary puddles, dams, streams, rivers, flooded fields and brackish lagoons.

7 RED-FRONTED COOT *Fulica rufifrons*   38cm
Rich yellow bill; base of bill and long, lanceolate frontal shield purply chestnut. The point of the shield juts slightly above crown, forming a bump on the head. Raises tail often to fan and show white undertail coverts. Lakes, marshes, roadside ditches, streams with much aquatic vegetation, especially reed-beds.

8 GIANT COOT *Fulica gigantea*   52cm
Huge and hefty. Bill reddish chestnut with yellow tip. Base of the maxilla and central frontal shield white. Base of the mandible and edge of shield bright yellow. Shield is grooved up the centre and ends in 2 lobes that push up into a 'double bump' on the forehead. Red legs. Open high Andean lakes with submerged vegetation.

9 HORNED COOT *Fulica cornuta*   50cm
Huge and hefty. Bill yellow-orange, culmen black; from the shield juts a strange black caruncle. Legs olivaceous grey. Open Andean lakes with submerged vegetation.

ROLRIGUEZ MATA 9

OYSTERCATCHERS (HAEMATOPODIDAE), STILTS AND AVOCETS (RECURVIROSTRIDAE) AND PLOVERS (CHARADRIIDAE)

Oystercatchers are red-billed shorebirds found on beaches and coasts. Rowdy; high-pitched whistles.

1 AMERICAN OYSTERCATCHER *Haematopus palliatus* 42cm
Head, neck, breast, upperparts, tail and wings brownish black. Underparts, rump, underwing and wing-bar white. White curls around bend of folded wing at rest. Red eye-ring, yellow iris. Legs pinkish. Sandy beaches and seashores.

2 MAGELLANIC OYSTERCATCHER *Haematopus leucopodus* 44cm
Upperparts, neck, tail and breast black. White underparts and secondary flight feathers which do not curl in front of wing. Eye-ring and iris yellow. Legs pale pinkish. Juv duller. Seashores, often inland on short-grass meadows in breeding season.

3 BLACKISH OYSTERCATCHER *Haematopus ater* 44cm
All dirty black. Red eye-ring and yellow iris. Legs pinkish. Rocky coasts.

Stilts and Avocets are long-legged waders of the shallows, often in flocks. Feed on insects, crustaceans and other aquatic invertebrates. High-pitched barking call when alarmed.

4 BLACK-WINGED STILT *Himantopus himantopus* 37cm
Unmistakable. Black and white. Long, fine, black bill. Legs extremely long, reddish pink. Juv: crown and back brownish black. Edge of fresh and saline inland waters from sea level to mountains. The two American races, *H. h. mexicanus* (Northern) and *H. h. melanurus* (Southern, illustrated) may each be valid species.

5 ANDEAN AVOCET *Recurvirostra andina* 46cm
White. Upper back, wings and tail black. Slender upturned black bill. Legs blue. High Andean Puna lakes, usually above 3,000m. Sweeps the surface of the water to catch its food.

Lapwings are larger than most plovers, aggressively noisy and territorial, with spurs on the bend of the broad wing. Sharply contrasting pattern in flight. Less dependent on shores and water, they are mostly found on short-grass meadows. Sociable, pairs, flocks.

6 SOUTHERN LAPWING *Vanellus chilensis* 35cm
Long, slender occipital crest (short in S race). Head and upperparts brownish grey. Purple and green sheen on wing coverts. Forehead, line down throat and neck, and breast black. Underparts white. Base of bill, eye and legs red. Calls include loud repeated *tay-oo*, while rare S form calls, *ray-oo….* Short grass and lawns, gardens, wet meadows.

7 ANDEAN LAPWING *Vanellus resplendens* 32cm
No occipital crest. Head, neck and breast pale greyish. Blackish through the face. Throat whitish. Back and upperparts greyish brown; greenish and purple sheen on wing coverts. Underparts white. Base of bill, eye and legs reddish. Voice a nasal and repeated *key-er*. Short-grass meadows near water in high Andes, cultivated land, puna above 3,000m.

RODRIGUEZ MATA

PLOVERS (CHARADRIIDAE)

1 PIED LAPWING *Vanellus (Hoploxypterus) cayanus* 25cm
Striking black on head, neck, breast and scapulars. Crown-patch, upper back and wing coverts brownish grey. Rest of crown and underparts white. Bill black. Eye-ring and legs pinkish red. Juv duller. Beaches, sand and mudbanks on forest rivers or edge of small lakes and other bodies of water in savannah.

Plovers (*Charadrius*) are smallish and active runners on flats near water, gravel or sandy beaches, dunes, and even short grass. Fast flyers with sharp, long wings. 1-note calls in alarm. Juvs are like non-br plumages but with feathers on head and upperparts edged tawny, giving a scaly effect. Solitary, pairs or small flocks.

2 PUNA PLOVER *Charadrius alticola* 18cm
Br plumage: black across crown, down to incomplete blackish collar; a second ill-defined pectoral collar brownish cinnamon. Crown and hind-neck pale cinnamon. Slight post-ocular streak. Upperparts pale brownish grey. Underparts white. Bill and legs black. Non-br duller, bands washed out. On flats around lakes in Puna above 3,000m.

3 SEMIPALMATED PLOVER *Charadrius semipalmatus* 18cm
Bill short, pinkish with black tip. Legs dirty pink. Non-br plumage: crown, lores, cheeks, pectoral collar and upperparts brownish grey. Forehead, brow, throat, collar and underparts white. Br plumage: fore-crown, lores and collar black. Upperparts darker than non-br. Eye-ring pink. Sharp *tweet* on taking flight. Estuaries, bays, mudflats, beaches. Migrant from N America.

4 WILSON'S PLOVER *Charadrius wilsonia* 19cm
Heavy black bill. Fore-crown, lores, cheeks and wide pectoral collar black (more cinnamon in S race). Cinnamon on ear-patch and nape. Forehead, brow, complete collar and rest of underparts white. Upperparts greyish brown. Legs pale pinkish. Non-br plumage less contrasted. Sandy beaches, mudflats, mangroves, coastal lagoons.

5 TWO-BANDED PLOVER *Charadrius falklandicus* 19cm
Bill and legs black. Double pectoral collar and fore-crown black. Crown, cheeks and hind-neck cinnamon. Upperparts brownish grey. Underparts white. Non-br duller; black and cinnamon turn grey. Sandy beaches, dunes, short grass by water.

6 COLLARED PLOVER *Charadrius collaris* 16cm
1 black pectoral collar. Fore-crown and lores black. Pale post-ocular streak. Cheeks and part of crown cinnamon. Upperparts brownish grey; underparts white. Bill black, legs pale pinkish. Non-br plumage duller. Sandy river beaches and banks, ocean beaches, mudflats of freshwater lakes, coast of saline lagoons, flooded short grass, estuaries.

7 SNOWY PLOVER *Charadrius alexandrinus* 16cm
Upperparts pale sandy grey. White collar round hind-neck. Black patch on sides of breast. Fore-crown black. Blackish post-ocular streak. Notable white brow. Underparts white. Bill and legs black. Lagoons and saline lakes near sea coasts, beaches.

8 KILLDEER *Charadrius vociferous* 24cm
Double black pectoral collar. Lores, cheeks and band across crown black. Brow and line under eye white. Long tail black, edged white. Rump and upper tail coverts cinnamon. Upperparts brown, underparts white. Bill black, eye-ring red. Legs creamy yellow. Onomatopoeic call *kill-deer, kill-deer....* Short grass, often far from water, beaches, saline lagoons near coasts.

172

2
non-br

2

2 br

3 br

3 br

3 br

3 non-br

4 br

4
non-br

4 br

6

5 br

5 non-br

5 br

6

5 juv

7

7

7

8

1

1

1 juv

8

8

RODRIGUEZ MATA

PLOVERS AND DOTTERELS (CHARADRIIDAE), AND TURNSTONE AND SURFBIRD (SCOLOPACIDAE)

1 AMERICAN GOLDEN PLOVER *Pluvialis dominica* 26cm
Non-br: upperparts to rump brownish grey, feathers edged paler (buffy in juv).
Whitish brow. Face, neck, breast and upper belly pale brownish grey, feather
edges paler. Throat and lower underparts whitish. Axillaries pale. Br: face,
fore-neck and underparts black. White line though forehead, brow, down sides
of neck to sides of breast. Whistled call in flight. Short grass, muddy shores of
bodies of fresh water, sandy beaches. Migratory from N America.

2 BLACK-BELLIED PLOVER *Pluvialis squatarola* 28cm
Non-br: pale and greyer version of 1. Bill heavier. Axillaries black. Upper tail
coverts white, tail feathers barred. Br: face, fore-neck, breast and upper belly
black. Rest of the head and neck, sides of breast and lower belly white. Usually
solitary, sometimes in small flocks. Shy. Quiet whistled call in flight. Tidal
mudflats, seashores, lake-shores, rarely in short grass. Migratory from N America.

3 RUFOUS-CHESTED DOTTEREL *Charadrius (Zonibyx) modestus* 21cm
Br: crown and upperparts dark brown. Long white brow. Face and upper neck
grey. Breast rufous. Black pectoral band. Rest of underparts white. Non-br:
head, neck and breast brownish, brow white. Upperparts uniform brown. Juv:
feathers on upperparts edged buff. Back of the beach, muddy shores, short-grass
pastures, seashores, lakes.

4 TAWNY-THROATED DOTTEREL *Oreopholus ruficollis* 28cm
Elegant and upright. Buff and grey. Black line through the eye and large spot at
mid-belly. Back streaked black and buff. Tawny bib. Legs dirty pink. Scattered
pairs. Flocks in winter. Melodious whistled flight-call. Steppe and desert in
lowlands and mountains, short grass, stony terrain, usually far from water;
agricultural land in winter.

5 DIADEMED PLOVER *Phegornis mitchellii* 16cm
Small. Blackish head with white band around crown and half-collar. Hind-
neck and upper back rufous. Rest of upperparts dark brown. Underparts white,
finely barred blackish brown. Legs pinkish orange. Juv: brown head and
upperparts barred dark brown. Brow and throat white. Shy, solitary or pairs.
Puna, high mountain bogs, shores of streams and lakes.

6 MAGELLANIC PLOVER *Pluvianellus socialis* 20cm
Head, upperparts and breast ash-grey. Underparts white. Black bill, red eye,
reddish-pink legs. Juv: feathers on upperparts edged whitish buff. Orange eye,
yellowish legs. Longish sad descending whistle. Stony shores of inland lakes,
on downwind side; seashores and tidal mudflats in winter.

7 RUDDY TURNSTONE *Arenaria interpres* 24cm
Short bill slightly upturned. Non-br: brownish-grey head, upperparts and
breast, back feathers edged whitish. Underparts, rump and throat white.
Contrasting black and white on wings and tail. Legs pinkish. Br: head, neck
and throat boldly patterned black and white. Upperparts mostly rufous. Sea
coasts, mudflats and stony beaches. Digs and turns pebbles in search of its food.
Sometimes on lake shores. Migratory from N America.

8 SURFBIRD *Aphriza virgata* 26cm
Non-br: head, upperparts and breast blackish grey. Brow and throat whitish.
Underparts white, streaked grey. Bold wing-bar seen in flight. Rump and tail
white, tail-tip black. Bill basally yellowish, legs yellowish. Br: paler and
streaked. Rocky seashores and beaches. Migratory from N America.

1
non-br

2 br

2 non-br

2 non-br

1
non-br

1 br

5 juv

5

3 br

5

4

3 br

4

3 non-br

7

8 non-br

7 non-br

8 non-br

7 br

6

8 br

6

RODRÍGUEZ MATA

JACANAS (JACANIDAE), **PAINTED SNIPE** (ROSTRATULIDAE) **AND SNIPE** (SCOLOPACIDAE)

1 WATTLED JACANA *Jacana jacana*   25cm
Long legs and toes. Black and reddish chestnut. Flight feathers yellow. Bill yellow, frontal shield and small wattles red. A Colombian race is all black except flight feathers. Juv: browner upperparts. Dark post-ocular streak. Brow and underparts whitish. Floating vegetation of fresh water.

2 SOUTH AMERICAN PAINTED SNIPE *Nycticryphes semicollaris*   21cm
♀: upperparts, head and breast blackish brown. White medial line on forehead and crown. Ochreous 'V' on back starts white from sides of breast. Large white spots on wing coverts. Underparts white. Bill down-curved at the tip and legs yellowish olive. ♂ duller. Low and erratic flight. Shy and silent. Emergent vegetation by lakes, marshes, streams, muddy shores.

Snipe have a very long yellowish-olive bill, are dumpy birds of cryptic coloration, probing mud for food. Flight displays include dives producing different mechanical sounds with outer tail feathers.

3 FUEGIAN SNIPE *Gallinago stricklandii*   30cm
Generally cinnamon-buff and fairly uniform. Back feathers edged cinnamon. Face and underparts ochre barred dark brown on breast and flanks. Solitary or small flocks in bogs and damp transition zones with woods. Sea level to 3,000m.

4 ANDEAN SNIPE *Gallinago jamesoni*   30cm (not illustrated)
Like 3 but brow, throat, face and underparts whiter, belly more barred. Open areas with grass in Páramos, boggy patches in woods and scrubby areas, coastal bogs. Often thought to be a race of 3.

5 NOBLE SNIPE *Gallinago nobilis*   30cm
A hefty version of 6. Head, neck and breast darker, pattern less marked, buffy brown, spotting more dense. Underwing and flight feathers darker. Proportionately shorter legs. Differs from 4 in having narrower base of the bill. Scapulars and back feathers edged white. Mid-belly white. Bogs, streams and small lakes in Páramos, damp grassland, savannah.

6 SOUTH AMERICAN SNIPE *Gallinago paraguaiae*   27cm
Bold face-pattern with 3 dark stripes on dirty white. Back feathers edged white contrasting with black. Lower underparts white, barred on flanks. Flight feathers uniform greyish-brown. Legs pale olive-grey. Damp grassland, peat bogs, edges of marshes and lakes, wet patches in open woods, boggy banks of rivers and streams, flooded savannah. The race Puna Snipe (*G. p. andina*) is a smaller version, with yellower legs, and proportionately shorter bill. Call differs. Replaces 6 in high Andean region. Some consider this a separate species (6R).

7 GIANT SNIPE *Gallinago undulata*   48cm
A giant version of 6. Bill broad at the base, seeming to flatten the forehead. Flight feathers dark brown, finely barred whitish. Unusually shy, hard to see. Tall grass in bogs, flooded grassland – sometimes drier, marshes in savannah.

8 IMPERIAL SNIPE *Gallinago imperialis*   31cm
Dark upperparts chestnutty cinnamon with black streaking and bars. No pale edges to feathers. Cinnamon breast heavily streaked blackish. Lower underparts and vent have broad black and white barring. Flight feathers dark brown, underwing coverts black. Very rare and local. At tree line in mountains, elfin woods, bogs, damp places with tall grass, cane and tree-ferns. Isolated places in Peru's Andes – Piura, Amazonas, La Libertad and Cuzco, possibly also in Colombia.

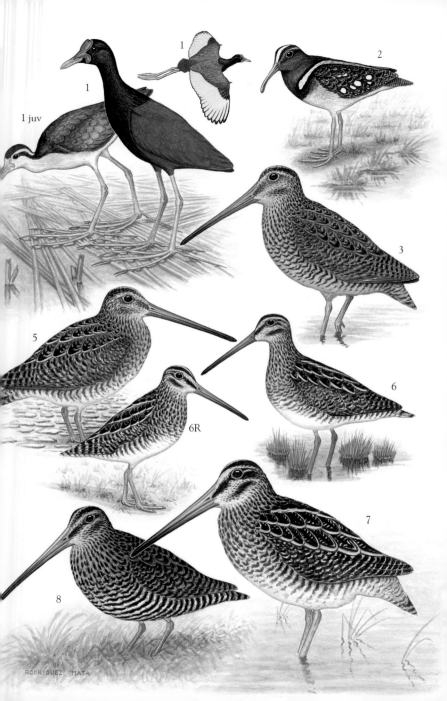

SANDPIPERS (SCOLOPACIDAE)

1 WILLET *Catoptrophorus semipalmatus*   40cm
Non-br: head, neck and upperparts brownish grey. Short white brow before the eye. Underparts whitish, breast washed brownish grey. Heavy bill. Bluish-grey legs. Wings with very bold black and white seen in flight. Br: streaked and barred. Rocky seashores, beaches, saline lakes, mangroves, bogs. Migratory from N America.

2 SPOTTED SANDPIPER *Actitis macularius*   19cm
Non-br: head, sides of breast and upperparts brownish grey washed olive. Brow and underparts white. Legs pinkish. White wing-bar. Barred outer tail feathers. Br: spotted black all over. Bobs hind part of body. Flight with wings below the horizontal. Generally solitary. Beaches, mangroves, rocky shores, tidal mudflats, lakes, bogs, forest rivers.

3 BUFF-BREASTED SANDPIPER *Tryngites subruficollis*   20cm
Generally cinnamon-buff. Upperparts have dark brown feathers edged buff. Spotting on sides of breast. Short, slender bill. Yellowish legs. Short grass in low-lying land, dunes. Migratory from N America.

4 STILT SANDPIPER *Calidris (Micropalama) himantopus* 22cm
Non-br: upperparts greyish, feathers bordered paler. Underparts whitish, somewhat streaked on neck and breast. Pale brow. Bill slightly down-curved at the tip. Long legs yellowish olive. White rump in flight. Tail grey. Br: cheeks cinnamon. Underparts barred. Tidal mudflats, edge of lakes and other bodies of water, flooded fields. Migratory from N America.

5 GREATER YELLOWLEGS *Tringa melanoleuca*   32cm
Non-br: like 6. Larger. Bill proportionately thicker and longer, slightly upturned, 1.5 times as long as head. In flight, white rump and barred tail. Long yellow legs. Br: more contrasted. Bobs head. Calls *tew tew tew…*, 3–5 times. Shores of fresh and saline water, tidal mudflats, estuaries. Migratory from N America.

6 LESSER YELLOWLEGS *Tringa flavipes*   26cm
Non-br: slight brow. Upperparts grey, spotted and barred darker and lighter. Neck and breast streaked greyish. Rest of underparts white. Slender, straight bill as long as the head. Long yellow legs. Br: more contrasted markings. Bobs head. Calls *tew* once or twice only. Shores of fresh or saline water, mangroves, estuaries, mudflats. Migratory from N America.

7 SOLITARY SANDPIPER *Tringa solitaria*   19cm
Upperparts, face and sides of breast dark brownish-grey. Mid-rump and central tail feathers blackish brown. Outer tail feathers barred. Underparts white. Notable whitish eye-ring. Legs greyish olive. Usually solitary. On taking flight, makes an emphatic *tweet*. Wooded freshwater shores, mangroves, mudbanks. Migratory from N America.

8 WANDERING TATTLER *Heteroscelus incanus*   28cm
Non-br: upperparts dark grey. Underparts white. Brow and eye-ring white. Straight bill longish, somewhat thick. Short yellowish legs. Flight feathers, rump and tail dark. Br: streaked and barred blackish. Active. Loud *weet weet weet* when alarmed. Beaches and rocky sea coasts. Rarely on inland water and muddy estuaries.

9 RUFF *Philomachus pugnax*   ♂ 29cm, ♀ 23cm
Non-br: upperparts brown, feathers edged buff. Face, neck and breast buffy, faintly streaked brown. Brow, throat and underparts white. Yellowish bill. Legs pinkish yellow. Br males sport ornamental feathers. Lake and marsh edges, short grass. Accidental.

1 non-br

1 non-br

2 br

2 non-br

1 br

4 non-br

2 non-br

4 non-br

3 ♀

3

4 br

5

6

6

5

7

7

9 ♂ br

8 non-br

9 ♂ non-br

8 non-br

8 br

9 ♀

DRIGUEZ MATA

SANDPIPERS (SCOLOPACIDAE)

1 WESTERN SANDPIPER *Calidris mauri*   17cm
Upperparts greyish, underparts white. Cheeks, hind-neck and sides of breast
densely streaked greyish. Bill longer than 2, with drooping tip. Legs black. In
flight, like 2. Br: face, upper back and scapulars partly rusty. Sea beaches,
mangroves, swamps, lake shores. Migratory from N America.

2 SEMIPALMATED SANDPIPER *Calidris pusilla*   15cm
Very like 1 but no drooping tip on shorter bill. In flight, narrow white wing-
bar. Mid-rump and central tail feathers blackish, outers grey. Br: feathers on
crown and scapulars black and rust, edged buff. Seashores, mangroves, salt
lakes, bogs, river banks. Migratory from N America.

3 CURLEW SANDPIPER *Calidris ferruginea*   23cm
Upperparts brownish grey. Underparts white. Pale brow. Longish down-curved
bill. White wing-bar and rump very notable in flight. Br: overall rufous.
Seashores, lakes and other bodies of water. Accidental.

4 WHITE-RUMPED SANDPIPER *Calidris fuscicollis*   18cm
Upperparts: feathers dark brownish grey edged paler. Head, neck and breast
streaked blackish grey, extending along flanks. Pale brow. Bill and legs black.
White rump seen in flight. Br: back feathers edged rufous and buff. Active. On
taking flight, makes a single or double *jeet*. Seashores, river banks, lake shore,
bogs, estuaries, mudflats. Migratory from N America.

5 BAIRD'S SANDPIPER *Calidris bairdii*   18cm
More buffy brown than 4. Speckling on face, neck and breast more uniform,
barely onto flanks. Bill and legs black. Dark line down centre of rump seen in
flight. Br: more contrasted and richer colours. Voice is a notable *crreeeek*.
Inland waters, pebbly shores, high Andean lakes, estuaries, short-grass
meadows, seashores. Migratory from N America.

6 SANDERLING *Calidris alba*   20cm
White with grey upperparts, feathers edged white. In flight, contrasting black
and white on wings. Mid-rump blackish onto tail. Bill and legs black. Br: head
and breast finely speckled brown. Back darker, feathers edged buff or rufous.
Active. Seashores and beaches, less inland. Migratory from N America.

7 LEAST SANDPIPER *Calidris minutilla*   14cm
Tiny. Bill black, legs yellow. Upperparts and breast brownish grey. Back
feathers edged pale. Underparts white. Black down mid-rump to tail. Br: more
contrasting pattern, back feathers edged whiter and rusty. Seashores,
mangroves, salt lakes, streams, flooded areas, river banks in forest. Migratory
from N America.

8 PECTORAL SANDPIPER *Calidris melanotos*   22cm
Breast brownish buff streaked blackish, neatly contrasting with white below.
Stance fairly upright. Neck longer than other sandpipers. Bill and legs olive-
yellow. In flight, rump has broad blackish midline. Freezes when alarmed. *Creek*
on taking flight. Br: brighter. Marshes, temporary puddles, roadside ditches, rice-
paddies, flooded fields, wet short grass, salt lakes. Migratory from N America.

9 RED KNOT *Calidris canutus*   25cm
Large and stocky. Non-br: upperparts grey, feathers edged pale. Underparts
white. Faintly barred grey on sides of breast and flanks. Bill black, legs washed
olive. Secondary flight feathers have white and black bars. White rump barred
grey. Tail grey. Br: face to upper belly cinnamon. Seashores, beaches and rocks,
bays, estuaries, nearby open lagoons. Migratory from N America.

1 br

2 br

3 br

3 non-br

on-br

2 non-br

3 non-br

on-br

5

5

4 non-br

4 br

6 non-br

7

6 br

7

6 non-br

8

9 non-br

8

9 br

9 non-br

RODRIGUEZ MATA

SANDPIPERS (SCOLOPACIDAE)
AND THICK-KNEES (BURHINIDAE)

1 HUDSONIAN GODWIT *Limosa haemastica*   40cm
Greyish, lower underparts whitish. Very long bill slightly upturned. White
wing-bar and rump contrast strongly in flight. Tail and flight feathers blackish.
Br: contrasting black and rufous. Muddy shores, tidal mudflats, estuaries, bays,
wet meadows. Migratory from N America.

2 MARBLED GODWIT *Limosa fedoa*   47cm
Mostly buffy cinnamon, barred, streaked and spotted blackish. Very long bill,
slightly upturned, blackish, base pinkish. Sea coasts, coastal lagoons, wet
pastures, tidal mudflats, bays, estuaries. Migratory from N America.

3 SHORT-BILLED DOWITCHER *Limnodromus griseus*   28cm
Very long straight bill. Greyish, whiter below. Flanks faintly barred. White lower
back. Rump and tail barred. Secondaries have narrow white bar and white tip.
Legs greenish grey. Br: upperparts blackish, feathers edged buff. Breast and upper
belly cinnamon paling towards vent. Voice somewhat like a Greater Yellowlegs'
tew tew tew. Seashores, mangroves, estuaries, bays, mudflats, sandy beaches.

4 LONG-BILLED DOWITCHER *Limnodromus scolopaceus* 30cm (not illustrated)
Very like 3. Bill and legs longer. Neat break between grey breast and white
belly. Br: underparts' cinnamon extends to vent, barred blackish on flanks and
sides of breast. Voice is a high-pitched, thin *kick* or *keek*. Fresh water, flooded
grassland, muddy lake-shores and saline lagoons.

5 ESKIMO CURLEW *Numenius borealis*   35cm
Small version of 6. Bill proportionately shorter and more slender. Buffy
cinnamon. Underwing and axillaries cinnamon. Flight feathers uniformly dark
brown. Grass, coastal and inland. Migrates from N America. Virtually extinct.

6 WHIMBREL *Numenius phaeopus*   45cm
Very long down-curved bill. Upperparts brownish, serratedly bordered buffy
white. Crown and eye-line dark brown. Mid-crown line and brow buffy white.
Underparts buffy white, neck and breast streaked, flanks barred. Underwing
coverts barred. Flight feathers faintly barred. Usually solitary. Loud whistle on
taking flight. Tidal mudflats and beaches, mangroves, bays, estuaries, sheltered
seashores. Migratory from N America.

7 UPLAND SANDPIPER *Bartramia longicauda*   28cm
Slender bill, yellowish with black tip. Yellowish legs. Upright stance. Upperparts
dark brown, feathers edged buff and cinnamon. Whitish buff grading to white
belly; neck finely streaked, breast and flanks barred. Mid-rump and central tail
blackish, outers barred. 3-syllable whistle in flight. Perches on fence posts.
Grassland, cultivated land, marshy areas. Migrates from N America.

Thick-knees are like a hefty, long-legged plover with a short thick bill. Very large
yellow eyes. Crepuscular and nocturnal. Far from water.

8 DOUBLE-STRIPED THICK-KNEE *Burhinus bistriatus*   46cm
Whitish brow bordered above by black line. Back feathers brown edged buff.
Runs. Active and rowdy at night. Call is a longish series of accelerating *prips*.
Dry savannah, short open grass, sometimes with scattered trees and bushes,
cultivated land, arid land.

9 PERUVIAN THICK-KNEE *Burhinus superciliaris*   40cm
White brow bordered by black line above. Upperparts brownish grey. Juv:
feathers on back and sides of breast edged whitish buff, giving a scaly effect.
Runs. Voice *way ray kay kay*. Arid and semiarid regions, open land with short
grass, cultivated land, scattered trees and bushes.

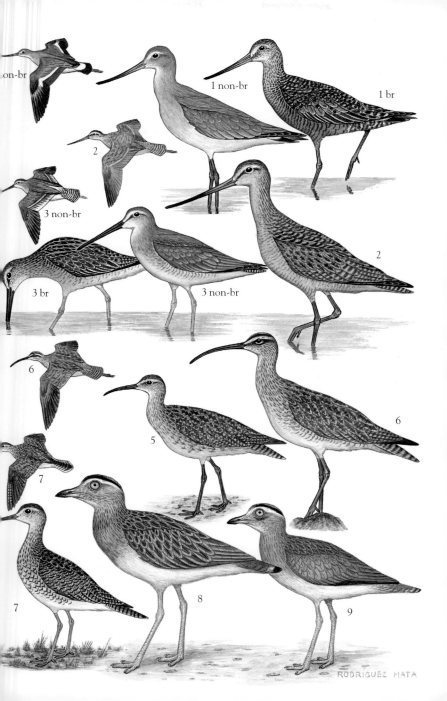

on-br

1 non-br

1 br

2

3 non-br

3 br

3 non-br

2

6

5

6

7

7

8

9

RODRIGUEZ MATA

PHALAROPES (SCOLOPACIDAE)
AND SEEDSNIPES (THINOCORIDAE)

Phalaropes are unlike others of the family in having lobed toes for swimming. Males duller in br plumage.

1 RED PHALAROPE *Phalaropus fulicarius*   20cm
Dumpier and with thicker bill than others. Non-br: eye-line, nape, line down hind-neck and upper back blackish. Upperparts grey. Face, neck and underparts white. Black and white wing-bar on flight feathers. Tail and mid-rump black. Br: reddish rufous. White face, rest of head black. ♂: black crown striped white. Yellow bill, black tip. ♀ brighter. Crown black. Pelagic. Rarely near shore. Accidental on inland waters. Migratory at sea from Arctic.

2 RED-NECKED PHALAROPE *Phalaropus lobatus*   18cm
Like 1 but blacker crown, upperparts blackish with 2 white lines and edge of feathers white. Bill more slender. Br: 2 buff lines along upperparts. Neck and brow cinnamon. Crown and eye-stripe black. Sides of forehead, lower cheek and throat white. Sides of breast blackish, flanks thickly streaked blackish. Rest of underparts white. ♀: blacker on head, neck rufous cinnamon. White only on throat. Sometimes in huge flocks. Pelagic, saline lakes, beaches and river banks. Migrates from Arctic.

3 WILSON'S PHALAROPE *Phalaropus tricolor*   23cm
Crown, post-ocular streak, hind-neck and upperparts grey. Face, neck and underparts white. Long slender bill like a needle. Olive legs. Dark flight feathers. White rump. Pale grey tail. Br: ♂ as non-br but cinnamon on sides of neck. ♀: line from eye to scapulars starts black, then chestnut. Another chestnut line on wing coverts. Fore-neck cinnamon. Forehead, crown, hind-neck and upper back pale grey. Swims gyrating and 'stitching' the surface. Wades in shallows. Sometimes in huge flocks. Lakes, often saline, high mountain lakes, streams, roadside ditches. Rarely seashore. Migratory from N America.

Seedsnipes are dove- or pigeon-shaped shorebirds. Cryptic coloration on upperparts. Squat. Fast, erratic snipe-like flight. Great walkers on short yellow legs. In pairs, family groups or small flocks, these larger in winter.

4 GREY-BREASTED SEEDSNIPE *Thinocorus orbignyianus*   22cm
♂: white throat bordered black. Face, neck and breast grey, this bordered by black pectoral band. White below. Crown and upperparts cryptically blackish, brown, cinnamon and buffy white. Underwing and axillaries blackish. ♀: head, neck and breast streaked. Throat and underparts white. Mountains and rolling country with pebbly steppe, grass and small bushes, wet valley bottoms and peat bogs. Migrates north in winter, or simply to lower elevations.

5 LEAST SEEDSNIPE *Thinocorus rumicivorus*   18cm
Like 4 but smaller. ♂: black border of throat and pectoral band joined by a line forming an 'anchor'. ♀: lacks grey but 'anchor' narrower. Juv lacks 'anchor'. Flat pebbly steppe, mountains, dunes, cultivated lands and short grasslands in winter.

6 WHITE-BELLIED SEEDSNIPE *Atagis malouinus*   28cm
Sexes alike. Like a large ♀ of 4 but no white throat and no black or grey. Generally more ochreous, designs more contrasted. Underwing white. Pairs or small flocks. High mountains and plateaux, grassy or pebbly terrain. Descends altitude in winter.

7 RUFOUS-BELLIED SEEDSNIPE *Atagis gayi*   30cm
Head, neck, breast and upperparts tawny buff scaled blackish. Underparts cinnamon. Underwing buffy white. Isolated race in Ecuador (*A. g. latreillii*) darker with rufous ventral parts and underwing. Mountain bogs with hummocky vegetation, Páramos, stony slopes, grassland, sheltered valleys.

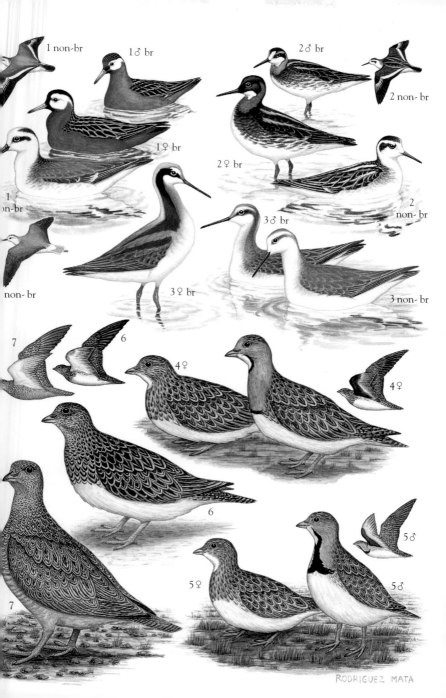

1 non-br
1 ♂ br
1 ♀ br
1 non-br
non-br

2 ♂ br
2 non-br
2 ♀ br
2 non-br

3 ♂ br
3 ♀ br
3 non-br

7
6
4 ♀
4 ♀

6

5 ♀
5 ♂
5 ♂

7

RODRIGUEZ MATA

SKUAS, JAEGERS (STERCORARIIDAE)
AND SHEATHBILLS (CHIONIDAE)

Skuas are rapacious gulls, hefty, aggressive and territorial. Coastal, they are found near colonies of other seabirds and mammals to steal eggs and chicks, feed on afterbirths and other waste. Displays include wings raised high, accompanied by vocalisations. Plumage varies with populations that some consider races or full species. Variation occurs within each form and hybridisation is common.

1 GREAT SKUA *Stercorarius (Catharacta) skua*   55cm
Overall dark brown, upperparts darker. Slight buff streaking on hind-neck. Heavy black bill and legs. White patch at base of primaries. Pairs or small flocks. Seashores and rocky coasts. Northern S America. Chilean Skua (*S. s. chilensis*) has cinnamon-brown on underparts and underwing. From Peru to Tierra del Fuego and up to Buenos Aires. Brown Skua (*S. s. antarctica*) is more uniformly dark blackish brown. Subantarctic islands and Antarctic peninsula, Tierra del Fuego and Falkland Is. Migrates north in winter. Many consider these two races valid species.

2 SOUTH POLAR SKUA *Stercorarius (Catharacta) maccormicki*   53cm
Head and body greyish buff, contrasting with dark brown back, wings and tail. White patch at base of primaries. A dark phase is all dark brown. Nests in coastal mainland Antarctica. Migrates N in winter at sea, as far as N hemisphere.

Jaegers arrive on migration at sea, occasionally coastal. They harass seabirds to make them regurgitate food, which they then feed on.

3 POMARINE JAEGER *Stercorarius pomarinus*   48cm
Hefty with broadish wings. Non-br: like juv but central tail feathers longer. Axillaries and underwing uniformly blackish brown. Scapulars and back some-what barred whitish brown. Br: top half of head black. Cheeks and neck ochreous and white. Upperparts blackish brown. Underparts white. Pectoral collar and flanks barred. Paler base of primaries and tail feathers. Base of the heavy bill pink-ish. Central tail feather long, shaped like a twisted spoon. A dark form is overall blackish brown. Juv duller; underparts brownish white, barred darker, as back. Central tail feathers barely extend beyond tail. Migratory at sea from Arctic.

4 PARASITIC JAEGER *Stercorarius parasiticus*   44cm
In all plumages like 3 but slender. Long, sharp wings. Central tail feathers long and pointed. In br plumage pectoral collar paler and more uniform. At sea in coastal waters, estuaries and bays with other seabirds. Migratory from Arctic.

5 LONG-TAILED JAEGER *Stercorarius longicaudus*   50cm
Smallest and most slender of genus. Like 3 and 4 in all plumages but upperparts paler and greyer (except dark form). White at base of primaries less contrasted. Non-br like juv but more uniform especially on underwing. Br: no pectoral collar. Very long, pointed central tail feathers. Far out at sea. Migrates from Arctic as far as subantarctic waters.

6 SNOWY SHEATHBILL *Chionis alba*   40cm
Dumpy. All white. Bill yellowish brown, horn-coloured sheath on basal half. Bare pink around eye. Blackish legs. Solitary or flocks. Seashores around colonies of seabirds and mammals to feed on eggs, chicks, afterbirths and excrement. Nests in the Antarctic and on subantarctic islands.

4 dark form

3 juv

3 dark form

3 pale form

4 pale form

4 juv

5 juv

5

1R

2

1R

6

1

ODRIGUEZ MATA

GULLS (LARIDAE)

1 **DOLPHIN GULL** *Leucophaeus scoresbii* 44cm
Br: grey, wings and back black. Tail white. White eye. Bill and legs bright red.
Non-br: head blackish. Bill and legs blackish red. Imm browner. Subterminal
black band on tail. Rowdy and aggressive. At colonies of seabirds and
mammals. Sea coasts, dumps, beaches, ports.

2 **GREY GULL** *Larus modestus* 45cm
Br: grey with whiter head. Flight feathers and band on tail black. Non-br: all
grey, dirtier on head. Imm overall greyish brown, back feathers edged pale.
Sandy beaches, follows fishing vessels. Nests inland in desert.

3 **LAVA GULL** *Larus fuliginosus* 53cm
Blackish hood, white eye-ring. Body and wings dark grey, belly and tail lighter.
Outer flight feathers darker. Bill and legs black. Juv: browner. Less noticeable
hood, no eye-ring. Feathers on upperparts edged blackish brown. Broad
blackish band at tip of tail. Desert islands, rocky shores, ports, follows ships,
sea-lion colonies. Galapagos.

4 **SWALLOW-TAILED GULL** *Creagrus furcatus* 57cm
Forked tail. Br: black bill with white tip and base. Eye-ring and legs red. Black
hood. Upperparts grey. Outer primaries black, rest of flight feathers white.
Non-br: white head. Black patch around eye. Juv like non-br but grey area on
upperparts brown, feathers edged whitish. Bill black, legs pale pinkish. Active
at night, when it feeds on squid and fish. Undulant flight. Seashores and at sea.

5 **BELCHER'S or BAND-TAILED GULL** *Larus belcheri* 50cm
Wings, back and subterminal band on tail black. Grey half-collar. Yellow bill,
red tip, black ring. Red eye-ring. Brown eye. Yellowish legs. Non-br: hood dark
brown. Juv: brownish, speckled whitish on underparts. Feathers on back darker,
edged whitish. Band on tail. Bill ivory, tip black. Imm whiter in general. Black
coming in to wing coverts. Feeds on crabs and fish remains. Does not follow
vessels. Estuaries, beaches, rocky coasts, ports, islands. The Atlantic population
is considered by some to be the separate species Olrog's Gull (*L. atlanticus*). This
has grey on back of the head in non-br, and no half-collar in br plumage.

6 **KELP GULL** *Larus dominicanus* 60cm
Black wings and back. Yellow bill with red spot near tip of mandible. Pale
yellow iris. Legs greyish yellow. Juv: speckled whitish and brownish grey. Head
and underparts paler. Bill all dark. Flight feathers and band on tail blackish
brown. Imm successively paler. Band on tail disappears in 3rd year. Aggressive
opportunist. Dumps, estuaries, inland lakes, seashores, ports, follows ships.

7 **HERRING GULL** *Larus argentatus* 55cm
Non-br: grey back. Outer flight feathers subterminally black, tipped white. Bill
yellow, mandible tipped red. Pinkish legs. Face and sides of neck finely
streaked greyish brown. Br: face and sides of neck white. Juv like 6 juv, but
underparts paler. Band of greyish-brown flecking round back of the head. Sea
coasts. Accidentally Trinidad, Venezuela and Colombia, from N America.

8 **RING-BILLED GULL** *Larus delawarensis* 50cm
Non-br: grey back. Outer flight feathers black with white spot and tip. Back of
the head and neck streaked brown. Yellow bill with black subterminal ring.
Legs yellow. Br: lacks streaking on head and neck. Accidental in Trinidad and
Colombia. Coasts and other bodies of water, dumps.

imm

5 non-br

7 br

7 non-br

5 juv

6 juv

6 imm

5R br

2 non-br

6 br

1 juv

3

1 br

n-br

4 br

2 br

6 br

1 br

2 juv

8 br

1 non-br

RODRIGUEZ MATA

GULLS (LARIDAE)

1 GREY-HEADED GULL *Larus cirrocephalus*   41cm
Grey hood, white body. Wings and back grey. Wing-tips show extensive black,
less white. White eye. Bill and legs red. Non-br: head white. Underwing dark grey. Non-br: head
white, greyish ear-patch extending towards nape. Brownish-grey eye, legs and
bill slightly duller, tip of bill blackish. Juv: brown upper wing coverts and band
at tip of tail. Follows the plough. Inland water and nearby fields, marshes,
seashores, protected bays, estuaries, rubbish dumps.

2 BROWN-HOODED GULL *Larus maculipennis*   37cm
Dark blackish-brown hood. Incomplete white eye-ring. Dark brown eye.
White, pale grey upperparts. White wing-tip patterned with little black. Bill
and legs dark red. Non-br: white head, dark spot on ear coverts. Bill and legs
duller, bill-tip blackish. Juv: back has brownish feathers. Blackish-brown band
on tail. Wing-tips darker. Bill and legs dirty pinkish. S race has less black on
wing-tip. Flocks, often huge. Follows the plough. Rubbish dumps, ports, inland
water, sea coasts.

3 ANDEAN GULL *Larus serranus*   48cm
Black-headed version of 2. Bill and legs reddish black. Non-br: white head,
black ear-patch. Bill and legs blackish. Juv very like 1 and 2 juvs. High
mountain bodies of water up to 5,300m. Winters lower, even to sea level on
Pacific coast.

4 LAUGHING GULL *Larus atricilla*   42cm
White. Black head, white eye-ring. Dark grey back. Wing-tips all black. Bill
deep red, legs reddish black. Non-br: blackish around eye, ear-patch and nape.
Bill blackish. Juv: back with brown on some wing coverts, crown and hind-
neck. Aggressive opportunist. Large flocks. Seashore, lagoons, dunes, ports,
saline lakes.

5 FRANKLIN'S GULL *Larus pipixcans*   36cm
Non-br: white. Upperparts grey. Back of the head blackish. Bill and legs
reddish black. Br: black hood, white eye-ring. Bill and legs red. Pattern on
wing-tip with black patch separated by white band from the grey of the back.
Tip of outer primaries white. Juv: upperparts have brown on coverts. Primaries
unpatterned blackish brown. Blackish band on tail. Head as in non-brs.
Seashores, estuaries, inland waters.

6 SABINE'S GULL *Xema sabini*   30cm
Unmistakable. Small. Tail slightly forked. Grey back. Non-br: head with
blackish on nape and hind-neck. Bill black tipped yellow. Legs black. Notable
wing pattern with black triangle on outer leading edge, grey coverts and white
triangle on inner flight feathers. Br: hood is slate-grey edged black on neck.
Juv: browner on wing coverts and back. Black band on tip of tail. Flies like a
tern. Plunges to capture prey. Migrates at sea and along coast from N America.

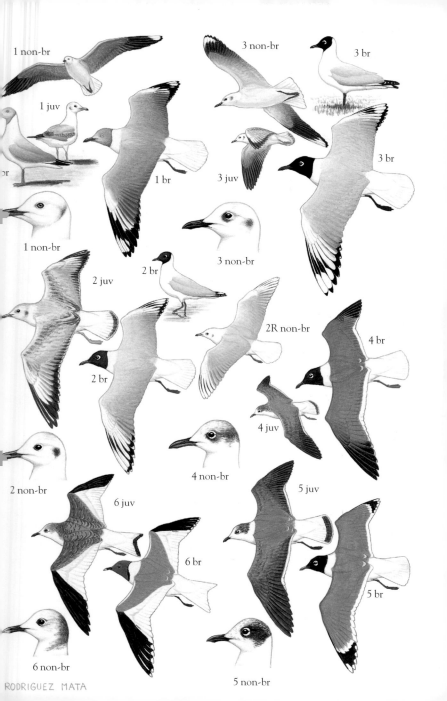

1 non-br

1 juv

1 br

1 non-br

3 non-br

3 br

3 br

3 juv

3 non-br

2 juv

2 br

2 non-br

2R non-br

4 br

4 juv

4 non-br

5 juv

6 juv

6 br

5 br

6 non-br

5 non-br

RODRIGUEZ MATA

TERNS (STERNIDAE)

Birds with long, sharp wings and fast flight. They are found at sea and on inland waters. Pointed bills and (often) forked tails. They dive from on high to catch their prey. Loud voices and gregarious, especially in nesting season.

1 SOOTY TERN *Sterna fuscata* 41cm
Bill and legs black. Eye-line, cap, hind-neck and upperparts smoky black. Forehead, cheek and underparts white. Deeply forked black tail edged white on outer feathers. Juv: all sooty black with white tips to feathers on upperparts. Follows warm currents. Feeds on squid, fish, crustaceans. Tropical islands and oceans.

2 BRIDLED TERN *Sterna anaethetus* 36cm
Slender bill and legs black. Eye-line and cap black. Forehead white. Upperparts smoky grey. Lower hind-neck and underparts white. Deeply forked tail, outer pair of feathers all white. Juv: crown and nape streaked. Post-ocular streak blackish. Back and scapulars scaled. Tropical seas, coral islands, coastal areas and sea.

3 WHITE TERN *Gygis alba* 32cm
Unmistakably all white. Black bill with blue base. Black eye. Bluish-grey legs. Forked tail. Tropical islands with bushes and trees where it nests, as it also does on cliffs; nearby seas.

4 BLACK NODDY *Anous minutus* 37cm
All blackish but for ash-grey crown, which is noticeably demarcated. Bill straight and black. Blackish legs. Wedge tail slightly notched on central feathers. Juv: back feathers barely edged buff. At sea, solitary or in small scattered flocks. Oceans and islands. Nests on cliffs, bushes and mangroves. Sedentary. Sea adjacent to roosts and nesting islands.

5 BROWN NODDY *Anous stolidus* 42cm
All brownish black. Crown and forehead ashy grey, diffusing at nape. Bill slightly heavier than 4, black and slightly down-curved at tip. Legs blackish. Juv: all brownish black. Wedge tail notched at tip. Very gregarious in nesting season; mixed colonies in mangroves with 4, sometimes on the ground. Fast flight near surface. Swims. Diurnal and nocturnal. Coastal and at sea.

6 INCA TERN *Larosterna inca* 40cm
Unmistakable. Overall slate-grey. Blackish cap and outer flight feathers. Heavy bill and bright red legs. Bare yellow patch at base of bill. White down-curled whiskery feather from base of bill. Juv: all brownish grey. Bill and legs reddish black, bill tipped reddish. Back feathers edged pale. Slightly forked tail. Gregarious, sometimes in large flocks. Feeds especially on anchovies, also squid; scavenges on scraps from feeding sea-lions. Cliffs and rocky coasts.

TERNS (STERNIDAE)

1 BLACK TERN *Chlidonias niger* 25cm
Non-br: bill and legs black. Crown, auriculars and around eye black. Forehead, brow, neck and underparts white. Upperparts and sides of breast mid-grey. Tail slightly forked. Br: head, neck and underparts black. Bill black. Legs blackish red. Juv: as non-brs but back feathers blackish edged pale. Blackish line along leading edge of upperwing. Adult transition plumage has black scalloping. Solitary or flocks. Often feeds on insects in flight. Coastal waters and at sea, estuaries, lagoons, inland lakes. Migratory from N America.

2 GREY NODDY *Procelsterna albivitta* 29cm
Bill black. Long legs blackish, big feet with pale webs. Hind-neck and upperparts grey. Head and underparts white. Eyes black. Nests on high cliffs. Rocky islands and adjacent seas. Off Chile on San Ambrosio, Juan Fernandez, San Felix and Easter Is.

3 PERUVIAN TERN *Sterna lorata* 24cm
Br: black cap and eye-line. Forehead white, as are cheeks and throat. Upperparts grey, darker than 4 and 5, paler grey below. Underwing white. 3 (sometimes 2 or 4) outer primaries black with white shafts, giving a paler effect than those on 4 and 5. Long slender bill black, dirty yellow at base. Legs orangy yellow. Tail forked. Non-br: blackish bill, duller legs. Crown uniform grey. Juv: crown and upperparts scaled blackish and brown. Blackish bill. Blackish line along leading edge of upperwing. Tail less forked and tipped darker. Nests on wide beaches, dunes and well inland in desert. Coastal. Beaches and adjacent waters.

4 YELLOW-BILLED TERN *Sterna superciliaris* 24cm
Br: eye-line and cap black. Forehead white, as are underparts. Upperparts pale grey. 3 (sometimes 4 or 5) outer primaries black, forming a triangle. Large and long bill yellow, as are legs. Shortish forked tail. Non-br: crown grey streaked blackish. Bill and legs duller yellow. Juv: crown and upperparts scaled blackish and brown. Bill blackish, yellow at base. Solitary, sometimes small flocks. Preferably fresh water. Big rivers and marshes, estuaries and lagoons, on sandbanks and island beaches.

5 LEAST TERN *Sterna antillarum* 24cm
Br: plumage virtually identical to 4 but smaller bill tipped black. Fewer (2 or 3) outer primaries black. Non-br: bill blackish. Legs yellowish grey. Crown white. Juv: upperparts paler than 4. Solitary, sometimes flocks. Sea coasts, lagoons, salt flats, estuaries. Occasionally inland, far from the sea. Migratory from N America, also resident, nesting on islands off Venezuela and NW Colombia. Some consider this a race of the Old World's Little Tern *S. albifrons*, to which it seems identical, but voices differ.

1 moulting

1 juv

1 br

2

3 br

3 juv

4 br

3 br

4 br

4 br

4 juv

5 br

5 br

5 juv

5 non-br

4 non-br

3 non-br

RODRIGUEZ MATA

TERNS (STERNIDAE)

1 TRUDEAU'S or SNOWY-CROWNED TERN *Sterna trudeaui* 35cm
Bill yellow with blackish subterminal ring. Legs yellow. White head with
blackish eye-line. Rest of the body washed pale grey. Forked tail. Non-br:
generally whiter. Bill black, tipped yellow. Legs darker yellowish. Tail shorter.
Juv: brown on crown, back and tail-tip. Bill blackish. Freshwater lakes and
marshes, sometimes seashores, especially estuaries, nearby lagoons.

2 SOUTH AMERICAN TERN *Sterna hirundinacea* 42cm
Fairly large. Br: large bill and legs bright red. Cap black. Upperparts pale grey.
Underparts whiter. Forked tail longer than folded wings, white. Outer
primaries edged blackish. Non-br: forehead and fore-crown white. Bill and legs
reddish black, bill-tip black. Juv: crown, back and tail-tip streaked and barred
blackish. Coastal waters, seashores, bays, peninsulas, estuaries.

3 ANTARCTIC TERN *Sterna vittata* 37cm
Short bill and legs. Br: bill and legs bright red. Black cap. White stripe through
cheeks. Body grey. Rump, undertail coverts and tail white, this slightly shorter
than folded wing. Non-br: whiter. Forehead white, crown streaked blackish.
Bill and legs blackish red, bill tipped black. Juv: blackish-brown feathers on
crown, back and tail. Subantarctic islands and Antarctic shores and at sea.
Migrates far out at sea.

4 ARCTIC TERN *Sterna paradisaea* 35cm
Very like 3 but seasonal plumage reversed. Non-br: forehead and crown white.
Black from eye round back of the head and nape. Bill black, some red at the
base. Short legs blackish washed reddish. Deeply forked tail white, this not
longer than folded wing. Br: tail extending beyond folded wing. Outer vane of
outer tail feathers blackish, but not always present. At sea as far as Antarctica,
rarely near land. From N American Arctic on world's longest migration.

5 COMMON TERN *Sterna hirundo* 37cm
Non-br: blackish line along leading edge of upperwing. Bill blackish to reddish
black at base. Legs blackish to reddish black. White tail with outer vanes of
outer feathers black; forked, does not protrude beyond folded wing. Outer
primaries blackish grey. Br: black cap. Legs and bill bright red, this with black
tip. Underwing shows dark outer primaries, rest tipped blackish, forming a 'V'.
Tail longer and more deeply forked. Juv: like non-br but shorter tail. Crown,
back, wings and tail with blackish on feathers. Blackish line on upperwing
along leading edge. Migrant from N America. There is a resident population
off Venezuela.

6 ROSEATE TERN *Sterna dougalli* 38cm
Br: bill black, a little red at the base. Legs bright red. Black cap. Long, deeply
forked tail exceeds the length of folded wing. Outer flight feathers dark grey
tipped white. Breast briefly has slight pink wash. Non-br: forehead and crown
white. Bill all black. Legs blackish red. Breast white. Tail shorter. Juv: much
paler upperparts than similar species. Breeds on islands off Venezuela. Coastal
regions, nearby lagoons, estuaries, bays. Resident and migratory.

7 FORSTER'S TERN *Sterna forsteri* 35cm
Non-br: bill blackish. Legs pinkish yellow. Head white. Black post-ocular
streak. Br: black cap. Bill reddish pink with black tip. Legs reddish pink.
Accidental, few records in Venezuela.

2 non-br

1 juv

1 non-br

1 br

2 juv

3 non-br

2 br

3 juv

3 br

4 juv

4 br

4 non-br

5 juv

5 br

5 non-br

6 juv

6 non-br

6 br

6 br

7 br

7 non-br

RODRIGUEZ MATA

TERNS (STERNIDAE) AND SKIMMERS (RYNCHOPIDAE)

1 GULL-BILLED TERN *Sterna (Gelochelidon) nilotica*   34cm
Short, heavy bill and longish legs black. Br: black cap. Upperparts and tail pale grey, darker on primaries. Underparts white. Wings long and pointed. Tail short and only slightly forked. Non-br: white head, black post-ocular streak. Hind-crown faintly streaked. Juv: well-marked brown on crown and upperparts. Estuaries, coastal lagoons, tidal mudflats, seashores, bays, dunes, rivers, inland lakes.

2 LARGE-BILLED TERN *Phaetusa simplex*   39cm
Unmistakable. Huge yellow bill and legs. Part of forehead white. Cap and auricular black. Neck and underparts white. Back, rump and tail grey. Wing boldly patterned: lesser coverts grey. Primaries black, rest of flight feathers and coverts white. Short tail slightly forked. Non-br: white forehead. Crown streaked with white. Juv: duller with brown on upperparts and less black on crown. Rivers, lakes, marshes, estuaries.

3 CASPIAN TERN *Sterna (Hydroprogne) caspia*   54cm
Huge and hefty. Non-br: heavy bill dull carmine tipped blackish. Legs black. Forehead crown and short nuchal crest white, streaked black. Broad black eye-patch. Upperparts pale grey, underparts white. Br: forehead, crown and short nuchal crest black. Bill bright carmine, barely tipped blackish. Juv: brown on crown and back. Sea coasts, nearby lagoons, estuaries, bays, mouths of large rivers. Migrates from N America to N Colombia and NW Venezuela.

4 ROYAL TERN *Sterna (Thalasseus) maxima*   48cm
Large and hefty. Br: large bill orangy red, legs black. Forehead, crown and longish nuchal crest black. Upperparts pale grey, underparts white. Primaries edged blackish. Non-br: forehead white, crown streaked black. Bill duller. Juv: brown on crown and back. Sea coasts and adjacent sea, estuaries, bays, peninsulas, small islands. Migratory from N America, and resident populations breeding off Venezuela and Patagonia.

5 ELEGANT TERN *Sterna (Thalasseus) elegans*   41cm
Smaller and more slender version of 4, with bill longer, slender and slightly down-curved, and paler, orangy yellow. Longer nuchal crest. Non-br has more black on crown than 4. At sea and in coastal waters, estuaries, bays, nearby islands and nearby saline lagoons. Migratory from N America.

6 SANDWICH TERN *Sterna (Thalasseus) sandvicensis*   40cm
Long slender bill, varying from yellow to black with yellow tip. Blackish legs. Br: forehead, crown and nuchal crest black. Primaries edged blackish. Non-br: forehead and crown white, streaked black. Bill duller. Juv: crown and upperparts with brownish black. Coastal areas and adjacent seas. Some consider the S form with all-yellow bill a separate species, Cayenne Tern *S. eurygnatha*, while the black-billed N birds would be the Sandwich Tern *S. sandvicensis acutiflavius*.

Skimmers are tern-like, large-winged birds with a peculiar bill in which the mandible is much longer than the maxilla. Strange flight, wings above the horizontal.

7 BLACK SKIMMER *Rynchops niger*   46cm
Strange bill red, tipped black. Upperparts and tail black, underparts white. Outer primaries edged black. Duller in non-br plumage, with blackish-brown crown and pale hind-collar. Juv: crown striped, upperparts browner, feathers edged whitish. Seashores, estuaries, mangroves, rivers, lakes.

198

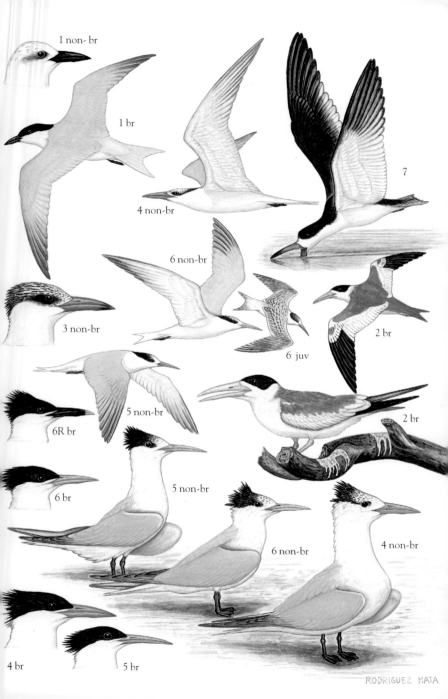

1 non- br

1 br

4 non-br

7

6 non-br

3 non-br

6 juv

2 br

5 non-br

6R br

5 non-br

2 br

6 br

5 non-br

6 non-br

4 non-br

4 br

5 br

RODRIGUEZ MATA

PIGEONS (COLUMBIDAE)

Columba pigeons are the largest of the family. Sexes are alike. Mostly pastel shades of greys and browns, many with patterns on hind-neck or wings. Perch in mid- to higher strata; they fly high, straight and very fast with short, powerful wing-beats. They come down to the ground to feed, or on fruit from the vegetation. Solitary, in pairs or variable-sized flocks. Low-pitched, deep, sonorous calls – the well-known 'cooing' – but some calls are rough, harsh or higher pitched.

ROCK DOVE *Columba livia*   33cm (not illustrated)
Introduced from Europe. Very variable and tied to towns and farm buildings, though some populations are truly wild, living and nesting on cliffs and vertical banks.

1 BARE-EYED PIGEON *Columba corensis*   32cm
Bill yellow, bare skin around eye sky-blue. Wing-bar white. Head, neck and underparts pale vinaceous, whiter on lower belly and undertail. Hind-neck finely barred pale blue, black and white. Deciduous woods, thorny thickets, cactus.

2 CHILEAN PIGEON *Columba araucana*   37cm
Mostly winy chestnut. Hind-neck with white nuchal collar, below which has scaled shiny coppery-bronze appearance. Open S beech woods in Patagonia.

3 BAND-TAILED PIGEON *Columba fasciata*   36cm
Yellow bill and legs. Cap, breast and upper belly dark vinaceous. Upperparts olivaceous brown. Tail grey, slightly darker on basal half. Nuchal collar white, below which has scaled shiny bronzy-green appearance. Tropical and temperate montane forest and cloud-forest, open woods, scattered trees, Páramos, bushy slopes with trees, alder woods, savannahs and cultivated land.

4 PICAZURO PIGEON *Columba picazuro*   36cm
Red eye. Mostly winy lead-grey. Back and wings grey-brown. Greater and middle coverts edged white, seen as a band in flight. Hind-neck scaled pale sky-blue, vinaceous and black, with metallic sheen. Woods, savannahs, edge, transition woods with clearings, copses, cultivated land, plantations, parks, gardens.

5 SPOT-WINGED PIGEON *Columba maculosa*   34cm
White eye. Overall lead-grey, back and wings darker. All wing coverts tipped white. Dry woods, scrubby savannah, open woods, scattered trees, copses and cultivated land, parks and gardens.

6 SCALY-NAPED PIGEON *Columba squamosa*   37cm
Red eye-ring. Red bill, yellow tip. Head, fore-neck and breast dark vinaceous. Nape purple. Hind-neck scaled light and dark purple with sheen. Woods and arid areas with trees on islands (Los Testigos and Los Frailes, off Venezuela).

7 PALE-VENTED PIGEON *Columba cayennensis*   32cm
Crown and nape shiny bronzy green. Cheeks lead-grey. Forehead and fore-crown, neck, breast and part of upperparts winy chestnut. Rest of underparts grey. Tail with paler terminal band. Rainforest, clearings, gallery forest, deciduous woods, open areas with scattered trees, dry woods, mangroves, cultivated land.

8 SCALED PIGEON *Columba speciosa*   32cm
Red bill with yellow tip. Neck scaled black and white. Underparts scaled pale vinaceous and reddish chestnut. ♀: dark brown on head and upperparts. Tropical and subtropical rainforest, gallery forest, edge, savannahs, scattered trees, open woods.

RODRIGUEZ MATA

PIGEONS AND DOVES (COLUMBIDAE)

1 RUDDY PIGEON *Columba subvinacea*   30cm
Dark coloration; no patterns. Upperparts very dark olivaceous brown. Purply
tint on crown, hind-neck and upper back. Underparts dark greyish vinaceous.
Cinnamon wash on forehead and lores. Tropical and subtropical rainforest and
cloud-forest, edge, secondary growth.

2 SHORT-BILLED PIGEON *Columba nigrirostris*   28cm
Dark colours with no pattern. Back, wings and tail dark brown. Head, neck
and breast vinaceous, lighter below. Hind-neck with a violaceous wash.
Tropical and subtropical rainforest, edge.

3 DUSKY PIGEON *Columba goodsoni*   25cm
Dark with no pattern. Head, fore-neck and breast light bluish lead-grey. Rest of
underparts vinaceous lead-grey. Hind-neck with violaceous tint. Upperparts
and tail very dark olive-brown. Lowland and montane rainforest.

4 PLUMBEOUS PIGEON *Columba plumbea*   33cm
Dark with no pattern. Head, neck and underparts dark greyish vinaceous.
Whitish on throat and fore-face. Violaceous wash on crown and hind-neck.
Rest of upperparts very dark olive-brown. Tropical and subtropical rainforest,
montane cloud-forest, edge, tropical dryland woods, secondary growth.

5 PERUVIAN PIGEON *Columba oenops*   33cm
Yellow bill tipped darker. Head, neck and breast vinaceous. Rest of underparts
lead-grey. Chesnutty vinaceous on back. Primaries blackish, secondaries
brownish, greater coverts narrowly edged white. Tail slate-grey, darker at tip.
Arid, subtropical woods and scattered trees.

Zenaida doves are medium sized. They perch on trees and shrubs, and feed on the
ground. Very fast, straight flight on shallow but powerful wing-beats. Gregarious,
sometimes flocks of many thousands.

6 WHITE-WINGED DOVE *Zenaida asiatica*   30cm
Bare patch around eye sky-blue. Greyish head with small blackish spot below
cheek. Bronzy sheen on sides of neck. Neck and breast vinaceous. Belly and
undertail coverts grey. Brownish-grey upperparts. White band on wing. Flight
feathers blackish. Outer tail feathers with broad white tip. Tropical and subtropical arid regions with trees or bushes, riverine woods, canyons, valleys, oases,
parks, gardens and plantations. Because of a difference in vocalizations, some consider the South American race a different species: Pacific Dove (*Zenaida meloda*).

MOURNING DOVE *Zenaida macroura*   28cm (not illustrated)
Virtually identical to 7 but much longer, pointed tail. Accidental in Colombia
from N or C America.

7 EARED DOVE *Zenaida auriculata*   25cm
Crown sky-bluish grey. Cheeks, neck and underparts vinaceous, grading to
lighter below. Line down hind-neck and upperparts brownish grey. Black spot
on ear coverts and more on wing coverts. Pinkish-bronze sheen on sides of
neck. Outer tail feathers with broad white tip, subterminally black. ♀ is more
buffy brown on crown, head and underparts. Almost any habitat with trees or
bushes: woods, plantations, parks, gardens, cultivated areas, cities, but not
dense rainforest and high mountains. Extremely abundant.

8 GALAPAGOS DOVE *Zenaida galapagoensis*   25cm
Long bill, short tail. Eye-ring brilliant turquoise. 2 black lines through the face.
Pale ear coverts. Head and neck brownish, the latter with pinkish-bronze
sheen on the sides. Rest of underparts buffy vinaceous. Upperparts darker
brown, patterned black and white. Scrub, arid bush, small trees, cactus. Only
on the Galapagos Is, Ecuador.

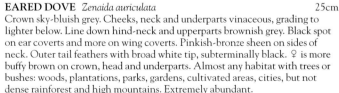

RODRIGUEZ MATA

DOVES (COLUMBIDAE)

Metriopelia ground-doves are terrestrial. Their outer tail feathers, flight feathers and underwing are black.

1 BLACK-WINGED GROUND-DOVE *Metriopelia melanoptera*   23cm
Bare orange skin around whitish eye. Whitish shoulders and leading edge of wing. Grey legs. Sandy and stony steppe, sparse grassland and scrub in high mountains. Puna, usually near water.

2 BARE-EYED GROUND-DOVE *Metriopelia morenoi*   17cm
Bare skin around eye orange. All buffy grey. High mountains, valleys, bushy and stony areas, steppe with sparse grass, puna.

3 GOLDEN-SPOTTED GROUND-DOVE *Metriopelia aymara*   17cm
Dumpy. Short neck and tail. Buffy brown. Shiny golden-bronze spots on wing coverts. Sandy and stony steppe with sparse grasses in high mountains, near habitations, corrals, and water.

4 BARE-FACED GROUND-DOVE *Metriopelia ceciliae*   18cm
Bare skin around eye orange. Pale scaling on upperparts. Tawny breast. Tail longish. High mountains (to sea level where arid), valleys, grasslands, stony steppe, cultivated land, near water, houses and corrals.

Leptotila doves are woodland species. All have rufous underwings. They feed on the ground, frequenting shady lower storeys. They fly low and weave through vegetation, and they seldom leave the trees. More often heard than seen.

5 LARGE-TAILED DOVE *Leptotila megalura*   30cm
Upperparts earthy chestnut-brown, washed violaceous on crown and hind-neck. Face and underparts buffy vinaceous. Three-syllable call *coooo-co-coooo*. Montane forest and woods, alder woods.

6 WHITE-TIPPED DOVE *Leptotila verreauxi*   30cm
Crown and hind-neck bluish with faint green sheen. Breast buffy grey. Upperparts brownish grey with olive wash. Call bi-syllabic *coo-cwoo*, 2nd note a tone lower. Open, shady woods, parks, forest edge, dry woods, plantations.

7 GREY-CHESTED DOVE *Leptotila cassini*   26cm
Head, neck and chest light greyish blue, lower breast and belly creamy grey. Back, rest of upperparts and tail dirty dark chestnut-brown. Call is a single deep long *cooooo*. Edge of rainforest and woods, trails and clearings.

8 GREY-FRONTED DOVE *Leptotila rufaxilla*   28cm
Forehead pale greyish blue. Eye-ring red. Upperparts dirty dark chestnut-brown, tinted purple on crown and neck. Face and underparts pinkish buff. Call is a low-pitched, resonant, descending *cooooo*. Rainforest, gallery forest, varzea, montane forest.

9 PALLID DOVE *Leptotila pallida*   26cm
Forehead white. Crown, nape and hind-neck lead-blue. Face, fore-neck and underparts creamy grey. Upperparts dull dark chestnut-brown. Call is a single *cooOOooo*, louder in the middle. Rainforest, old secondary growth, edge. W Colombia and W Ecuador.

10 GREY-HEADED DOVE *Leptotila plumbeiceps*   26cm
Virtually the same as 9 but less white on forehead, deeper blue on crown and hind-neck. Double-note call *who, who*? Dry forest, secondary woods, edge, copses. NW Colombia.

11 OCHRE-BELLIED DOVE *Leptotila ochraceiventris*   26cm
Forehead sky-blue and white. Crown, nape and hind-neck purple. Face tawny ochre. Breast vinaceous pink. Rest of underparts ochre. Edge of tropical and subtropical forest on plains and foothills. SW Ecuador.

12 TOLIMA DOVE *Leptotila conoveri*   26cm
Sky-blue and whitish forehead. Crown and hind-neck dark violaceous blue. Cheeks, fore-neck and underparts pinkish vinaceous. Rainforest edges with bushes and thickets. Endemic of E slope of C Andes in Colombia.

RODRIGUEZ MATA

GROUND-DOVES AND QUAIL-DOVES (COLUMBIDAE)

Claravis ground-doves are found on the forest floor and in the lower storeys. Sexes differ, with contrasting patterns on wing coverts. Hard to see. Calls are a series of deep, hollow *coos*.

1 PURPLE-WINGED GROUND-DOVE *Claravis godefrida*   24cm
Upperparts darkish bluey grey, paler below. 2 dark purple bands and 1 dark blue band on wing coverts. Outer tail feathers white. ♀: brownish version of the above. Rainforest, cane-brakes, montane forest.

2 MAROON-CHESTED GROUND-DOVE *Claravis mondetoura*   24cm
Upperparts darkish bluey grey. Breast purply chestnut. Underparts grey, white below. 2 purple bands, 1 blue on wing coverts. Outer tail feathers white. ♀ very like ♀ 1 but has cinnamon fore-face and is darker. Cloud-forest, open forest and upland woods in mountains.

3 BLUE GROUND-DOVE *Claravis pretiosa*   22cm
Yellow bill. Feet pale pink. Light bluish-grey upperparts, whiter on face and below. Outer tail feathers black. Black markings on wing coverts. ♀: brownish with purple wing-spots; rump and tail rufous. Rainforest, edge of woods, tropical arid woods, open woods, savannah, deciduous woods, riverine woods, plantations and cultivated land.

Quail-doves are dumpy, with short rounded tail and wings and long legs. Hard to see on the forest floor. They perch low and fly low and only for short distances. Most have patterns on the head, and showy colours.

4 VIOLACEOUS QUAIL-DOVE *Geotrygon violacea*   24cm
Bill red. Face greyish. Crown, hind-neck and back purple, rump chestnut. Breast pale buffy vinaceous. Underparts creamy white. ♀: hind-neck and upper back brownish. Rainforest, valleys and slopes in mountains.

5 OLIVE-BACKED QUAIL-DOVE *Geotrygon veraguensis*   23cm
Very dark olive-brown. Buffy lower underparts. Forehead white and bluish. Broad pure white line across face. Rainforest and tall secondary growth in lowlands and foothills, valleys. W Colombia and NW Ecuador.

6 LINED QUAIL-DOVE *Geotrygon linearis*   28cm
Forehead and cheeks buffy cinnamon, crown rufous. Behind eye to nape greyish sky-blue. Black line below cheek. Upperparts chestnut, violet sheen on upper back. Underparts cinnamon. Montane rainforest and cloud-forest, tall secondary growth, thickets on steep slopes.

7 SAPPHIRE QUAIL-DOVE *Geotrygon saphirina*   22cm
Forehead, top half of cheek and belly white. Lower cheek black. Crown and nape very deep blue. Breast bluish grey. Hind-neck shiny golden, violaceous and purple. One race with crown and nape green. Rainforest and tall secondary growth in lowlands, low mountains.

8 WHITE-THROATED QUAIL-DOVE *Geotrygon frenata*   32cm
Face vinaceous, crown and nape violaceous. Line round lower face black. Upperparts chestnut, scaled on hind-neck with green and violet sheen. Throat whitish, underparts greyish. Rainforest and cloud-forest in mountains, secondary growth, bushes and thickets. A dark-headed race with a darker breast occurs in Ecuador, considered by some a separate species (Dark Quail-dove, *G. erythropareia*).

9 RUSSET-CROWNED QUAIL-DOVE *Geotrygon goldmani*   32cm
Differs from 8 in having a buffy-cinnamon face. Crown and nape rufous. Rainforest. NW Colombia.

10 RUDDY QUAIL-DOVE *Geotrygon montana*   24cm
Red bill. Mostly purply chestnut. Pale line through face. Breast washed violaceous. Lower underparts buffy cinnamon. ♀ duller, darker brown. Rainforest, cloud-forest in mountains, secondary growth, plantations.

1♂

2♀ 2♂

1♀

3♀

3♂ 4♂

4♀

5 6 7R

7

9

8 10♂ 10♀

RODRIGUEZ MATA

GROUND-DOVES (COLUMBIDAE)

Columbina ground-doves are tiny and terrestrial. Very often in pairs. There is sexual dimorphism in some species. All have contrasting patterns in wings and tail that may help in their identification.

1   SCALED DOVE *Columbina (Scardafella) squammata* 20cm
Scaled black all over. Rufous primaries. White band on greater coverts. Call is a clear, repeated *ooo puru poo*. Dry fields, scattered trees in scrubland, savannah, edge of copses, stubble fields, gardens and parks.

2   CROAKING GROUND-DOVE *Columbina cruziana*   18cm
Bill yellow with black tip. Notable purplish band across lesser coverts. Underparts vinaceous. ♀: head and underparts greyish buff and whitish. Voice a deep, throaty *ghee gwa gwa*. Trees and bushes in arid areas, valleys and oases, riverine woods, parks, gardens, farmland and plantations.

3   COMMON GROUND-DOVE *Columbina passerina*   15cm
Breast scaled pale on black ground. Flight feathers strong rufous and black. ♀: head and scaling less contrasted. Monotonous, repeated, low-volume, triple cooing. Fields, cleared land, scattered trees in thickets, sparse scrub, edge of woods and gallery forest, cultivated land, gardens.

4   ECUADOREAN or PALE GROUND-DOVE *Columbina buckleyi*   17cm
Overall brownish grey, greyer on crown and hind-neck. Black spots and lines on wing coverts. Flight feathers and outer tail feathers blackish. ♀ more brownish buff. Dry tropical areas with trees and shrubs. Some consider this a race of 5.

5   RUDDY GROUND-DOVE *Columbina talpacoti*   17cm
Overall ruddy chestnut, more vinaceous pink below. Cap greyish blue. Black spots and lines on wing coverts. ♀ generally browner. Voice monotonous *cooroo*. Open areas in savannah, with trees or shrubs, palm groves, often near water, open fields with scattered trees, edge of rainforest, gallery forest and cloud-forest, cities.

6   PICUI GROUND-DOVE *Columbina picui*   17cm
Upperparts pale brownish grey. Black line on lesser wing coverts. Underparts pale vinaceous cream, whitish below. White wing-bar. Outer tail feathers notably white. ♀ browner. Voice a double, high-pitched *cooroo*. Open areas, earth and sandy roads, scattered trees and bushes, dry land with thorny scrub and cactus, savannah, farmland, cities.

7   PLAIN-BREASTED GROUND-DOVE *Columbina minuta*   14cm
Short tail. Crown, nape and hind-neck greyish blue. Breast and underparts vinaceous. Wing coverts have black dots and lines. Flight feathers strong rufous and black. ♀ more brownish grey. Voice a repeated, insistent *oo ark oo ark....* Dry bushy areas, savannah with low scrub, fields with scattered trees and bushes, deciduous woods, edge of rainforest and gallery forest, cultivated land.

8   BLUE-EYED GROUND-DOVE *Columbina cyanopis*   16cm
Head, upper tail coverts and wing coverts chestnut-rufous. Neck chestnut with violaceous sheen. Black spotting on coverts. Tail black. ♀ paler. Open areas and savannah. Very rare and local.

9   LONG-TAILED GROUND-DOVE *Uropelia campestris*   18cm
Long tail. Forehead and lores greyish blue. Two purple, black and white bands on wing coverts. Outer feathers black with outer vane and tip white. ♀ paler. Long *teeeee* call. Open areas in savannah, fields, grasslands, near water, sparse woods and edge, scrubby parkland.

RODRIGUEZ MATA

MACAWS (PSITTACIDAE)

Macaws are the giants of the parrot family. They are spectacularly coloured, with proportionately enormous bills and very long pointed tails.

1 HYACINTH MACAW *Anodorhynchus hyacinthinus* 100cm
The largest. Enormous hefty black bill. Bare skin around eye and at base of mandible bright yellow. Overall cobalt-blue. Call is a very loud *kraah, kraah* (♂) and *wracker, wracker* (♀), all with rolled r's. Palm groves and water, forests and gallery forests nearby.

2 GLAUCOUS MACAW *Anodorhynchus glaucus* 68cm
Very like 3. Blue with green wash, approaching turquoise. Gallery forest with stands of palms. Nests and roosts in river banks and hollow trees. NE Argentina and adjacent Paraguay, Brazil and Uruguay. Extinct.

3 INDIGO MACAW *Anodorhynchus leari* 71cm
Bill black. Bare skin around eye and at base of mandible (semicircular) pale yellow. General colour metallic blue, darker than 2 and paler than 1. Voice is a harsh *arah, arah* and *trrarah*, relatively high pitched. Deep canyons, where it roosts and nests in holes and on ledges; nearby palm groves, where it feeds on the fruit. Only NW of Bahía at Raso da Catarina. Endangered.

4 SPIX'S MACAW *Cyanopsitta spixii* 57cm
Bill and bare skin around eye blackish. General coloration blue, pale greyish blue on head. Voice: *kraah, kraah* and *kree, kree*. Arid-zone palm groves and scattered trees in savannah, riverine woods with Caraiba trees that have been extirpated. Extinct in the wild.

5 BLUE-AND-YELLOW MACAW *Ara ararauna* 85cm
Bill black. Bare face white with lines of small black feathers. Black bib. Rest of underparts bright yellow. Forehead greenish. Rest of upperparts blue. Voice is a loud, harsh, deep *ruaaark*. Palm groves and scattered trees in savannah, often near rivers and marshes, gallery forest.

6 BLUE-THROATED MACAW *Ara glaucogularis* 85cm
Like 5 but blue forehead, lines of blue feathers on bare face and a larger and blue bib. Seasonally flooded grasslands with palms and small patches of forest. Once considered a race of 5. Very localized in Bolivia, department of Santa Cruz. Endangered.

7 MILITARY MACAW *Ara militaris* 75cm
Bill blackish. Bare face pink with concentric lines of tiny black feathers. Red pompom on forehead. Mostly green, blue flight feathers, tail dorsally red and blue. Voice a harsh *crrraaahk*. Montane forest and woods in arid and semiarid zones, tall trees and open woods near cliffs. Only occasionally and seasonally in rainforest.

8 GREAT GREEN MACAW *Ara ambiguus* 80cm
Very like 7, bill heavier and paler at tip. Lighter green faintly washed yellow. Tail feathers paler, orangy. Rainforest in lowlands. Some consider this a race of 7.

⑨ SCARLET MACAW *Ara macao* 85cm
Ivory maxilla, black at the base, black mandible. Bare face white. Mostly scarlet. Blue wings with yellow greater and median coverts. Voice deep, harsh and loud *rowaaark*. Lowland and gallery forest, rainforest, copses and palm groves in savannah, large isolated trees near water.

10 RED-AND-GREEN MACAW *Ara chloroptera* 90cm
Differs from 9 in being slightly darker red and having concentric lines of tiny red feathers on face; greater and median wing coverts green. Voice like 9. Crowns of the rainforest's tallest trees, edges, savannah with scattered trees, gallery forest; usually in the lowlands.

RODRÍGUEZ MATA

MACAWS (PSITTACIDAE)

Small macaws are mostly green with bare faces. In flight, most show some of the yellow-olive underwing coverts, and yellow-olive underside of tail feathers and flight feathers. They fly high over the forests in flocks or pairs, straight and with continuous wing-beats, emitting raucous calls, less loud than those of the large macaws and higher-pitched. Perch preferably in the crowns of trees. They feed in silence. When frightened they take flight, making a cacophony of sounds.

1   RED-FRONTED MACAW *Ara rubrogenys*   55cm
Blackish bill. Small patch of bare skin around eye pink. Forehead, crown, auricular, shoulders and underwing strikingly orange. Voice a medium-pitched *crew-ack*. Montane forests, wooded uplands, thorny woods.

2   CHESTNUT-FRONTED MACAW *Ara severa*   48cm
Bill black, bare face white. Narrow forehead and chin blackish chestnut. Edge of the wing scarlet. Underwing coverts scarlet and green. Flight and tail feathers reddish purple from below. Voice a medium-pitched *arrrrow* with very rolled r's. Edge of forest near wetlands, swampy forest, gallery forest, copses in grassland, plantations, palm groves.

3   RED-BELLIED MACAW *Orthopsittaca (Ara) manilata*   46cm
Bill black. Extensive bare face pale yellowish. Crown, part of the cheeks and forehead blue. Notable dull red patch on belly. Calls include loud *chewiak* and *chee-ak*. Riverine forests, savannah with palm groves and scattered palms.

4   BLUE-WINGED MACAW *Primolius (Ara) maracana*   43cm
Bill black. Bare face creamy white. Forehead orange-red and blackish blue. Crown and part of the cheek bluish. Irregular orange-red patch on belly. Topside of the tail reddish chestnut, underside yellowish olive. Lower back red. Edge of the forest, swamps, gallery forest, palm groves.

5   BLUE-HEADED MACAW *Primolius (Ara) couloni*   41cm
Bill black, greyish-ivory tip. Small bare patch around eye greyish. Head bluish. Tail reddish chestnut from above. Wet tropical forest near water.

6   RED-SHOULDERED MACAW *Diopsittaca (Ara) nobilis*   33cm
Small. Bill: ivory maxilla and black mandible, or all black according to race. Bare face white. Fore-crown blue. Bend of the wing and primary underwing coverts bright red. Voice is high-pitched for the genus, like *Aratinga* parakeets', *creek creek, airk airk*. Sandy savannah with scattered trees and palm groves, scrubby areas, plantations, edge of the forest, cultivated clearings, coastal areas.

7   GOLDEN-COLLARED MACAW *Primolius (Ara) auricollis*   38cm
Bill blackish, paler at tip. Bare white face. Black forehead and part of the cheeks. Crown and rest of the cheeks washed blue. Yellow hind-collar variable. Tail dorsally chestnutty red and blue. Pink legs. Calls like *Aratinga* parakeets. Forests and woods, gallery forests, wooded swamps and clearings, montane forests.

RODRIGUEZ MATA

PARAKEETS (PSITTACIDAE)

Parakeets of the genus *Aratinga* are medium sized, all with longish, pointed tails.

1 BLUE-CROWNED PARAKEET *Aratinga acuticaudata*   35cm
Bill: buffy-ivory maxilla, blackish mandible, or entirely buffy ivory, according to race. Bare skin around eye white. Head (or only forehead) pale blue. Tail from below has orange wash, underwing coverts green. Calls are series of *guack-crewack*, harsh and all together creating a cacophony. Dry and arid woods, savannah, scattered trees, palm groves, riverine woods, near swampy areas, gardens, city parks.

2 GOLDEN PARAKEET *Guarouba (Aratinga) guarouba*   35cm
Bill greyish ivory. Bare skin around the eye white. Almost entirely bright yellow but for green flight feathers. Call is series of quietish *gra, gra, gra*. Tropical forests, edges, palm groves, transition woods.

3 MITRED PARAKEET *Aratinga mitrata*   38cm
Heavy bill buffy ivory. Bare skin around the eye white. Scarlet on forehead and onto face, less so in the ♀, but always irregular and variable. A few scattered red spots on the head and body. Variable orangy red on shoulder. Underwing coverts green. Call like others of the genus but strident and high-pitched. Subtropical rainforest in mountains and adjacent valleys, upland woods, plantations.

4 SIERRAN PARAKEET *Aratinga alticola*   35cm
Bill buffy-ivory, bare skin around the eye white. Scarlet forehead and scattered spots on face. Green underwing coverts. High-altitude temperate forests in mountains. Some consider this a race of 3.

5 SCARLET-FRONTED PARAKEET *Aratinga wagleri*   35cm
Very like 4 but scarlet on forehead extends onto fore-crown. Scarlet garters. Dorsally lighter green than 4. Cloud forests, rainforest, semi-open areas of the Andes, valleys, plantations, foothills.

6 RED-MASKED PARAKEET *Aratinga erythrogenys*   34cm
Most of the head bright scarlet. Underwing coverts scarlet, also visible on leading edge when wing is folded. Scarlet garters. Dry woods.

7 WHITE-EYED PARAKEET *Aratinga leucophthalma*   35cm
Differs from the previous 4 species in having only few scarlet spots on head. In flight, primary underwing coverts shine red and yellow. The red is also seen on the leading edge when wing is folded. The calls are a series of penetrating, rough *cheerrry cheerrry* with rolled r's. Open woods and forest, palm groves, savannah, mangroves, gallery forest, scattered trees, plantations, copses, rainforest, gardens, parks.

8 JANDAYA PARAKEET *Aratinga jandaya*   30cm
Bill blackish. Bare skin around eyes greyish. Conspicuous orange and yellow head and body. Green on lower belly and back. Orange underwing coverts. Loud and penetrating *creek, creeek*. Edge of forest, palm groves, open woods.

9 SUN PARAKEET *Aratinga solstitialis*   30cm
Differs from 8 in having bright yellow upperparts, wing coverts and leggings. Underwing coverts yellow. Savannah, open woods and forests, edges, palm groves. Some consider this a race of 8.

PARROTS AND PARAKEETS (PSITTACIDAE)

1 GOLDEN-CAPPED PARAKEET *Aratinga auricapillus* 30cm
Bill blackish grey. Bare skin around eye greyish. Forehead and upper face orange, grading to yellow at back of crown. Belly rusty orange, flanks and underwing coverts orange. Voice is a loud, penetrating *kreee, kreeee*. Edge of forest, secondary growth, savannah, open woods and cultivated areas.

2 DUSKY-HEADED PARAKEET *Aratinga weddellii* 28cm
Bill black. Bare skin around eye white. Fore-crown, forehead and face lead-grey. Underparts and underwing coverts light green. Voice penetrating nasal *gee-eek*. Edge of the forest, savannah, copses, transition woods, scrubby areas, varzea and gallery forests.

3 BROWN-THROATED PARAKEET *Aratinga pertinax* 25cm
Variable. All races have blackish-grey bills, bare skin around eye white. One race has forehead, cheeks and throat yellow. Fore-neck and breast pale greyish brown. Underwing coverts light green. Another race has bare facial skin bordered orange. Forehead and cheeks brownish streaked orange. Fore-neck and upper breast brownish, faintly scaled orange. Mid-belly has irregular pale orange spots. Yet another race has forehead pale yellow, crown washed blue, cheeks, fore-neck and breast greyish brown. Other races are intermediate. Loud and penetrating *creeeks….* Open woods, scrubby dry areas, cactus, thorny woods, transition to forest, grasslands with scattered trees, mangroves, savannah, gallery forest, plantations, gardens.

4 CACTUS PARAKEET *Aratinga cactorum* 25cm
Bill greyish ivory. Skin around eye white. Forehead, crown, lower cheek, fore-neck and breast greyish brown. Ear-patch and upperparts green. Belly and flanks yellow. Underwing light green. Voice *cree….* Bushy areas with cactus, open woods and savannah.

5 PEACH-FRONTED PARAKEET *Aratinga aurea* 25cm
Bill blackish. Forehead and feathering around eye yellowish orange. Cheek, fore-neck and breast pale brownish grey. Underwing pale green. Copses in open country, open woods, savannah, scrub, cultivated areas.

6 NANDAY or BLACK-HOODED PARAKEET *Nandayus nenday* 32cm
Bill black. Front half of head black. Flight and tail feathers notably black. Extremely noisy; penetrating harsh screams. Savannah, woods, palm groves, scattered trees, copses, cultivated land, plantations.

7 YELLOW-EARED PARROT *Ognorhynchus icterotis* 43cm
Bill black. Forehead, lores and ear coverts bright yellow. Feathers of these are long and give the impression of ears. Lower cheeks and sides of the neck somewhat scaled. Underparts and underwing yellowish green. Tail ventrally dull orange. Voice is distinctive, nasal, bisyllabic like a goose. Subtropical and temperate forests in mountains, especially semi-open areas with palm groves.

8 GOLDEN-PLUMED PARROT *Leptosittaca branickii* 35cm
Bare skin around eye white. Narrow forehead orange, ranging to yellow under eye to form a tufted ear-patch. Belly scaled dull orange. Underside of tail dull orange. Flanks and underwing green. Temperate cloud-forest, Podocarp woods and above to tree line, dwarf woods, areas of brush.

9 BURROWING PARROT *Cyanoliseus patagonus* 46cm
Dark olive-brown. Lower underparts, rump and lower back dirty yellow. Pale red at centre of belly. Dark race has dull olive-brown where former is yellow. Raucous ugly screams. Colonies at cliffs. Scrubland, Andean woods and brushland, agricultural land, orchards, scattered trees, near rivers with tall banks.

RODRIGUEZ MATA

PARAKEETS (PSITTACIDAE)

1 AUSTRAL PARAKEET *Enicognathus ferrugineus* 35cm
Overall dark green, feathers edged dark, giving scaly effect. Forehead, belly patch and tail rusty red. Small bill blackish. Rowdy in flight, silent when perched or feeding. Feeds in trees, bushes and on the ground. Pairs and flocks of up to 100. Subantarctic woods, S Andes and ecotone.

2 SLENDER-BILLED PARAKEET *Enicognathus leptorhynchus* 41cm
Long, slender straightish maxilla blackish. Overall dark green, feathers edged dark, looking like scales. Reddish forehead, tail and belly patch. Pairs or groups up to 300. Rowdy. S Andean woods and farmland, forestry plantations, *Araucaria* woods.

3 MONK PARAKEET *Myiopsitta monachus* 30cm
Forehead, fore-crown, cheeks, breast and upper belly grey, scaly on breast. Rest bright green, flight feathers bluish. Bill ochreous ivory. Very rowdy. Pairs and flocks of up to hundreds. Huge stick community nests with many entrances high in trees or pylons. Woods, plantations, copses, palm groves, city parks, tree-lined avenues, farmland, savannah.

Pyrrhura parakeets are small, slender and multicoloured. All have white bare skin around eye, long, pointed tails and sharp wings. Fast flight on constantly beating wings. Rowdy in flight. Hard to see when perched and silent. Social, pairs, small flocks, and sometimes large flocks.

4 SANTA MARTA PARAKEET *Pyrrhura viridicata* 25cm
Mostly green with two irregular bands across belly and flanks. Underwing, bend of the wing and narrow forehead all scarlet. Ear-patch chestnut, undertail chestnutty red. Bill ochreous ivory. Humid subtropical montane forests. Endemic to Santa Marta mountains in N Colombia.

5 BLUE-THROATED PARAKEET *Pyrrhura cruentata* 29cm
Ochre on sides and back of neck. Lores, ear-patch and rump reddish chestnut. Cap dark brown streaked even darker. Breast blue. Belly patch and underside of tail chestnutty red. Rest green. Forest, in canopy.

6 CRIMSON-BELLIED PARAKEET *Pyrrhura perlata* 25cm
Startling crimson belly and underwing. Lower belly, leggings and undertail coverts blue. Head and neck dark, scaled lighter; cheeks bluish to yellowish green. Tail blackish below. Riverine forests.

7 MAROON-BELLIED PARAKEET *Pyrrhura frontalis* 26cm
Green cap. Ear-patch pale brownish grey. Side of neck, throat and upper breast brownish ivory scaled blackish. Belly and undertail reddish chestnut. Top of the tail green. The rest of upperparts all green. Noisy flocks. Erratic fast flight through trees. Rainforest edges, upland forest, palm groves, *Araucaria* plantations, farmland, riverside forests.

8 BLAZE-WINGED PARAKEET *Pyrrhura devillei* 26cm
Differs from 7 only in bright orange, red and yellow underwing coverts. Savannah, woods, forest, scattered trees. Possibly only a race of 7 as they seem to interbreed in N Paraguay.

9 GREEN-CHEEKED PARAKEET *Pyrrhura molinae* 26cm
Differs from 7 in having a dark brown cap, slightly scaled darker. Tail all chestnutty red. Flocks fly rowdily. Edge and clearings in montane forests, wooded valleys, semi-open woods, copses. 9* is a mutation once considered a separate species, Yellow-sided Parakeet (*P. hypoxantha*), in SW Mato Grosso, Brazil.

RODRIGUEZ MATA

PARAKEETS (PSITTACIDAE)

1 MAROON-FACED PARAKEET *Pyrrhura leucotis* 22cm
Several races. Purply-chestnut cheeks. White ear-patch varies with race.
Breast scaled green, black and white or just black and white. Dark red on belly,
lower back and rump. Underside of tail feathers dull red. Tropical and
subtropical forest, cloud-forest, edges and clearings. The race *P. l. pfrimer*,
without ear-patch is, for some, a separate species: Pfrimer's Parakeet: 1*.

2 PAINTED PARAKEET *Pyrrhura picta* 22cm
Blue forehead. Crown and nape dark brown. Cheeks purply chestnut and
whitish. Markedly scaled on neck and breast. Red patch at mid-belly.
Underside of tail dull red. Another race has forehead and crown pinky red.
Intermediates. Tropical and subtropical forest and cloud-forest, coastal forest,
varzea. The races *P .p. subandina* and *P. p. caerleiceps* are, for some, separate
species: Sinu and Todd's Parakeets, respectively.

3 FIERY-SHOULDERED PARAKEET *Pyrrhura egregia* 25cm
Small ear-patch chestnut. Cream and black scales on breast. Patch of reddish
chestnut on mid-belly. Underwing orangy yellow, redder at leading edge. Dark
tail, topside purply chestnut and underside blackish. Forest on the slopes of the
tepuis, tropical forest.

4 PEARLY PARAKEET *Pyrrhura lepida* 25cm
Cap dark greyish brown. Cheek blue, auricular whitish brown. Scaling on neck
and breast brown and whitish brown. Lower underparts all green. Underwing
carmine. Tail topside chestnutty red, underside blackish. Rainforest, gallery
forest.

5 MAROON-TAILED PARAKEET *Pyrrhura melanura* 25cm
Cap scaled blackish on dark green. Cheeks all green. Extensive scaling on
breast. Short red line on leading edge of wing. Tail topside reddish chestnut,
underside blackish. Some forms have light auricular and area of reddish-
chestnut marks on mid-belly. Tropical and subtropical forests from lowland to
cloud-forest, edges, semi-open areas.

6 EL ORO PARAKEET *Pyrrhura orcesi* 22cm
Ivory bill, red forehead and lores. Breast slightly scaled. Underwing green.
Highland, very humid tropical forest. Very local in El Oro province, SW Ecuador.

7 BLACK-CAPPED PARAKEET *Pyrrhura rupicola* 26cm
Cap dark brown. Cheeks all yellowish green. Neck and breast yellowish white,
broadly scaled blackish brown. Short red line on leading edge of wing. Tail
topside green, underside blackish. Tropical rainforest.

8 WHITE-NECKED PARAKEET *Pyrrhura albipectus* 25cm
Yellow-orange ear-patch (green in one race). Whiter on neck forming a nuchal
collar. Yellow breast. Basal half of tail topside green, distal half reddish
chestnut, underside blackish. Subtropical forest in mountains, Podocarp
woods. Local in SE Ecuador (Loja).

9 BROWN-BREASTED PARAKEET *Pyrrhura calliptera* 25cm
Bill ivory. Head scaly, auricular rusty. Extensive blackish-brown scaling on
ochreous-buff fore-neck and breast. Patch of chestnut-red markings at mid-
belly. Yellow line on leading edge of the wing. Tail reddish. Edge of subtropical
and temperate forest in mountains, upland woods to paramo.

10 ROSE-HEADED PARAKEET *Pyrrhura rhodocephala* 25cm
Bill ivory. Scarlet cap. White line on leading edge of wing. All reddish-
chestnut tail. Subtropical forests in mountains, as high as paramo.

11 RED-EARED PARAKEET *Pyrrhura hoematotis* 25cm
Ear-patch scarlet. Patch of reddish-chestnut markings at mid-belly. All
reddish-chestnut tail. Subtropical montane forests, cloud-forests, open areas,
scattered trees in temperate zone.

PARAKEETS AND PARROTLETS (PSITTACIDAE)

Brotogeris parakeets are smallish, the sexes alike, mostly green, and have a shortish sharp tail (except in the first 2 species). Their bills are less robust than others in the family and less flattened onto the chin – pointed forward.

1 CANARY-WINGED PARAKEET *Brotogeris versicolorus*   23cm
Longish sharp tail. Mostly light green but for contrasting yellow and white wing-bar (or just yellow according to race). Upperparts and wing olivaceous. Topside of flight feathers dark green, underside bluish green. Underwing coverts pale green. Call noisily in flight, a penetrating, loud *cheerie, cheerie*. Open woods and forest edge, savannah, scrubby areas, palm groves, parks and gardens. The race *B. v. chiriri* may be a valid species: Yellow-chevroned Parakeet. 1R.

2 PLAIN PARAKEET *Brotogeris tirica*   24cm
Longish, pointed tail. All light green but shoulders brownish olive and flight feathers blue. Underwing light green. Edge of the forest, palm groves, gardens and parks.

3 COBALT-WINGED PARAKEET *Brotogeris cyanoptera*   19cm
Green. Orange chin. Yellowish forehead, or lacking this in another race, which has yellow at the bend of the wing. Underwing coverts green, flight feathers cobalt-blue. Lowland rainforest, edges, humid secondary growth, riverine forest, varzea, savannah, woods.

4 GOLDEN-WINGED PARAKEET *Brotogeris chrysoptera*   19cm
Short pointed tail. Mostly green. Narrow forehead orange (or brownish black in one form). Chin orange. Orange on primary coverts (or yellow in one race). Underwing green, flight feathers cobalt-blue. Call *chill, chill, chill*.... Cloud-forest, primary rainforest, coastal forest, savannah, gallery forest, woods, town parks.

5 ORANGE-CHINNED PARAKEET *Brotogeris jugularis*   19cm
Overall green. Chin-spot orange. Shoulders conspicuously brown. Underwing contrasting yellow. Flight feathers blue-green. Call in flight a harsh, continuous, single-note chatter *ack, ack, ack*.... Dry woods, scrubby areas with trees, open forest, gallery forest, parks, plantations, gardens.

6 TUI PARAKEET *Brotogeris sanctithomae*   17cm
Tiny, with short, pointed tail. Pale green. Bill horn-grey. Forehead and ear-patch yellow, the latter lacking in one race. Underwing coverts pale yellow, flight feathers bluish green. Call is a loud, dry, repeated *screek*. Near water, secondary growth, gallery forest, varzea, edges, palm groves.

7 GREY-CHEEKED PARAKEET *Brotogeris pyrrhoptera*   19cm
Short-tailed and dumpy. Mostly light green. Forehead and cheeks pearl-grey. Crown and nape pale blue. Chin-spot and conspicuous underwing flame-orange. Flight feathers darker green. Evergreen forest and woods, tropical scrubby areas, open cultivated areas, plantations.

8 TEPUI PARROTLET *Nannopsittaca panychlora*   14cm
Tiny. Short square tail. Bill horn-brown, longer and more slender than other parrotlets. Mostly dark green, paler below. Forehead, lores and line below the eye greenish yellow. Underwing dark green, flight feathers greyish green. Montane forest, cloud-forest, lowlands around tepuis. Locally in N, S, E Venezuela, S Guyana, N Brazil.

9 AMAZONIAN PARROTLET *Nannopsittaca dachilleae*   14cm
Bright green, paler below. Crown and forehead blue. Black allula. Bill pinky cream, legs orange. Short tail. Recently discovered in Manu National Park SE Peru. Humid forest near big rivers.

RODRIGUEZ MATA

PARAKEETS AND PARROTLETS (PSITTACIDAE)

Bolborhynchus and *Psilopsiagon* parakeets are small and modestly coloured. Small flocks. Feed on tops of bushes or on the ground. All are from mountainous areas.

1 GREY-HOODED PARAKEET *Psilopsiagon (Bolborhynchus) aymara*   18cm
Cap brownish grey. Cheeks, fore-neck, breast and part of belly very pale grey. Clicking calls in flight. Arid mountains, bushy slopes with grass and cactus, sheltered valleys.

2 MOUNTAIN PARAKEET *Psilopsiagon (Bolborhynchus) aurifrons*   18cm
Mostly green, paler below. Other races have variable yellow on underparts and/or face. Arid mountains, puna, scrubby grass slopes with small trees, upland steppe, cultivated areas.

3 BARRED PARAKEET *Bolborhynchus lineola*   16cm
Green, barred and scaled black all over. A musical chatter. Mountains with subtropical and temperate forest, cloud-forest, cane-brakes, open woods, plantations.

4 RUFOUS-FRONTED PARAKEET *Bolborhynchus ferrugineifrons*   18cm
Broad tail. Overall dull green. Olivaceous wash on cheeks and breast. Narrow rusty forehead and lores. Mountains, temperate scrubby slopes at or above tree line. Local in C Andes of Colima and Cauca in Colombia.

5 ANDEAN PARAKEET *Bolborhynchus orbygnesius*   17cm
Broad tail. All dull green, brighter tail. Head, breast and upper belly washed olive. Forehead pale green. High mountains, stunted forest, *Polylepis* woods, bushy ravines in open country.

Forpus parrotlets are the smallest of the family, with short tails. Dumpy and large-headed. Sexes differ. High-pitched calls. Only one ♀ has any blue.

6 BLUE-WINGED PARROTLET *Forpus xanthopterygius (crassirostris)*   12cm
Green, yellowish wash on underparts (and face of one race). ♂: lower back and rump dark blue (or turquoise); blue underwing. ♀'s forehead and face yellowish. Call *tsip, tsip, tsip*. Savannah, brushland and cactus, open semiarid woods, edge of rainforest, palm groves, parks.

7 GREEN-RUMPED PARROTLET *Forpus passerinus*   12cm
♂ all green (no blue on lower back and rump), blue greater coverts and underwing. ♀ paler. Call *chee, chee*. Scattered trees, savannah, arid and semiarid brushland sometimes with cactus, gallery forest, plantations, parks.

8 SPECTACLED PARROTLET *Forpus conspicillatus*   12cm
Dull green with bluish wash around eye. Forehead and cheeks brighter green. Lower back and rump dark blue. Underwing blue. ♀ much paler. Calls are chortled and musical, like those of a finch. Open tropical forest, gallery forest, semi-open woods, grassland with trees, plantations, agricultural land.

9 DUSKY-BILLED PARROTLET *Forpus sclateri*   12cm
Bill blackish. Dark green washed olive. Dark blue lower back, rump and underwing. ♀ underparts and face yellowish green. Tropical rainforest, clearings with trees, thickets, gallery forest.

10 PACIFIC PARROTLET *Forpus coelestis*   12cm
Forehead, face and crown bright green. Post-ocular streak light blue. Nape and neck greyish. Upper back and wings olivaceous grey. Lower back and rump blackish blue. ♀ greenish, paler below. Voice is a high-pitched chattering. Arid scrub with scattered trees, open woods, gallery forest.

11 YELLOW-FACED PARROTLET *Forpus xanthops*   15cm
Bright yellow on most of the head. Post-ocular streak, nape, neck and breast grey. Lower back and rump very dark blue. ♀: slightly lighter blue parts. Arid tropical montane scrub with cactus. Only N C Peru (Libertad, Marañón valley).

RODRIGUEZ MATA

PARROTLETS AND PARROTS (PSITTACIDAE)

Touit parrotlets are small, dumpy and large-headed. The tail is short and square.

1 LILAC-TAILED PARROTLET *Touit batavicus* 15cm
Parts of back and wings black and yellow. Tail lilac. Underwing very dark blue.
Penetrating call *eee, eeeth*. Montane areas from deciduous woods to temperate,
tropical, cloud, gallery and coastal forests.

2 SAPPHIRE-RUMPED PARROTLET *Touit purpuratus* 16cm
Dark brownish scapulars. Crown, ear coverts and hind-neck olive-brown.
Lower back to rump very dark blue. Outer tail feathers carmine. ♀: tail with
green subterminal band. Call *kerreee, ke, ke*. Tropical and subtropical forest in
mountains, savannah, coastal forest, woods, varzea.

3 BROWN-BACKED PARROTLET *Touit melanonotus* 15cm
Back and scapulars dark brown. Crown and hind-neck brownish green. Outer
tail feathers carmine. Call is a harsh and sharp *tiree*. Humid forest on lower
mountain slopes.

4 SCARLET-SHOULDERED PARROTLET *Touit huetii* 15cm
Forehead black, upper cheeks dark blue. Crown and ear-patch yellowish.
Leading edge of wing blue and red. Undertail bright yellow. Outer tail feathers
carmine (♂) or light green (♀). Underwing red. Calls *touit*. Tropical rainforest
near rivers, varzea.

5 BLUE-FRONTED PARROTLET *Touit dilectissimus* 17cm
Forehead and upper cheek blue. Lores and line under the eye red. Crown, nape
and hind-neck olivaceous brown. Red on leading edge of wing (less in ♀).
Underwing and outer tail bright yellow, the latter greenish yellow in ♀. Call is
a high-pitched and nasal *too eet*. Humid forest and cloud-forest in mountains,
tall secondary growth, foothills.

6 GOLDEN-TAILED PARROTLET *Touit surdus* 16cm
Scapulars brown. Forehead, lores and part of cheeks ochreous yellow. Outer
tail feathers golden yellow (yellowish green in ♀). Lowland evergreen forest,
coastal forest.

7 SPOT-WINGED PARROTLET *Touit stictopterus* 17cm
Wing coverts contrasting dark brownish grey with whitish spots (plain green
in ♀). Call a rough *ch, ch, ch*. Tropical and subtropical montane forest.

Hapalopsittaca parrots are generally slender, with contrasting patches of colour. Tail
medium length and somewhat rounded. In Andean forests.

8 BLACK-WINGED PARROT *Hapalopsittaca melanotis* 24cm
Mostly green, bluish on neck. Black spot on ear coverts (or yellowish brown in
one race). Black wing coverts. Humid temperate forest in Andes, cloud-forest
and stunted forests.

9 RUSTY-FACED PARROT *Hapalopsittaca amazonina* 23cm
Red face, darker on crown (rusty in one race). Cheeks striped yellow. Golden
wash on breast (brownish olive in another). Red shoulders and leading edge of
wing. Tail dark carmine with blue terminal band. Call is a repeated *check*. Subtropical humid and temperate forest, cloud-forest, open, low woods near tree line.

10 RED-FACED PARROT *Hapalopsittaca pyrrhops* 23cm
Like 9 but darker and duller, crown dark green. Tail green with blue terminal
band, blue underside. Underwing coverts red. Dripping cloud-forest to
transition shrubbery near paramo. Local in SW Ecuador and NE Peru. Some
consider this a race of 9.

11 INDIGO-WINGED PARROT *Hapalopsittaca fuertesi* 23cm
Differs from 9 in having yellow forehead, lores and ear-patch. Crown and nape
bluish. Red patch at mid-belly. Underwing coverts red. Upper temperate
cloud-forest. Local in C Andes of Colombia (Quindio reserves). Some
consider this a race of 9.

RODRIGUEZ MATA

PARROTS (PSITTACIDAE)

Pionus parrots are medium sized, with short, broad, square to rounded tails. Broad wings. All have undertail coverts and base of the tail bright red. Rowdy in flight, wing-beat below the horizontal.

1 BLUE-HEADED PARROT *Pionus menstruus* 28cm
Bill black and red. Hood and breast cobalt-blue, ear coverts blackish. Faint red scaling on fore-neck (lacking in one race). Rest dark green, slightly scaled. Call in flight is a double *key-wenk*. Lowland tropical forest, gallery forest, rainforest, deciduous forest, scattered trees and copses in cleared areas, occasionally in tropical forest in mountains.

2 RED-BILLED PARROT *Pionus sordidus* 28cm
Notable red bill. Head dark green with blackish scaling. Breast dark blue. Rest dull dark green. Underwing green. Another race has red and horn bill, paler head. Upperparts olive brown, underparts greyer, somewhat scaled. Call very noisy *key-ank* or *pee-unt*. Tropical and subtropical forest in mountains, rainforest and cloud-forest, woods, partially cleared areas, scattered trees, plantations, occasionally in more arid areas.

3 SCALY-HEADED PARROT *Pionus maximiliani* 28cm
Bill blackish and ivory. All green, scaled blackish. Bluer on breast. Underwing green. Call in flight continuous resonant *crack, mytak, mytak* and *chack chok, choklock* according to race. Lowland forest and open woods, copses, *Araucaria* woods, savannah, woods in marshy areas, transition woods, humid montane forest.

4 SPECKLE-FACED PARROT *Pionus tumultuosus* 28cm
Forehead, crown, nape and neck purply red. Scaled black on hind-neck. Cheeks flecked with contrasting blackish purple and pale pinkish white. Rest dark green with slightly scaled violaceous blue on breast. Humid tropical and subtropical montane forest.

5 WHITE-CROWNED PARROT *Pionus senilis* 28cm
Whitish head with transverse blackish barring on crown. Forehead whiter. Speckled on cheeks and throat. Breast and upper belly greyish pink with black barring. Rest of upperparts green. Call is a low *chank* of laughing quality. Subtropical and temperate forests in mountains, cloud-forest and open areas with scattered trees near paramo.

6 BRONZE-WINGED PARROT *Pionus chalcopterus* 28cm
Mostly dark blue. Throat and breast pinkish white scaled blue. Upper wing coverts brown. Underwing coverts dark blue, flight feathers blue. Call like that of 1. Tropical and subtropical humid montane forests, edges and clearings with scattered trees, tropical dry forest.

7 DUSKY PARROT *Pionus fuscus* 27cm
Bill blackish and pinky horn. Overall dark. Head dark dull blue, ear coverts black, streaked white on the border. Upperparts blackish-brown scaled buff, wings and topside of tail very dark blue. Underparts chestnutty purple, browner and scaled on breast. Call in flight 3 or 4 hoarse *craaaks*. Tropical and subtropical montane forest, gallery forest, edges, clearings, coastal forests on dunes, savannah and plantations.

PARROTS (PSITTACIDAE)

Pionites parrots are dumpy and large-headed. The tail is short and square.

1   BLACK-HEADED PARROT *Pionites melanocephalus*   23cm
Bill black. Cap black. Cheeks yellow, sides and back of the neck orange-ochre.
Breast and mid-belly whitish. Leggings orange-ochre (or yellow in one race).
Underwing in flight like 2, axillaries orange. Call a high-pitched *cleeeoo, cleeeoo*.
Rainforest, open tropical forest, edges, woods, savannah, coastal forest.

2   WHITE-BELLIED PARROT *Pionites leucogaster*   23cm
Bill ivory. Crown and hind-neck tawny orange. Cheeks bright yellow. Breast
and upper belly whitish. Leggings, lower belly green (or yellow, as is the tail, in
another race). Underwing coverts green, flight feathers blackish from below.
Call *zrrree, zrrree*. Gallery forest, varzea, dry forest. The race *P. l. xanthomeria* is
considered a separate species by some. It has more chestnut on hind-neck,
yellowish ochre on cheeks, cream breast and upper belly, faintly scaled darker.

3   SHORT-TAILED PARROT *Graydidascalus brachyurus*   24cm
Dumpy and very large-headed. Tail extremely short. Heavy black bill. All
green. Call a gentle *kyerick* and strident *kia kia kia*. Tropical forest, mostly near
water, tall gallery forest, edge of varzea.

Pionopsitta parrots are variously colourful around the head. The tail is shortish,
broad and rounded, wings broad.

4   PILEATED or RED-CAPPED PARROT *Pionopsitta pileata*   22cm
Sexes differ. Bill black. Bare skin around eye dark. Red forehead, crown and
part of face (variable). Rest green. Flight feathers, tail and underwing bluish. ♀
lacks red; rusty ear-patch. Calls include *chee chee, cheely cheely* and *kloo-louie*.
Hill forest, copses, woods, rural areas.

5   BROWN-HOODED PARROT *Pionopsitta haematotis*   21cm
Ivory bill. Dark brown hood. Nape and hind-neck olive-washed. Red dot on
ear coverts, red half-collar on fore-neck. Breast olive. Leading edge of wing,
underwing coverts and flight feathers blue. Axillaries and part of flank bright
red. Base of tail feathers when seen from below show rusty orange. Some races
have all underwing coverts red. Calls in flight *check* or *cheek*. Cloud-forest, wet
lowland forest, piedmont forest.

6   ROSE-FACED PARROT *Pionopsitta pulchra*   22cm
Pink face, edged black and white. Calls *skreek skreek*. Humid tropical and
subtropical forest, tall secondary growth, clearings with scattered trees,
plantations. Some consider this a form of 5.

7   ORANGE-CHEEKED PARROT *Pionopsitta barrabandi*   23cm
Bill black. Hood black, cheeks yellowish orange. Breast yellowish olive.
Shoulders with orangy yellow and red. Leading edge of wing and underwing
scarlet. One form has shoulders and cheeks bright orange. Calls *chew-it* and
choyet, distinctive and bi-syllabic. Humid forest, varzea, isolated stands of trees,
sandy-soil woods.

8   CAICA PARROT *Pionopsitta caica*   23cm
Greyish-ivory bill. Short black hood. Wide tawny-chestnut collar with darker
scaling. Strident *illit* call. Rainforest, tropical, gallery and piedmont forests.

9   SAFFRON-HEADED PARROT *Pionopsitta pyrilia*   21cm
Hood yellow, orange wash on ear coverts. Cere and bare skin around eye dark.
Breast olive. Shoulders and leading edge of the wing yellow and red.
Underwing scarlet. Call *cheweek*. Lowland humid forest to cloud-forest, tall
secondary growth.

RODRIGUEZ MATA

PARROTS AND AMAZONS (PSITTACIDAE)

1 **VULTURINE PARROT** *Pionopsitta (Gypopsitta) vulturina*   23cm
Bill blackish and horn coloured. Remarkable bare, black head with forehead and
high collar yellow. Bend of the wing and leading edge red. Underwing coverts
scarlet. Tail from below blue and yellow. Juv: feathered head, dirty yellow. Call is
terek terek and *tray, trayer*. Lowland tropical forest, varzea, also terra firme forest.

2 **ORANGE-HEADED VULTURINE-PARROT**
Pionopsitta aurantiocephala   23cm
Differs from 1 in having featherless orange head with black bristles.
Underwing coverts scarlet. Recently recognised as a species, once thought to
be an immature plumage of 1. Rainforest at mid-Tapajos river, possibly also
lower Madeira river, C Brazilian Amazonia.

3 **BLUE-BELLIED PARROT** *Triclaria malachitacea*   29cm
Ivory bill. Large blue area on mid-belly. Very large and broad bluish squarish
tail. ♀ lacks blue belly. ♂ has fluted, thrush-like voice, with *ee-ay ee-a*y and
jillids, while ♀ joins with *diot, diot*. At mid-elevation in mountain forests and
escarpments, adjacent drier woods, towns, plantations.

4 **RED-FAN PARROT** *Deroptyus accipitrinus*   35cm
Large crest of erectile blue-bordered red feathers around head. Forehead and
crown speckled. Breast and upper belly also scaled red and blue. In another race
forehead and crown are ivory-white. Strident nasal calls of *kyah, ghee* and *he-ah*.
Terra firme forest, clearings, coastal dune forest, savannah, transition woods.

Amazons are largish and dumpy with square tails. Heavy bill, broad and somewhat
rounded wings. Some species have wing flashes of combinations of bright colours,
and most have dark blue primaries. Notable bare skin around eye.

5 **VINACEOUS AMAZON or PARROT** *Amazona vinacea*   34cm
Bill reddish with ivory tip. Red lores. Hind-collar pale blue, scaled black.
Breast and upper belly vinaceous scaled black. Red on leading edge of wing.
Underwing green. Tail green, base of outer feathers carmine. Calls *tay-oh* and
cryee-creeoh. Forest with *Araucaria*, isolated patches of woods in open country,
Araucaria plantations, dry woods, humid forest with cane.

6 **TUCUMAN AMAZON or PARROT** *Amazona tucumana*   32cm
All green, scaled blackish. Forehead and primary coverts red. Underwing
green. Upper montane forest, mostly alders and Podocarps. Some consider this
a race of 7.

7 **RED-SPECTACLED AMAZON or PARROT** *Amazona pretrei*   32cm
Forehead, crown and around eye red; leading edge of wing and 'garters' also
red. Underwing green. Calls include strident whistles interspersed with word-
like *spee-ah, krek, clow* and *kayro*. Forest, especially with *Araucaria*.

8 **YELLOW-FACED AMAZON or PARROT** *Amazona xanthops*   26cm
Head yellow, pectoral collar scaled green. Breast and upper belly yellowish
orange. Flanks orange. Tail green, dull orange at base. Immature has yellow
forehead, crown and cheeks. Underparts scaled green. Yellowish orange on
flanks. Calls in flight *cree-ay, gray-oh* and *tottoto*. Scattered low trees in
cerrado, or with cactus in caatinga, gallery forest.

3♀

2

1 juv

1

3♂

5

4

4

1

6

8

7

8

7

8 juv

RODRÍGUEZ MATA

AMAZONS (PSITTACIDAE)

1 **BLUE-CHEEKED AMAZON or PARROT** *Amazona dufresniana* 37cm
Bill grey and reddish. Forehead yellowish orange grading to scaled yellowish green on crown. Bluish cheeks. Forests in mountains, irregularly coastal forests.

2 **RED-BROWED AMAZON or PARROT** *Amazona rhodocorytha* 37cm
Differs from 1 in paler bill, reddish-orange forehead and crown, yellow lores and fore-part of cheek (all reddish orange in some individuals). Rest of cheek bluish. Calls include clear *koiok, cow-ow* and *ullo ullo ullo; cray-oh* in flight. Humid lowland forest, ranging into highlands. Some believe it is a race of 1.

3 **BLUE-FRONTED AMAZON or PARROT** *Amazona aestiva* 37cm
Forehead and fore-face have varying extents of turquoise. Crown and rest of face yellow to a variable extent, sometimes nearly all the head. Red and yellow shoulder very variable to absent. Call *arrow, how rrow, rrackow*. Dry or humid forest, palm groves, gallery forest, savannah, copses, dry woods, plantations.

4 **ORANGE-WINGED AMAZON or PARROT** *Amazona amazonica* 34cm
Centre of crown and of forehead yellow; sides blue. Cheeks yellow. Voice with *koorik, keeroh* and *dlue dlue*. Dry woods, savannah, rainforest, gallery forest, varzea, swampy areas, palm groves, mangroves, grasslands with scattered trees, plantations.

5 **YELLOW-SHOULDERED AMAZON or PARROT** *A. barbadensis* 35cm
Extensive face and shoulders yellow. Savannah with scattered trees, thorny vegetation, brushland with cactus, plantations. Falcón and Anzoategui (N coastal Venezuela) and nearby islands.

6 **RED-TAILED AMAZON or PARROT** *Amazona brasiliensis* 37cm
Forehead, crown and lores pinkish red (forehead only in ♀). Face pale mauve (less in ♀). Touch of red on leading edge of wing. Calls *krah, clee* and *kalik* and *cree-oh*. Coastal forest. E São Paolo and Parana states in SE Brazil.

7 **MEALY AMAZON or PARROT** *Amazona farinosa* 41cm
All dull green scaled darker. Some with yellow on crown. Bluish wash and heavily scaled blackish on hind-neck. Red on part of leading edge of wing. End of tail pale green. Calls *creek, cooreek* and *krop*, low-pitched and musical. Tall, dense tropical forest, gallery forest, coastal sand-ridge forest, palm groves, deciduous woods, semi-open secondary growth. A previously presumed form of this may instead be a separate species: Kawall's Parrot (*A.kawalli*), 7R

8 **FESTIVE AMAZON or PARROT** *Amazona festiva* 34cm
Lores and part of forehead deep red. Hind-brow blue. Lower back and rump bright red, lacking in some forms. Calls in flight nasal and laughing *whah whah*. Gallery forest, varzea, rainforest, savannah, grassland with scattered trees, secondary growth, plantations.

9 **SCALY-NAPED AMAZON or PARROT** *Amazona mercenaria* 34cm
All scaly green (more scaled on nape and hind-neck), with touch of yellow on leading edge of wing. Call *calee calee*. Subtropical and temperate forest in Andes, cloud-forest, partially open terrain at higher elevations.

10 **RED-LORED AMAZON or PARROT** *Amazona autumnalis* 36cm
Forehead red. Crown, nape and hind-neck lilac-blue, slightly scaled blackish. Flight calls harsh *cheekack cheekack* and *oorrack oorrack*. Rainforest, gallery, open lowland and dry scrubby forests, scattered trees in cleared areas, plantations.

11 **YELLOW-CROWNED AMAZON or PARROT** *Amazona ochrocephala* 38cm
Forehead and crown yellow (or yellow crown and face in one race). Shoulder red. Calls *kerah* and *bow-wow*. Tropical rainforest, gallery forest, varzea, swampy forest, arid open woods, scrubland, savannah, scattered copses, coastal forest, deforested areas, plantations.

RODRÍGUEZ MATA

CUCKOOS (CUCULIDAE)

Cuckoos of the genus *Coccyzus* are stealthy and hide well amongst the dense foliage.

1 YELLOW-BILLED CUCKOO *Coccyzus americanus* 28cm
Black bill with notable yellow mandible. Eye-ring grey, yellow in juv. Brownish olive above, underparts white, throat and breast slightly tinted grey. Rufous primaries seen in flight. Savannah, open woods, gallery forest, tropical deciduous forest, thorny woods, thickets, secondary growth, parkland. Migratory from N America; silent on 'winter' range.

2 PEARLY-BREASTED CUCKOO *Coccyzus euleri* 28cm
Like 1 but with no contrasting primaries, these being brownish grey. Call a slow *kuope* at 1 per sec, also a rattle followed by *tooks*, then *twops*. Rainforest, gallery forest, edge, woodland on sandy soils, regrowth, scrub.

3 BLACK-BILLED CUCKOO *Coccyzus erythrophthalmus* 29cm
Red eye-ring. Black bill. Upperparts bronzy brown, underparts white with creamy wash on throat and undertail coverts. Cinnamon primaries seen in flight. Tail: greyish underside, feathers with dirty white tip. Juv washed rufous on underparts. Woods, forest, scrub, secondary growth, plantations, open woods. Migrant from N America, silent on wintering grounds.

4 DARK-BILLED CUCKOO *Coccyzus melacoryphus* 27cm
Mask and bill black. Eye-ring yellow or grey. Malar region, sides of neck bluish grey, rest of underparts buffy cream. Cap slate-grey. Juv duller. Voice deep, hollow accelerating series of *coos* descending in pitch; also *churrs*. Rainforest, deciduous forest, gallery forest, varzea, dryland forest, mangroves, thorny woods, trees and bushes, secondary growth, thickets, regrowth, savannah, plantations.

5 MANGROVE CUCKOO *Coccyzus minor* 31cm
A large version of 4 but mandible orangy yellow and underparts cinnamon or buff. Low, guttural *gawks*; also a single *whit*. Mangroves, forests, thorny woods, brushland, thickets.

6 DWARF CUCKOO *Coccyzus pumilus* 20cm
The smallest of the genus. Face, throat and breast tawny rufous. Short and slender bill black. Rest of underparts creamy white. Shortish tail less graduated. Calls of *churr* and *trrrr*. Gallery forest, rainforest, deciduous tropical forest, savannah, open woods, thorny woods, shrubby areas, scattered trees, parks and gardens.

7 ASH-COLOURED CUCKOO *Coccyzus cinereus* 23cm
Small. Short, slender bill. Eye and eye-ring red. Upperparts brownish grey. Shortish tail not graduated. Throat and breast buffy grey, rest of underparts whitish. Juv: eye-ring yellowish, eye dark brown. Generally browner. Voice dovelike *cow-w cow-w cow cow*. Lowlands, tropical deciduous forest, gallery forest, savannah, thorny woods, cerrado, regrowth, woods and thickets near water.

8 GREY-CAPPED CUCKOO *Coccyzus lansbergi* 27cm
Bill black. Cap, ear coverts and hind-neck slate-grey. Rest of upperparts rufous brown. Throat, breast and undertail coverts cinnamon, rest of underparts buffy cinnamon. Call rapid, hollow *coos*. Tropical deciduous, gallery, and arid forest, brushland, low thickets near water.

RODRIGUEZ MATA

CUCKOOS AND GROUND-CUCKOOS (CUCULIDAE)

Dromococcyx cuckoos have somewhat pointed chestnut crests and a notable post-ocular streak. Upper tail coverts are huge, covering most of fanned tail. Solitary and secretive, very hard to see.

1 PHEASANT CUCKOO *Dromococcyx phasianellus* 36cm
Throat and breast washed buff, streaked and spotted blackish brown. Voice a melancholy whistled *fee fee whirrrrrr* (trill or quaver on last note), also rising *sah, say, seesay*; clucking growl when angry. Forests, lowland flooded forest, thickets and undergrowth, lower cloud-forest, edge, secondary woods, cane-brakes.

2 PAVONINE CUCKOO *Dromococcyx pavoninus* 27cm
Throat, neck and breast uniform cinnamon-buff. Upperparts darker. Voice a high-pitched rhythmic *we see thee titee*, rising a tone on last 4 notes. Understorey thickets, dense tangled vegetation in forests, transition forests, secondary woods, seasonally flooded forest.

3 STRIPED CUCKOO *Tapera naevia* 28cm
Cap tawny rufous striped black; bushy topknot. Whitish brow and post-ocular stripe. Upperparts brown and buff striped black. Underparts whitish, buffy-grey wash on neck and breast. Juv more rufous. Crown and back dotted buff. Call is a high-pitched 2-note whistle, second note a semitone higher, insistently repeated. Dry woods and scrub, clearings, scattered trees, edge, secondary growth.

Ground-cuckoos have heavy curved bills, with notable crest and large tails. Legs are somewhat long. Very shy, terrestrial and hard to see in deep forest.

4 RUFOUS-WINGED GROUND-CUCKOO *Neomorphus rufipennis* 50cm
Bill black with greenish-yellow tip. Bare skin around eye red. Crested hood blackish blue. Cheeks, throat and upper breast grey, scaled dark blue. Underparts pale greyish. Tropical forest in lowlands, foothills and lower slopes.

5 BANDED GROUND-CUCKOO *Neomorphus radiolosus* 50cm
Bill bluish black. Bare skin around eye pale blue. Dark blackish blue with green and deep purple sheen. Scaled buffy white on fore-parts. Evergreen forest on foothills and lower slopes of Andes, tropical forest in lowlands. Rare and local.

6 RED-BILLED GROUND-CUCKOO *Neomorphus pucheranii* 50cm
Bill and bare skin around eye bright red. Cap dark blue. Cheeks and neck pale brownish grey. Breast scaled black. Black pectoral collar. Rest of underparts cinnamon or buffy, according to race. Calls like bellowing with your mouth closed. Lowland tropical forest.

7 RUFOUS-VENTED GROUND-CUCKOO *Neomorphus geoffroyi* 50cm
Bill yellow and greenish. Bare skin around eye pale blue. Crest dark blue. Head, neck and upper breast scaled dark brownish and whitish. Black pectoral collar. Underparts buffy white grading to rufous. Other races have blackish head, or more buffy, yet others with blue back and wings, or more coppery, or are generally rustier. Call is dove-like *oooo oop*, chacks and bill-snapping. Forest in lowland and foothills, seasonally flooded transition forest, cane-brakes, thickets.

8 SCALED GROUND-CUCKOO *Neomorphus squamiger* 50cm
Differs from 7 in lack of collar. Forehead, crown, cheeks, neck, breast and part of flanks cinnamon and buffy white, brown V-shaped scaling. Upperparts brownish with purply copper sheen. Forest on lower Tapajos river. Some consider this a race of 7 but differs in design of scaling.

RODRIGUEZ MATA

ANIS AND CUCKOOS (CUCULIDAE), AND HOATZIN (OPISTHOCOMIDAE)

Anis are wobbly birds both perched and in flight. They have long floppy tails.

1 GREATER ANI *Crotophaga major*   45cm
White eye. Shiny black with bright blue and green sheen. Highly arched culmen with 'keel' on top. Noisy. Voice all *roodle-toodle-toodle* with 'sizzling' background accompaniment. Always low, by water. Edge of riverine vegetation, mangroves, flooded forest.

2 SMOOTH-BILLED ANI *Crotophaga ani*   33cm
All black. High, arched culmen on smooth black bill. Voice high-pitched *ooeee* whistles, longish and rising, perched or in flight. Edge of forest, open woods, tall scrub, grassland with scattered trees, thorny woods, cleared areas and secondary growth, savannah, parks and gardens. Hunts through the grass, often near cattle.

3 GROOVE-BILLED ANI *Crotophaga sulcirostris*   31cm
Like 2 but culmen less arched, all grooved. Voice a series of *wickers*, also dry *quilk*. Evergreen tropical forest to dryland scrub and trees, grasslands, edge of rainforest, gallery forest, secondary growth, cleared areas, marshes, deciduous woods, parks and gardens, often near cattle.

All in the genus *Piaya* are very long tailed. Agile and sneaky through the vegetation.

4 SQUIRREL CUCKOO *Piaya cayana*   47cm
Huge tail. Greenish-yellow bill. Bare skin around eye pale green or red. Head and neck buffy vinaceous. Back, wings and topside of tail rusty red. Underparts grey. Undertail black or rust and black, and white. Calls *pit-wheew* and a series of *wheeps*. Dense foliage in gallery and rainforest, dry forest, thickets, secondary growth, open deciduous woods, mangroves, savannah, plantations, parks and gardens.

5 BLACK-BELLIED CUCKOO *Piaya melanogaster*   40cm
Bill red. Eye red, bare skin around it yellow and pale green. Cap and nape grey. Throat, neck, breast and upperparts rufous. Belly and undertail coverts black. Underside of tail rufous with subterminal black, and white tip. Call an explosive *djit, djitjitjit*, also a descending *yaaaaah* followed by dry rattle. Humid forest, sandy soil forest, rainforest, savannah.

6 LITTLE CUCKOO *Piaya minuta*   28cm
Smallest of the genus. Bill greenish yellow. Eye and bare eye-ring red. Overall rufous. Belly and undertail coverts brownish grey. Underside of tail black with white terminal spots. Call a muted *pit-whew*, also *checks*, *kyenk* and a descending chatter. Rainforest, gallery forest, edge, secondary growth, shrubs and thickets, deciduous woods, usually near water, mangroves, cane-brakes, swampy areas.

7 GUIRA CUCKOO *Guira guira*   40cm
Untidy appearance. Long 'uncombed' crest. White back and rump. Voice is a series of slow descending *kee-ay kee-ay kee-eh kee-orr keeoh cure cure*; *keeerrrrrrr* rattle in alarm, slow quiet *yews* in flight. Trees in open spaces, savannah, plantations, bushes and thickets, edge of woods, urban gardens and parks.

The following species is an oddity, having its own order and family. Probably related to the Cuculiformes, it looks somewhat like a giant *Guira* cuckoo.

8 HOATZIN *Opisthocomus hoazin*   62cm
Unmistakable appearance. Long untidy crest, bare blue face, red eye. Upperparts dark brown with buff streaks and feather-edges. Throat and breast buff. Rest of underparts and primaries chestnut. Reptile-like huffing and puffing sounds. Forest waterside thickets, shrub and low trees.

RODRIGUEZ / MATA

BARN OWL (TYTONIDAE) & TYPICAL OWLS (STRIGIDAE)

1 BARN OWL *Tyto alba*   35cm
Slender and long-legged with heart-shaped facial disc and black eyes.
Upperparts grey and ochre with blackish and white spotting. Underparts all
white with sparse faint dots. Dark phase ochre on underparts. In flight in the
dark seems all white. Call is a long series of vocal clicks. Also *shhhh* rising.
Urban areas and farmsteads, open fields, hedgerows, roadsides, arid terrain.

Typical owls are nocturnal hunters, usually solitary. Daylight is spent hiding in
woods or forest foliage. Usually low-pitched calls. Strong talons on feathered tarsi.

2 BUFF-FRONTED OWL *Aegolius harrisii*   21cm
Dark chocolate-brown and cinnamon-ochre. White spots on wings and tail.
Call a warbled rolling *rrrrrrrr….* Humid and montane forest, podocarp and
alder woods to tree line, *Araucaria* and dry chaco woods, edge, bushy terrain
with steep banks and valleys, cerrado, caatinga, plantations.

Pygmy-owls are tiny, crepuscular and often diurnal, and have 'false eyes' on the nape.
The iris is yellow. Often on exposed perches. They twitch tail sideways when nervous.
Much mobbed by dicky-birds.

3 FERRUGINOUS PYGMY-OWL *Glaucidium brasilianum*   17cm
Variable. Upperparts streaked and marked white. Upper back and scapulars
uniform. Crown finely streaked. Underparts whitish and irregularly streaked,
this denser on breast and flanks. Tail blackish brown with 4–6 white bands. In
rufous phase, some specimens lack barring on tail. Call a long series of whistles
at 3 per sec. Woods, forests, gardens, to 2,000m. The Tucuman Pygmy-owl *G.
tucumanum* and Peruvian Pygmy-owl *G. peruanum* may be races.

4 AUSTRAL PYGMY-OWL *Glaucidium nanum*   20cm
A large version of 3 with 8 or 9 rufous-cinnamon bands on tail. Also a rufous
phase. S Patagonian Andean woods and ecotone. Migrates N to dry woods.

5 ANDEAN PYGMY-OWL *Glaucidium jardinii*   15cm
Very like 3 but smaller. Crown has white dots. Scaling on sides of breast, upper
back and scapulars. Tail blackish with 3 visible white bars (really 4). Also a
rufous phase. Call a single (S race) or double (N race) low-pitched whistle.
Montane forest and woods, to tree line, grasslands, scrub, 900–4,000m. Perhaps
an upland race of 3. The Jungas Pygmy-owl *G. bolivianum* is possibly a race of 5.

6 CLOUDFOREST PYGMY-OWL *Glaucidium nubicola*   16cm
Like a rufous phase 5, but all uniform chestnut-brown on sides of breast and
upper back. Tail shorter, dark brown with 3 visible whitish bands. Call a series of
double whistles rapidly repeated. Primary humid cloud-forest, 1,400–2,000m.

7 LEAST PYGMY-OWL *Glaucidium minutissimum*   13cm
Tiny. Brownish-grey head with tiny white dots. Upperparts dark brown with
whitish markings. Tail blackish brown with 3 visible white bands edged
blackish. Underparts heavily streaked chestnutty rufous, especially towards
flanks. There is a brown phase like 3. Tropical humid, terra firme, varzea,
subtropical evergreen forests on Andean slopes. Some consider the western
race, *G. m. parkeri*, a separate species (Subtropical Pygmy-owl), and the
northern race, *G. m. hardyi*, another (Amazonian Pygmy-owl).

8 LONG-WHISKERED OWLET *Xenoglaux loweryi*   14cm
Small and dumpy. Long whiskers from sides of facial disc. Upperparts and breast
chestnutty brown vermiculated dark brown. Brow, dotting and nape-band
white. Paler below. Local, rare. Humid cloud-forest with dense undergrowth.
1,900–2,200m. N Peru, Mayo river valley NE of San Martin.

9 BURROWING OWL *Athene (Speotyto) cunicularia*   25cm
Very visible. Long legs. Patterned in brown and whitish. Juv more uniform and
darker. Open grass, cultivated land, savannah, stony scrubby steppe, desert
and mountains to 4,500m, golf courses.

RODRIGUEZ MATA

SCREECH-OWLS (STRIGIDAE)

There is a lot of work to be done on screech-owls. Their classification seems somewhat confused.

1 BARE-SHANKED SCREECH-OWL *Otus clarkii*   25cm
Rufous, with unframed face. Yellow iris. Crown and underparts have heavy bar-crossed streaks. Line of white spots on scapulars. Bare tarsi. Call 3 deep *wouks*. Montane forest.

2 CLOUDFOREST SCREECH-OWL *Otus marshalli*   23cm
Dark rufous with contrasting streaks, bars and white markings. Facial disc rufous, framed black. Dark eyes. White spots around nape. Call a series of *eees*. Cloud-forest with dense undergrowth. C and S Peru, Pasco (Yanachaga Mts) and Cuzco (Vilcabamba Mts).

3 PERUVIAN SCREECH-OWL *Otus roboratus*   21cm
Like 4 but streaks on breast broader at lower tip, somewhat drop-shaped. Cap blackish. Pale nuchal collar. Call a harsh rising trill. Dry woods, bushes with cactus, from coastal plains to foothills.

4 TROPICAL SCREECH-OWL *Otus choliba*   22cm
Variable. Contrasting design. Crown streaked black on pale form. Upperparts irregularly streaked and barred blackish. White spots down scapulars and patch on coverts. Face framed with black. Underparts streaked. Iris yellow to orangy yellow. Forests, woods, savannah, scrubby areas, open areas with trees, plantations, parks, gardens. The race *O. c. koepckeae* may be a valid sp.

5 BLACK-CAPPED SCREECH-OWL *Otus atricapilla*   24cm
Like 4 but crown dark, dense streaks arrow-shaped. Brown or dull yellow iris. Whitish nuchal collar varies. More uniform upperparts and face. Breast streaks broader at lower end. There are also rufous and blackish-brown forms. Rainforest, dense undergrowth, forest edge. Long-tufted Screech-owl (*O. a. sanctaecatarinae*) is a hefty version with less dark cap and yellow iris. Call is similar but longer, slower and lower pitched. Some consider this a separate species. Some consider the identical *Otus a. hoyi* a valid species: Montane Forest Screech Owl.

6 VERMICULATED SCREECH-OWL *Otus vermiculatus*   21cm
Pale face with white brow. More finely and uniformly patterned. Yellow iris. There are brown and rufous phases. Call a long trill growing in volume and fading at end. Humid lowland tropical forest to mountain slopes.

7 RUFESCENT SCREECH-OWL *Otus ingens*   28cm
Least contrasting design; all vermiculated cinnamon and dark brown. Eyes yellowish brown to dark brown. Faint streaking on underparts. There is a rufous form. Call a long series of rapid *tootootoo*.... Dense humid cloud-forest and scrub on steep slopes. Colombian Screech-owl *O. i. colombianus* is considered a separate species by some. Slightly larger with richer lower underparts.

8 CINNAMON SCREECH-OWL *Otus petersoni*   21cm (not illustrated)
A small version of 7 but basically buffy brown. Tarsi feathered onto toes. SW Ecuador (Cutucú Mts) and adjacent NW Peru. Possibly a race of 7.

9 TAWNY-BELLIED SCREECH-OWL *Otus watsonii*   22cm
Little contrast in designs, mostly vermiculated. Iris yellowish brown to blackish brown. Several morphs, from brownish cinnamon to rufous and blackish brown. All have tawny-buff lower underparts, finely streaked black, and facial disc bordered dark. A long call, accelerating, rising, then falling in pitch and volume. Lowland rainforest, clearings and edge, gallery forest.

10 WHITE-THROATED SCREECH-OWL *Otus albogularis*   25cm
No 'ears'. Dark brown dotted and barred buff. Dark face. White throat. Yellow iris. Call is a very long series of *cheroos* and *choos*. Humid montane and stunted forest, clearings and edge, scattered trees.

1

3

4 dark form

4 rufous form

4 brown form

4 grey form

4 cinnamon form

2

7

4

5 brown form

5 rufous form

6

9 amon form

9 brown form

10

10

RODRIGUEZ MATA

TYPICAL OWLS (STRIGIDAE)

1 GREAT HORNED OWL *Bubo virginianus*   55cm
Large and hefty. Prominent 'ears'. Bright yellow iris. Upperparts irregularly
patterned blackish brown, buffy and cinnamon. Underparts buffy barred
blackish. Face, breast and upperparts may be browner, more rufous or paler
according to race. Call is a powerful low-pitched hooted *who whowho... who
who*, carries far. From tropical forest to woods, scrub and grasslands, lowlands
to high puna; mangroves, parks and gardens. The grey race in Patagonian
Andes is considered a different species by some, *B. magellanicus*.

2 STRIPED OWL *Pseudoscops (Rhinoptynx) clamator*   35cm
Perches upright. Long 'ears'. Whitish face framed blackish. Upperparts
irregularly marked cinnamon, buff, whitish and blackish brown. Underparts
buffy white (or ochre-buff according to race) with prominent blackish streaks.
Iris pale brown, orange or dark brown. Call loud whistled descending
pheeeeeew, series of yaps as a small dog. In flight like 3. Gallery forest, edge,
marshes, grassland with scattered trees and bushes, savannah, patches of
woods, agricultural areas, plantations, suburban areas.

3 SHORT-EARED OWL *Asio flammeus*   36cm
Often hunts by day over grassland. Low flight, exaggerated wing-beat. Short
'ears', seldom seen. Upperparts buffy cinnamon with blackish-brown streaks
and barring. Underparts buffy with fine blackish-brown streaks. Face blackish
brown and buff with white brow. Flight feathers barred. Iris pale yellow. Perches
on ground, fence posts. Open savannah, edge of gallery forest, wet grasslands,
open grassland, cultivated land, areas with scattered trees and shrubs.

4 STYGIAN OWL *Asio stygius*   37cm
Hides in uppermost branches of trees, perching erect. Upperparts brownish
black, also face. Whitish brow. Underparts buffy or buffy white with broad
brownish-black streaks. Outer flight feathers blackish. Much longer 'ears' than
3. Juv: upperparts and face as 3. Call low-pitched, loud single *hoo* repeated at
longish intervals. Humid montane forest, woodland patches in savannah,
upland woods, wet chaco woods, *Araucaria* woods, deciduous forest, open areas
with scattered trees, plantations, parks.

5 SPECTACLED OWL *Pulsatrix perspicillata*   50cm
Large and hefty. Lacks 'ears'. Crown, head, upperparts and breast-band
blackish brown or dark chocolate. 'Spectacles' and throat white. Underparts
buffy. Iris yellow. Juv: mostly whitish with black face and yellow iris. Call is
motmot-like *boo boo boo boo boo...*, descending. From humid tropical and
subtropical to gallery and dry forest, savannah, transition woods, montane
woods, swamps, secondary growth.

6 TAWNY-BROWED OWL *Pulsatrix koeniswaldiana*   42cm
Smaller than 5. 'Spectacles' buffy cinnamon. Underparts cinnamon-buff with
variable rusty scaling. Tail blackish grey with 2 visible fine whitish bars. Iris
brown. Juv like 5's but iris dark. Call a series of descending and diminishing,
ventriloquial *brrrs* or *urrrs*. Humid tropical and subtropical forest, *Araucaria*
woods, edge and clearings. Some consider this a race of 7 but voices differ.

7 BAND-BELLIED OWL *Pulsatrix melanota*   42cm
Differs from 6 in having underparts all barred buffy white and rusty. Wing and
scapulars barred buff. Pectoral collar has diffuse scaling. Some specimens are
intermediate and look more like 6. Call a short deep trill ending in 4–5 rapid
pops; in Peru, deep *hoots*. Humid tropical and montane forest, open woods,
700–1,600m, sometimes lower.

RODRIGUEZ MATA

TYPICAL OWLS (STRIGIDAE)

1 CRESTED OWL *Lophostrix cristata* 41cm
'Ear' tufts disproportionately long, starting at base of bill and rising through brow, partially white. Rufous face. Upperparts buff with white spots on wings. Underparts paler. Dark form with upperparts blackish brown, underparts dark brown grading to buff, all finely barred. Call a toad-like rolling *K-K-Krrrrrrrr…* Humid heavy forest, riverine woods, tall secondary growth.

2 BLACK-BANDED OWL *Ciccaba (Strix) huhula* 34cm
All black, finely barred white. Bill and legs yellow. Eye blackish brown. Call low-pitched *hoo hoo hooo HOOOO* and variations. Terra firme, varzea and humid rainforest and clearings, *Araucaria* woods, plantations.

3 BLACK-AND-WHITE OWL *Ciccaba (Strix) nigrolineata* 34cm
Face, crown and upperparts black. Brow, hind-neck and underparts white, barred black. Tail black with fine white bars. Bill and legs yellow. Iris blackish brown. Call like that of 2. Cloud-forest, humid, gallery and deciduous forests, clearings and edge, scattered trees near paramo, tall secondary growth, tall mangroves, plantations.

4 RUFOUS-BANDED OWL *Strix (Ciccaba) albitarsis* 35cm
Upperparts cinnamon-rufous barred and scaled blackish brown. Underparts cinnamon-buff grading to buffy white, scaled blackish brown. Brow whitish. Iris orangy yellow. Call *hoo… hoo-hoo-hoo HOOO.* Cloud-forest and humid forest, edge and clearings, scattered trees, high, near paramo.

5 RUSTY-BARRED OWL *Strix hylophila* 36cm
Very like 4 but paler on head, back and breast, smaller scaling. Call a raucous *hoo, hoo, HOO* followed by descending *HOO…hoo, hoo, hoo-hoo-hoo.* Humid forest edge, woods, tropical mountain forest and lowlands, secondary growth, sometimes near human habitation.

6 MOTTLED OWL *Strix (Ciccaba) virgata* 35cm
Upperparts dark brown finely barred cinnamon-buff. Brow and edge of face whitish. Underparts buffy, barred brown, especially on breast and flanks (or streaked in 1 form). Iris brown or orangy brown. Call a series of low-pitched, short and rising *gwoo gwoo….* ♀'s call like that of a cat. Tropical rainforest, gallery, deciduous, cloud-forest, woods, *Araucaria* and open areas with scattered trees, bushes and thickets, thorny woods, plantations, around towns.

7 RUFOUS-LEGGED OWL *Strix rufipes* 40cm
Upperparts barred dark greyish brown and buffy white. Face paler, finely barred whitish and dark brownish grey. Underparts whitish barred dark greyish brown. Lower belly, vent, underwing and undersurface of tail buffy, barred greyish brown. Tarsus and toes cinnamon. Iris brown. Calls vary with races: S race low *brrrrs* followed by a long series of *oo ooAhOO oo oo oo oo …*; N race *crew crew crew (crew crew) CRAW CRAW.* Dry chaco woods with cactus and scrub, Patagonian Andes' woods and forest. The N population may be valid species, Chaco Owl *S. chacoensis.*

2

2

1 light form

1 dark form

3

6

6 streaked form

4

5

barred form

7

7

OILBIRD (STEATORNITHIDAE), **POTOOS** (NYCTIBIIDAE) AND NIGHTHAWKS (CAPRIMULGIDAE)

1 OILBIRD *Steatornis caripensis* 46cm
Rufous with white spots and narrow black bars. Nocturnal. Roosts and nests in caves. Tropical and subtropical montane forest down to sea level.

Potoos are nocturnal. During daylight they perch on branches, vertically for better effect. They look like extensions of branches; very hard to see. Feed at night on insects.

2 GREAT POTOO *Nyctibius grandis* 52cm
Paler than others. Ash-grey, all finely spotted and streaked, and other patterns in black, whitish and brown. Shoulders rusty. Eye dark brown. Voice a long, harsh *wow*. High in big trees of open forest, savannah.

3 LONG-TAILED POTOO *Nyctibius aethereus* 55cm
Like large 4 with longer, broader graded tail. Yellow eye. One Amazon form (*N. a. longicaudus*) somewhat more rufous, median wing coverts whitish. Voice a plaintive *ra-OOH* repeated at 5–10 sec intervals. Deep, unspoilt forest, from very humid to relatively dry.

4 COMMON POTOO *Nyctibius griseus* 35cm
Brownish grey to cinnamon-brown with everything in between, all streaked, spotted and barred black, chestnut, buff and whitish. Yellow eye. Blackish malar stripe. Irregular black markings on scapulars, breast and post-ocular. Dark shoulders. Median coverts sometimes very pale. Voice 5–8 mournful whistled notes descending in pitch. Forest, woods, mangroves, plantations.

5 WHITE-WINGED POTOO *Nyctibius leucopterus* 27cm
Like 4 but smaller. Wing coverts whitish with some few faint blackish streaks. Eyes yellow. One long descending *feeeeooooo*. Atlantic forest and montane forest. The mountain race, Mountain Potoo *N. l. maculosus*, is larger and differs in voice, which is like a higher-pitched call of 3; some believe this to be a separate species.

6 RUFOUS POTOO *Nyctibius bracteatus* 23cm
Small. Cinnamon-rufous with white dots and black barring. Yellow eye. Lowland rainforest, terra firme forest, swampy areas, with palms.

Nighthawks and nightjars are cryptically coloured nocturnal birds that mostly roost on the ground during daylight hours. Very hard to see. Flush only at last moment. Voices can be important to find them and for identification.

7 PAURAQUE *Nyctidromus albicollis* 28cm
Pale cinnamon (or reddish cinnamon). White band on throat. Scapulars black with chestnut, feathers edged whitish. Black flight feathers with white medial band. Outer tail feathers black, next pair inwards white. ♀: white outer tip of tail, buffy wing-band. Voice *coo wee ahh ooh*. Open areas and edge of forest, savannah, near marshes, open woods, arid regions, plantations, from sea level to mountains.

8 SEMI-COLLARED NIGHTHAWK *Lurocalis semitorquatus* 24cm
Swallow-like. Short square tail. Blackish. Tertials white, barred blackish. White triangle on throat. Lower underparts cinnamon-rufous, barred. Perches and nests in trees. Voice *whit…whoo it…chew it* in flight. Forests, woods, plantations, open areas with scrub. The Andean form is considered by some a separate species, Rufous-bellied Nighthawk *L. rufiventris*. Call a series of evenly pitched or descending *kwa*.

9 NACUNDA NIGHTHAWK *Podager nacunda* 30cm
Unmistakable. Big. Large rounded wings. Band at base of black primaries, triangle on throat, lower underparts and underwing white. ♀: lacks white tail-tips. Crepuscular, often also diurnal. Flies low in gentle wobbly flight. Savannah, open grass near woods or water.

7 rufous form

ODRÍGUEZ MATA

NIGHTHAWKS AND NIGHTJARS (CAPRIMULGIDAE)

1 BAHIAN NIGHTHAWK *Chordeiles vielliardi* 17cm
Tiny. Chestnut. Streaks, scaling and barring black and rufous. No white or black on wings. Calls a series of *wick-wicks*. Caatinga along rivers, near dunes and rocky outcrops. Discovered 1994. E Brazil in state of Bahía along San Francisco river (Januária and Mocambinho).

2 LEAST NIGHTHAWK *Chordeiles pusillus* 17cm
Tiny. Upperparts dark. White on throat. Secondaries blackish brown with buff following edge. From below, tip of central tail feathers white. White band on primaries. Underparts whitish buff barred black. Stuttering *k k k k kuree*. Edge of rainforest, savannah, open areas, cerrado, caatinga, rocky slopes.

3 SAND-COLOURED NIGHTHAWK *Chordeiles rupestris* 22cm
Pale sandy with darker spots, bars and streaks on breast and back. Underparts white. Tail tipped black. Outer primaries black, forming a contrasting triangle. Dunes, rocky outcrops, sandbanks and river banks in open rainforest and marshes, near towns.

4 COMMON NIGHTHAWK *Chordeiles minor* 23cm
Upperparts barred, spotted and streaked black, buff, greyish brown and cinnamon. White on throat. Underparts barred. Tail barely forked, tipped black with white subterminal band. White band near base of primaries. Perches on roofs or along cables and branches. High erratic fast flight, emitting *tsips*. Open areas, grassland with scattered trees, cultivated land, marshes, barren hillsides, open forest and woods, edge, dunes, beaches, urban areas, roadsides. Migratory from N America.

5 LESSER NIGHTHAWK *Chordeiles acutipennis* 20cm
Like 4 but smaller, white band at mid-primaries. Barred underparts buffy. Call is a trill. Open areas, desert, suburban areas, cultivated land, beaches, mangroves. Some are migratory from N America.

6 BAND-TAILED NIGHTHAWK *Nyctiprogne leucopyga* 20cm
Dark. No white on wing. White on throat split. Black tail with white bar midway. Voice a triple-note *gole kwok quack*. Perch in clusters on branches. Savannah, near watercourses, rainforest, gallery forest, deforested areas, edge.

7 OCELLATED POORWILL *Nyctiphrynus ocellatus* 20cm
Dumpy and large-headed. Blackish, finely barred chestnut. Narrow white collar on lower throat. White spots on wing coverts. Outer tail feathers narrowly tipped white. There is a rufous form. Voice repeated trill *preeeoh*. Clearings in humid lowland forest, open understorey. The race *N. o. rosenbergi* is, for some, a separate species: Choco Poorwill.

8 CHUCK-WILLS-WIDOW *Caprimulgus carolinensis* 29cm
Very like 9 and hard to separate in the field. Difference is in the tail: 3 outer pairs of tail feathers are white on inner web. ♀s are virtually identical. Scrub thickets, secondary growth, woods, forest, suburban areas, pastures.

9 RUFOUS NIGHTJAR *Caprimulgus rufus* 30cm
Tinged rufous cinnamon. Heavily dotted, barred, streaked black, buff and white. Cheek and throat barred. Buff half-collar. Flight feathers and tail barred. ♂: white on inner web of 3 outer pairs of tail feathers, cinnamon from below. ♀: tail all barred. Call 4-syllabled and insistent *chuck whipwhip wheeew*. Forest and edge, gallery forest, secondary growth, open woods, grass and scrub, savannah, suburbs.

10 SILKY-TAILED NIGHTJAR *Caprimulgus sericocaudatus* 29cm
Like 9 but browner. Blackish cheeks. Flight feathers dark and almost uniform. Tail blackish, irregularly barred dark brown. Outer 3 pairs with white tip, finely edged buff. ♀: tail all barred and paler. Voice 3-syllabled *do, wheeu-weeu*. Forest clearings, cane, secondary growth and edge.

RODRIGUEZ MATA

NIGHTJARS (CAPRIMULGIDAE)

1 BAND-WINGED NIGHTJAR *Caprimulgus longirostris* 20–27cm
S races: upperparts have very contrasting designs. Buff hind-collar. Upper
breast streaked white. Lower breast and flanks barred. Primaries have medial
white band. Tail: all but central pair broadly tipped white. Medial white band.
♀: tail all barred, wing-band buffy. *C. l. decussatus* (Peru and N Chile) paler
and smaller. *C. l. roraimae* from Tepuis (S Venezuela) much darker. Rufous
collar. Crown dotted rufous (may be a separate species). Call a thin *psee-wheet*.
Edge and clearings in forest and woods, scrub, steppe, to paramo.

2 WHITE-TAILED NIGHTJAR *Caprimulgus cayennensis* 22cm
Upperparts very mottled. Lores and throat white, framing dark triangle. Hind-
collar buffy cinnamon. All but central tail feathers black and white; white
from below with black medial band. Flight feathers with 3 white bands. ♀
more uniform. Underparts spotted and barred. No white on tail. Wing-band
cinnamon-buff. Grassland with scattered trees, edge of gallery forest, cloud-
forest and rainforest, arid scrub, towns.

3 WHITE-WINGED NIGHTJAR *Caprimulgus candicans* 21cm
Pale brownish grey. Dark face. Black and white streaks very contrasting. Lower
breast and rest of underparts white. Flight feathers white, primaries broadly
tipped black. Outer tail all white. ♀ lacks white. Wings and tail barred.
Grassland, scattered trees, bushes, palms and termite mounds, arid, open
savannah, wood edge, cerrado.

4 LITTLE NIGHTJAR *Caprimulgus parvulus* 20cm
White on throat. Narrow malar stripe. Nuchal collar buffy cinnamon. Outer
flight feathers with white band. Tail feathers tipped white except central pair.
♀: wing-band buffy, tail all barred. Call a warbled *chorreee, froo-froo-froo-froo*.
Open dry woods, savannah, scrubby hills, plantations, parks.

5 SCRUB NIGHTJAR *Caprimulgus anthonyi* 20cm
Differs from 4 only in outer 2 pairs of tail feathers having all-white inner web.
Wing-band longer and nearer base of feathers. ♀: tail with buffy white on
inner web of outer 2 pairs. Call *wheeeeoo*. Semiarid areas with scattered trees,
woods, deciduous forest.

6 CAYENNE NIGHTJAR *Caprimulgus maculosus* 23cm (not illustrated)
Known from only 1 specimen. Tamanoir waterfall, French Guiana.

7 SPOT-TAILED NIGHTJAR *Caprimulgus maculicaudus* 22cm
Blackish crown and face. Long buffy-white brow. Nuchal collar tawny. Spotted
breast. No white in wings. From above, all but central pair of tail feathers tipped
white with black subterminal band; from below 3 white spots along inner webs.
♀: tail all barred. Savannah, edge of forest and woods, secondary growth, slopes
of dry hills.

8 BLACKISH NIGHTJAR *Caprimulgus nigrescens* 21cm
Very dark. White on throat. Blackish flight feathers with short white bar on 2 to
4. Outer 3 pairs of tail feathers tipped white. ♀: no white on tail or wings. Call:
soft purring *crrrrrrrc*. Rocky outcrops along rivers, edge of rainforest, savannah.

9 RORAIMAN NIGHTJAR *Caprimulgus whitelyi* 22cm (not illustrated)
Very like 8. Upperparts darker with less contrasting pattern. ♀: narrow wing-bar
buffy. Tepuis; wet forest. SE Venezuela and possibly adjacent Brazil and Guyana.

10 PYGMY NIGHTJAR *Caprimulgus hirundinaceus* 15cm
Tiny. Pale with little contrast. White band on dark outer primaries. Tail has
white tips on inner web of outer 2 pairs. ♀: no white on tail and smaller or
absent wing-band. Open areas, woods, rocky areas.

1R

1♂

3♂

1R

1

1♂

2♂

2♂

2♀

2♂

4♂

4♂

5♂

4

♀

7♂

7

7♂

8♂

8♂

8

8♂

10♂

10♂

10

RODRIGUEZ MATA

NIGHTJARS (CAPRIMULGIDAE)

1 **LYRE-TAILED NIGHTJAR** *Uropsalis lyra* ♂ 90cm, ♀ 26cm
Unmistakable. Inordinately long 'lyre'-shaped tail, 3 times body length,
blackish tipped white. Overall dark, brownish black. Short buffy and
cinnamon bars on breast, spots and dots on upperparts. Crown streaked black.
Collar rufous and buffy. ♀: brownish black. Tail slightly forked, all barred buffy
brown and blackish. Several ♂s follow 1 ♀. Rainforest and cloud-forest in
mountains, edge and clearings, especially where there are banks, rocks and
caverns, open woods near water, alder woods, transition scrub.

2 **SWALLOW-TAILED NIGHTJAR** *Uropsalis segmentata* ♂ 67cm, ♀ 23cm
Like 1 but smaller and tail shorter (2× body length), browner, long feather tips
more slender, inner webs finely barred whitish. Crown blackish brown flecked
buff. ♀ like 1 but crown flecked. Bushy slopes, edge of woods, to tree line and
paramo, grassland with shrubs and canes, cloud-forest (higher than 1).

3 **LADDER-TAILED NIGHTJAR** *Hydropsalis climacocerca* ♂ 28cm, ♀ 24cm
Upperparts with contrasting designs, blackish, white and buff. Underparts,
underwing and tail mostly white. Outer primaries blackish with white band; rest
of flight feathers barred blackish and white. Tail forked, with central pair longer
than the rest, as long as outers when tail folded. Tail feathers white, tipped
greyish and basally barred blackish. ♀: all cinnamon-buff with varying markings
black and buff. Buffy-cinnamon wing-band. Tail all barred buffy cinnamon and
blackish, same shape as ♂'s. Gallery forest, rainforest, edge, rocky outcrops on
rivers, sandbanks, grassland with bushes, savannah, open woods.

4 **SCISSOR-TAILED NIGHTJAR**
Hydropsalis torquata (brasiliana) ♂ 60cm, ♀ 30cm
Tail long, deeply forked, 1.5 times body length. Nuchal collar rufous. Face pale.
Blackish triangle on lower cheek. Crown streaked black. Upperparts
contrastingly marked on coverts and scapulars, tips and edges buffy white
forming a line. Shoulder dark. Flight feathers blackish barred cinnamon-buff.
♀: shorter tail, forked, central feathers protruding slightly from 'V'. Call a
short *tsip, tsip tsip*. Edge and clearings in forest, woods, savannah, grassland
with scattered trees and bushes, near marshes, cerrado, plantations, parks.

5 **LONG-TRAINED NIGHTJAR**
Macropsalis creagra (forcipata) ♂ 80cm, ♀ 34cm
Like 4 but larger. Tail longer, 3 times body length. Inner vane broadly edged
white. Upperparts darker, less contrasted. Crown and upper back speckled buff.
Scapulars notably bordered buffy white. Whitish on breast. ♀: outer tail
feathers much shorter, barred. Tail forked, central pair not longer. Both sexes
call *tsip tsip tsip*. Forest and woods, edge and clearings, rolling and hilly country,
secondary growth, suburban areas.

6 **SICKLE-WINGED NIGHTJAR** *Eleothreptus anomalus* 19cm
Dumpy. Short tail and wings. Strange shape in flight: inner flight feathers
much shorter than outers. Overall pattern not markedly contrasting. Crown
and scapulars streaked black, these with buffy-white edges. Breast streaked
whitish. ♀: 'normal' wings, flight feathers barred blackish and buffy cinnamon.
Edge of gallery forest, woods, transition zones, low marshy grassland with trees
and shrubs, savannah with palms, marshes interspersed with woods.

RODRIGUEZ MATA

SWIFTS (APODIDAE)

1 WHITE-COLLARED SWIFT *Streptoprocne zonaris*   22cm
Large. Sooty black, white collar. Tail slightly forked. Juv: less or no collar.
Forest, savannah and open land, mountains, rock-faces of caves and waterfalls,
over cities.

2 BISCUTATE SWIFT *Streptoprocne biscutata*   21cm
Like 1 but collar interrupted on sides of neck. Square tail. Over all manner of
habitats, including urban areas.

3 CHESTNUT-COLLARED SWIFT *Streptoprocne (Cypseloides) rutila*   15cm
Sooty black with throat, neck and breast chestnut, chin dirty. Long square tail.
♀ and juv have less or no chestnut. Mountains, forest, grassland, towns.

4 TEPUI SWIFT *Streptoprocne (Cypseloides) phelpsi*   16.5cm
Like 3 but chin, throat, neck and breast orange-rufous. Long tail slightly forked.
♀ like ♂ but blackish brown among the rufous. Mountains near rock-faces and
waterfalls. S Venezuela and neighbouring mountains in Brazil, NW Guyana.

5 GREAT DUSKY SWIFT *Cypseloides senex*   18cm
Hefty. Sooty blackish brown, pale head. Notable black before eye. Square tail.
Juv: darker head. Rainforest, farmland, over cities, associated with waterfalls.

6 SOOTY SWIFT *Cypseloides fumigatus*   15cm
Sooty black, square tail with emerging barbs. Juv: belly feathers white-edged.
Over forest, cleared land, flooded land, hills, waterfalls. The race *C.f. rothschildi*
from NW Argentina and S Bolivia, considered by some a separate species,
(Rothschild's Swift), is lighter and browner, 'softer' tail lacks emergent barbs.

7 WHITE-CHINNED SWIFT *Cypseloides cryptus*   14cm
Smoky black, white chin hard to see or absent. Short square tail with emergent
barbs. Savannah, forest, mountains, lowlands.

8 SPOT-FRONTED SWIFT *Cypseloides cherriei*   14cm
Dots at base of bill and behind the eye white, smaller in ♀. Belly faintly
spotted paler. Juv with clearer belly spotting. Rest smoky blackish. Tail short
and square, shafts emergent. Always in forested mountains with deep valleys.

9 BLACK SWIFT *Cypseloides niger*   15cm
Sooty black. Lores and brow whitish, tail slightly forked. Mountains.
Occasional as northern migrant.

10 WHITE-CHESTED SWIFT *Cypseloides lemosi*   15cm
Sooty black with white patch on breast. Tail slightly forked. Juv with less or no
white. Upland and mountain grasslands and eroded foothills. Upper Cauca
valley, SW Colombia, NC Colombia, NW Peru.

11 FORK-TAILED PALM-SWIFT *Tachornis (Reinarda) squamata*   14cm
Small. Slender, long deeply forked tail. Smoky blackish. Underparts whitish
with variable dirty markings except on belly. Flanks and undertail coverts
scaled white. In mixed flocks, with certain swallows, occupying lower deck.
Uses nest as roost year-round. Open ground, forest, marshes, savannah, palm
groves and urban areas.

12 PYGMY SWIFT *Tachornis (Micropanyptila) furcata*   10cm
Miniature 11. Upper tail has white base. Dirty white only on throat and mid-
belly. Very fast wing-beats. Uses nests as roost year-round. Forest, open land,
cleared areas, scattered trees, palm groves where it nests.

RIGUEZ MATA

SWIFTS (APODIDAE)

1 ASHY-TAILED SWIFT *Chaetura andrei*   13.5cm
Short square tail, short barbs protruding. Upperparts dark smoky brown. Contrasting rump and tail coverts pale smoky grey. Throat dirty whitish, rest of underparts smoky brown. Over woods and cloud-forest in mountains, near cliffs and steep rocky slopes. Lowlands over forest, secondary growth, open areas. The southern race (*C. a. meridionalis*) is considered by some a separate species: Sick's Swift; some regard *C. andrei* as a race of 6.

2 CHIMNEY SWIFT *Chaetura pelagica*   13.5cm
Short square tail, longish barbs protruding. Upperparts dark smoky brown, rump and tail coverts slightly paler. Throat whitish. Underparts greyish brown, noticeably paler than above. Over woods, open country, towns, suburban areas, farmland, secondary growth, tropical forest, mountains, coastal areas. Migrates from N America.

3 CHAPMAN'S SWIFT *Chaetura chapmani*   13.5cm
Short square tail with protruding barbs. Mostly uniform dark smoky brown. Throat barely paler. Tail coverts and rump slightly paler and greyer. Over wooded hills and plains with trees, tropical forest, secondary forest, swamps, mangroves, coastal areas. Th race *C. c. viridipennis*, for some, a separate species: Amazonian Swift.

4 GREY-RUMPED SWIFT *Chaetura cinereiventris*   10.5cm
Small. Short square tail, long barbs protruding. Upperparts lustrous black but rump and tail coverts contrasting pale grey. Throat and breast whitish grey. Belly pale grey contrasting with blackish underwing and undertail coverts. Over forested broken terrain near cliffs and steep banks, wooded hills, tropical forest and secondary growth from plains to mountains.

5 PALE-RUMPED SWIFT *Chaetura egregia*   10.5cm
Like 4 but rump and tail coverts white, belly and flanks greyish brown. Over tropical lowland forest, hills and mountains, open areas. Sometimes considered conspecific with 4.

6 VAUX'S SWIFT *Chaetura vauxi*   11cm
Small. Short square tail with long barbs. Upperparts smoky black contrasting with pale greyish-brown rump and tail coverts. Throat dirty whitish. Rest of underparts greyish brown. Rainforests from plains to montane cloud-forest. Northern Venezuela.

7 BAND-RUMPED SWIFT *Chaetura spinicauda*   10.5cm
Differs from 5 and 6 in having a white band across lower back; rump, upper tail coverts and tail smoky black; underparts all darker. Lowland and montane forest, secondary growth, cleared areas, open habitats.

8 SHORT-TAILED SWIFT *Chaetura brachyura*   10cm
Short but hefty. Very short square tail with protruding barbs. Black with lower body and tail pale brownish grey. Secondary flight feathers form an aileron next to the body. Over forest and partially open areas in lowlands and mountains, grassland, semiarid areas, coastal areas, beaches and mangroves.

9 LESSER SWALLOW-TAILED SWIFT *Panyptila cayennensis*   13cm
Long tail forked, feathers pointed. Blackish. Bib, nuchal collar, patch on lower flank and base of outer tail feathers white. Over forest, cleared areas, open fields in plains and mountains, slopes and foothills.

10 WHITE-TIPPED SWIFT *Aeronautes montivagus*   12.5cm
Blackish. White bib extends in a line down mid-breast to belly. White patch on lower belly and part of flanks. Montane forest, semi-open areas, secondary growth and cleared areas, slopes, deep gorges and valleys. Occasionally in lowlands.

11 ANDEAN SWIFT *Aeronautes andecolus*   14.5cm
Fast and rowdy. Long forked tail. Upperparts dark greyish brown. Collar, rump and underparts whitish, contrasting with greyish-brown underwing, tail and vent. Rocky and arid mountains, scrub with bushes, open woods, cactus-studded slopes.

RODRIGUEZ MATA

HUMMINGBIRDS (TROCHILIDAE)

1 **BLUE-FRONTED LANCEBILL** *Doryfera johannae* 10.5cm
Long, slender black bill slightly upturned. Forehead shiny violaceous blue. Nape coppery. Rest of upperparts greenish. Rounded tail bluish black. Underparts greenish black. ♀: paler below, tail finely tipped greyish white. Edge of tropical and subtropical forest on lower slopes and ravines, adjacent lowlands.

2 **GREEN-FRONTED LANCEBILL** *Doryfera ludovicae* 12cm
Long, slender black bill slightly upturned. Forehead shiny green. Crown to hind-neck coppery. Tail coverts blackish and bluish. Rounded tail bluish black, tip grey. Cloud-forest with epiphytes in mountain terrain, low and on edges.

3 **TOOTH-BILLED HUMMINGBIRD** *Androdon aequatorialis* 13.5cm
Very long upturned black bill with yellow mandible, some with hook at tip. Crown and rump coppery. Tail coverts white and blackish. Rounded tail grey, tip white. Underparts whitish streaked blackish. Wet forest in lowlands and base of hills, low and at edge.

4 **SAW-BILLED HERMIT** *Ramphodon maevius* 15cm
Hefty. Black and yellow down-curved bill. Upperparts coppery brown. Rounded tail with cinnamon outer feathers. Bib tawny with black streaking on chin. Rest of underparts whitish streaked blackish. Low in humid and shady forest with bromeliads.

5 **HOOK-BILLED HERMIT** *Glaucis (Ramphodon) dohrnii* 12.5cm
Curved bill black, mandible yellow. Upperparts bronzy green. Tail rounded, tips white. Post-ocular brow and malar streak white. Underparts tawny. Low in lowland primary forest with *Heliconia*.

6 **RUFOUS-BREASTED HERMIT** *Glaucis hirsutus* 13cm
Curved bill black, mandible yellow. Upperparts bronzy green. Central tail feathers as back, rest rufous with black subterminal band and white tip. Slight pale malar stripe. Throat and breast cinnamon, lower underparts dirty whitish. Forest, woods, thickets, swamps, grassland, copses.

7 **BRONZY HERMIT** *Glaucis aeneus* 9.5cm
Small. Curved bill black, mandible yellow. Upperparts dark coppery with green sheen. Post-ocular and malar stripes whitish. Tail somewhat rounded, basally rufous, then black, tip white. Underparts tawny rufous. Low in modified forest, edge, thickets, swamps, near streams, coastal areas.

8 **BAND-TAILED BARBTHROAT** *Threnetes ruckeri* 11cm
Curved bill black, mandible yellow. Upperparts dark bronzy green. Ear coverts blackish brown bordered by whitish-cinnamon post-ocular and malar streaks. Throat browny grey. Fore-neck cinnamon. Rest of underparts greyish. Outer tail feathers bluish black with white base and tips. Low in disturbed forest, thickets, edge, plantations.

9 **PALE-TAILED BARBTHROAT** *Threnetes leucurus* 11cm
Curved bill black, mandible yellow. Upperparts dark bronzy green. Post-ocular and malar stripes whitish cinnamon. Throat cinnamon, chin blackish. Breast greenish black. Rest of underparts buffy green grading paler. Central tail feathers as back, outers white, buffy or blackish (*T. loehkeni*). Wet forest, scrub and thickets, plantations, regrowth, near rivers. Some think these are races of 10.

10 **SOOTY BARBTHROAT** *Threnetes niger* 11cm
Curved bill black, mandible yellow. All blackish with bronzy-olive sheen. Tropical forest.

RODRIGUEZ MATA

HUMMINGBIRDS (TROCHILIDAE)

1 SOOTY-CAPPED HERMIT *Phaethornis augusti*   14cm
Crown and mask blackish grey. Throat finely flecked blackish grey. Rump and
tail coverts rufous. Central tail feathers coppery green, outers black, tips white.
Underparts whitish grey. Montane and cloud-forest, thickets in mountains,
edges, plantations, secondary growth, parks and gardens.

2 PALE-BELLIED HERMIT *Phaethornis anthophilus*   13cm
Crown and mask blackish grey. Throat scaled blackish grey. Upperparts bronzy
green, rump and tail coverts edged ochreous. All tail feathers greenish black,
tipped white. Underparts whitish grey. Semi-deciduous forest, dry woods,
thickets, edge, gallery forest, plantations.

3 GREAT-BILLED HERMIT *Phaethornis malaris*   16cm
Dark. Crown and mask blackish brown. Very long bill. Throat blackish.
Upperparts blackish green with bronzy sheen, feathers edged dirty buff. Outer
tail feathers tipped buff. Underparts dirty buffy grey. Wet and upland forest,
edge, cane-brakes, thickets and shrubs.

4 LONG-TAILED HERMIT *Phaethornis superciliosus*   14cm
A smaller version of 3 with shorter tail and whitish-tipped outer tail feathers.
Slightly buffier underparts. Throat buff and blackish. The W population is
considered by some a separate species, Western Long-tailed Hermit *P. longirostris*.

5 WHITE-BEARDED HERMIT *Phaethornis hispidus*   15cm
Mostly grey, darker on head and tail. Sub-malar stripe dark grey scaled whitish.
Central throat white. Upper tail coverts and lower underparts paler. Undertail
coverts grey, edged white. Wet, flooded and gallery forest, woods and
plantations, edge, thickets and scrub.

6 STRAIGHT-BILLED HERMIT *Phaethornis bourcieri*   14cm
Bill almost straight. Less contrast on face. Upperparts blackish grey. Upper tail
coverts barred buff. Underparts brownish grey, more whitish centrally.
Undertail whitish. Thickets, lowland forest, varzea forest, secondary growth,
plantations.

7 PLANALTO HERMIT *Phaethornis pretrei*   14cm
Underparts rich cinnamon. Upper tail coverts cinnamon-rufous. Throat buffy
between brownish-grey sub-malar streaks. Outer tail feathers tipped white.
Gallery forest, dry forest, secondary growth, thickets, edge, parks, gardens.

8 TAWNY-BELLIED HERMIT *Phaethornis syrmatophorus*   14cm
Lower back and rump feathers edged tawny. Upper tail coverts rich tawny.
Throat white between brownish-grey sub-malar stripes. Underparts tawny,
centrally paler. Outer tail feathers tipped tawny buff. Montane forest, cloud-
forest, thickets and edge.

9 NEEDLE-BILLED HERMIT *Phaethornis philippii*   13.5cm
Bill only slightly curved. Small mask, no malar stripe. Lower back and rump
scaled tawny buff and dark greenish. Upper tail coverts cinnamon. Outer tail
feathers tipped tawny buff. All underparts tawny buff. Lowland rainforest,
varzea, thickets, plantations. Some consider Koepcke's Hermit *P. koepckeae*
(an upland form with a dark brown sub-malar stripe) a valid species.

10 SCALE-THROATED HERMIT *Phaethornis eurynome*   14cm
Post-ocular brow tawny buff. Rump and upper tail coverts blackish green edged
coppery. Throat blackish, scaled white. Sides of body greyish, belly and
undertail buffy. Tail feathers dark green and black with white tips. Low in
forest, thickets, edge, regrowth.

RODRIGUEZ MATA

HUMMINGBIRDS (TROCHILIDAE)

1 GREEN HERMIT *Phaethornis guy* 14cm
Dark green. Underparts grey, centre of belly ochreous. Throat tawny. Tail blackish blue. Humid montane forest, thickets, clearings, edge, woods, plantations.

2 WHITE-WHISKERED HERMIT *Phaethornis yaruqui* 14cm
Like 1, but dark green underparts, whitish chin. Humid montane forest, thickets, secondary growth, plantations.

3 BROAD-TIPPED HERMIT *Anopetia (Phaethornis) gounellei* 10cm
Sides of the nape rusty. Chin blackish, throat rusty. All tail coverts tawny buff. Tail black with white tips, lacks long pointed central feathers. Thickets and damper areas in caatinga and cerrado.

4 BUFF-BELLIED HERMIT *Phaethornis subochraceus* 11cm
Dull. Upperparts dull bronzy green, rump and tail coverts edged cinnamon. Chin slightly flecked blackish. Underparts dirty buffy white. Dry forest in undergrowth, secondary growth, open woods.

5 STREAK-THROATED HERMIT *Phaethornis rupurumii* 11cm
Very like 4 but throat blackish scaled grey; upper tail coverts cinnamon. Low at rainforest edge, dryer or gallery forest, savannah, thickets, secondary growth, scrub.

6 DUSKY-THROATED HERMIT *Phaethornis squalidus* 11cm
Like 5 but underparts browner. Chin and throat all dark brown. Low in forest, thickets, open cleared areas.

7 WHITE-BROWED HERMIT *Phaethornis stuarti* 9cm
Differs from 8 in that topside of tail is bronzy olive and brownish, smaller black spot on breast, sometimes absent. Transition between varzea and terra firme forest, savannah, hills, thickets and secondary growth. Some believe this to be a race of 8. SE Peru to C Bolivia.

8 REDDISH HERMIT *Phaethornis ruber* 7.5–9cm
Variable. Underparts and upper tail coverts rufous. Black spot on breast (some ♀s lack this). Upperparts coppery olive. Tail feathers coppery brown with browny-buff tip, white in one race. Smallest form (illustrated here as 8R) has dark green upperparts, band on breast, and coppery-blackish tail with hardly any pale tips. Forest, copses, edge, transition, woods, thickets, savannah, regrowth, parks and gardens. The Black-throated Hermit *P. atrimentalis* differs only in having a dark brown throat and whitish vent. It may be a race of 8.

9 GREY-CHINNED HERMIT *Phaethornis griseogularis* 9cm
Upperparts light coppery green. Black tail with white tip. Underparts all buffy. An E form is like 8 but lacks spot on breast, tail feathers black. Rainforest and cloud-forest, edge, clearings. The very similar NW population (Stripe-throated Hermit *P. g. striigularis*) is considered by some to be a separate species.

10 MINUTE HERMIT *Phaethornis idaliae* 8cm
Small. ♂ dark. Throat blackish grading to chestnut on fore-neck and upper breast. Rest of underparts grey. Vent white. ♀: in upperparts coppery olive, upper tail coverts and underparts rufous, throat brownish. Forest, thickets in craggy terrain in hills, edge, patches of forest. Bahía to Rio de Janeiro, Brazil.

11 LITTLE HERMIT *Phaethornis longuemareus* 9cm
Black chin with faint streaking. Underparts buffy cinnamon, vent whiter. Tail shortish and broad, tipped whitish. Low in open forest, swamps, cleared areas, thickets and plantations.

12 CINNAMON-THROATED HERMIT *Phaethornis nattereri* 9.5cm
Upperparts light bronzy olive. Upper tail coverts, hind-neck and tips of outer tail feathers buffy rufous. Underparts all buffy. Lowland thickets, secondary growth, edge, copses and gallery forest. *P. n. maranhaoensis* is at present considered the adult ♂ of this species

RODRIGUEZ MATA

HUMMINGBIRDS (TROCHILIDAE)

 1 WHITE-TIPPED SICKLEBILL *Eutoxeres aquila* 12cm
Unmistakable bill. Tail feathers greyish brown with white tip. Underparts streaked. Mountainous areas, dense thickets, wet forest, edge, near *Heliconia*.

 2 BUFF-TAILED SICKLEBILL *Eutoxeres condamini* 14cm
Unmistakable bill. Central tail feathers blackish with white tip, outers cinnamon buff. Throat blackish, underparts streaked. Humid montane forest, ravines, open areas, shady cane-brakes, cultivated areas and plantations.

 3 RUFOUS-BREASTED SABREWING *Campylopterus hyperythrus* 11cm
Dorsally bronzy green, underparts and outer tail feathers cinnamon-rufous. Montane and cloud-forest, scrub on Tepuis.

 4 BUFF-BREASTED SABREWING *Campylopterus duidae* 11.5cm
Upperparts bronzy green. Central tail feathers coppery, outers basally blackish coppery, distal half buff. Underparts dirty buffy grey. Montane forest, Tepuis, thickets.

 5 GREY-BREASTED SABREWING *Campylopterus largipennis* 14cm
Upperparts shiny metallic green. Central tail feathers dark green, outer tail feathers blackish blue, greyish-white tip. Underparts grey, vent white. Humid forest, secondary growth, woods, plantations, thickets.

 6 LAZULINE SABREWING *Campylopterus falcatus* 12cm
Dark green with large violaceous blue bib. Tail and undertail coverts rufous chestnut. ♀: throat blue. Underparts pale greyish. Tail paler than ♂'s. Montane forest, cloud-forest to near paramo, plantations, gardens.

 7 SANTA MARTA SABREWING *Campylopterus phainopeplus* 13cm
Shiny green, bib shiny dark blue. Tail blackish blue. ♀: whitish grey below; green flanks and vent. Whitish-grey tip to outer tail feathers. Low in humid montane forest, edge, plantations. Endemic to Santa Marta mountains, N Colombia.

 8 WHITE-TAILED SABREWING *Campylopterus ensipennis* 13cm
Bright green, bib shiny dark blue. Outer tail feathers white, black at the base. ♀: blue throat, central underparts greyish white with green spots. Montane cloud-forest, clearings, edge, plantations. NE Venezuela – Caripe and Paria peninsula mountains.

 9 NAPO SABREWING *Campylopterus villaviscensio* 13cm
Dark shiny green, bib dark blue. Tail dark violaceous blue. ♀: grey underparts, narrow white tip to tail. Cloud-forest.

 10 SWALLOW-TAILED HUMMINGBIRD
Eupetomena (Campylopterus) macroura 20cm
Shiny violaceous-blue hood. Long forked tail and undertail coverts dark blue. Open savannah, gardens, secondary growth, plantations, forest, edge.

 11 SCALY-BREASTED HUMMINGBIRD
Campylopterus (Phaeochroa) cuvierii 12cm
Bronzy green, belly cinnamon scaled green. Tail bright green, outer feathers with large white spot at tip. Thickets, scrub, edge, woods, gardens. Coastal N Colombia.

 12 WHITE-NECKED JACOBIN *Florisuga mellivora* 11cm
Head and breast shiny dark blue. White spot on back. Belly, vent and outer tail feathers white, the latter edged blackish. ♀ bronzy green. Bib and undertail coverts dark green, scaled white. Forest, gallery forest, woods, secondary growth, plantations, gardens.

RODRIGUEZ MATA

HUMMINGBIRDS (TROCHILIDAE)

1 GREEN VIOLETEAR *Colibri thalassinus* 11cm
Shiny dark green. Dark blue ear-patch. Blackish-blue subterminal band on tail.
Edge of cloud-forest, scrubby slopes, thickets, scattered trees in upland
pastures, plantations, gardens.

2 SPARKLING VIOLETEAR *Colibri coruscans* 14cm
Shiny dark green. Throat dark blue. Violaceous-blue ear-patch and upper belly.
Large undertail coverts whitish. Blackish-blue subterminal band on tail.
Cloud-forest edge, open woods, scrubby upland valleys, gardens, paramo.

3 WHITE-VENTED VIOLETEAR *Colibri serrirostris* 13cm
Shiny green. Purply-violet ear-patch. Lower belly and undertail coverts white.
Blackish-blue subterminal band on tail. Mountain scrub, open forest, woods,
thickets, savannah, grassland.

4 BROWN VIOLETEAR *Colibri delphinae* 11.5cm
Greyish brown, paler below. Violet-blue ear-patch. Feathers on lower back and
rump bordered buffy rufous. Throat scaled green and blackish. Hills and low
mountain slopes, lowlands. Arid scrub, secondary growth, clearings, edge and
canopy of forest, plantations.

5 PLOVERCREST *Stephanoxis lalandi* 8.5cm
Unmistakable. Long straight crest. Large dark blue or black area on underparts.
♀ lacks crest; underparts all grey. Mountains and lowlands; forest, thickets,
scrub and along watercourses.

6 BLACK JACOBIN *Florisuga (Melanotrochilus) fusca* 13cm
Unmistakable. Black with lower flanks and tail white. Juv has wide chestnut
malar area. Woods, gardens, open areas with scattered trees, secondary growth,
plantations, forest edge.

7 RUBY TOPAZ *Chrysolampis mosquitus* 8cm
Unmistakable. Blackish brown. Shiny ruby crown. Golden bib. Undertail
coverts and tail chestnutty rufous. ♀: coppery crown, upperparts bronzy green,
underparts grey. Tail orange-rufous and black, tip white. Gallery forest, woods,
gardens, parks, scrub, savannah, mangroves, open country.

8 FIERY-TAILED AWLBILL *Anthracothorax (Avocettula) recurvirostris* 8cm
Bill upturned at tip. Shiny dark green. Black band on belly. Tail reddish
chestnut. ♀: white from chin to upper belly, with wide central black streak.
Blue-black tail, outer feathers tipped white. Forest, thickets, scrub, savannah,
edge of secondary vegetation, near rivers.

9 BLACK-THROATED MANGO *Anthracothorax nigricollis* 12cm
Shiny dark green. Huge black area from throat to belly. Undertail coverts
blackish. Outer tail feathers purply violet. ♀: white below with wide black central
streak. Outer tail purply violet and black, tip white. Rainforest, secondary growth,
clearings, shrubby areas, thickets, gallery forest, plantations, parks, gardens.

10 GREEN-BREASTED MANGO *Anthracothorax prevostii* 12cm
Differs from 9 in having a small black area from throat to breast, bordered
bluish green. ♀: virtually identical to that of 9 but has some green and blue in
central underparts' streak. Base of outer tail feathers darker, more white at tip.
Forest, edge, open woods, scrub and thickets, grassland with scattered trees,
parks, gardens, mangroves. Coastal N Venezuela, Colombia (Guajira peninsula
and Upper Cauca valley), extreme SW Ecuador and NW Peru.

11 GREEN-THROATED MANGO *Anthracothorax viridigula* 12cm
Differs from 9 and 10 in having green throat. ♀ virtually identical to that of 9.
Thickets, shrubs, open woods, mangroves, coastal regions, marshy savannah,
swampy places, open areas with scattered trees.

RODRIGUEZ MATA

HUMMINGBIRDS (TROCHILIDAE)

1 SPANGLED COQUETTE *Lophornis stictolophus* 6.5cm
Remarkable rufous crest, feathers with black tips. Bib emerald. ♀: rufous forehead; whitish bib with rufous spotting; double pectoral collar green. Forest, clearings, thickets, scrubby areas, edge of woods, in hills.

2 RUFOUS-CRESTED COQUETTE *Lophornis delattrei* 6.5cm
Rufous crest of long, slender feathers with black tips. Coppery ear-coverts and sides of neck. Bib coppery emerald. Another race has more slender tawny crest without black tips and emerald bib. ♀ virtually the same as that of 1 but more cinnamon below and less marked pectoral collars. Scrub, edge of woods and humid forest, clearings.

3 TUFTED COQUETTE *Lophornis ornatus* 6.5cm
Rufous crest of slender feathers. Tuft of very long cinnamon-rufous feathers with round, blackish-green tips forms a fan from cheeks. ♀: forehead and crown bronzy green. Underparts cinnamon, greenish on lower flanks and belly. Gallery forest, rainforest, savannah, scrub, thickets, plantations and cultivated land, near water.

4 DOT-EARED COQUETTE *Lophornis gouldii* 6.5cm
Fan of long white feathers with greenish-black tips from cheek. ♀ undistinguishable from that of 3. Edge of forest, scrub and thickets, savannah, cerrado.

5 FRILLED COQUETTE *Lophornis magnificus* 6.5cm
Fan of large white feathers edged black, like scales, from cheek. ♀: rufous forehead, white bib with greenish spotting and rufous edge. White pectoral collar. Rest of underparts dirty bronzy green. Edge of humid forest, scrub, secondary growth, cerrado, regrowth, smallholdings, gardens, plantations.

6 FESTIVE COQUETTE *Lophornis chalybeus* 7cm
Big green fan covers cheek and neck, narrow feathers tipped white. Centre of dirty white breast streaked black. NW race has elongated crown feathers forming a crest. Underparts blacker. ♀: underparts dirty greyish, faintly barred blackish. Blackish chest-spot. White malar streak. Forest and edge, secondary growth, thickets, cerrado, grassland with bushes.

7 PEACOCK COQUETTE *Lophornis pavoninus* 8.5cm
Fan from cheek, broad green feathers with black spots at the tip. Underparts and upper tail coverts dark green. ♀: throat, cheek and underparts streaked black and white. Montane forest, cloud-forest and rainforest, edge, bushes, thickets.

8 GREEN THORN-TAIL *Discosura (Popelairia) conversii* ♂ 12cm, ♀ 8cm
All green with bluish wash. Long blue tail of pointed feathers. ♀: short, white-tipped tail, malar area and sides of belly. Humid forest, edge, woods, clearings.

9 BLACK-BELLIED THORNTAIL
Discosura (Popelairia) langsdorffi ♂ 12cm, ♀ 8cm
Emerald bib bordered orange below. Black breast, white on sides of belly. ♀ as that of 10. Rainforest, scrubby areas, gallery forest, montane and lowland forest edge.

10 WIRE-CRESTED THORNTAIL
Discosura (Popelairia) popelairii ♂ 12cm, ♀ 8cm
Very long slender crest. Black breast. ♀ lacks crest. White malar area, white on sides of belly. Blackish breast-patch. Short, white-tipped tail. Humid forest, edge, thickets, bushy areas, groves at foot of hills.

11 COPPERY THORNTAIL *Discosura (Popelairia) letitiae* ♂ 12cm, ♀ 8cm
Like 9. Coppery green. Shiny golden-emerald forehead and bib with golden border below. ♀ unknown. Probably rainforest along rivers. Lowlands in NE Bolivia.

1♂   5♀   5♂

1♀

3♀   3♂

2R

2♂   7♀

6R   6♀   10♂

8♂   9♂

8♀   10♀

RODRIGUEZ MATA

HUMMINGBIRDS (TROCHILIDAE)

1 RACQUET-TAILED COQUETTE *Discosura longicaudus* ♂ 10cm, ♀ 7.5cm
Long tail with 'racquets' on outer feathers. ♀: tail lacks 'racquets' and is grey and purply brown with white tips on outer feathers. Buff band across rump. Black throat bordered white. Fields with scattered trees, gallery forest, scrubby savannah, plantations.

2 VIOLET-HEADED HUMMINGBIRD *Klais guimeti*   8.5cm
Forehead, crown and bib violaceous blue. Lower underparts whitish grey. Tail bronzy green with blackish subterminal band and white tip. ♀: forehead and crown bluish. Throat and lower underparts whitish grey. Ill-defined pectoral collar green. Humid forest on mountain slopes, woods, edge, thickets, shrub, clearings.

3 BLUE-CHINNED SAPPHIRE *Chlorostilbon notatus*   9cm
Black bill with red at base of mandible. Dark shiny green, blue wash on throat. Square blue tail. ♀: dorsally paler and bronzy. Underparts greyish white heavily spotted green on breast, finer on throat. Tail dark blue, no white tip. Gallery forest, rainforest, edge, woods, bushy areas, savannah, plantations, fields, gardens.

4 GLITTERING-BELLIED EMERALD *Chlorostilbon aureoventris*   9cm
Red bill, tip black. Shiny dark green, bib washed blue. Dark blue tail, slightly forked. ♀: base of bill pale pinkish. Dorsally paler and bronzy. Underparts greyish white. Tail dark blue, white tips to outer feathers. Woods, edge of forest, isolated trees, savannah, secondary growth, thickets and scrubby areas, plantations, parks, gardens.

5 RED-BILLED EMERALD *Chlorostilbon gibsoni*   8cm
Differs from 6 in having red on mandible. Longish, more forked tail. ♀: pinkish mandible. White post-ocular streak. Dark brown ear-patch. Dorsally paler and bronzy. Underparts greyish white. Tail dark blue with white tips to outer feathers, slightly forked. Thorny woods and thickets, deciduous forest, rainforest, plantation, hill vegetation. Some believe this to be a race of 6.

6 BLUE-TAILED EMERALD *Chlorostilbon mellisugus*   7.5cm
Shiny dark green. Tail square and dark blue. Bill black. ♀: like that of 5 but bill black, tail square. Gallery and deciduous forest, rainforest, savannah, thorny scrub, plantations, parks, gardens. The race *C. m. olivaresi* is considered by some a valid species: Chiribiquete Emerald.

7 GREEN-TAILED EMERALD *Chlorostilbon alice*   7.5cm
Very like 6 but square tail green. The bill is the most slender and shortest of the genus. ♀ very like those of 8 and 9. Rainforest, cloud-forest, edge, secondary growth, plantations, open areas.

8 SHORT-TAILED EMERALD *Chlorostilbon poortmani*   7.5cm
Identical to 7 but green tail slightly forked. Bill longer and heavier. ♀ same as that of 9. Humid forest, edge, open woods, secondary growth, plantations.

9 NARROW-TAILED EMERALD *Chlorostilbon stenurus*   7.5cm
Like 7 but slightly forked green tail, feathers narrow and pointed. ♀: upperparts paler and bronzy, ear-coverts brownish. Underparts greyish white. Tail feathers unlike ♂'s in shape, dark greenish blue with white tip. Thickets and cloud-forest in high mountains, secondary growth.

10 COPPERY EMERALD *Chlorostilbon russatus*   7.5cm
Nape and upperparts coppery with golden and green sheen. Tail coppery rufous. ♀: brown cap and ear-patch. Underparts extensively greyish white. Tail has dark subterminal band and white tip. Montane forest and edge, scrub, rainforest, plantations.

RODRIGUEZ MATA

HUMMINGBIRDS (TROCHILIDAE)

1 VIOLET-BELLIED HUMMINGBIRD *Damophila julie* 8.5cm
Head and back emerald. Rump bronzy. Breast and belly violaceous blue. ♀:
underparts greyish white spotted green, insinuating a breast-band. Humid
forest, edge, thickets and scrub, lowlands and foothills.

2 FORK-TAILED WOODNYMPH *Thalurania furcata* ♂ 10.5cm, ♀ 8.5cm
Upperparts dark bronzy green. Blacker on cap. Bib brilliant green. Underparts
purply blue. Heavy forked tail blackish blue. A purple-crowned form (*T. f.
colombica*) and a green-crowned form (*T. f. fannyi*) may be a valid species,
named accordingly. ♀: underparts greyish white. Coppery bronze on crown.
Thickets, cloud-forest, rainforest, woods, open areas with trees, lowlands and
mountains, plantations, parks, gardens.

3 VIOLET-CAPPED WOODNYMPH *Thalurania glaucopis* ♂ 11cm, ♀ 8.5cm
Green. Forehead and crown dark purply blue. Blackish-blue tail, longish and
forked. ♀ as that of 2 but green crown. Forest, edge and clearings, bushes and
thickets, secondary growth, parks, gardens.

4 LONG-TAILED WOODNYMPH *Thalurania watertonii* ♂ 13cm, ♀ 10cm
Green. Back dark blue. Undertail coverts and long forked tail blackish blue. ♀:
like that of 3 but tail longer, tail feathers narrower. Thickets, shrubs and copses
on plains, coastal rainforest, cerrado, plantations, parks, gardens.

5 SHINING-GREEN HUMMINGBIRD *Lepidopyga goudoti* 9.5cm
Green. Mandible red. Tail dark blue and forked. Undertail feathers edged white.
♀: belly slightly marked white. Arid scrub, scattered trees, open woods,
deciduous forest, edge of gallery forest, plantations, gardens. Plains to mountains.

6 SAPPHIRE-THROATED HUMMINGBIRD
Lepidopyga coeruleogularis 9.5cm
Green. Violaceous-blue bib. Blackish-blue tail somewhat forked. ♀:
underparts whitish marked with green. Tail tipped white. Edge of mangroves,
arid scrub and woods, near sea level.

7 SAPPHIRE-BELLIED HUMMINGBIRD
Lepidopyga lilliae 9.5cm (not illustrated)
Like 6 but underparts shiny blue, throat more purply. Tail forked, blackish
blue. ♀ unknown. Mangroves, thorny scrub. Very restricted area in N
Colombia. Endangered.

8 BLUE-HEADED SAPPHIRE *Hylocharis grayi* 9cm
Red bill. Bronzy green. Blue head. Blue tail slightly forked. ♀: underparts white
spotted blue on throat, green on rest of underparts. Humid woods and forest,
mangroves, edge, arid bush, open woods, cultivated land, sea level to hills.

9 RUFOUS-THROATED SAPPHIRE *Hylocharis sapphirina* 9cm
Rufous throat, blue bib. Tail rufous chestnut. ♀: pale rufous throat. Rest of
underparts whitish spotted blue on fore-neck. Forest, edge, regrowth,
savannah, brushland, woods, scattered trees, cleared land, sea level to hills.

10 WHITE-CHINNED SAPPHIRE *Hylocharis cyanus* 9cm
Red bill. Violet-blue head and bib. White spot on chin. Upper tail coverts
coppery chestnut. Square tail dark blue. ♀: blue-spotted throat. Upper tail coverts
coppery chestnut. Woods, forest, regrowth, edge, scrub, thickets, plantations.

11 GILDED HUMMINGBIRD *Hylocharis chrysura* 9cm
Red bill. All golden bronze with green sheen. ♀ slightly greener. Gallery forest,
woods, arid bush, secondary growth, thickets, edge, savannah, parks, gardens.

12 BLUE-THROATED GOLDENTAIL *Hylocharis eliciae* 9cm (not illustrated)
Like 10, but only bib blue, tail bronzy green, belly and undertail coverts buff. ♀:
underparts whitish. Throat dotted blue and breast spotted green. Tail bronzy
green. Only NW Colombia bordering Panama.

1♂ 1♀ 2♀ 3♀ 3♂ 5 4♂ 11 6 8♂ 8♀ 9♂ 9♀ 10♂ 10♀

RODRIGUEZ MATA

HUMMINGBIRDS (TROCHILIDAE)

1 VIOLET-CAPPED HUMMINGBIRD *Goldmania violiceps* 9.5cm
Forehead and crown violaceous blue. Crimson-chestnut tail broadly tipped olive-brown. ♀: forehead and crown green. Underparts whitish spotted green. Tail like ♂'s. Humid forest, edge, foot of the hills. Extreme NW Colombia bordering Panama.

2 PIRRE HUMMINGBIRD *Goethalsia bella* 8.5cm
Chin and lores rufous. Cinnamon patch on wing. Short tail buffy cinnamon and black. Undertail coverts buffy white. ♀: underparts all buffy cinnamon, whiter on breast. Humid forest, edge, foothills to mountains (Mount Pirre in NW Colombia bordering Panama).

3 TEPUI GOLDENTHROAT *Polytmus milleri* 12cm
Upperparts coppery, stronger on cap. Rounded tail, outer feathers green, white band at base and white tips. Throat and belly speckled green and white. ♀ similar but has more white on throat and belly. Cloud-forest edge, open country with scattered bush and trees. Endemic to tepuis in E Venezuela and Roraima.

4 WHITE-TAILED GOLDENTHROAT *Polytmus guaynumbi* 10.5cm
Reddish bill. White post-ocular and malar stripes. Upperparts coppery, underparts emerald. Tail rounded, outer feathers white, outer edge of each and subterminal band dark green. ♀: lower underparts buffy. Central tail feathers green, outers dark green with white outer edge and tip. Marsh edge, open country, deforested areas, tall savannah with scrub, edge of gallery and deciduous forests.

5 GREEN-TAILED GOLDENTHROAT *Polytmus theresiae* 8.5cm
Post-ocular streak and lores white. Rounded tail bright green. Underparts green. ♀: fine white speckling on throat and lower belly. Forest edge, thickets and bushes, savannah, grassland.

6 GOLDEN-TAILED SAPPHIRE *Chrysuronia oenone* 9cm
Cap (just crown in one race) blue. Tail coppery golden. Undertail coverts golden cinnamon. ♀: green cap. Whitish underparts with green spotting. Tail like ♂'s. Deciduous, gallery and rainforest, woods, edge and clearings, shrubs, thickets, scattered trees, plantations, gardens. Sea level to hills.

7 WHITE-THROATED HUMMINGBIRD *Leucochloris albicollis* 10.5cm
Dark green with white throat, belly and undertail coverts. Regrowth, bush, thickets, edge of subtropical forest, trees, parks, plantations, gardens.

8 MANY-SPOTTED HUMMINGBIRD *Taphrospilus hypostictus* 13cm
Hefty. Post-ocular and malar stripes white. Underparts dark green scaled white. Arid upland thickets, forest and edge, ravines in foothills.

9 BUFFY HUMMINGBIRD *Leucippus fallax* 10cm
Underparts buffy cinnamon. Central tail feathers light green, outers greyish brown with white tips. ♀ duller. Thorny trees and bushes, edge of mangroves.

10 TUMBES HUMMINGBIRD *Leucippus baeri* 9cm
Dull. Upperparts pale golden green. Underparts greyish. Cap and cheeks brownish. Square tail green, outer feathers and subterminal band browner. Dry scrub, coastal and deciduous forest. Extreme NW Peru and SW Ecuador.

11 OLIVE-SPOTTED HUMMINGBIRD *Leucippus chlorocercus* 10cm
Underparts whitish with faint greyish-olive spotting, especially on throat and flanks. Square tail green, outer feathers browner. Secondary growth, shrub and thickets at humid forest edge, near rivers.

12 WHITE-BELLIED HUMMINGBIRD *Amazilia (Leucippus) chionogaster* 10.5cm
All underparts white. Upperparts pale bronzy green. Forest and woods edge in hills, bush and thickets, dry brushland.

13 SPOT-THROATED HUMMINGBIRD *Leucippus taczanowskii* 10.5cm
Dull. Green spotting on white throat. Forehead and ear coverts dirty brown. Underparts dirty whitish. Square tail green, outer feathers browner. Bush and scrub in arid uplands with cactus, plantations. N and C Peru, W slope of Andes.

6♀

3

5

4♂

7

1♂

4♀

10

12

9

11

13

8

RODRIGUEZ MATA

HUMMINGBIRDS (TROCHILIDAE)

1   GREEN-AND-WHITE HUMMINGBIRD
Amazilia (Leucippus) viridicauda   9.3cm
Upperparts and sides of breast brilliant green. Tail darker and olivaceous, slightly forked. Underparts white. Arid upland bushy terrain to subtropical forest.

2   RUFOUS-TAILED EMERALD *Amazilia tzacatl*   9.2cm
Bill red, tip black; or black, red only on mandible. Brilliant green, dirty white on lower belly. Tail and tail coverts rufous. Arid bush to cloud-forest, rainforest, edge, open woods, cultivated land along streams, savannah, plantations.

3   CHESTNUT-BELLIED EMERALD *Amazilia castaneiventris*   8.5cm
Upperparts coppery. Tail reddish chestnut. Bib green. Underparts rufous-chestnut. Lower montane humid forest, edge, bushy canyons. Endemic to W slope of E Andes (N Boyaca, S Bolivar, N end of San Lucas range), NC Colombia.

4   AMAZILIA EMERALD *Amazilia amazilia*   9cm
Upperparts coppery. Forehead and crown more coppery green. Rufous-chestnut tail, barely forked. Large bib shining green, feathers edged white, or most of bib white (one race). Rest of underparts cinnamon. Coastal arid scrub and open woods, plantations, parks, gardens.

5   LOJA EMERALD *Amazilia alticola*   9cm (not illustrated)
Virtually the same as white-bibbed race of 4. Differs in having central underparts white. Cloud-forest edge, clearings, open scrub, bushy savannah below mountains. Very local in S Ecuador (Loja). Probably a race of 3.

6   WHITE-CHESTED EMERALD *Amazilia (Agyrtria) brevirostris*   9cm
Upperparts and sides bronzy green. Upper tail coverts and tail coppery bronze, dark subterminal band seen from below. Throat and underparts white. Edge of woods, rainforest, gallery and deciduous forest, secondary growth, semi-open scrub, savannah. Formerly *A. chionopectus*.

7   PLAIN-BELLIED EMERALD *Amazilia (Agyrtria) leucogaster*   9cm
Upperparts and sides brilliant green. Upper tail coverts and central tail feathers brownish bronzy olive, outers bluish black. Throat and underparts white. Open forest, edge, shrubs, mangroves, cerrado, caatinga, plantations, secondary growth, parks, gardens.

8   ANDEAN EMERALD *Amazilia (Agyrtria) franciae*   9.2cm
Dark blue cap (green in ♀). Rest of upperparts brilliant green. Tail and upper coverts bronzy olive. Throat and underparts white. Humid forest edge, wooded hills, thickets and scrub, secondary growth, arid brushy areas.

9   VERSICOLOURED EMERALD *Amazilia (Agyrtria) versicolor*   8.3–9cm
Upperparts bronzy green. Upper tail coverts and tail brownish bronzy olive. Dark brown subterminal band on tail. Bib white speckled emerald-green. Rest of underparts bronzy green, white on central and lower belly and undertail coverts. Another race has green upperparts and sides of body, dark bluish-green cap. Bib with less white, belly dirty white. Yet another race, once considered the Collared Emerald *A. hollandi* in SE Venezuela, has blue cap and cheeks. Underparts mostly white. Gallery forest, humid and cloud-forest, savannah, open arid woods, edge, thickets and bushes, secondary growth, plantations, parks, gardens.

10 BLUE-GREEN EMERALD *Amazilia rondoniae*   9cm
Like the nominal race of 8 but has a blue face and bib. Forest, cerrado, open woods. Along Madeira river (right bank) in WC Brazil and N Bolivia. Usually considered a race of 8.

RODRIGUEZ MATA

HUMMINGBIRDS (TROCHILIDAE)

1 PURPLE-CHESTED EMERALD *Amazilia (Polyerata) rosenbergi* 9cm
Bronzy green with violaceous-blue chest. Throat slightly flecked whitish.
Lower underparts brownish grey. Undertail coverts white. Central tail feathers
brownish olive, outers blackish blue. ♀: whiter on throat and upper breast.
Outer tail feathers tipped white. Humid forest edge, thickets, shrubs and
regrowth, edge of woods, coastal scrubby areas.

2 BLUE-CHESTED EMERALD *Amazilia (Polyerata) amabilis* 9cm
Like 1 but bib bluish mauve. Lower underparts greyish. Tail all violaceous
black. Edge of forest, open woods, thickets, secondary growth, riverside
vegetation, clearings, plantations, parks, gardens.

3 SAPPHIRE-SPANGLED EMERALD *Amazilia (Polyerata) lactea* 9cm
Upperparts brilliant dark green with bronzy sheen. Brilliant violet-blue bib.
Central tail feathers dark green, bluer towards tip; outers dark blue, edged
green. From below, the tail is all blackish blue. Sides of belly dark green, centre
and undertail coverts white, varying with race. Rainforest and gallery forest
edge, bushes and thickets, secondary growth, clearings, parks, gardens.

4 GLITTERING-THROATED EMERALD *Amazilia (Polyerata) fimbriata* 9cm
Bill red. Upperparts brilliant green, upper tail coverts bronzy green. Central
tail feathers greenish bronze, outers blacker. Tail from below bronzy black.
Shining emerald-green bib. Sides of belly brownish green, centre and undertail
coverts white (to throat in ♀). Gallery forest, woods, regrowth, mangroves,
caatinga, savannah, bush and thickets, edge, thorny scrub in arid areas,
plantations, parks, gardens.

5 COPPER-RUMPED EMERALD *Amazilia (Saucerottia) tobaci* 9cm
Overall dark brilliant green. Back, rump, upper tail coverts and wing coverts
coppery. Tail brilliant blackish blue. Undertail coverts coppery blackish.
Woods, rainforest, savannah, cloud-forest, gallery forest, thorny brush, cleared
areas, edge, plantations, parks, gardens.

COPPER-TAILED EMERALD
Amazilia (Saucerottia) cupreicauda 9cm (not illustrated)
Differs from 5 only in having a coppery-chestnut tail and glittering golden-
green underparts. Forest edge, clearings and scrub, slopes and tepuis.

6 GREEN-BELLIED EMERALD *Amazilia (Saucerottia) viridigaster* 9cm
Overall brilliant dark green. Rump and all tail coverts bronzy olive. Tail
vinaceous black. Edge and clearings, forest, scattered trees, foothills to
uplands, secondary growth, plantations.

7 STEELY-VENTED EMERALD *Amazilia (Saucerottia) saucerrottei* 9cm
Overall brilliant dark green. Tail blackish blue, undertail coverts greyish edged
whitish (or blackish blue in one form). Woods, edge, arid scrub, cultivated
land, parks and gardens, to high elevations.

8 INDIGO-CAPPED EMERALD *Amazilia (Saucerottia) cyanifrons* 9cm
Overall dark shining green. Cap dark blue. Rump and all tail coverts bronzy
olive. Tail blackish blue. Humid forest edge, open woods, brushy clearings,
plantations, foothills to lower mountains.

RODRIGUEZ MATA

HUMMINGBIRDS (TROCHILIDAE)

1   WHITE-VENTED PLUMELETEER *Chalybura buffoni*   11.5cm
Hefty. Overall bright green, undertail coverts white. Slightly forked tail
blackish blue. ♀: greyish from chin to belly. White tips to outer tail feathers.
Rainforest, deciduous forest, dry forest, semi-open and secondary growth,
woods, edge, bushes and thickets, swamps.

2   BLUE-BELLIED PLUMELETEER *Chalybura caeruleogaster*   11.5cm
Like 1, but dark blue chin, throat, breast and upper belly. ♀: virtually same as
that of 1, but flanks more marked green. As 1 but more often inside the forest,
on *Heliconia*; for some, just a race of the former.

3   BRONZE-TAILED PLUMELETEER *Chalybura urochrysia*   11.5cm
Same as 1 but tail bronzy olive. ♀ identical to 2's. Rainforest, deciduous forest,
edge, secondary growth, shrubs and thickets, plantations, gardens. Prefers
shady places.

4   SOMBRE HUMMINGBIRD *Aphantochroa (Campylopterus) cirrochloris*   11cm
All dull smoky brown. Greener on head and upperparts. Tail dull grey, blackish
distal half. Humid forest, edge, secondary growth, small farms, plantations.

5   BLOSSOMCROWN *Anthocephala floriceps*   8cm
Buffy-white forehead, rufous-chestnut crown. Underparts greyish. ♀: crown
and forehead brownish. Humid montane forest, open woods, thickets and
bushes, secondary growth. Santa Marta mountains and Magdalena valley (E
slope of C Andes) Colombia.

6   SPECKLED HUMMINGBIRD *Adelomyia melanogenys*   8.5cm
Dull. Long white post-ocular streak. Upperparts brownish green with bronzy
sheen. Underparts cinnamon-buff (or dirty buff in other races), spotted blue on
throat, brown markings on sides of body. Undertail cinnamon (buffy white in
other races). Tail blackish blue with broad cinnamon tips (or buffy white in
other races) to all outer feathers. Montane forest, cloud-forest, edge, thickets
and bushes along mountain streams.

7   RUFOUS-VENTED WHITETIP *Urosticte ruficrissa*   ♂ 9.3cm, ♀ 8.5cm
Mostly brilliant green. Shiny dark green bib. Breast feathers edged white. Long,
deeply forked tail greenish black, central feather with broad white tip. Undertail
coverts buffy. ♀: underparts white, spotted green. Short white malar stripe.
White tip to outer tail feathers. Montane forest and humid forest, cloud-forest,
edge. E-facing slope of Andes. For some, just a race of 8.

8   PURPLE-BIBBED WHITETIP *Urosticte benjamini*   ♂ 8.8cm, ♀ 8cm
Differs from 7 in having lower half of bib purple. Green undertail coverts. ♀ same
as that of 7. Montane, cloud- and rainforest, edge. Pacific-facing slopes of Andes.

9   ECUADORIAN PIEDTAIL *Phlogophilus hemileucurus*   8cm
Upperparts brilliant green. Rounded tail blackish blue with distal third of
outer feathers white. Throat white with lines of blackish spots. White collar,
green half-collar below. Mid-belly whitish, greyish green on flanks. Humid
forest, foot and slopes of mountains.

10   PERUVIAN PIEDTAIL *Phlogophilus harterti*   8cm
Upperparts brilliant green with bronzy sheen. Rufous lores. Underparts buffy
cinnamon. Faint collar. White tail with diagonal blackish band across outer
feathers. Central feathers greenish with distal half blackish brown. Rainforest
at base of mountains, secondary growth, edges.

1♀

1♂

2♂

4

5

3

6

7♀

7♂

10

9

8♂

RODRIGUEZ MATA

HUMMINGBIRDS (TROCHILIDAE)

1 BRAZILIAN RUBY *Clytolaema rubricauda*   12.3cm
Brilliant green overall. Forehead and breast shining green. Throat ruby-red.
Tail reddish rufous. ♀: underparts cinnamon. Forest, edge, thickets and bushes,
parks, gardens.

2 GOULD'S JEWELFRONT *Heliodoxa (Polyplancta) aurescens*   12cm
Overall darkish brilliant green. Forehead purplish blue. Chin and upper throat
black. Rufous-orange patch on breast. Tail reddish rufous. ♀ paler, forehead
bronzy green. Chin and throat speckled blackish and buffy green. Humid
rainforest, woods, damp places and along streams, sandy areas, varzea.

3 VIOLET-CHESTED HUMMINGBIRD *Sternoclyta cyanopectus*   13cm
Hefty. Overall brilliant dark green. Shining emerald-green throat. Violet
breast. Tail bronzy brown. Lower belly and undertail coverts brownish grey.
From below, distal third of outer feathers' inner vane white. ♀: throat and
breast buffy white spotted green. Belly and vent buffy spotted green towards
flanks. Cloud-forest, rainforest, coffee plantations, shady places with *Heliconia*.

4 RUFOUS-WEBBED BRILLIANT *Heliodoxa branickii*   11.8cm
Overall dark brilliant green. Throat-patch pinkish ruby. Undertail coverts white.
Slightly forked tail blackish blue, central feathers bluish green. Inner flight
feathers pale rufous. Foothill rainforest, woods, edge, plantations. Between
Cuzco and Manu (E Andean foothills, Peru) and extreme NW Bolivia.

5 PINK-THROATED BRILLIANT *Heliodoxa gularis*   11.5cm
Overall dark brilliant green. Central line of shining emerald on forehead and
crown. Throat ruby-pink. Vent white. Tail slightly forked blackish-greenish
bronze. Humid montane forest.

6 EMPRESS BRILLIANT *Heliodoxa imperatrix*   14.3cm
Hefty. Overall dark green. Long forked tail black. Violet throat-spot. Lower
belly paler green. ♀: throat and breast white with lines of green dots. Lower
cloud-forest, edge, secondary growth, foot of the mountains.

7 FAWN-BREASTED BRILLIANT *Heliodoxa rubinoides*   13cm
Upperparts brilliant green. Pinkish-topaz patch on throat. Rest of underparts
cinnamon-buff, faintly marked green. Underwing coverts cinnamon. Longish
forked tail olive-bronze from below. Montane cloud-forest, rainforest, edge, on
slopes.

8 VELVET-BROWED BRILLIANT *Heliodoxa xanthogonys*   11cm
Very dark brilliant green. Cinnamon malar stripe. Tail bluish black. ♀:
underparts white, spotted green. Tip of tail feathers white. Montane forest,
edge, cleared areas.

9 GREEN-CROWNED BRILLIANT *Heliodoxa jacula*   12cm
Overall dark brilliant green. Forehead and crown shining deep emerald. Dark
violet spot on throat. Longish forked tail violaceous black. ♀ like that of 10.
Montane forest, cloud-forest.

10 VIOLET-FRONTED BRILLIANT *Heliodoxa leadbeateri*   12cm
Overall very dark green with bronzy sheen. Forehead and crown shining violet.
Face blackish brown. Bib shining emerald-green. Upper tail coverts coppery
violet. Longish tail forked, violaceous black. ♀: underparts white spotted
green. Tip of tail white. Montane forest, cloud-forest and rainforest to open
woods, edge, cleared areas, coffee plantations.

11 BLACK-THROATED BRILLIANT *Heliodoxa schreibersii*   12cm
Overall dark brilliant green. Lower face and throat black. Fore-neck shiny
purple. Centre of belly black. Vent and longish forked tail bluish black. ♀:
malar stripe white, throat blackish green, belly greenish grey. Tail shorter and
less forked. Humid montane forest and scrub.

1♂

1♀

7

2

4

3

8♂

11♂

11♀

9

6♀

6♂

10♂

10♀

RODRIGUEZ · MATA

HUMMINGBIRDS (TROCHILIDAE)

1 SCISSOR-TAILED HUMMINGBIRD
Hylonympha macrocerca ♂ 21cm, ♀ 12cm
Dark metallic green overall. Forehead and crown shiny dark violet. Very long forked tail. Bib shining emerald-green. ♀: throat and breast white spotted green. White malar stripe. Belly and vent tawny. From above, central feathers blackish purple with green at base, outers with rufous base, tip white. Cloud-forest, woods, edge, clearings. NE Venezuela (endemic to Paria peninsula).

2 CRIMSON TOPAZ *Topaza pella* ♂ 18cm, ♀ 15cm
Black hood. Glittering shiny pale green bib with golden sheen. Fiery-crimson body. All tail coverts greeny gold. Rufous-chestnut tail with 2 long, black curved feathers surpassing the rest. ♀: like that of 3 but 2 pairs of outer tail feathers rufous chestnut. Rainforest and trees, usually along watercourses.

3 FIERY TOPAZ *Topaza pyra* ♂ 18cm, ♀ 15cm
Like 2 but tail vinaceous black. ♀ brilliant green. Throat pale green, golden and fiery. Tail coverts bright green. Underwing coverts rufous. Outer tail feathers' outer web white. Central feathers shorter than in ♂. Rainforest, trees in rocky areas, mostly near waterfalls and streams, edge of savannah. Some believe this to be a race of 2.

4 GREAT SAPPHIREWING *Pterophanes cyanopterus* 16.5cm
Large and hefty. Brilliant dark green. Wing coverts blue. Slightly forked tail dark olive-green. ♀: throat to mid-belly cinnamon. Outer tail feather edges and tips whitish. High mountains, scrubby slopes and thickets, scattered bushes and trees in paramo, edge of montane forest.

5 WHITE-TAILED HILLSTAR *Urochroa bougueri* 15cm
Dark green overall. Rufous malar stripe. Bib shining blue. Belly and vent grey. Outer tail feathers white, edge and tips blackish. ♀: notable rufous malar stripe, shining blue throat. Rest of underparts brownish grey. Rainforest and cloud-forest in mountains, edge, shrubs and thickets.

6 MOUNTAIN VELVETBREAST *Lafresnaya lafresnayi* 10cm
Overall brilliant green with bronzy sheen. Centre of belly black. Square tail, central feathers green, outers whitish or buff with outer edge and tip blackish. ♀: underparts buff (or whitish in one race) with scattered greenish markings. Tail from below buffy with broad blackish tip. Thickets and bushes in montane forest, edge of cloud-forest, upland meadows with scattered bushes.

7 SWORD-BILLED HUMMINGBIRD *Ensifera ensifera* 20cm
Inordinately long bill. Dark brilliant green overall, bronzy sheen on head. ♀: whitish underparts spotted green. High mountain forest, edge, cloud-forest, low trees and shrubs, scrubby slopes, scattered trees.

8 GIANT HUMMINGBIRD *Patagonas gigas* 22cm
Huge and unmistakable. Cinnamon or rufous-cinnamon underparts, vent whitish. Upperparts browny olive with slight bronzy sheen. White rump. ♀ duller. Arid mountains with cactus and scrub.

4♀

4♂

1♂

2♂

1♀

3♂

3♀

5♀

7♀

5♂

8

7♂

6♂

6♀

GUEZ MATA

HUMMINGBIRDS (TROCHILIDAE)

1 WHITE-SIDED HILLSTAR *Oreotrochilus leucopleurus*　　　　10cm
Shining green bib tinged golden. Collar black. Upperparts dull brownish olive.
Underparts white with blackish-blue median line on central breast and belly.
Rounded tail mostly white, slender outer feathers blackish. ♀ dull, whitish bib
dotted brown. Rest of underparts whitish brown. High arid mountain scrub,
steppe with rocky outcrops near streams, sometimes with cactus.

2 ANDEAN HILLSTAR *Oreotrochilus estella*　　　　12cm
Like 1 but larger bib protrudes from sides of neck. Mid-belly stripe chestnut.
White tail, central feathers dark, outers variably black. ♀: whitish throat
dotted brown, rest of underparts pale greyish brown. Base and tip of outer tail
feathers white. Upland grassland and brush, near human habitations, edge of
Polylepis woods and *Puya*.

3 GREEN-HEADED HILLSTAR *Oreotrochilus stolzmanni*　　　　11.5cm
Like 1 but head and upperparts greenish olive, broader outer tail feathers
blackish, base white. Bib shiny green. ♀ like that of 1 but upperparts greener.
High mountain steppe, puna, rocky terrain, brush, thickets, stunted trees. For
some, a race of 2.

4 ECUADOREAN HILLSTAR *Oreotrochilus chimborazo*　　　　12cm
Head and neck brilliant dark blue. Green throat present or not. Underparts
have black median line. ♀: dull brownish-green upperparts. White bib dotted
brownish. Rest of underparts light brownish grey. Outer tail greenish black
with white tip and base. Arid rocky high mountain steppe, bush, thickets,
grassland, scattered low trees, woods, montane forest.

5 BLACK-BREASTED HILLSTAR *Oreotrochilus melanogaster*　　　　11cm
Underparts black. ♀: paler above, greenish cap with coppery sheen. Throat
white spotted blackish. Rest of underparts pale brownish grey. Central tail dark
green, outers blackish with white tip and base. High mountain rocky steppe,
grassland, thickets, scrub, temperate montane woods and forest, scattered trees.

6 WEDGE-TAILED HILLSTAR *Oreotrochilus adela*　　　　12cm
Breast and mid-belly black. Chestnut flanks. Graded tail tawny buff bordered
brownish black. ♀: white bib spotted brown. Underparts tawny buff. High-
mountain arid stony steppe, bushes, thickets, grassland.

7 BLACK-HOODED SUNBEAM *Aglaeactis pamela*　　　　10cm
Mostly black. Lower back to upper tail shining emerald. Tail and vent
chestnut-rufous. Patch of white spots at mid-breast. Very high arid temperate
scrub, thickets and stunted trees, edge of montane woods.

8 SHINING SUNBEAM *Aglaeactis cupripennis*　　　　12cm
Cap, ear-patch and upper back chocolate-brown. Back to rump glittering
purple, pink, golden yellow and green. Brow and underparts cinnamon-rufous.
Patch of buffy-white spots on breast. Forked tail. ♀: duller, colour patch on
back smaller. Edge of high montane woods, low and stunted trees, bushes,
thickets, paramo, gardens.

9 WHITE-TUFTED SUNBEAM *Aglaeactis castelnaudi*　　　　12cm
Head, upperparts and breast-band dark chocolate-brown. Patch of white marks
on breast. Rump shiny purple. Brow, collar (or throat-patch) and underparts
tawny rufous. Very high arid scrub, thickets and stunted trees, above montane
woods and forest.

10 PURPLE-BACKED SUNBEAM *Aglaeactis aliciae*　　　　12cm
Mostly dark chocolate-brown. Lores, pectoral collar, wing coverts, central
belly and vent white. Lower back and rump glittering purple. Very high arid
scrub, thickets and edge of montane woods.

♀

1♂

2♂

2♀

3♂

4♂

4♀

5♂

5♀

6♂

6♀

7

8

9

10

DRIGUEZ MATA

HUMMINGBIRDS (TROCHILIDAE)

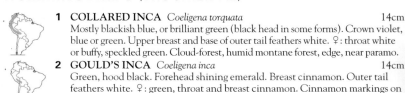
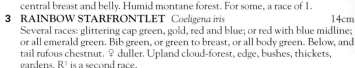

1 COLLARED INCA *Coeligena torquata* 14cm
Mostly blackish blue, or brilliant green (black head in some forms). Crown violet, blue or green. Upper breast and base of outer tail feathers white. ♀: throat white or buffy, speckled green. Cloud-forest, humid montane forest, edge, near paramo.

2 GOULD'S INCA *Coeligena inca* 14cm
Green, hood black. Forehead shining emerald. Breast cinnamon. Outer tail feathers white. ♀: green, throat and breast cinnamon. Cinnamon markings on central breast and belly. Humid montane forest. For some, a race of 1.

3 RAINBOW STARFRONTLET *Coeligena iris* 14cm
Several races: glittering cap green, gold, red and blue; or red with blue midline; or all emerald green. Bib green, or green to breast, or all body green. Below, and tail rufous chestnut. ♀ duller. Upland cloud-forest, edge, bushes, thickets, gardens. R[1] is a second race.

4 VIOLET-THROATED STARFRONTLET *Coeligena violifer* 14cm
Cap to breast green. Rest tawny. Shiny violet patch on throat. Faint pale pectoral collar. ♀: light green head, cinnamon malar streak and lacks violet on throat. Very high cloud-forest and elfin forest, bushes and thickets.

5 BROWN INCA *Coeligena wilsoni* 13cm
Dark brownish with greenish sheen. White patch on side of breast. Cloud-forest, montane forest, edge.

6 BLACK INCA *Coeligena prunellei* 14cm
Blackish. Shining blue upper wing coverts. White patch on sides of breast. Humid montane forest, open country and gallery forest. Andes in NC Colombia (Quindío, SE Santander, W Boyaca, W Condinamarca).

7 BLUE-THROATED STARFRONTLET *Coeligena helianthea* 14cm
Overall greenish black. Forehead glittering emerald-green. Throat shining violaceous blue. Belly and flanks shining pinkish purple. ♀: head and upperparts bright green. Throat cinnamon spotted green. Belly cinnamon with pinkish-purple marks. Cloud-forest, montane forest, scattered trees, edge, thickets, bushes, parks, gardens.

8 GOLDEN-BELLIED STARFRONTLET *Coeligena bonapartei* 14cm
Forehead glittering emerald. Cap black. Body green but belly and upper tail coverts golden olive. Tail and vent bronzy olive. ♀ like that of 11 but tail, vent and upper tail coverts like ♂. Cloud-forest, montane forest, scattered trees and bushes near paramo.

9 BRONZY INCA *Coeligena coeligena* 14cm
Blackish brown or cinnamon brown. Throat scaled white. Wing coverts and shoulders tinged reddish chestnut. Green sheen on back and rump. Cloud-forest, montane forest, edge, coffee plantations, scattered trees and bushes.

10 WHITE-TAILED STARFRONTLET *Coeligena phalerata* 14cm
Brilliant dark green. Tail coverts and tail white. ♀: upperparts green, underparts tawny rufous. Tail olive-green, tips buff. Cloud-forest and montane forest, edge, shrubs and thickets. Endemic to Santa Marta Mtns, extreme N Colombia.

11 CINNAMON STARFRONTLET *Coeligena eos* 14cm
Forehead brilliant emerald-green. Crown and nape black. Rest of head, breast and upper back dark green grading to tawny rufous below. Underwing coverts and inner flight feathers rufous. ♀: cap green. Bib tawny, spotted green. Cloud-forest, montane forest, stunted upland woods, scattered trees and bushes near paramo.

12 BUFF-WINGED STARFRONTLET *Coeligena lutetiae* 14cm
Upperparts black. Forehead glittering emerald-green. Violet throat-patch. Underparts dark green. Inner flight feathers buff. ♀: green, throat buffy cinnamon. Cloud-forest, montane forest, edge, thickets and bushes, scattered stunted trees near paramo.

RODRIGUEZ MATA

HUMMINGBIRDS (TROCHILIDAE)

1 LONGUEMARE'S SUNANGEL *Heliangelus clarisse* 9.5cm
Bib glittering rosy amethyst. Collar white. Underparts buffy grey spotted green, all green on flanks. Vent blackish grey, feathers edged whitish. Slightly forked tail, central feathers bronzy green, outers blackish. ♀: bib brown. Cloud-forest, upland woods with low, stunted trees, bushy copses on paramo. The form in NW Venezuela (Merida Sunangel *H. c. spencei*) with a broader white collar was once considered a separate species, while some consider this (1) a race of 2.

2 AMETHYST-THROATED SUNANGEL *Heliangelus amethysticollis* 9.5cm
Like 1 but blackish chin and cinnamon-buff collar and underparts. Vent dirty white. ♀: throat tawny, streaked green on sides. Some races have white collar. Cloud-forest, upland woods with small or stunted trees, edge, open slopes with shrubs and scattered trees, scrubby ravines. Some consider this to include 1 and its races.

3 GORGETED SUNANGEL *Heliangelus strophianus* 9.5cm
Like white-collared forms of 2 but breast and belly green. Tail longer and somewhat forked, all blackish blue. ♀: throat blackish cinnamon streaked white. Humid montane forest, edge, scrubby ravines along watercourses. Extreme SW Colombia (Nariño) and NW Ecuador.

4 ORANGE-THROATED SUNANGEL *Heliangelus mavors* 9.5cm
Large bib shining golden orange. Collar tawny. Underparts tawny spotted green towards flanks. Vent tawny and buff. ♀: throat buffy cinnamon flecked green. Cloud-forest, montane forest with low and stunted trees, slopes with scattered trees and shrubs, edge, scrubby grassland.

5 LITTLE SUNANGEL *Heliangelus micraster* 9cm
Dark green. Chin black, throat golden orange. Vent white. Somewhat forked tail with central feathers coppery dark green, rest blackish blue. ♀ like ♂ but chin and upper throat white. Montane temperate moss-laden woods, grassland with scrub, edge, slopes with scattered trees and shrubs.

6 ROYAL SUNANGEL *Heliangelus regalis* ♂ 10cm, ♀ 7.5cm
All brilliant dark blue. Long tail deeply forked. ♀: underparts buffy cinnamon spotted blackish on throat, green on breast and flanks. Buffy collar. Small blackish eye-patch. Low montane forest, cloud-forest, dry grassland, scrub, wooded ravines, edge, stunted trees. Near San Martin, Peru.

7 TOURMALINE SUNANGEL *Heliangelus exortis* 10.3cm
Dark green. Chin violaceous black, bib shining pink. Vent white. Tail somewhat forked, central feathers dark green, outers purply black. ♀: throat white speckled blackish. Montane forest, cloud-forest, dwarf forest with cane, edge, upland slopes with trees and bushes, scrubby grassland.

8 PURPLE-THROATED SUNANGEL *Heliangelus viola* 11.7cm
Glittering green. Forehead shining blackish blue. Bib shining purply violet. Deeply forked tail, central feathers blackish green, outers blackish. Vent greenish edged buffy. ♀ lacks shining bib. Throat greenish black. Cloud-forest, montane forest, edge, shrubs and thickets, slopes with trees or bushes, alder woods.

9 JUAN FERNANDEZ FIRECROWN *Sephanoides fernandensis* 12cm
All reddish chestnut. Cap fiery red. ♀: upperparts green, underparts white spotted greenish black. Cap blue. Thickets, bushes, gardens.

10 GREEN-BACKED FIRECROWN *Sephanoides sephanoides* 9.5cm
Cap fiery red. Mostly bronzy green. Bib white spotted bronzy black. ♀: cap bronzy green. S Andean woods, edge, clearings, thickets, parks, gardens.

RODRIGUEZ MATA

HUMMINGBIRDS (TROCHILIDAE)

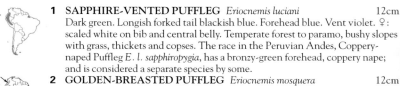

1 SAPPHIRE-VENTED PUFFLEG *Eriocnemis luciani*   12cm
Dark green. Longish forked tail blackish blue. Forehead blue. Vent violet. ♀:
scaled white on bib and central belly. Temperate forest to paramo, bushy slopes
with grass, thickets and copses. The race in the Peruvian Andes, Coppery-
naped Puffleg *E. l. sapphiropygia*, has a bronzy-green forehead, coppery nape;
and is considered a separate species by some.

2 GOLDEN-BREASTED PUFFLEG *Eriocnemis mosquera*   12cm
Dark bronzy green. Coppery sheen on breast and face. Vent brownish grey.
Longish forked tail blackish green. Low montane woods and bushes, dwarf
copses, thickets at tree line in paramo.

3 BLUE-CAPPED PUFFLEG *Eriocnemis glaucopoides*   9cm
Dark green, bluer underparts. Forehead and vent dark blue. Slightly forked tail.
♀: cinnamon bib, central underparts buffy, spotted green. Montane forest,
edge, bushes and thickets.

4 EMERALD-BELLIED PUFFLEG *Eriocnemis alinae*   7.5cm
Huge pantaloons. Upperparts bronzy green. Shining emerald underparts and tail.
White breast-patch spotted green. Montane forest and cloud-forest, less on edge.

5 GLOWING PUFFLEG *Eriocnemis vestita*   9cm
Dark green. Throat and vent violet. Slightly forked tail. ♀: throat scaled
violet. Sides of throat and breast cinnamon spotted green. Mid-belly whitish,
spotted green. High montane forest and cloud-forest, edge, elfin woods, bushy
areas, upland grasslands, copses in paramo.

6 COPPERY-BELLIED PUFFLEG *Eriocnemis cupreoventris*   9cm
Dark green. Lower belly shining copper. Vent violet. Somewhat forked tail.
paramo, scattered stunted trees and bushes, temperate montane forest, edge,
thickets.

7 BLACK-THIGHED PUFFLEG *Eriocnemis derbyi*   8.7cm
Dark coppery green. All tail coverts brilliant light green. Outer tail feathers
pointed. Leggings blackish. ♀: underparts scaled white. Leggings greyish.
Temperate montane forest and woods, edge, shrubby areas, thickets,
neighbouring grassland, bushy slopes, ravines.

8 BLACK-BREASTED PUFFLEG *Eriocnemis nigrivestis*   9cm
Blackish blue-green. Throat and vent violet. ♀: dark bronzy green. Throat
violaceous blue. Breast scaled cinnamon. Mid-belly scaled white. Upland
temperate woods, edge, bushes, thickets bordering paramo. On ridges around
Quito, Ecuador – Frutillas, Yanacocha, Alaspungo and Pugsi mountains.
Critically endangered.

9 TURQUOISE-THROATED PUFFLEG *Eriocnemis godini*   9cm
Coppery green. Throat and vent shining blue. Upper tail coverts pale green. Tail
slightly forked. Bushy upland slopes and ravines, edge of upland forest, thickets.

10 COLOURFUL PUFFLEG *Eriocnemis mirabilis*   8.5cm
Emerald forehead. Vent orangy vermilion. Belly dark shining blue. Tail greenish
bronze. ♀: throat and mid-breast white, spotted green. Rest of underparts
white, spotted coppery orange. Montane forest, cloud-forest, clearings and
edge, bushes and thickets. W slope of W Andes, Cauca, Colombia.

11 GREENISH PUFFLEG *Haplophaedia aureliae*   9cm
Upperparts coppery green. Underparts dark green faintly scaled greyish. Tail
slightly forked. Cloud-forest and montane forest, edge and clearings, bushes
and thickets. S Peru's race (*H. a. assimilis*), all bronzy green on upperparts; and
N Peru's (*H. a. affinis*) with tawny-rufous leggings, constitute for some a
separate species: Buff-thighed Puffleg.

12 HOARY PUFFLEG *Haplophaedia lugens*   9cm
Upperparts coppery green. Underparts blackish grey, scaled white on throat.
Montane forest, cloud-forest, forest at foot of mountains, edge, thickets.

RODRIGUEZ MATA

HUMMINGBIRDS (TROCHILIDAE)

1 RACQUET-TAILED PUFFLEG *Ochreatus underwoodii* ♂ 12cm, ♀ 7.5cm
Unmistakable. ♂: long tail, outer feathers racquet-tipped. Bib shining
emerald. Big white leggings (tawny in some races). ♀: underparts white dotted
green on breast and flanks (more so in S races). Small white line on blackish-
green malar stripe. Undertail coverts buff. Short tail barely forked, outer
feathers blackish blue tipped white. Montane tropical to temperate forest,
cloud-forest, dwarf forest, ravines with dense, humid vegetation, coffee
plantations, edge, bushes, thickets.

2 BLACK-TAILED TRAINBEARER *Lesbia victoriae* ♂ 25cm, ♀ 15cm
Extremely long forked tail purply black with green tips. Shining green bib.
Mid-belly and undertail coverts cinnamon-buff. ♀: shorter forked tail.
Underparts white and buff spotted green. Montane bushy terrain, slopes, banks
and ravines, dwarf woods, scrubby grassland, plantations, bushy copses in
paramo.

3 GREEN-TAILED TRAINBEARER *Lesbia nuna* ♂ 16cm, ♀ 11cm
Very long forked tail, feathers green but for purply-black outer pair. Bib shining
green. Undertail coverts green. ♀: forked tail shorter. Underparts white and
buff spotted green. Bushes and thickets on edge of upper montane forest,
grasslands with shrubs, scattered trees, parks and gardens.

4 RED-TAILED COMET *Sappho sparganura* ♂ 18cm, ♀ 13cm
Back brilliant purply carmine. Tail long and forked, fiery red, feathers tipped
black. ♀: tail shorter. Underparts buffy white spotted green. Temperate and
subtropical woods and bushy areas in mountainous and hilly country, near
slopes and banks, scrubby grassland, copses, thickets, parks, gardens.

5 BEARDED HELMETCREST *Oxypogon guerinii* 11cm
Unmistakable. Striking crest and green and white 'beard'. Rest of head
blackish. White collar. ♀ similar but lacks crest and 'beard'. Paramo and
nearby bushes, slopes with shrubby grassland, ecotone with dwarf woods.

6 BRONZE-TAILED COMET *Polyonymus caroli* 13cm
Bronzy green. Bib shining carmine. White lores. Long, deeply forked tail
brilliant green and coppery purple. ♀: underparts white spotted green and
blackish. Some carmine dots at mid-throat. Edge of montane woods, copses of
low trees and shrubs, arid temperate areas, thickets.

7 PURPLE-BACKED THORNBILL *Ramphomicron microrhynchum* 8cm
Tiny sharp bill. Upperparts shining violaceous purple. Bib shining golden
green. Longish tail forked, purply black. ♀: upperparts brilliant green.
Underparts buffy white spotted green. Tail with white tip to outer feathers.
Edge of cloud-forest and dwarf forest, bushes and thickets, scattered trees.

8 BLACK-BACKED THORNBILL *Ramphomicron dorsale* 9.5cm
Tiny sharp bill. Upperparts shining black. Upper tail coverts fiery red. Bib
shining golden green. ♀: bright green upperparts. Underparts buffy white
spotted green on breast and flanks. Undertail coverts buffy white. Outer tail
feathers purply black tipped white. Edge of montane forest and cloud-forest,
dwarf woods at great elevations, shrubs and thickets on slopes, paramo, even
above snowline.

RODRIGUEZ MATA

HUMMINGBIRDS (TROCHILIDAE)

1 VIRIDIAN METALTAIL *Metallura williami*   10cm
Very dark shining green. Brilliant purply-blue tail. Bib brilliant green. Other races have green underside of tail, and one has black bib. ♀: upperparts like those of ♂. Cinnamon-buff throat spotted green. Lower belly and undertail coverts buffy cinnamon. Tail like corresponding ♂'s. Bushy areas in ecotone between montane forest and paramo.

2 BLACK METALTAIL *Metallura phoebe*   13cm
Overall shining black. Bib glittering emerald. Tail shining purply red. Semiarid open scrub and woods in uplands, canyons, bushy slopes.

3 SCALED METALTAIL *Metallura aeneocauda*   10cm
Bronzy green. Shining emerald-green bib. Tail has bronzy-green underside, with bluish or coppery sheen dorsally. Breast, upper belly and undertail coverts edged buff, giving slight scaly effect. Temperate montane forest, bushy areas, edge.

4 FIRE-THROATED METALTAIL *Metallura eupogon*   10cm
Bronzy green. Fiery-red bib. Tail has bronzy-green underside, topside with bluish sheen. ♀: throat buffy cinnamon spotted green. Feathers of lower underparts edged cinnamon-buff. Montane bushy areas and upper edge of forest.

5 NEBLINA METALTAIL *Metallura odomae*   10cm (not illustrated)
Like 4 but fiery-red bib much larger. Cheeks chestnutty copper. Topside of tail blue, underside bronzy green. All outer tail feathers tipped white. ♀: bib whitish spotted red. Above tree line, open paramo, dwarf copses.

6 VIOLET-THROATED METALTAIL *Metallura baroni*   10cm
Blackish coppery green. Shining violet bib. Slightly forked tail shining green, with purple-coppery sheen dorsally. ♀: bib buff, spotted shining violet. Underpart feathers edged buffy cinnamon. Edge of temperate woods and bushy areas at great elevations.

7 COPPERY METALTAIL *Metallura theresiae*   11cm
Bright coppery purple. Violaceous-purple tail, greener underside. Bib shining greenish gold. A race has blue undertail surface and reddish-bordered bib. Thickets and edge of montane forest, moss-hung dwarf forest, edge of bogs.

8 REDDISH METALTAIL *Metallura malagae*   10cm
Like 3 but tail bright purply red. Maybe just a race of it. Bushy areas and edge of montane forest.

9 PERIJA METALTAIL *Metallura iracunda*   10cm
Black with coppery and green sheen. Forehead and bib shining emerald. Tail shining rufous red. ♀ like 4's but tail longer and square. Bushes and grassland at great elevations, above montane forest.

10 TYRIAN METALTAIL *Metallura tyrianthina*   9cm
Bronzy green with coppery sheen. Bib shining emerald-green. Lower belly and undertail coverts cinnamon-buff. Slightly forked tail purply red (violaceous blue or shining bronzy-purple in other races). ♀: underparts cinnamon-buff spotted green. Outer tail feathers tipped white. Cloud-forest, dwarf forest, bushes in paramo.

HUMMINGBIRDS (TROCHILIDAE)

1 RUFOUS-CAPPED THORNBILL *Chalcostigma ruficeps* 10cm
Bronzy green. Cap rufous. Pointed bib rainbow colours. Bronzy-olive tail
somewhat forked. Vent and lower belly cinnamon-buff. Bushes and edge of
montane forest.

2 BRONZE-TAILED THORNBILL *Chalcostigma heteropogon* 13cm
Bronzy green. Forehead and beard emerald, this ending in bright violaceous-
carmine tip. Rump and upper tail coverts coppery purple. Somewhat forked
tail bright bronzy olive. Belly and vent cinnamon-buff. Low and open
montane woods, edge, bushy areas, copses, paramo, ravines.

3 RAINBOW-BEARDED THORNBILL *Chalcostigma herrani* 13cm
Greenish black. Forehead and crown rufous, ending in an ochre crest. Long
narrow beard rainbow coloured. Rump coppery red. Tail blackish blue, broadly
tipped white. Vent white. ♀ lacks beard. Underparts dark brown. Open or
scattered woods, dwarf woods, copses, bushes, paramo.

4 OLIVACEOUS THORNBILL *Chalcostigma olivaceum* 14cm
All brown, olive sheen on upperparts. Long beard rainbow coloured. Arid
bushes, thickets at high elevations, dwarf woods, copses, paramo.

5 BLUE-MANTLED THORNBILL *Chalcostigma stanleyi* 14cm
Blackish. Slight green sheen on shoulders. Forehead and beard shining
emerald-green, tip of the beard glittering violaceous carmine. Tail shining
bluish black. Undertail coverts edged whitish. ♀: forehead and throat black.
Thickets, dwarf woods and edge at great elevations.

6 VELVET-PURPLE CORONET *Boissonneaua jardini* 12cm
Overall dark. Head and breast black. Belly dark blue with purple sheen. Outer
tail feathers white, outer edge and tip black. Shoulders greenish blue.
Rainforest at foot of mountains, moss-hung trees, scrub on lower slopes, edge.

7 BUFF-TAILED CORONET *Boissonneaua flavescens* 12cm
Overall bright green, scaled whitish buff on lower belly. Undertail coverts
greyish, edged cinnamon-buff. Outer tail feathers creamy buff, outer edge and
tip greenish. Montane forest and cloud-forest to upper edge, low stunted trees,
bushy slopes, thickets and bush, edge.

8 CHESTNUT-BREASTED CORONET *Boissonneaua matthewsii* 12cm
Underparts rufous chestnut. Outer tail feathers tawny rufous, outer edge and
tip greenish. Humid montane forest, treetops, edge.

1♂

3♂

3♀

5♂

4

2

6

7

8

RODRIGUEZ MATA

HUMMINGBIRDS (TROCHILIDAE)

1   BEARDED MOUNTAINEER *Oreonympha nobilis*   16cm
Large. Head blackish blue. Cap purply violet, some with feathers edged white.
Beard green above, glittering carmine below. Upperparts brown. Underparts
brownish white. Outer tail feathers mostly white. ♀ similar, duller, tail shorter,
less beard. Uplands, arid bush, thickets, copses, ravines.

2   GREEN-TAILED SYLPH *Aglaiocercus emmae*   17cm
Very long forked tail glittering green. Cap and throat shining emerald.
Underparts bronzy green. ♀ like that of 3. Clearings and edge of montane
forest and cloud-forest, bushes, thickets, plantations, parks, gardens. Some
believe this to be a race of 3.

3   LONG-TAILED SYLPH *Aglaiocercus kingi*   18cm
Glittering dark green. Very long forked tail brilliant dark blue. Cap shining
emerald. ♀: upperparts bronzy green. Tail short, outer feathers tipped white.
Green malar stripe, white line above. White throat spotted green, cinnamon
below, spotted green on flanks. Edge of humid forest in mountains, cloud-
forest, clearings, edge of woods, shrubs, thickets, plantations, parks, gardens.

4   VIOLET-TAILED SYLPH *Aglaiocercus coelestis*   18cm
Differs from 3 in having coppery-olive underparts. Cap shining emerald. Very
long forked tail violaceous blue, all but outer pair of feathers broadly tipped
greenish blue. ♀: tail short, outer feathers bronzy green, subterminal band dark
blue, tips white. Green malar stripe, white line above. Throat whitish, densely
spotted greenish. Broad white pectoral collar. Belly and flanks cinnamon. Vent
buff. Moss-hung montane forest and cloud-forest, edge, scrub, copses.
Considered by some to be a race of 3.

5   GREY-BELLIED COMET *Taphrolesbia griseiventris*   16cm
Upperparts and tail bronzy green, this long and forked with golden and bluish
sheen; bluish undertail. Bright blue bib. Underparts pale grey. ♀: upperparts
and tail like ♂'s though tail is shorter. Underparts whitish buff spotted
brownish on throat, flecked green on flanks. Bushes and thickets in arid
temperate zone of high elevations, hillsides, ravines.

6   MOUNTAIN AVOCETBILL *Opisthoprora euryptera*   10cm
Short bill slightly upturned at tip. Green with coppery sheen on head, bronzy
on upperparts. Slightly forked tail, brilliant dark green, outer feathers blackish
blue-green with narrow white tip. White on throat and breast grading to rufous
on belly and vent, nearly all heavily spotted green. Temperate montane forest
at high elevations, bushes, thickets, edge, slopes in paramo.

7   HOODED VISORBEARER *Augastes lumachella*   9cm
Fore-face and bib shining golden green, ending in scarlet point. Cap and sides
of bib black. Divided white pectoral collar. Rest of body bronzy green with
coppery sheen. Tail reddish purple. ♀ similar, no black. Stony semiarid upland
terrain with cactus and shrubs.

8   HYACINTH VISORBEARER *Augastes scutatus*   8cm
Fore-face and bib shining emerald-green. Fore-crown, face and tufted ear
coverts bluish black. Collar white. Wide dark blue band down mid-breast and
belly. Flanks and upperparts bronzy green. Vent white. Underside of tail
brilliant green. ♀: duller; head bronzy green. Underparts grey flecked green.
Smaller bib. Blue and white collars. Stony areas with bushes, thickets and low
vegetation in uplands. The race *A. s. ilseae* from gallery forest at lower
elevations has band on breast and belly pinkish, upperparts bluish green.

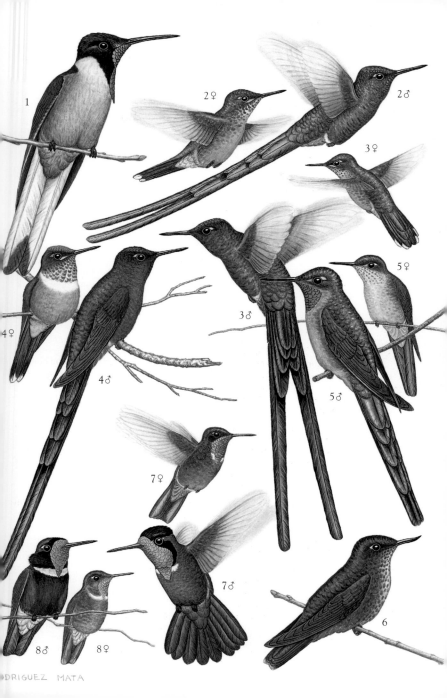

ODRIGUEZ MATA

HUMMINGBIRDS (TROCHILIDAE)

1 OASIS HUMMINGBIRD *Rhodopis vesper* ♂ 13.5cm, ♀ 10cm
Upperparts bronzy olive. Upper tail coverts cinnamon. Bib shining purply red.
Tail longish and forked, blackish; feathers narrow and pointed. Central
underparts whitish. ♀: throat white. Shorter tail with broad outer feathers
tipped white. Oases in desert, lowlands and mountains, gardens, coastal hills.

2 HORNED SUNGEM *Heliactin bilophus* (= *H. cornuta*) 11cm
Shining rainbow-coloured 'horns'. Forehead glittering blue. Pointed black bib.
Tail long and pointed. ♀: bronzy-green cap, whitish throat. Savannah, gallery
forest, bushes, thickets, gardens, hills, plains.

3 BLACK-EARED FAIRY *Heliothryx auritus* 12cm
Black 'ear'. Upperparts and throat brilliant green. Underparts white. Rounded
tail, central feathers blue, outers white. ♀: white throat spotted greyish.
Lowland forest, edge, secondary growth, thickets and bushes. A race, Purple-
crowned Fairy (*H. a. barroti*) from W of Andes, differs in white throat and
shining purply-violet forehead and crown; considered by some a valid species.
♀: plain white throat though occasionally grey-marked.

4 PERUVIAN SHEARTAIL *Thaumastura cora* ♂ 13cm, ♀ 8cm
Purply red and shining blue bib. Broad white collar. Very long tail, central
feathers slender. Mid-belly to vent white. ♀: tail short and rounded. Throat
and rest of underparts buffy white. Incomplete bronzy-green collar. Shrubs and
thickets in ravines, oases and desert, lower slopes to coast.

5 WEDGE-BILLED HUMMINGBIRD *Schistes (Augastes) geoffroyi* 8.5cm
Mask dark green. Violet and white marks on sides of neck. Coppery upper tail
coverts. Underparts emerald, mid-belly and vent dirty white. Rounded tail
bronzy green and blue, narrowly tipped white. ♀: white throat. Rainforest,
dense cloud-forest, edge, shrubs, thickets.

6 MARVELLOUS SPATULETAIL
Loddigesia mirabilis ♂ 17cm (tail 12cm), ♀ 9.5cm
Very long racquet tail. Bib bluish green and golden. Ventral mid-line black. ♀:
dirty white throat and underparts, spotted on sides of breast and flanks. White
undertail coverts extend beyond bluish-black tail. Outer tail feathers paddle-
shaped. Humid temperate and tropical montane forest, bushes and thickets, edge.

7 STRIPE-BREASTED STARTHROAT *Heliomaster squamosus* 10cm
Dark bronzy green. Cap shining blue. Gorget glittering purply red. White stripe
down mid-belly. Undertail coverts edged white. ♀: underparts dirty white.
White throat scaled blackish brown. White malar stripe. Tail green, subterminal
band black, tip white. White spot on side of body. Tropical rainforest, edge,
savannah, bushes and thickets, woods and scrub in hills, copses.

8 BLUE-TUFTED STARTHROAT *Heliomaster furcifer* 10cm
Upperparts bronzy green, underparts dark blue. Gorget purply red and shining
dark blue. Vent dark green. ♀: underparts plain dirty white. Tail black, basally
green, tipped white. Dry woods, arid scrub, savannah, forest, edge, copses,
parks, gardens.

9 LONG-BILLED STARTHROAT *Heliomaster longirostris* 10cm
Brownish olive with bronzy sheen. Cap glittering emerald. Purply-red bib
bordered white. Central underparts dirty white. Tail brownish olive, white
tips. ♀: brownish-olive cap, notable white malar stripe and blackish-spotted
throat. White mark on side of body. Open woods, edge, copses, scattered trees,
open areas, bushes, thickets, savannah, plantations, parks, gardens.

1♂ 1♀ 2♂ 2♂ 3♂ 3R♂ 3♀ 4♂ 4♀ 5♂ ♀ 6♂ 6♀ 7♀ 7♂ 8♀ 8♂ 9♀ 9♂

RODRIGUEZ MATA

HUMMINGBIRDS (TROCHILIDAE)

1 CHILEAN WOODSTAR *Eulidia (Myrtis) yarrellii*   ♂ 8cm, ♀ 7cm
Bib shining purply red and blue. Tail forked, outer feathers narrow, pointed. ♀:
throat and collar white, underparts mostly cinnamon. Shrubs, thickets and
gardens in arid regions. Tacna (S Peru) to Antofagasta (N Chile).

2 SHORT-TAILED WOODSTAR *Myrmia micrura*   6.5cm
Shining violaceous-red gorget. Very short rounded tail. ♀: all underparts buffy
white. Tail tipped white. Shrubs and thickets in arid tropical regions.

3 PURPLE-COLLARED WOODSTAR *Myrtis fanny*   ♂ 9cm, ♀ 7.5cm
Longish forked tail, outer feathers curving inwards. Bib brilliant blue and
purply red. ♀: outer tail feathers black, tips buffy white. Underparts plain buffy
cinnamon. Arid shrubs and thickets in tropical and temperate regions, coastal
plains to high mountains.

4 SLENDER-TAILED WOODSTAR *Microstilbon burmeisteri* ♂ 8.5cm, ♀ 7cm
Strangely forked tail. Narrow shining purply-red gorget. Throat and mid-belly
grey. ♀: underparts buffy cinnamon. Shrubs and thickets in mountains, edge of
montane forest.

5 AMETHYST WOODSTAR *Calliphlox amethystina*   ♂ 9cm, ♀ 6.5cm
Forked tail, outer pair pointed. Shining purply-red bib. White collar. ♀: throat
buff, spotted green. Green and buff collars. Rest of underparts cinnamon-
rufous. Edge of humid and gallery forest, clearings, shrubs, thickets, savannah.

6 PURPLE-THROATED WOODSTAR
Calliphlox (Philodice) mitchellii   ♂ 9cm, ♀ 7.5cm
Forked tail, feathers narrow. Shining purply-red gorget. Rufous lower belly. ♀:
buffy-white throat with green and red centre. Collar buffy white. Breast green,
rufous below. Humid montane and cloud-forest, edge, bushes, thickets.

7 WHITE-BELLIED WOODSTAR
Chaetocercus (Acestrura) mulsantii   ♂ 8.5cm, ♀ 7.5cm
Shining purply-red bib. Collar and mid-belly white. Forked tail, feathers
pointed. Vent white and green. ♀: throat, collar and mid-belly buffy, flanks
and vent rufous cinnamon. Incomplete green collar. Edge of humid forest,
bushes, thickets, copses, grassland, cultivated areas in mountainous terrain.

8 ESMERALDA'S WOODSTAR
Chaetocercus (Acestrura) berlepschi   ♂ 6.2cm, ♀ 5.5cm
Strange tail: outer feathers like long thorns. Bib shining purply red. ♀:
underparts white. Outer tail tipped white. Edge of subtropical and temperate
montane forest, shrubs, thickets.

9 LITTLE WOODSTAR *Chaetocercus (Acestrura) bombus*   ♂ 6.8cm, ♀ 6cm
Bib shining red. Collar buffy. Tail forked, outer feathers thorn-like. ♀:
underparts cinnamon. Incomplete green collar. Bushes and thickets at edge of
tropical and subtropical forest, mountains, valleys and plains.

10 GORGETED WOODSTAR
Chaetocercus (Acestrura) heliodor   ♂ 6.4cm, ♀ 5.7cm
Gorget brilliant purply red. Breast grey. Tail forked, feathers very narrow. ♀:
underparts cinnamon-rufous. Incomplete green collar. Montane and cloud-
forest, clearings, edge, bushes, thickets, copses, plantations. The Santa Marta
Woodstar *C. h. astreans* from Santa Marta Mtns in extreme N Colombia has
lower body bluish. ♀'s underparts paler. May be a valid species.

11 RUFOUS-SHAFTED WOODSTAR *Chaetocercus jourdanii* ♂ 7.2cm, ♀ 6.5cm
Bright purply-red bib (pinkish red in one race). Broad white collar. Forked tail,
outer feathers very narrow with cinnamon base. ♀: underparts cinnamon and
white. White collar. Incomplete green collar. Somewhat rounded tail. Montane
and cloud-forest, edge, bushes, thickets, woods, coffee plantations.

1♂   1♀   7♂   7♀   2♀   3♂   8♂   2♂   3♀   8♀   4♂   5♀   9♂   9♀   4♀   5♂   0♀   10♂   11♀   11♂

RODRIGUEZ MATA

QUETZALS AND TROGONS (TROGONIDAE)

1 CRESTED QUETZAL *Pharomachrus antisianus*   30cm
Crest from forehead. Very brilliant emerald-green head, breast and upperparts.
Underparts bright red. Central tail feathers black, outers white. Upper tail
coverts green and longer than the tail. ♀: head and underparts greyish brown.
Breast bright green. Vent bright red. Blackish tail with outer feathers partially
barred and tipped white. Cloud-forest and edge.

2 WHITE-TIPPED QUETZAL *Pharomachrus fulgidus*   33cm
Upperparts and breast bright emerald-green. Head with strong golden sheen.
Underparts bright red. Tail blackish with distal third of outer feathers white.
Upper tail coverts brilliant green, longer than tail. ♀: head greyish brown with
golden-green gloss. Breast bright green. Vent pinkish red. Blackish tail
partially barred and tipped white. Humid forest, cloud-forest, edge, coffee
plantations.

3 GOLDEN-HEADED QUETZAL *Pharomachrus auriceps*   33cm
Differs from 2 only in its entirely black tail. Yellow bill. ♀ differs from those of
1 and 2 in all-blackish tail and pinkish red on to lower belly. Humid forest,
cloud-forest, dwarf copses, open country with scattered trees.

4 PAVONINE QUETZAL *Pharomachrus pavoninus*   33cm
Very like 3 but bill red and tail more graded, outer feathers very short. ♀ like
that of 1 but bill dirty red. Terra firme and rainforest in lowlands.

5 BLACK-THROATED TROGON *Trogon rufus*   25cm
Face and throat black. Only trogon with head, breast and upperparts green.
Underparts rich yellow. Wing coverts vermiculated black and white. Tail
underside barred black and white, tipped white. Bill yellow. 3 races differ in
green, blue or coppery central tail feathers. ♀: head, breast and upperparts
cinnamon-brown. Underparts yellow. Underside of tail like ♂'s. Rainforest,
gallery forest, cloud-forest, upland open woods, edge.

6 WHITE-TAILED TROGON *Trogon viridis*   28cm
Head and breast blue. Back bright green. Wing coverts black. Underparts rich
yellow. Tail has white outer feathers, basally black (or all white in one race).
Eye-ring pale blue. ♀: head, breast and upperparts slate-grey. Underparts yellow.
Wing coverts finely vermiculated black and white. Underside of tail black, 3
outer pairs tipped and externally bordered white, this serrated with black. Eye-
ring complete and narrow, pale blue. Montane forest, rainforest, deciduous and
gallery forest, edge, scattered trees in deforested areas, plantations.

7 VIOLACEOUS TROGON *Trogon violaceus*   23cm
A small version of 6, but eye-ring orange, undertail barred and slight pectoral
collar white. Central tail feathers bluish green or blue, according to race. ♀
differs from 6's only in white eye-ring being incomplete and broader.
Rainforest, edge, scattered trees in deforested areas, open woods, woods along
streams, humid to arid regions.

RODRIGUEZ MATA

TROGONS (TROGONIDAE)

1 BLACK-TAILED TROGON *Trogon melanurus*   30cm
Glossy green head, breast and back, with golden sheen. Face and throat
blackish. Eye-ring orangy red. Bill yellow. Wing coverts finely vermiculated
black and white. Central tail feathers green washed blue. Underparts bright
red. Pectoral collar white. Undertail slaty. ♀: slate-grey, belly and vent pinkish
scarlet. Blackish bill, yellow mandible. Orange eye-ring. Humid rainforest,
edge, secondary growth.

2 SLATY-TAILED TROGON *Trogon massena*   30cm
Very like 1 but lacks pectoral collar. Bill red. ♀ also has red bill. Some
specimens have slight white markings on outer vane and tip of outer tail
feathers. Humid rainforest, edge, scattered trees, clearings, secondary growth.

3 BLUE-TAILED TROGON *Trogon comptus*   28cm
Like 1 but smaller. White eye. Black eye-ring. No pectoral collar. ♀ like that of
1 but darker slate, especially on head and breast. Eye and eye-ring like ♂'s.
Humid rainforest, edge, foothills, broken terrain.

4 COLLARED TROGON *Trogon collaris*   25cm
Head, breast and upperparts green with strong golden and bronzy sheen. Blue
tint on central tail feathers. Face and throat blackish. Wings finely barred black
and white (vermiculated in one race). Pectoral collar white. Rest of underparts
bright red. Undertail variably barred black and white. Eye-ring orangy red. ♀:
head, breast and upperparts tawny brown. Face and throat dark brown. Bill
blackish with yellow mandible. Upper tail more tawny. Pectoral collar white.
Rest of underparts pale rosy red. Undertail white, finely vermiculated grey,
outer feathers with narrow subterminal band. Central feathers black. Cloud-
forest, varzea, gallery forest, rainforest, edge, tall secondary growth.

5 MASKED TROGON *Trogon personatus*   25cm
Very like 4 but upper tail green with golden or bronzy sheen. Wings darkly
vermiculated. Undertail very finely barred black and white (almost seems
silvery in some), broader white tips. ♀ like that of 4 but bill all yellow. Face,
throat and forehead blackish. Undertail barred, tipped white. Cloud-forest,
rainforest, edge, open woods at higher elevations.

6 BLUE-CROWNED TROGON *Trogon curucui*   25cm
Face and throat blackish. Head and neck metallic blue with greenish sheen.
Upperparts metallic green with bronzy sheen. Central tail feathers bluish
green. Narrow pectoral collar white. Underparts bright red. Underside of tail
barred black and white, tips white. ♀ like that of 7 but white pectoral collar
and more extensive rosy-red underparts. Outer vane of tail feathers serrated
black and white. Greyish culmen. Cloud-forest, montane forest, varzea, terra
firme and gallery forests, tall secondary growth.

7 SURUCUA TROGON *Trogon surrucura*   26cm
Head, neck and breast metallic blue. Upperparts metallic green with bronzy
sheen. Central tail feathers green washed blue. Underparts bright red.
Undertail white, base blackish. ♀: mostly dark slate-grey, darker on head,
lighter on upper belly. Wings black, finely barred white. Lower belly and vent
pinkish red. Undertail outer vane white, tip white. Bill yellowish. Montane
and lowland forest, gallery forest, edge, cerrado. A race in SE Brazil (*T. s.
aurantius*) has orange underparts.

♀

2♂

1♀

4♂

5♂

5♀

6♀

6♂

7♀

7♂

RODRIGUEZ MATA

KINGFISHERS (ALCEDINIDAE)

1 BELTED KINGFISHER *Megaceryle alcyon* 30cm
Medium-sized. Erectile crest. Upperparts and pectoral band greyish blue.
Throat, collar and underparts white. ♀: 2 pectoral bands, greyish blue and
chestnut-rufous. Swamps, trees bordering lakes, rivers and streams, freshwater
bodies, sea coasts, estuaries, mangroves. Migrates from N America.

2 RINGED KINGFISHER *Megaceryle torquata* 40cm
Large. Erectile crest. Upperparts greyish blue. Throat, collar and vent white.
Underparts chestnut-rufous. ♀: breast-band greyish blue. S race brighter.
Tree-lined rivers, streams, lakes, fresh water, cables and bridges over water,
mangroves.

3 AMAZON KINGFISHER *Chloroceryle amazona* 28cm
Medium-sized. Proportionately long and heavy beak. Erectile nuchal crest.
Upperparts shining dark green. Throat, collar and underparts white. Breast
chestnut-rufous. Flanks partly streaked green. ♀: 1 incomplete green pectoral
collar. Trees by lakes, marshes, streams, rivers, bodies of open water. Less in forest.

4 GREEN KINGFISHER *Chloroceryle americana* 19cm
Small, dumpy. Small version of 3 but bill proportionately smaller. Upperwings
dotted white. More chestnut-rufous on breast. Belt of green spots. ♀: double
breast-band of green dots. Lakes, marshes, roadside ditches, mangroves,
watercourses with trees or reeds.

5 GREEN-AND-RUFOUS KINGFISHER *Chloroceryle inda* 22cm
Upperparts dark shining green. Spotted white on wings and tail. Throat and
collar rufous ochre. Rest of underparts chestnut-rufous. ♀: dark green breast-
band scaled white. Shady forest streams, swamps and ponds, flooded forest,
varzea, mangroves.

6 AMERICAN PYGMY KINGFISHER *Chloroceryle aenea* 13cm
Miniature version of 5. Centre of belly and vent white. Small shady streams
and ponds in forest, flooded forest, varzea, mangroves.

1♂

6♀   6♂

1♀

3♀

2♂   2♀   3♂

5♂   5♀   4♀   4♂

RODRIGUEZ MATA

MOTMOTS (MOMOTIDAE)
AND NUNBIRDS (BUCCONIDAE)

Motmots are large birds with heavy black bills, large heads and black face-masks. Long tail with or without 'racquets'.

1 BROAD-BILLED MOTMOT *Electron platyrhynchum*   33cm
Head and breast rufous, chin green. Face-mask black, narrowing towards ear coverts. Topside of tail blue with 'racquets'. Low-pitched, nasal, resonant *ornk* or *quoonk*. Rainforest, secondary growth, lowland forest and at the foot of mountains.

2 RUFOUS MOTMOT *Baryphthengus martii*   46cm
Like 1 but larger and lacking green chin. Rufous reaches belly. Tail seldom has 'racquet'. Broader face-mask. Series of owl-like, low-pitched *hoot hoot ….* Rainforest, secondary growth, lowland forest and at the foot of mountains. Considered a race of 3 by some.

3 RUFOUS-CAPPED MOTMOT *Baryphthengus ruficapillus*   44cm
Cap rufous and ventral band cinnamon-rufous. Rectangular face-mask. Tail with ill-defined 'racquets', topside blue. Calls: deep, guttural *hoorooroo hoorooroo* and long rolled *oorrrrrrrrrrrr*. Rainforests and gallery forests.

4 BLUE-CROWNED MOTMOT *Momotus momota*   43cm
Blue cap with black centre. Irregular face-mask. Underparts green (or more or less cinnamon-green according to race). Notable 'racquets' on tail. Call *hooroop… hooroop* and deep *whoodledoodledoo*. Rainforest, gallery forests, forest edge, open woods, secondary growth, plantations. The race *M. m. aequatorialis* may be a separate species (Highland Motmot).

5 TODY MOTMOT *Hylomanes momotula*   18cm
Small; tail proportionately shorter. Whitish line across face. Head rufous, brow blue. Call a loud, resonant *kwakwakwakwa…* or long tremulous *cooooooo-o-o-oo*. Humid forest at foot of mountains.

Monasa is a genus of 4 large slaty-black puffbirds. They are large-headed but not dumpy. The bills provide the only touch of bright colour.

6 BLACK NUNBIRD *Monasa atra*   28cm
Nearly all black, belly slaty. 'Shoulders' and borders of upper wing coverts white. Bill bright coral-red. Voice is loud, a three-syllable *tree-de-lee*. At lower to highest storeys of the vegetation in rainforest, gallery forest, scrubby thickets and forest edge.

7 BLACK-FRONTED NUNBIRD *Monasa nigrifrons*   28cm
Entirely slaty black, darker on face, cap and throat. Bright coral-red bill. Juv: rufous-brown forehead and chin, yellowish bill. Voice: a quiet *keeor* or a long phrase of melodious whistles lasting for several minutes. At all levels of the vegetation. Edge of rainforest, gallery forest, varzea, forested islands on rivers, secondary growth, scattered trees, palm groves.

8 WHITE-FRONTED NUNBIRD *Monasa morphoeus*   28cm
Like 7 but with white forehead and chin. Juv: buffy-cinnamon forehead and chin, whitish bill. The race *M. m. pallescens* has only forehead white. Calls as does 7, in noisy choruses. At mid-levels to below the crowns, occasionally to lower levels in rainforest, gallery forest and dryland forest.

9 YELLOW-BILLED NUNBIRD *Monasa flavirostris*   24cm
Yellow bill. Black with white 'shoulders', slatier on belly. Perches quietly on exposed limbs at upper levels of trees. Sallies to snap up prey from the air or the foliage. Drylands forests, edges of forests, scattered trees in forest clearings, secondary growth, forest at the foot of hills.

RODRIGUEZ MATA

PUFFBIRDS (BUCCONIDAE)

Puffbirds on this plate (genera *Notharchus, Bucco, Hypnelus*) are those that have the most massive black bills (bar one orange/red-billed species). All have notable breast-bands or collars.

1 WHITE-NECKED PUFFBIRD *Notharchus macrorhynchus* 25cm
Huge. White head with black crown and mask. Broad black breast-band. Rest of underparts white, flanks barred. *N. m. swainsoni* has ochreous-buff underparts. Forest to open country with scattered trees, in treetops.

2 BLACK-BREASTED PUFFBIRD *Notharchus pectoralis* 20cm
Head black, white only on ear-patch and throat. Neck and breast black. Lower underparts white, flanks barred. Whistled *whets, whews* and combinations. From mid-storey upwards in rainforest, secondary growth, edge of forest.

3 BROWN-BANDED PUFFBIRD *Notharchus ordii* 18cm
Breast-band black over brown. Head white but for black cap. Black barring on white belly and flanks. Base and tips of tail feathers white. Rainforest.

4 PIED PUFFBIRD *Notharchus tectus* 15cm
Small. Cap black with white speckling, black mask, long white eyebrow. Broad black breast-band. Scapular patch white. The race *N. t. subtectus* has a narrower breast-band. High-pitched *pee-peed, pee-peedit, peedit, peedit, peeah, pee, pee, pee*. Rainforest to mangroves, open areas with trees and stubble fields.

5 CHESTNUT-CAPPED PUFFBIRD *Bucco (Argicus) macrodactylus* 15cm
Chestnut cap. Long brow whitish. Black mask and neck-band. Cinnamon hind-collar. Underparts buffy, finely barred brown. Upperparts brown. Series of *pips* and *peeps* ending in *piz twitter*; series of *weeahs* rising slightly. Perches at lower levels especially near water and flooded areas. Rainforest, its edge and woodland, gallery, dryland and varzea, secondary growth and thickets in clearings.

6 SPOTTED PUFFBIRD *Bucco (Nystactes) tamatia* 18cm
Brow and bib tawny. Cap and mask brown. Long white malar streak. Long black streak on lower cheek. Upperparts brown. Breast and rest of underparts white with black scaling simulating barring. Long series of whistled *chewys* at 2 per sec, ending emphatically with strong *petchowees*. Trusting, in lower branches. Edges of rainforest, varzea and sandy savannah along rivers, edge of woods and thickets.

7 SOOTY-CAPPED PUFFBIRD *Bucco (Nystactes) noanamae* 18cm
Cap and mask sooty. Lores, brow and throat white. Broad black breast-band. Rest of underparts buffy, spotted dark, emulating barring. Trusting; low in rainforest and secondary growth.

8 COLLARED PUFFBIRD *Bucco capensis* 19cm
Orange bill with black. Mostly rufous and white. Black breast-band. Call: *kwa wheel, kwa wheel*. Perches quietly from mid-height to just below the crown of trees. Dryland and rainforest.

9 RUSSET-THROATED PUFFBIRD *Hypnelus ruficollis* 23cm
Cap, back and tail dirty brown, feathers tipped and edged whitish buff. Narrow forehead and throat cinnamon-russet. Ear-patch and narrow hind-collar whitish. Lower cheek darkish brown. Black breast-band. Rest of underparts ochreous buff, barred on flanks. The race *H. r. bicinctus* differs in having a double collar/breast-band and a buffy-white throat. Noisy, usually a duetted rhythmic *oo-dooks*, ending with a half-speed solo. Quiet and trusting, perches low on outer branches of isolated trees or thorny bushes. Deciduous forest and dryland woods and thickets.

RODRIGUEZ MATA

PUFFBIRDS (BUCCONIDAE)

Malacoptila puffbirds are dumpy and large-headed. Most have white down from the base of the bill – a droopy moustache. Bills are down-curved at the tip. They are particularly passive and trusting, mostly frequenting the darker areas of forest, usually at mid- to lower levels.

1 CRESCENT-CHESTED PUFFBIRD *Malacoptila striata*   22cm
Lores, small brow and chin tawny. Moustache and band across fore-neck white, pectoral collar black. Breast and flanks from tawny to buffy. Bill black. Calls are a thin whistled *bee-ee, bee-ee…* and series of 10+ uniform *pee-u*. Rainforest and edges, in shadier parts.

2 WHITE-CHESTED PUFFBIRD *Malacoptila fusca*   20cm
Lores, moustache and band on fore-neck white. Breast and flanks streaked dark brown and white. Bill orange with black culmen and tip. Voice: a thin whistled *seeee…* sometimes lasting up to 2 sec, descending in pitch. Perches on branches from mid-levels to near the ground. Rainforest, plantations, dryland forest, secondary growth, edges.

3 SEMICOLLARED PUFFBIRD *Malacoptila semicincta*   20cm
Practically identical to 2 but has a rufous half-collar on hind-neck. Rainforest. Some consider this a race of 2.

4 BLACK-STREAKED PUFFBIRD *Malacoptila fulvogularis*   22cm
Similar to 2 and 3, but lores, chin and patch across throat buffy. Scapulars and wing coverts edged lighter, giving a scaly effect. Tail relatively longer. Bill black. Forested slopes in the damp understorey.

5 RUFOUS-NECKED PUFFBIRD *Malacoptila rufa*   20cm
Cap and auricular grey, finely streaked white. Forehead and lores rufous cinnamon. Cheeks, sides of the neck and hind-neck rufous. Moustache and band across upper breast white, the latter with slight dark barring below. Call: a rising phrase *ee, ee, ee, ee, ee*. Rainforest and varzea.

6 WHITE-WHISKERED PUFFBIRD *Malacoptila panamensis*   20cm
Sexes differ. ♂ mostly rufous. White moustache, fine streaking on cheeks. Upper breast rufous; lower breast, flanks and belly streaked. ♀ greyish brown where ♂ is rufous. Upper breast ochre. Voice in alarm a thin *seee*; in territorial flight a high-pitched squeaky, repeated *seeet, hee, hee*. Rainforest and secondary growth.

7 MOUSTACHED PUFFBIRD *Malacoptila mystacalis*   24cm
Head, upperparts and tail brown, speckled buffy on back and wing coverts. Lores and moustache white. Breast tawny rufous, somewhat streaked brown, this extending onto the flanks. Rainforest, cloud-forest and open or deciduous woods, in lower storeys.

8 WHITE-FACED NUNBIRD *Hapaloptila castanea*   25cm
Large. No streaking. Lead-grey cap. White around the base of the black bill. Black band across forehead. Cheeks olive. Rest of upperparts and tail dark brownish grey. Underparts orange-rufous. Call an owl-like hoot, rising; sometimes a trill. In pairs or small flocks. Treetops of rainforest or lower on the edge of forest or small clearings.

9 SWALLOW-WINGED PUFFBIRD *Chelidoptera tenebrosa*   16cm
Unlike any other puffbird. Long wings, short tail. Mostly black, lower belly cinnamon. Rump, all tail coverts and underwing coverts white. Hunts insects on the wing in acrobatic flight. Perches in exposed positions in a variety of open habitats and edges of forest, rivers, savannah, woods.

RODRIGUEZ MATA

PUFFBIRDS (BUCCONIDAE)

Nystalus puffbirds are squat, large-headed and short-necked. They have large bills with a hooked tip. Mostly silent.

1 SPOT-BACKED PUFFBIRD *Nystalus maculatus*   19cm
Bill orange and blackish. Lower throat and upper breast ochre. Belly and flanks white, streaked black. Crown and face streaked. Back and tail barred. Duets: a whistled *to you, to you, to you, to you…*. Low, thorny arid scrub and open woods.

2 WHITE-EARED PUFFBIRD *Nystalus chacuru*   19cm
Bill orange. Face black, auricular white. Underparts and hind-collar whitish. Duets: *turutee turutay turutee turutay…*, descending. On telegraph wires and posts by roads at the edge of forest, trees in fields, secondary growth, transition forest.

3 STRIOLATED PUFFBIRD *Nystalus striolatus*   20cm
Bill blackish and yellowish horn. Face and underparts ochre and buff streaked blackish. Upperparts barred. Edge of the forest, open woods, arid scrub with trees.

4 BARRED PUFFBIRD *Nystalus radiatus*   20cm
Bill blackish and yellowish horn. Crown and rest of upperparts rufous. Face, hind-neck and underparts buffy ochre, all finely barred blackish. Call a long, slow *wheeeeeet wheeeeeew* like a wolf-whistle, repeated twice a minute. Edge of rainforest, open damp areas with scattered trees, secondary growth. W Colombia and W Ecuador.

5 LANCEOLATED MONKLET *Micromonacha lanceolata*   13cm
Very small. Black bill. Tail proportionately shorter. Upperparts brown, underparts white with blackish drip-shaped streaks. White around base of bill. Edge of rainforest, secondary growth near clearings.

Nunlets are dull and fairly uniformly coloured. Strong bill down-curved at the tip. They live low in the depth of forests. Often overlooked. Apparently silent.

6 RUSTY-BREASTED NUNLET *Nonnula rubecula*   15cm
Bill black and yellowish. Eye-ring pale. Upperparts and cheeks olive-brown; crown greyish. Lores buffy white. Throat, breast and flanks buffy cinnamon, lower belly lighter. Rainforest, varzea, gallery forests.

7 FULVOUS-CHINNED NUNLET *Nonnula sclateri*   15cm
Like 6 but face greyish, lores and chin tawny buff, crown olive-brown. Tropical rainforest.

8 BROWN NUNLET *Nonnula brunnea*   16cm
Bill black, bluish horn on mandible. Upperparts, cheeks and sides of the neck dark brown. Lores and underparts tawny, lighter on belly. Eye-ring pink. Tropical rainforest, dryland forest, lowland forest at the base of the Andes, secondary growth.

9 RUFOUS-CAPPED NUNLET *Nonnula ruficapilla*   15cm
Bill black and blue. Face and sides of the neck all bluish grey. Cap rufous. Rest of upperparts and tail brown with olive wash. Throat, breast, flanks and rest of underparts tawny, ranging to white at lower belly. Eye-ring pink. Race *N. r. frontalis* differs in having lower face and hind-neck more olive-brown, cap tawny rufous; for some a valid species: Grey-cheeked Nunlet. Edge of rainforest and gallery forest, especially in climbers and lianas; secondary growth in damp areas.

10 CHESTNUT-HEADED NUNLET *Nonnula amaurocephala*   15cm
Head and breast tawny rufous, belly and undertail coverts white. Tropical forests.

RODRIGUEZ MATA

JACAMARS (GALBULIDAE)

1 WHITE-EARED JACAMAR *Galbalcyrhynchus leucotis* 20cm
Somewhat like a kingfisher. Large pale pink bill. Overall strong chestnut and
black. Cheeks white. Bare patch around eye bright pink. Iris red. Calls: single
or repeated *keeew* or rising trill. Edge of the varzea and gallery forest, secondary
growth. The S race lacks the white ear and is considered by some a separate
species, G. *purusianus*, the Chestnut Jacamar.

Jacamars of the genus *Brachygalba* are the smallest and dullest of the family with
dark, non-shiny plumage.

2 BROWN JACAMAR *Brachygalba lugubris* 17cm
Mostly blackish brown. Crown feathers edged whitish, giving a scaly effect.
Some streaking on cheeks. Whitish throat finely streaked dark brown. Buff-
lined white triangle from centre of breast to lower belly. Undertail coverts
black. A dark form is black on breast and flanks, with whitish throat streaked
chestnut. Another has yellow on lower mandible, base of upper mandible and
eye-ring. Call is a high, descending, accelerating insect-like stuttering trill.
Edge of forest plantations, scrubby and bush vegetation in rainforest, cloud-
forest and gallery forest, clearings, trees in open areas.

3 PALE-HEADED JACAMAR *Brachygalba goerengi* 17cm
The only jacamar with a buffy-white post-ocular streak and collar. White throat.
Dirty brown crown and cheeks, darker upper breast and back. Lower breast, lower
belly and undertail white. Broad chestnut band across belly. Call: single *weet*, or a
series, rising and accelerating to a trill. Edge and clearings in deciduous riverine
forests, open woods, edge of savannah, stubble fields, scrub vegetation, bushes.

4 DUSKY-BACKED JACAMAR *Brachygalba salmoni* 17cm
Overall slaty black with slight blue sheen. Throat white. Belly, flanks and
undertail cinnamon with sparse black speckling. Call: high-pitched, insistent
pe pe pe peet or *pe peet*, often in a long series. Edge and clearings in rainforest,
gallery forest and secondary growth with tall trees.

5 WHITE-THROATED JACAMAR *Brachygalba albogularis* 17cm
Ivory-yellow bill slightly decurved. Face and throat white, creamier on cheeks.
Overall blackish brown. Large chestnut spot at mid-belly. Edges and clearings
in forest, riverside forests, stubble fields, brushland and bushes at forest edge.

6 THREE-TOED JACAMAR *Jacamaralcyon tridactyla* 18cm
Mostly dull slate-grey. White streaking on head, which is more chestnut in
some individuals. Breast and belly white, flanks and undertail feathers
narrowly tipped whitish, giving effect of slight barring or large scales. Only 3
toes, unlike all others of the family. Series of high, short, whistled notes. Forest
along mountain rivers, patches of primary and secondary forest, forestry
plantations; usually near earth banks of riversides.

7 GREAT JACAMAR *Jacamerops aureus* 30cm
Huge and hefty for the family. Large slightly decurved black bill. Head, sides of
the breast, back, tail and wings all glittery bright green with bronze, coppery and
purple sheen. Underparts bright rufous. ♂: white upper breast. Infrequent, long
melancholy whistled *weeeeee…eeeeeer* somewhat raptor-like. Edge and clearings
of rainforest and gallery forest, of woods and stubble fields. Shy, keeps still for long
periods in the foliage at all levels beneath the crowns. Rarely emerges to hunt.

JACAMARS (GALBULIDAE)

All *Galbula* except one have green backs, rufous below; the ♂ of most species has a white throat, while that of the ♀ is buffy to cinnamon. All have long, slender, sharp-pointed bills.

1 YELLOW-BILLED JACAMAR *Galbula albirostris*   19cm
Bill mostly yellow and appears slightly decurved. Forehead, crown and part of cheeks browny purple. ♂: white throat, green above with bronze and coppery sheen, rufous below, paler on lower belly. Yellow eye-ring and lores. ♀: buffy cinnamon throat. Call: sharp *peek* or series accelerating to trill. Bushes and scrub at edge of rainforest and varzea.

2 BLUE-CHEEKED JACAMAR *Galbula cyanicollis*   20cm
Similar to 1. Bill straight. Forehead, crown and part of the cheeks dark blue. ♂: rufous throat. Edge of rainforest. Some think this is a race of 1.

3 GREEN-TAILED JACAMAR *Galbula galbula*   21cm
Upperparts and broad band across breast metallic green with bronzy and coppery sheen. Forehead, crown and part of the cheeks bluish green. Throat white (♂) or buffy cinnamon (♀). Rest of underparts rufous. Tail green above, blackish blue below. Call: *peer* repeated, or rhythmic *peep peep*…. Edge of rainforests and gallery forest, riverine forest, tall secondary growth, scrub and bushes.

4 WHITE-CHINNED JACAMAR *Galbula tombacea*   21cm
Both sexes have white chin; throat and breast metallic green. Forehead, crown and part of the cheeks brown. Rest of underparts rufous, ♀ paler. Call: repeated *keelip*, and *pee pee pe pe*… accelerating. Edge and clearings of varzea, gallery forest, and thickets.

5 BLUISH-FRONTED JACAMAR *Galbula cyanescens*   22cm
Plumage differs from 4 only in bluish-green forehead, crown and part of the cheeks. Slightly larger than 4. ♀ paler below. Edge of gallery forest. Possibly a race of 4.

6 COPPERY-CHESTED JACAMAR *Galbula pastazae*   23cm
Similar to 5 though slightly larger; heavier bill slightly down-curved; narrow yellowish-orange eye-ring. ♂ has white chin-spot, ♀ chin and throat rufous. Edge of montane rainforest.

7 RUFOUS-TAILED JACAMAR *Galbula ruficauda*   23cm
Upperparts, breast and central tail feathers metallic green with bronzy and purple sheen. Blue wash on forehead. Chin and throat white or buffy cinnamon (♀). Rest of underparts rufous; outer tail feathers rufous with darker tip. A NW race has blackish chins in both sexes, longer tail, and outer tail feathers lacking dark tips. Some consider this a species – Black-chinned Jacamar (*G. melanogenia*), 7R. Call: sharp *pee-up*, accelerating *pee pee pe pe pe e e e*… ending in trill. Edge and clearings in wet or dry forest, gallery forest, nearby bushes and thickets, copses, plantations, savannah, isolated trees in deforested areas and secondary growth.

8 BRONZY JACAMAR *Galbula leucogastra*   20cm
Mostly coppery purple. Throat white (buffy cinnamon in ♀). Lower belly and undertail coverts white. Undertail blackish. Edge of dryland rainforest, gallery forest, secondary growth, forest in sandy soils. The race *G. l. chalcothorax* is considered by some a separate species: Purplish Jacamar.

9 PARADISE JACAMAR *Galbula dea*   30cm
Metallic bluish black with white throat. Very long slender tail. Call: descending *peep peep pee pee pe pe pe*… accelerating but quieter at end. Rainforest, by bodies of water, in sandy soils, dryland forest, scattered trees in deforested areas, woods and savannah.

RODRIGUEZ MATA

BARBETS (CAPITONIDAE)

Chunky, large-headed, colourful, forest birds with heavy bills and short necks. Bills horn-coloured or blackish.

1 SCARLET-CROWNED BARBET *Capito aurovirens*   19cm
Big yellowish-orange bib. Red cap. Mask and upperparts dark brown. Belly and undertail brownish olive. ♀: forehead, crown and nape whitish, faintly marked brown. Call a rapid, frog-like *crew crew....* Varzea, edge, tall secondary growth.

2 SPOT-CROWNED BARBET *Capito maculicoronatus*   17cm
Crown white streaked black. Mask, upperparts and tail black. Malar region and throat white, breast yellow. Rest of underparts white, flanks with broad black drop-shaped streaks, these orange in part. ♀: malar region, throat and breast black. Edge of humid rainforest, forest in hilly country, valleys, ravines, secondary growth.

3 SCARLET-BANDED BARBET *Capito wallacei*   19cm
Red cap. White brow; black mask, upperparts and tail. Lower cheek, throat and fore-neck white. Pectoral band red. Rest of underparts yellowish, browner on flanks. Humid montane and stunted forest all dripping with mosses. Recently discovered. Very local, NC Peru, E of the Andes, NW of Contamana on a low plateau between Huallaga and Ucayali rivers.

4 WHITE-MANTLED BARBET *Capito hypoleucus*   18cm
Forehead and fore-crown red. Hind-crown, nape and upper back white, speckled black. Mask, rest of upperparts and tail black. Underparts white, pectoral collar pale brown. Flanks washed greyish yellow. Call a deep croak. Humid forest at base of hills.

5 FIVE-COLOURED BARBET *Capito quinticolor*   18cm
Forehead and mask black. Crown and nape red. Upperparts and tail black, upper back bordered with yellow in a 'V'. Greater coverts and edge of scapulars yellow. Throat white, rest of underparts yellow, flanks with broad black drop-shaped streaks. ♀: cap streaked black and yellow. Mask finely streaked. Upperparts' feathers edged yellow. Underparts all dotted and spotted blackish. Call is a series of whooping notes for several seconds and guttural *churr*. Rainforest, edge, tall secondary growth.

6 BLACK-SPOTTED BARBET *Capito niger*   18cm
Forehead, fore-crown and throat red. Hind-crown and nape yellow streaked black. Yellow line from brow to middle of back. Mask, upperparts and tail black. White bar on wing coverts. Underparts yellowish with drop-shaped spots on flanks. ♀: mask streaked. Upperpart feathers edged yellow. Breast and flanks with black drop-shaped spots. Another race (*C. n. imperatus*) differs in having an ochreous forehead and crown. Throat pale orange. Underparts duller yellow streaked blackish grey. *C. n. auratus* has an orange forehead and throat, orangy-yellow underparts and orange line from brow to back; some consider this a separate species: Gilded Barbet. Call is a deep, frog-like, hollow, ventriloquial *hoot-oot*. Rainforest, humid terra firme forest, swampy forest, secondary growth, edge, plantations, occasionally in varzea.

7 ORANGE-FRONTED BARBET *Capito squamatus*   17cm
Forehead orange. Crown and nape white flecked black. Mask, upperparts and tail black. White outer vane on tertials. Underparts white, breast washed yellow, flanks streaked blackish. ♀: throat and breast black. Call is a deep, fast, quiet purring trill, and a single or double *yit*. Humid rainforest, lowland and hill forest, secondary forest, orchards, isolated fruiting trees, plantations, farms.

5♂

3

4

1♂

1♀

5♀

6♀

6♂

2♀

6♂

R♀

7♀

6R♀

7♂

6R♂

6R♂

RODRIGUEZ MATA

BARBETS (CAPITONIDAE)

1   BROWN-CHESTED BARBET *Capito brunneipectus*   18cm
Forehead and pectoral collar brown. Crown, nape and throat yellowish buff.
Rest of underparts dirty yellowish streaked blackish grey. Mask, upperparts and
tail black. Yellow line from nape to back. Outer vane of tertials yellowish buff.
♀: throat dotted black. Upper back feathers edged buff and yellow. Call is a
trilled *whooo*, rising and then ending *brrrrrr*. Canopy of lowland rainforest.

2   BLACK-GIRDLED BARBET *Capito dayi*   17cm
Cap and undertail coverts red. Mask, upperparts and tail black. White on side of
upper back and on flight feathers. Black flanks and striking incomplete girdle.
Throat barred concentrically dark brown (lacking in some individuals). Breast
and belly whitish buff. ♀ has black cap. Gallery forest, rainforest, forest in
lowlands and slopes in foothills, secondary forest with fruiting trees, plantations.

Eubucco barbets are smaller and very colourful, with yellow or grey bills. Most have
green backs and tails, and stripes on flanks and belly.

3   LEMON-THROATED BARBET *Eubucco richardsoni*   15cm
Yellow bill. Several races. *E. r. aurantiicollis* has crown, sides of head and chin-
spot deep red, barred black. Bib and nuchal collar yellow. Pectoral collar
scarlet. Flanks and belly striped green and yellow. ♀: grey bill and throat, green
crown, black mask, yellow post-ocular brow. Yellowish-orange upper breast. *E.
r. richardsoni* has wider pale blue nuchal collar. *E. r. nigriceps* has crown, sides of
head and chin all purply black with broad pale blue nuchal collar. There are
intermediate forms. Call is a series of fast *todoos* or *toodledoos*. Terra firme forest
and varzea, lowland forest, clearings, tropical hill forest, gallery forest.

4   RED-HEADED BARBET *Eubucco bourcierii*   16cm
Hood and bib bright red, the latter varying in extent with race. Chin and
around eye black. Narrow, very light blue hind-collar. ♀: forehead, around eye
and chin black. Throat and face pale greenish blue. Crown olive-green. Breast
orangy yellow. Rainforest and transition with cloud-forest, secondary growth,
wood edges.

5   SCARLET-HOODED BARBET *Eubucco tucinkae*   17cm
Bright red hood. Hind-collar pale orange. Upperparts and tail bronzy olive. ♀:
crown and nape olive, malar region and throat yellow. Call a longish series of
rapid *oopoopoops*. Thickets with cane in gallery forest, islands, tropical forest
near rivers in the Andes.

6   VERSICOLOURED BARBET *Eubucco versicolor*   16cm
Head mostly bright red with blue malar stripe and narrow collar. Breast rich
yellow. Pale red band across upper belly. ♀: crown and hind-neck olive-green.
Forehead, face and throat blue. Narrow red collar on fore-neck. Breast light
green. One race (*E. v. glaucogularis*) has yellow malar region and most of the
throat blue, breast pale yellow; another (*E. v. steerii*) has malar region, throat
and breast yellow, all hind-neck pale blue. Call is a low-pitched even trill.
Tropical forest, rainforest, secondary growth with epiphytes and mosses, dry
forest on lower slopes.

7   TOUCAN-BARBET *Semnornis ramphastinus*   20cm
Large and multicoloured. Cap and foreface black, white patch on hind-crown.
Cheeks and throat bluish grey. Breast red. Long series of fast, foghorn-like
honks, sometimes duetted. Montane forest, edge, secondary growth, isolated
fruiting trees.

RODRIGUEZ MATA

TOUCANETS (RAMPHASTIDAE)

Aulacorhynchus toucanets are small and green, with a long, slender, graduated tail.

1 YELLOW-BILLED TOUCANET *Aulacorhynchus calorhynchus*   33cm
Bill yellow with black at the base of the maxilla and basal half of the mandible. Narrow white line at the base of the bill. Bare skin around eye grey. Bright blue below the eye and slight eyebrow. No chestnut on tail. Calls include *wicks* or *wahks* at the rate of about 2 per sec. Cloud-forests and edges, scattered trees, gardens. Some consider it a race of 2.

2 GROOVE-BILLED TOUCANET *Aulacorhynchus sulcatus*   35cm
Like 1 but bill is reddish chestnut with part of the maxilla and mandible black. Base of mandible yellow, fine ivory line at the base of the bill. Pale post-ocular brow. Lacks chestnut tip to the tail. Voice similar to that of 1 but more nasal. Rainforest and cloud-forest, plantations, copses, even gardens.

3 CHESTNUT-TIPPED TOUCANET *Aulacorhynchus derbianus*   35cm
Bill varies according to race: black with basal third reddish chestnut; or black with culmen and base of the mandible reddish chestnut; or practically all black but for reddish tip and basal area and lower base of the maxilla. All have a narrow white line at the base. Bare skin around eye salmon-pink. Throat white. Tip of tail chestnut. Calls deep *guah…gawk…hawk…gahk* at the rate of 1 per sec. Montane forest.

4 EMERALD TOUCANET *Aulacorhynchus prasinus*   35cm
Many races. The bills are black with a variable yellow area on the maxilla, some races with reddish spots at the base of the mandible; all have an ivory or white line at the base of the bill. The bare skin around the eye is blackish, salmon-pink or grey according to race. Throats also vary between black, blue, white or bluish grey. All have chestnut undertail coverts, blackish underside of tail, chestnut tip. Temperate cloud-forest and alder woods in mountains, edge, scattered trees, secondary growth, plantations, gardens.

5 CRIMSON-RUMPED TOUCANET *Aulacorhynchus haematopygus*   42cm
Bill black with broad reddish-chestnut longitudinal stripe on the maxilla, white line at the base. Bare skin around eye salmon-pink. Throat green. Blue wash on breast. Bright red rump. Tip of tail chestnut. Montane evergreen forests, basal forests, edges, isolated trees, gardens.

6 BLUE-BANDED TOUCANET *Aulacorhynchus coeruleicinctis*   40cm
Bill blackish and grey, ivory towards the tip, lacking white at base. Blackish bare skin around eye, pale blue or yellow below. Part of the cheeks, small eyebrow and throat white. Ill-defined blue band across upper belly. Greenish undertail coverts. Rump bright red. Rainforest and cloud-forests in mountains, edges and secondary growth.

7 YELLOW-BROWED TOUCANET *Aulacorhynchus huallagae*   38cm
Black and grey bill with ivory tip. Ill-defined blue band across upper belly. Blackish bare skin around eye, pale blue or yellow below. Very like 6 but with white line at base of bill. Yellow post-ocular brow. Golden-yellow undertail coverts. Very local in San Martín and La Libertad in NE Peru.

RODRIGUEZ MATA

TOUCANETS (RAMPHASTIDAE)

Selenidera toucanets are smallish, and are dumpier than other small toucans. Sexes differ though the bills are the same in both; bare faces vary from turquoise to greenish. All *Selenidera* have eyes like certain reptiles, with what appears to be a horizontal pupil. All have green backs and tails, red undertail coverts and chestnut leggings; tips of tail are cinnamon in all but 1 species. Both sexes have yellowish-orange or yellowish flanks, most have yellow and/or orange ear tufts and hind-collar. ♂: black breast and cap. ♀s of all species show less or more chestnut on some part of the head, neck or breast. They frequent denser vegetation where they are very hard to see when still. These toucanets are hardly ever exposed or in the open. Mostly solitary or in pairs.

1 YELLOW-EARED TOUCANET *Selenidera spectabilis* 38cm
Bill slate-grey, culmen broad yellow with a greenish wash. Only species with neither hind-collar nor cinnamon tip to tail. ♀: all underparts black and lacks auricular patch. Crown and hind-neck chestnut. Voice a slow, weak, rhythmic, 2-syllable *krek-ek*. Rainforest. Usually not in lowlands.

2 GUIANAN TOUCANET *Selenidera culik* 35cm
Bill black with dark red at the base, more on mandible. Flanks greenish yellow. ♀: throat, lower cheeks, breast and upper belly lead-grey, chestnut only on hind-neck. Rattly voice. Tropical rainforest, lowlands.

3 GOLDEN-COLLARED TOUCANET *Selenidera reinwardtii* 33cm
Bill chestnutty red with black culmen, tip and cutting edge. ♀: chestnut where ♂ is black, with ear tufts dull yellowish olive. Voice longish series of froggy croaks. Rainforests, sometimes in varzea. Occasionally in mixed flocks.

4 GREEN-BILLED TOUCANET *Selenidera langsdorffi* 33cm
Differs from 3 only in having black bill, pale grey at the base. Some consider this to be a race of 3. Voice: deep-toned growling barks. Rainforest.

5 TAWNY-TUFTED TOUCANET *Selenidera nattereri* 33cm
Bill reddish chestnut, culmen and tip yellow, black spot at the base and 'teeth' along the white cutting edge. ♀: chestnut where ♂ is black, and lacks contrasting flank-patch. Voice is a series of deep-toned, quiet, frog-like notes. Rainforest in sandy soils, tropical forest.

6 SPOT-BILLED TOUCANET *Selenidera maculirostris* 33cm
Shortish pale greyish-blue bill with yellower culmen and tip, and irregular black marks across it. Dull yellowish-olive ear tufts. ♀: chestnut where ♂ is black. Call is a series of 4 or 5 deep, hollow *wawks*. The N race has mostly black upper mandible, and extensive white on lower; Some believe it to be a separate species, Gould's Toucanet (*S. gouldii*), 6R. Rainforest.

RODRIGUEZ MATA

ARAÇARIS (RAMPHASTIDAE)

Araçaris are slender, smallish, colourful toucans with large, relatively boldly patterned bills. The tail is long, slender and graduated. All species have olive back, wings and tail; rump and upper tail coverts are red. The best way to identify them is to note the patterns on the bill and colours of the head, breast and underparts. Sexes are the same except in 3 species. They take sun on exposed branches early in the day, but during the rest of the day they frequent the denser vegetation at upper levels of the forest in pairs or small flocks where they hunt for small vertebrates and invertebrates, or for ripe fruit. Flight is alternately fast flapping interspersed with gliding.

1   CHESTNUT-EARED ARAÇARI *Pteroglossus castanotis* 46cm
Bill mostly black with a broadening ochreous-yellow band along maxilla, ochreous-yellow base and 'teeth'. Iris white. Bare skin around eye bluish grey. Head chestnut, cap black in some forms. Chest black. One red cummerbund across yellow underparts. Chestnut leggings. Voice like scraping glass – high-pitched *tcheeeecheeek* jarring on the teeth. Rainforest, gallery and varzea forest, clearings, savannah, secondary growth, plantations.

2   BLACK-NECKED ARAÇARI *Pteroglossus aracari* 46cm
Maxilla and base of bill ivory; mandible, culmen and sub-basal line black. Skin around eye bluish grey. Hood bluish black (auricular chestnut in one race). One red cummerbund across yellow underparts. A tinkling high-pitched 2-syllable *biditz*. Rainforests, gallery forests, open woods, edges, scattered trees.

3   RED-NECKED ARAÇARI *Pteroglossus bitorquatus* 37cm
Bill: maxilla chrome-yellow, mandible black with white at the base, or entirely black (one race), or almost all white with black at the tip (another race); line of black along cutting edge. Bare skin around eye red, eye-ring blue. Head black. Back of the neck, upper back and breast dark red. Pectoral collar and rest of underparts yellow. Call: *wheat, wheat.* Rainforest, gallery forest and edges, scattered trees.

4   GREEN ARAÇARI *Pteroglossus viridis* 37cm
Sexes differ. Base of the bill reddish, wide culmen yellowish ochre, sides chestnut; mandible black; serrated white line along cutting edge. Bare skin around eye red and blue. Hood black (♂), dark chestnut (♀). Both sexes have lemon-yellow underparts. Call is a rattled *ticker, ticker, ticker….* Rainforests and gallery forests.

5   LETTERED ARAÇARI
Pteroglossus inscriptus 34cm (E race) and 44cm (W race)
Sexes differ. The small E, lowland race: yellowish-ivory bill with irregular blackish 'teeth' along cutting edge. Culmen, tip, below and sub-basal line black. Base yellowish ivory. Bare skin around eye pale blue with a red spot behind the eye. Hood black, ♀ with chestnut cheeks and fore-neck. Underparts all lemon-yellow. Call like a large kingfisher's explosive rattle and *tarack, rack-ack.* The large W, mountain form is considered another species by some (*P. humboldti*) and differs only in its size and an all-black mandible (5R).

2

1

3R

5♀

3

4♀

5♂

5R♂

5R♀

4♂

RODRÍGUEZ MATA

ARAÇARIS AND TOUCANETS (RAMPHASTIDAE)

1 COLLARED ARAÇARI *Pteroglossus torquatus*   43cm
Bill: ivory maxilla with chestnut wash near base, blackish culmen and 'teeth',
black mandible, white line at base. Bare skin around eye red, eye-ring blue.
Hood black. Hind-collar chestnut. Underparts yellow with red flecking, black
chest spot and cummerbund, both edged red. Call is a high-pitched, sneezy
kiyik. Rainforest and edge, secondary growth, open forest and scattered trees.
May be conspecific with 2 and 3. The race *P. t. frantzii* may be a separate
species: Fiery-billed Araçari.

2 STRIPE-BILLED ARAÇARI *Pteroglossus sanguineus*   43cm
Very like 1 but has black stripe on maxilla, bare skin around eye is mostly blue
and it lacks collar. Call and habitat similar to those of 1.

3 PALE-MANDIBLED ARAÇARI *Pteroglossus erythropygius*   45cm
Bill: mostly ivory with black stripe along cutting edge of maxilla, black and
blue tip of mandible, red sub-basal patch, thin white line at base. Bare skin
around red eye, eye-ring blue. Hood black. Underparts yellow with red
flecking, black chest spot and cummerbund. Extensive red lower back, rump
and upper tail coverts. Rainforest, edges, scattered trees. Some consider this a
form of 2, above.

4 MANY-BANDED ARAÇARI *Pteroglossus pluricinctus*   44cm
Bill: ivory maxilla with black on culmen and sub-basally, reddish tip, black
mandible; ivory line at base. Bare skin around eye bright blue. Hood black. 2
black bands across yellow underparts, flecked with red. Voice like scraping
glass, a jarring screech; also a high *pitchew*. Rainforest, varzea.

5 IVORY-BILLED ARAÇARI *Pteroglossus azara*   38cm
Bill ivory with variable reddish chestnut on mandible (some races) or maxilla
(others); notable 'teeth'. Bare skin around eye red and blue. Hood dark
chestnut, ♂ with even darker cap. Red chest. Black breast and upper belly,
lower belly yellow. Calls include a sharp *kissick* and a rattled, croaked *co..ark...
cro..ark...* about 1 per sec. Rainforests, edges, gallery forest, copses,
plantations. A race with a chestnut mandible is considered a separate species
by some, *P. mariae*.

6 CURL-CRESTED ARAÇARI *Pteroglossus beauharnaesii*   44cm
Multicoloured bill with chestnut, turquoise, ivory, white and ochre tip. Bare
skin around eye pale blue. Curly cap-feathers black. Cheeks and throat whitish
yellow speckled black. Breast and rest of underparts yellow with wide red and
black cummerbund. Voice is a loud and gruff, low-pitched, *rreeep* and *rree-
rreee-rreee*. Tropical rainforest, gallery forest, edge.

7 SAFFRON TOUCANET *Baillonius bailloni*   37cm
Unpatterned. Bill greenish yellow with chestnut-red at base. Bare skin around
eye pinkish orange. Eye pale. Upperparts pale olive-green; rump red.
Underparts greenish yellow with olive wash. Call is a whistled *gwee...gwee*;
also quiet sneezed *spitz...spitz*. Rainforests in lowland and rolling hills.

RODRIGUEZ MATA

TOUCANS (RAMPHASTIDAE)

Mountain-toucans live in montane forests. They all have bluish on the underparts and brownish-olive backs, black cap and red undertail coverts.

1 PLATE-BILLED MOUNTAIN-TOUCAN *Andigena laminirostris*   48cm
Bill black with red basal half and buffy-white rectangle near base. Bare face yellow and green. Rump yellow, patch on flanks ochre-yellow. Active and vocal. Voice a series of nasal *waaahs*, each note rising. Montane rainforest with many bromeliads and mosses.

2 GREY-BREASTED MOUNTAIN-TOUCAN *Andigena hypoglauca*   48cm
Bill: culmen red, basally yellow with black transverse band. Bare skin around eye black. Greyish blue hind-collar. Yellow rump. Voice at dawn and dusk a series of rising catlike *yaaaahs*, or repeated *eeeeeeks*. Rainforest and cloud-forest with bromeliads and mosses, woods up to near tree line and in epiphyte-free *Cecropia*.

3 HOODED MOUNTAIN-TOUCAN *Andigena cucullata*   48cm
Bill yellow (or greenish), black tip and spot at base of mandible. Bare face blue. Hood black. Hind-collar greyish-blue. Rump and upper tail coverts olive-green. Voice a series of nasal *was*, irregular *ke.. keke… ke…* and whining *ueeeee*. Shy. Montane cloud-forest with many epiphytes.

4 BLACK-BILLED MOUNTAIN-TOUCAN *Andigena nigrirostris*   51cm
Bill black. Bare face pale blue and yellow. (Other races have deep red at the base of the bill or only of maxilla; face salmon-pink and pale blue.) Throat, cheeks and part of neck white. Rump yellow. Voice a scraping, nasal *too-aaat* rising. In epiphyte-loaded cloud-forest, rainforest, scattered trees.

Ramphastos toucans are the largest of the family. Their plumage is mostly black, contrasting with white, yellow or orange on throat, part of the neck and breast. All have red undertail coverts. Huge bills. There are 2 groups: smaller species with relatively smaller bills that have a runnel along the side of the upper mandible and different vocalisations; larger species with huge, smooth bills. Many hybrids have been recorded as well as gradations between species. There is much work to be done on their taxonomy.

5 KEEL-BILLED TOUCAN *Ramphastos sulphuratus*   49cm
Bill green and yellowish with a red tip and orange stripe on the side. Blackish 'teeth' on cutting edge. Bare face greenish and yellowish. Cheeks down to breast bright yellow. Rump white. Voice a series of hoarse croaks or grunts. Rainforest, partly deforested areas, forestry plantations, dry, stunted coastal woods.

6 YELLOW-BREASTED TOUCAN *Ramphastos ambiguus*   58cm
Huge bill black with broadly yellow culmen, which, seen from in front, is rounded, like an inverted 'U'. Bare face pale blue. Cheeks to breast bright yellow, narrowly edged white and red below. Upper tail coverts white. Another race (*R. a. swainsoni*) differs in that the bill has chestnut instead of black, and is considered by some a separate species: Chestnut-mandibled Toucan. Voice yelping *kyoss today today* repeated at short intervals. Rainforest and cloud-forest, lower montane forest, mostly in the highest branches.

7 CHOCO TOUCAN *Ramphastos brevis*   54cm
A smaller version of black-billed race of 6, with which it is largely sympatric. Bill relatively shorter (though this varies between individuals), but all have a higher arched culmen, which, seen from in front, is sharp, like an inverted 'V'. Call: croaking grunts in series. Rainforest.

6R

7

6

5

4

R

3

1

2

RODRÍGUEZ MATA

TOUCANS (RAMPHASTIDAE)

1 RED-BREASTED TOUCAN *Ramphastos dicolorus* 45cm
Yellow bill with greenish wash, slightly 'toothed'; black base. Face salmon-pink and yellow. Pale eye. Cheeks and throat yellow, fore-neck orange. Chest-band yellow, rest of underparts and rump red. Voice: harsh tenor croaks, *yehhhks* repeated. Rainforests and edges, on plains and in rolling hills.

2 CHANNEL-BILLED TOUCAN *Ramphastos vitellinus* 46cm
Various races. Black bill, with blue base of the bill (nominal race), blue bare skin around eye, white cheeks and yellow breast. Broad chest-band, under tail coverts and upper tail coverts red. Others have bill yellow at base, bare skin around eye orange and paler orange on cheeks, throat and breast. Grunting bi-syllabic *yah*, *eah*. Rainforest, edges, scattered trees, gallery forest, forestry plantations.

3 CITRON-THROATED TOUCAN *Ramphastos citreolaemus* 50cm
Bill blackish purple, tip and culmen yellow, basally yellow and pale blue bands. Skin around the eye pale blue. Cheeks and fore-neck white, with yellow wash on upper breast. Pectoral collar red. Upper tail coverts pale yellow. Call is a series of frog-like *creeop* croaks at 1 per sec. Rainforests and edges. For some, a race of 2.

4 YELLOW-RIDGED TOUCAN *Ramphastos culminatus* 47cm
Virtually the same as 3 with narrower yellow base only on the maxilla, pale blue only on the mandible; also yellow-orange upper tail coverts. Intermediates exist through hybridisation with several other species. Behaviour and call same as those of 3. Rainforests, edges, scattered trees and occasionally savannah. For some, also a race of 2.

5 CUVIER'S TOUCAN *Ramphastos cuvieri* 58cm
A large version of 3 and 4 with a proportionally longer and heavier bill. Upper tail coverts yellowish orange. Yelping call. Rainforest, scattered trees, edge of forest, gallery forest. This species is considered by some to be a race of 6.

6 WHITE-THROATED TOUCAN *Ramphastos tucanus* 58cm
Differs from 5 in having the blackish-purple part of the bill dark chestnut or orangy chestnut, in either case with a black sub-basal band. Upper tail coverts yellow. There are many intermediate plumages. Voice: a loud series of rhythmic, whistled yelps. Rainforests, edges and scattered trees.

7 TOCO TOUCAN *Ramphastos toco* 59cm
Bill orangy yellow with a black base and a black spot at the tip; faint orange 'teeth'. Bare skin around eye orangy pink, eye-ring blue. Cheeks and bib white as are the upper tail coverts. Call is a deep, raucous croaking *aaaarks*. Rainforests, open areas with scattered trees, plantations, gardens.

2R

2

7

7

1

6R

6

3

6R

5

4

5

RODRÍGUEZ MATA

PICULETS (PICIDAE)

Piculets are tiny wren-sized woodpeckers, energetically active and unafraid on slender branches and twigs. They can best be located by their continuous Morse-like tip-tapping as they work. Very acrobatic, and sometimes even hang from twigs. High-pitched calls. Sexes differ.

1 CHESTNUT PICULET *Picumnus cinnamomeus*   10cm
Overall reddish chestnut. Forehead and lores white. Pink eye-ring and legs. Cap black speckled yellow and white (♀ speckled only white on hind-crown). A dark race is very dark chestnut with pinky-buff forehead. Rainforest and deciduous forest, scattered trees, arid scrubby areas, woods, mangroves.

2 RUFOUS-BREASTED PICULET *Picumnus rufiventris*   10cm
Reddish chestnut with olive-brown back. Front part of cap dotted red, hind-part spotted white. ♀ lacks red. Eye-ring grey. Terra firme forest and varzea, woods, secondary growth, scattered trees, clearings, bushes and thickets, climbers and creepers, cane-brakes.

3 TAWNY PICULET *Picumnus fulvescens*   10cm
Tawny underparts with faint whitish streaks. Cheeks, hind-neck and upperparts brown. Front part of cap dotted red, white spots behind (♀ lacks red). Atlantic forest, secondary thickets, palm groves, caatinga.

4 RUSTY-NECKED PICULET *Picumnus fuscus*   9.5cm
Underparts tawny buff, slightly scaled, paler centrally and on undertail coverts. Cap black with red dots on crown, no white (uniformly black in ♀). Eye-ring and legs salmon-pink. Lowland riverine forest, varzea. Locally in El Beni, Guaporé watershed (NE Bolivia), and WC Brazil (western Mato Grosso).

5 OCHRACEOUS PICULET *Picumnus limae*   9cm
Underparts greyish buff slightly streaked paler on throat and breast. Cap dotted red before, spotted white behind (all spotted white in ♀). Back greyish brown. Call is a thin, high *seeer, seeer* like a hummingbird's. Semi-deciduous forest, caatinga, in bushes, thickets and stunted trees, canes. Locally NE Brazil (NC Ceará).

6 PLAIN-BREASTED PICULET *Picumnus castelnau*   9.5cm
Underparts dirty whitish, upperparts olivaceous brown. Eye-ring pinkish. Hind-neck barred whitish and blackish. Black cap, fore-part dotted red in ♂, plain black in ♀, no white in either. Varzea, low islands, swampy forest, secondary growth, bushes and thickets.

7 FINE-BARRED PICULET *Picumnus subtilis*   9.5cm
Like 6. Underparts dirty whitish faintly barred greyish on sides of breast. Slight barring on hind-neck. White spotting on hind-cap, red on front part of cap (all white spotting in ♀). Humid tropical forest, lowlands to foothills. May be a race of 6.

8 WHITE-BELLIED PICULET *Picumnus spilogaster*   9cm
Dirty white underparts, slightly scaled on sides of breast and flanks (absent in one form), whitish face, brownish ear coverts. Olivaceous-brown upperparts. Black cap with dense red dotting on fore-crown, spotted white on hind-crown (no red in ♀). Rainforest, gallery forest, deciduous forest, bushes, thickets, scattered trees, mangroves.

9 GREYISH PICULET *Picumnus granadensis*   9cm
Dirty white underparts with very faint darker streaking (absent in one form). Sides of breast brownish. Upperparts and ear coverts olivaceous brown. Cap has small yellow dots on front part, white dots behind (all white dots in ♀). Deciduous forest, rainforest edge, secondary growth, bushes and thickets, open woods.

1R♂ 4♀ 4♂ 1♀ 1♂ 5♀ 5♂ 3♂ 3♀ 2♀ 2♂ 8♀ 6♀ 8♂ 9♀ 6♂ 7♀ 9♂ 7♂

RODRIGUEZ MATA

PICULETS (PICIDAE)

1 OLIVACEOUS PICULET *Picumnus olivaceus*   9cm
Back and pectoral collar olive-brown. Cheeks, hind-neck and throat
cinnamon-buff scaled brown. Underparts yellowish cream streaked blackish
brown. Cap has fine red streaking on fore-crown, spotted white behind (♀
lacks red). Foothills to higher elevations; rainforest, cloud-forest, open woods,
deciduous forest, edge, bushes and thickets, cultivated land.

2 MOTTLED PICULET *Picumnus nebulosus*   10cm
Ear coverts and pectoral collar tawny brown, back brown. Malar region and
throat whitish barred blackish. Underparts tawny buff, heavily streaked black.
Red streaks and white spots on cap (♀ lacks red). Woods, copses, savannah,
edge, bushes, thickets, cane-brakes.

3 VARZEA PICULET *Picumnus varzeae*   10cm
Overall chestnut-brown scaled blackish and whitish on cheeks, throat, neck,
breast and flanks, fainter on mid-belly and undertail coverts. Black cap, fore-
part heavily dotted red, tiny white spots behind (♀ lacks red). Varzea forest,
forest on river islands, bushes and thickets.

4 SPOTTED PICULET *Picumnus pygmaeus*   10cm
Overall chestnut-brown with all neck and underpart feathers tipped black and
white like little arrow-points. Dorsal markings more scaly. Cap black streaked
red, finely spotted white behind (♀ lacks red). Dry, open woods, caatinga,
thickets.

5 GUTTATE PICULET *Picumnus guttifer*   10cm
A version of 6 with whiter and blacker markings, more contrasting, on
underparts. Considered a race of 7. Forest and edge, bushes and thickets,
gallery forest, dry cerrado woods, savannah.

6 GUIANAN PICULET *Picumnus minutissimus*   10cm
Dorsally brown, feathers bordered buffy whitish. Underparts white, feathers
finely edged blackish, giving a scaly effect. Black cap with red streaking on fore-
part, spotted white behind; ♀ lacks red. Secondary forest, vegetation near rivers
and lagoons, plantations, montane forest, mangroves. May include 5 and 7.

7 WHITE-WEDGED PICULET *Picumnus albosquamatus*   10cm
Like 5 and 6 above but belly buffier, and breast whiter with feathers edged
black, leaving white wedges, and below edged brown, giving a scaly effect. Cap
as in most other species, with red dots and white spots on black ground (♀
lacks red). Forest, gallery forest, edge, thickets, bush, savannah. May be a race
of 6, close to 5.

8 SCALED PICULET *Picumnus squamulatus*   9cm
Underparts white, feathers edged blackish, giving a scaly effect. Upperparts
brownish olive, feathers edged darker. Black cap with very fine red streaks, rest
spotted white (♀ lacks red). Gallery forest, edge, secondary growth, deciduous
woods, scattered trees, bushes, thickets.

RODRIGUEZ MATA

PICULETS (PICIDAE)

1 OCELLATED PICULET *Picumnus dorbygnianus* 9cm
Underparts whitish with black markings, arrow-pointed on breast. Cap black with red dots and white spotting (♀ lacks red). Humid montane forest, transition forest, tropical and subtropical regions.

2 WHITE-BARRED PICULET *Picumnus cirratus* 9cm
Face and all underparts barred blackish and white. Cap black with red dots dense to the point of a patch, white spots behind; uniform and browner ear coverts. One race has red dots (red lacking in both ♀), ear-patch barred. Woods, transition to arid zones in low mountains and lowlands, copses, scattered trees, gallery forest, savannah, bushes and thickets.

3 OCHRE-COLLARED PICULET *Picumnus temminckii* 9cm
Face and hind-neck ochre. All underparts white barred black. Cap black, red dots on fore-part, white spots behind (♀ lacks red). Humid forest, edge, tall canes and thickets, regrowth.

4 SPECKLE-CHESTED PICULET *Picumnus steindachneri* 8.5cm
Breast and upper belly black with white drip-shaped spots. Rest of underparts barred. Black cap with red dots and white spots behind (♀ lacks red). Rainforest in mountains, tropical and subtropical regions, bushes and thickets, cane-brakes. NC Peru, Huallaga river.

5 ECUADORIAN PICULET *Picumnus sclateri* 9cm
Throat and breast barred, belly streaked, undertail barred, all black on white and contrasting. Black cap with short yellow streaks on forehead, rest spotted white (♀ lacks yellow). There is a paler, less contrasted race. Woods and edges, scrub with cactus, bushes and thickets in tropical and subtropical arid regions, more humid montane forest.

6 ORINOCO PICULET *Picumnus pumilus* 9cm
Yellowish-white underparts all barred blackish brown. Upperparts olivaceous brown barred tawny. Dark chocolate-brown cap with tiny yellow dots before and tiny white spots behind (♀ lacks yellow dots). Humid forest, edge of gallery forest, dense thickets, savannah. Some think this a race of 7.

7 LAFRESNAYE'S PICULET *Picumnus lafresnayi* 9cm
Very like 6 but forehead dotted red and upperparts more noticeably barred. Very humid rainforest, secondary growth, clearings, thickets. Very closely related to 6.

8 GOLDEN-FRONTED PICULET *Picumnus aurifrons* 8cm
Underparts yellowish white barred blackish on chest, streaked blackish below. Upperparts olivaceous brown, barred and scaled yellowish. Cap very dark chocolate with yellow dots in front, white spots behind (♀ lacks yellow). Rainforest, varzea and terra firme forest, copses, bushes and thickets.

9 BAR-BREASTED PICULET *Picumnus borbae* 8.5cm
Like 8 but red dots on cap and faint markings on upperparts. Face and throat whitish. Rainforest, bushes and thickets, tropical forest. Some believe this to be a race of 8.

10 GOLDEN-SPANGLED PICULET *Picumnus exilis* 9cm
Face whitish all finely barred blackish. Underparts yellowish barred black. Feathers of upperparts spangle-tipped black and yellow. Cap black, red dots in front, white spots behind (♀ lacks red). Rainforest, cloud-forest, savannah, open woods, mangroves, dense riverine vegetation with cane, regrowth.

11 BLACK-DOTTED PICULET *Picumnus nigropunctatus* 9cm
Very like 10 but lower breast and belly dotted black. Humid lowland tropical forest, varzea, terra firme forest, secondary growth, bushes and thickets, woodland. May be a race of 10. Amacuro Delta, Orinoco river, Venezuela.

FLICKERS AND WOODPECKERS (PICIDAE)

Flickers are mostly barred on upperparts, spotted on underparts. All have a white or whitish lower back seen in flight. They frequent more open country than other woodpeckers, including treeless landscapes, and are often active on the ground.

1 CHILEAN FLICKER *Colaptes pitius*   30cm
Generally barred blackish and whitish except grey cap, malar stipe flecked blackish, rest of face and throat greyish ivory. ♀: no malar stripe. Call is sharp, high-pitched *pitee-you*. Cool temperate S beech woods and ecotone, bushes, open fields in Patagonian Andes.

2 CAMPO FLICKER *Colaptes campestris*   31cm
Black cap and throat, malar region flecked crimson. Fore-face creamy white, hind-face, neck and breast yellow. Rest of upperparts barred black and whitish, underparts more finely barred blackish and whitish. ♀: no red on malar region. S form has whitish throat, the ♀ with black flecking in malar region. Open country, isolated trees, copses, palm groves, stony ground in hilly regions, cleared areas in forest, woodland edge, roadsides. The whitish-throated race (Field Flicker C. c. campestroides) was once considered a separate species.

3 ANDEAN FLICKER *Colaptes rupicola*   32cm
Long bill. Cap grey. Malar stripe red, somewhat streaked dark. Rest creamy, upperparts heavily barred black, underparts spotted black, especially on breast. ♀: blackish-grey malar stripe. Other races are warm cream, or ochre, barred on breast. Treeless upland steppe in puna, paramo scrub.

The following 3 species are sometimes referred to as 'forest flickers' and may compose a separate genus (*Chrysoptilus*).

4 GREEN-BARRED WOODPECKER *Colaptes melanochloros*   27cm
Mostly yellowish green barred black on upperparts, spotted black on underparts. Forehead and crown black, nape and malar streak red. Face whitish cream. Throat streaked blackish. ♀: blackish-streaked malar stripe. S race generally less greenish with golden yellow on breast and upper belly, pale yellow on rest of underparts. Some consider these to be separate species Golden-breasted Woodpecker C. *melanolaimus*. Edge of woods and forest, open country with trees, clearings, arid woods, scrub, cane-brakes, savannah, caatinga, palm groves, plantations, plains, mountains.

5 BLACK-NECKED WOODPECKER *Colaptes atricollis*   26cm
Forehead and fore-crown slate-grey. Nape, hind-neck and malar region red. Face creamy white. Throat, fore-neck and breast black. Upperparts olive barred blackish, underparts whitish barred blackish. ♀: black malar region. Semiarid woods and cloud-forest, riverside vegetation, irrigated areas, shrubby slopes, scattered bushes, plantations, gardens.

6 SPOT-BREASTED WOODPECKER *Colaptes punctigula*   23cm
Forehead and crown black, nape and malar region red. Face creamy white. Throat white finely dotted black. Upperparts olive scaled and barred black. Rest of underparts all spotted black on strong olivaceous yellow, breast washed redder. ♀: black malar region. Gallery forest, rainforest, varzea, deciduous forest, open woods, edge, deforested areas, bushes and thickets, mangroves, palm groves, savannah, cultivated areas.

1♂ 1♀ 2♂ 2R♂ 2♀ R♂ 5♀ 5♂ 6♀ 6♂ 3R♂ 3♀ 4R♀ 4♂ 4♀ 3♂

RODRÍGUEZ MATA

WOODPECKERS (PICIDAE)

Melanerpes woodpeckers are small to medium-sized with contrasting colours, combining black with lighter hues – including white, red and yellow. Most are very noisy, active, operating at all levels, singly, in pairs or family groups. Sexes differ. All have black bill. Nearly all have white lower back and rump.

1 ACORN WOODPECKER *Melanerpes formicivorus*   21cm
Mask and area at base of bill black. Forehead, line before the eye and bib yellow. Nape red. Back, wings, tail and breast black. Rest of underparts white, partly streaked black. Edge of forest, open woods, deforested areas, scattered trees, especially oaks.

2 RED-CROWNED WOODPECKER *Melanerpes rubricapillus*   18cm
Crown, nape and hind-neck red. Forehead yellowish. Rest of the head and underparts plain olive-buff. Central belly red. Upperparts and tail barred whitish and black. ♀: red on hind-neck only. Gallery forest, arid woods, thorny scrub with cactus, bushes and thickets, secondary growth, mangroves, scattered trees, gardens.

3 BLACK-CHEEKED WOODPECKER *Melanerpes pucherani*   19cm
Crown, nape and belly-patch red. Mask (with fine white brow) and rest of upperparts black, finely barred white on back and flight feathers. Forehead, lower face and rest of underparts olive-buff, barred black on breast, belly, flanks and undertail coverts. ♀: black hind-crown, red only on nape. Humid forest, edge, rainforest, secondary growth, scattered trees.

4 GOLDEN-NAPED WOODPECKER *Melanerpes chrysauchen*   19cm
Crown, nape and mid-belly red, narrow hind-collar golden. Mask black. Rest of upperparts black but white line down back. Forehead, lower face and rest of underparts olive-buff barred black on breast, belly, flanks and undertail coverts. ♀: black crown, red only on nape. Resonant *churr*. Humid forest, secondary growth, edge.

5 YELLOW-FRONTED WOODPECKER *Melanerpes flavifrons*   19cm
Crown, nape, hind-neck and lower half of breast red. Mask and rest of upperparts black. Forehead, lower face and fore-neck bright yellow. Upper breast and flanks pale olive-grey, these barred black. ♀: black crown and nape. Humid forest, gallery forest, edge, palm groves, secondary vegetation.

6 YELLOW-TUFTED WOODPECKER *Melanerpes cruentatus*   19cm
Mostly black. Fore-crown and belly red. Brow yellow ending in golden nape. Eye-ring yellow. Flanks and undertail coverts whitish barred black. Back white. ♀ lacks red on crown. One form (Red-fronted Woodpecker M. *c. rubrifrons*) lacks yellow brow and nape. Call is a double *wrack-up*. Edge of and clearings in rainforest, secondary growth, scattered trees, gardens.

7 WHITE-FRONTED WOODPECKER *Melanerpes cactorum*   18cm
Black mask, line down side of neck and back. White forehead and malar stripe. Mid-crown red. Neck, breast and rest of underparts buffy grey barred blackish lower down. Whitish-grey line from nape to mid-back. Rest of upperparts, upper tail coverts and tail barred black and white. ♀ lacks red on crown. Calls *weep-weep* and *wee-beep*. Thorny woods, scrub, cactus, palm groves.

1♂ 1♀ 3♂ 3♀ 2♀ 6R♂ 6R♀ 6♀ 2♂ 4♀ 4♂ 5♂ 7♂ 7♀ 5♀ 6♂

RODRIGUEZ MATA

WOODPECKERS (PICIDAE)

1 WHITE WOODPECKER *Melanerpes (Leuconerpes) candidus*   24cm
Mostly white. Post-ocular streak, upperparts and tail black. Nape and mid-belly yellow (♂) or white (♀). Very loud and noisy *wheerrrr…keeerrr*. In pairs and family groups. Open woods, savannah, palm groves, scattered trees, edge of woods, copses, plantations.

Piculus woodpeckers are medium sized, all but one with olive upperparts, and scaled or barred underparts; heads have bold patterns and colours, always with red. Singly, in pairs or family groups they frequent trees at mid- to upper levels.

2 YELLOW-THROATED WOODPECKER *Piculus flavigula*   18–23cm
Forehead, crown, nape and malar region red, face and throat golden yellow. Upperparts olive, underparts whitish scaled olive. ♀: forehead and crown olive, malar region yellow. One race has an all-red throat, another lacks red malar stripe. Infrequent hissed *queer* or *shreer*, sometimes doubled. Humid tropical forest, terra firme forest, gallery forest, edge, caatinga.

3 LITA WOODPECKER *Piculus litae*   18cm
As 2 but black throat and brown flight feathers. ♀: yellow forehead and crown. Formerly thought a form of 2. Humid forest, edge, secondary growth, in lowlands and foothills.

4 GOLDEN-OLIVE WOODPECKER *Piculus rubiginosus*   23cm
Forehead and crown grey. Nape and malar stripe red. Face ivory-white, slightly barred on hind-cheeks. Throat finely speckled white on blackish. Rest of underparts greenish yellow barred blackish. Upperparts golden olive. ♀: no red malar stripe. One race has red forehead and crown as well as nape. Montane and cloud-forest, clearings, secondary growth, open woods, lowland forest, deltas, edge, scattered trees.

5 GOLDEN-GREEN WOODPECKER *Piculus chrysochloros*   22cm
Cap and malar region red. Mask and lower malar region olive. Throat and line though face yellow. Upperparts olive. Underparts golden yellow barred olive. ♀ has no red. One race has olive malar region and barred throat. Woods, savannah, humid terra firme forest, varzea, gallery forest, edge, deciduous woods, xerophytic vegetation, scattered trees.

6 YELLOW-BROWED WOODPECKER *Piculus aurulentus*   21cm
Forehead, crown, nape and malar streak red. Mask and lower malar region olive. 2 yellow lines on face. Throat yellow. Underparts yellowish barred olive. Upperparts olive. ♀: forehead and crown olive, red only on nape. Transition woods and forest in hills and plains.

7 WHITE-THROATED WOODPECKER *Piculus leucolaemus*   20cm
Cap and malar area red. Golden line through face. Lores and upper cheek ochreous olive. ♀: forehead and crown olive. Throat whitish faintly speckled olive. Underparts olive with whitish markings: fore-neck streaked, breast with drip-shaped spots, belly barred and undertail scaled. Upperparts olive. Gallery forest, humid forest in foothills, plains.

8 CRIMSON-MANTLED WOODPECKER *Piculus rivolii*   28cm
Large. Notably crimson. Yellowish-ivory face, black throat. Breast scaled crimson and black, rest of underparts yellow with markings on flanks. ♀: forehead, fore-crown and malar region black. Flicker-like calls. Humid montane forest, cloud-forest, dwarf forest, gnarled trees and bushes at paramo line.

WOODPECKERS (PICIDAE)

Woodpeckers of the genus *Veniliornis* are small. Most are olive on upperparts, and have pale underparts with barring.

1 LITTLE WOODPECKER *Veniliornis passerinus*   15cm
Cap red, spotted grey on forehead. Face buffy brown. Throat and rest of underparts barred whitish and blackish grey. Upperparts olive with faint barring; pale spotting on wing coverts. ♀: cap grey flecked white. In other races ♂ has forehead and crown greyish, or brow and narrow malar stripe white. Gallery and terra firme forest, cloud-forest, varzea, savannah, deciduous woods, secondary growth.

2 RED-RUMPED WOODPECKER *Veniliornis kirkii*   16cm
Red cap, upper tail coverts and rump. Hind-neck golden yellow. Brownish-grey face slightly streaked. Throat whitish. Underparts whitish barred blackish grey. Upperparts plain golden olive. ♀: forehead and crown brownish, somewhat finely scaled. Gallery forest, rainforest, secondary growth, scattered trees, mangroves, deciduous woods, savannah, thorny vegetation, plantations.

3 YELLOW-EARED WOODPECKER *Veniliornis maculifrons*   17cm
Narrow forehead cinnamon, rest and fore-crown blackish flecked white. Rest of the crown and nape red, slightly mottled. Hind-neck yellow. Cheeks streaked whitish and blackish. All underparts whitish barred blackish grey. Upperparts dark olive, with sparse yellowish streaking on back and white dots on upper wing coverts. ♀: no red on crown, nape yellow. Forest, secondary growth, parks and gardens, montane forest.

4 DOT-FRONTED WOODPECKER *Veniliornis frontalis*   17cm
Forehead whitish, streaked grey. Crown, nape and hind-neck red, speckled dark (♀ lacks red). Whitish cheeks faintly streaked brown. All underparts densely barred blackish and whitish. Upperparts dark olive, sparse yellow streaking on back, white dots on upper wing coverts. Montane and cloud-forest, transition woods, upland subtropical and temperate zone.

5 YELLOW-VENTED WOODPECKER *Veniliornis dignus*   18cm
Forehead and throat blackish. Crown, nape and hind-neck red (♀: forehead, crown and nape grey); back has red markings. Face whitish with grey ear coverts. Underparts yellow with dark barring, grading to all-yellow undertail coverts. Montane forest and transition woods, subtropical and temperate zones.

6 GOLDEN-COLLARED WOODPECKER *Veniliornis cassini*   18cm
Blackish forehead and crown, this streaked red, nape redder. ♀: crown dotted yellow. Hind-neck yellow. Face greyish, ear coverts markedly streaked black. Underparts all densely and evenly barred blackish and whitish. Rainforest, clearings, open country with trees, shrubberies, lowlands. Considered by some to be a race of 7.

7 RED-STAINED WOODPECKER *Veniliornis affinis*   19cm
Forehead and crown black, slight red streaking. Nape and hind-neck red. Face dirty yellow, slightly streaked dark on cheeks. Underparts barred browny black and whitish. Sides of neck golden yellow. Upperparts olive, paler spotting on upper wing coverts. ♀: yellow hind-crown, nape and hind-neck (no red). One form has red forehead and crown, dirty buff face, yellower behind. Coverts tinted reddish. Humid forests, terra firme forest, varzea, secondary growth, edge, thickets.

1♀
2♀
2♂
3♂
1♂
3♀
6♀
5♀
4♀
4♂
5♂
6♂
7♀
7♂
7R♂

RODRIGUEZ MATA

WOODPECKERS (PICIDAE)

1 **WHITE-SPOTTED WOODPECKER** *Veniliornis spilogaster*   17cm
Dark and modest plumage. All dark blackish olive, mottled whitish below and
barred yellowish white above. Forehead, face and throat whitish, ear coverts
streaked black. Cap blackish, finely speckled red and white. ♀: blackish crown
speckled white. Humid forest and woods, riverine forest, isolated copses, open
woods, parkland, thorny trees.

2 **SCARLET-BACKED WOODPECKER** *Veniliornis callonotus*   14cm
Unmistakable. Scarlet upperparts. White underparts finely barred. Forehead
and crown streaked black, ear coverts dirty blackish. ♀: forehead, crown, nape
and hind-neck black. One race has tawny-brown auriculars and sides of the
neck, less streaking on cap. Dry deciduous forest, arid scrub, scattered trees,
cactus, dense waterside vegetation.

3 **BLOOD-COLOURED WOODPECKER** *Veniliornis sanguineus*   14cm
Unmistakable. Crown, nape, hind-neck, upperparts crimson. Face dark greyish
brown. Underparts dark greyish brown barred white. ♀: crown brownish grey
speckled white. Mangroves, swampy forest, coffee plantations, lowlands.

4 **SMOKY-BROWN WOODPECKER** *Veniliornis fumigatus*   16cm
Unmistakable. Crown and nape red. All the rest uniform, dark and modest
smoky brown. Face and undertail coverts paler. ♀: black forehead, crown and
nape. Humid montane forest, cloud-forest, woods, secondary growth, bushes,
thickets, coffee plantations.

5 **BAR-BELLIED WOODPECKER** *Veniliornis nigriceps*   18cm
Forehead, crown and nape red, streaked blackish. All smoky olive, barred
yellowish on underparts, lighter round eye, brushed reddish on back. ♀:
forehead and crown black. Humid montane forest, cloud-forest, clearings with
dense thickets and cane-brakes, temperate upland forest, stunted woods in
high mountains.

Picoides (*Dendrocopus*) woodpeckers are small, with black and white all over the
body. They are dumpy and large-headed. The sexes differ. Singly or in pairs, they
frequent the thinner branches and twigs in bushes and small trees.

6 **CHEQUERED WOODPECKER** *Picoides* (*Dendrocopus*) *mixtus*   15cm
Forehead, crown and nape black, the first two flecked white. Red marks on
either side of nape. White face, black ear-patch and malar stripe. Upperparts
spotted and barred black and white. Underparts white, streaked and scaled
black. ♀ lacks red on nape. Savannah, dry woods, riverine vegetation, trees
and thorny bushes, copses, palm groves.

7 **STRIPED WOODPECKER** *Picoides* (*Dendrocopus*) *lignarius*   18cm
Large version of 6 with red on all nape. S beech woods in Patagonian Andes,
edge, scattered trees in fields and slopes, gardens, plantations.

1♀

1♂

2♀

2♂

3♀

3♂

4♀

4♂

5♂

5♀

6♂

6♀

7♂

7♀

RODRIGUEZ MATA

WOODPECKERS (PICIDAE)

Celeus woodpeckers are relatively large to medium with remarkable bushy crests. Most are dominantly chestnut, some black and yellow, one buffy cream. Ivory or greyish-ivory bills. Singly or in pairs. Woods and forests, preferably in the denser, darker areas.

1 BLOND-CRESTED WOODPECKER *Celeus flavescens*   27cm
Dark form: head and prominent crest yellow but for red malar stripe and spot on forehead. Rest black scaled and barred yellow on upperparts. Rump and underwing yellow, flight feathers barred black and yellow. ♀: all-yellow head (sometimes malar stripe speckled blackish). Pale race: differs in having head tawny-ochre. Underparts blackish brown. Upperparts buffy ochre all marked and barred blackish brown There is a wide gradation between these 2 forms. Call a series of long-spaced *weep*s, also *wick*s. Humid forest and gallery forest, savannah, palm groves, secondary growth, edge, orchards.

2 PALE-CRESTED WOODPECKER *Celeus lugubris*   27cm
Brown race: big untidy bushy crest, warm ivory. Red malar area. Brown around eye. Fore-neck and rest of body brown, slightly scaled and barred ivory on top half of upperparts, wings barred chestnut. Rump and underwing warm ivory; flight feathers barred brown and dark ivory. ♀: malar region all brown. Blackish race: brown is replaced by dull blackish, and the ivory is 'dirty'. Calls *wee-wee-week*. Dense woods, patches, palm groves, savannah, open woods.

3 RUFOUS-HEADED WOODPECKER *Celeus spectabilis*   27cm
Head brownish chestnut, nuchal crest and malar region red. Breast and tail black, contrasting with rest of yellowish-ochre body, scaled and barred black. Flight feathers brownish chestnut. Underwing yellowish ochre. ♀ lacks red malar region. Calls *squeear* followed by *klooklookloo…*. Humid tropical forest, especially riverine forest, cane-brakes, *Cecropia* and *Heliconia* in lower storeys.

4 CREAM-COLOURED WOODPECKER *Celeus flavus*   26cm
Unmistakable. Nearly all tawny cream (or all cream in one race, or this with blackish markings on breast and upper back in another); red malar region. Wing coverts brown edged cream. Flight feathers chestnut and blackish chestnut. Underwing cream, tail blackish. ♀ lacks red malar region. Call loud *pweer pweer purr paw, kew, kew…* and *wheejah*. Humid forest, rainforest and varzea, all near water, mangroves, deciduous and open woods, secondary growth, plantations.

WOODPECKERS (PICIDAE)

1 CINNAMON WOODPECKER *Celeus loricatus* 22cm
Short-crested head cinnamon-chestnut, throat and malar region red.
Upperparts cinnamon-chestnut finely barred blackish. Underparts and tail
buffy cinnamon scalloped black. One race has no markings on upper- or
underparts. Flight feathers chestnutty cinnamon barred black. ♀ lacks red.
Loud call accelerating, descending *peee peeew pew poo puh*. Rainforest, humid
forest, secondary growth, clearings.

2 WAVED WOODPECKER *Celeus undatus* 20cm
Shortish crest, head and neck cinnamon streaked black (lacking in one race).
Part of cheek and malar region red. Upperparts rufous cinnamon, markedly
barred black. Underparts buffy cinnamon, densely scalloped black. Primary
flight feathers and tail-tip black. ♀ lacks red. Call is a loud *whick coer*. Dense
rainforest, edge, riverine forest, dryland forest.

3 SCALE-BREASTED WOODPECKER *Celeus grammicus* 21cm
Head chestnut, cheek and malar region red. Rest chestnut, finely barred and
scaled blackish, but lower belly, rump and upper tail coverts plain tawny
chestnut. Primary flight feathers and tail black. ♀ lacks red. Call a clear, sharp
curry-coo. Rainforest, humid forest and varzea, edge, secondary growth and
savannah with scattered trees. Closely related to 2.

4 RINGED WOODPECKER *Celeus torquatus* 27cm
Head buffy cinnamon, malar area red. Breast, upper belly, neck and upper back
black. Rest of underparts buffy cinnamon. Rump and upper tail coverts light
chestnut. Upperparts, wings and tail light chestnut, irregularly barred blackish.
In other races no black on upper back, underparts buffy (or white), barred and
scaled black. Tail, rump and upper tail coverts heavily barred black. ♀: no red
on face. Call is a series of 5 even-pitched *deeees*. Rainforest, gallery forest,
dryland forest, varzea, woods, tall secondary growth, clearings.

5 CHESTNUT WOODPECKER *Celeus elegans* 28cm
Mostly chestnut. Red malar region. Ochreous-yellow forehead, crown, crest
(this sometimes tawny) and hind-half of body. Upperparts with small yellowish
markings. Flight feathers faintly barred darker. Tail blackish. ♀ lacks red. Dark
form is dark chocolate-chestnut, lacking yellow on head. Part of flanks and
rump yellowish ochre. There is a whole gradation between the extremes. Call
is a descending *weewah ewewewewewewew* and mocking *ha hahahahaha*. Tall,
dense forest, gallery forest, varzea, edges, plantations. The dark form was
considered a separate species by some (*C. jumanus*).

1♀ 2♂ 2♀ 3♀ 3♂ 1♀ 1♂ 5R♀ 5R♂ 4♂ 4R♂ 5♂ 5♀ 4♀

RODRIGUEZ MATA

WOODPECKERS (PICIDAE)

Members of the genera *Dryocopus* and *Campephilus* are the largest in the family, and are basically black, white and red in patterns peculiar to each species. All have prominent crests. The sexes differ. They are found in woods and forests, on the larger trees and their boughs (preferably dead). The 'double-tac' drumming is characteristic of *Campephilus* and helps to locate them.

1   LINEATED WOODPECKER *Dryocopus lineatus*   33cm
Bill greyish-horn. Rounded crest and malar region red. Ear coverts grey. Chin and throat whitish flecked blackish. White line through face, down side of black neck, onto back (lacking in some individuals). Underparts whitish scaled blackish. Underwing and base of flight feathers white. ♀: black malar stripe. Call is a *wickwickwickwick* and *pickrrrr*. Humid, transition and fairly dry forest, rainforest, patchy forest, clearings and edge, gallery forest, thorn scrub, plantations, mangroves, gardens.

2   HELMETED WOODPECKER *Dryocopus galeatus*   31cm
Bill greyish-horn. Bushy rounded crest and malar region red. Lores, auricular and throat cinnamon, ear coverts finely barred blackish. Line on neck, lower back and rump white. Neck, upperparts and tail black. Underparts barred whitish and blackish. Underwing and base of flight feathers cinnamon. ♀: entirely cinnamon face. Call a series of up to 12 strident *keer* notes. Rainforest, gallery forest. Endangered.

3   BLACK-BODIED WOODPECKER *Dryocopus schulzi*   31cm
Bill greyish-horn. Conspicuous red crest and malar region. Ear-patch grey, chin and throat whitish grey. White line across face and down sides of neck. Body black. Underwing and base of flight feathers white. ♀: black malar region and forehead. Call *wick wick wick….* Unmodified dry Chaco woods.

4   CRIMSON-CRESTED WOODPECKER *Campephilus melanoleucos*   36cm
Bill bone-white. Head red. White at base of the bill, ear coverts black and white. Chin, throat, neck and breast black. White line down sides of neck, onto scapulars, forming a 'V'. Rest of upperparts, rump and tail black. Underwing and basal half of flight feathers white. ♀: white line through black cheeks. Fore-crown and fore-crest black. Call *queer queerer*. Cloud-forest, rainforest, gallery forest, deciduous forest open woodlands, savannah, secondary growth edges, semi-open country, palm groves, swampy areas, scattered trees.

5   CREAM-BACKED WOODPECKER *Campephilus leucopogon*   34cm
Bill ivory. Head and neck red. Ear-patch black and white. Back cream. Rest of the body black. Underwing buffy cinnamon, base of flight feathers cinnamon. ♀: black and white triangle through face, black forehead and fore-crest. Call *pee-aw* or *kwee-or*. Thorny woods, transition woods, savannah, palm groves, open woods, transition forest in mountains.

6   RED-NECKED WOODPECKER *Campephilus rubricollis*   34cm
Head, neck and breast red. Underparts, flight feathers and underwing chestnut. Upperparts black. ♀: white triangle bordered black through face. Call is explosive and nasal *nkaaah, kyah* and *kerra kerra*. Rainforest, terra firme forest and varzea, cloud-forest, edges, savannah, semi-open forest, riverine woods, light secondary growth.

2♂ 2♀ 1♀ 1♂ 3♀ 3♂ 6♂ 4♂ 4♀ 6♂ 5♀ 5♂ 6♀

ODRÍGUEZ MATA

WOODPECKERS (PICIDAE)

1   CRIMSON-BELLIED WOODPECKER *Campephilus haematogaster*   34cm
Bill black. Head with prominent red crest, face black and yellow with yellow post-ocular line. Throat and fore-neck black. Hind-neck, underparts and rump crimson. In one race the underparts are barred chestnut and blackish, washed carmine. Upperparts, wings and tail black. ♀: sides of neck yellow. Humid rainforest, edges, montane forests.

2   POWERFUL WOODPECKER *Campephilus pollens*   34cm
Bill black. Mask, throat and neck black, split by white line through face, down sides of neck and along scapulars to form a 'V'. Red crest, black in ♀. Upperparts and tail black. Central rump whitish. Underparts ochre, all barred blackish. Calls are nasal *kyaaah* and *peeyour*, often repeated, also *kikikikikaw*. Humid rainforest, cloud-forest, montane forest and edge.

3   ROBUST WOODPECKER *Campephilus robustus*   37cm
Bill ivory. Head and neck red. Black and white ear-spot. Buffy white along back, rump and upper tail coverts. Rest of upperparts black. Upper back, breast and belly barred whitish and blackish. Flight feathers cinnamon barred black. ♀: a black-bordered white triangle through face. Calls *pseew, keeew* perched or in flight. Humid forest, *Araucaria* woods, forest in hills, edges, cane-brakes.

4   GUAYAQUIL WOODPECKER *Campephilus gayaquilensis*   34cm
Greyish-ivory bill. Red head. Ear-spot black and white, throat and chin black. White line down sides of neck, onto scapulars to form a 'V'. Back and tail black, lower back barred whitish and blackish. ♀: wide white line through face. Underparts whitish barred blackish. Call *quick quickerrrrr*. Humid to dry deciduous forest, edge and secondary growth. Considered by some to be a race of Crimson-crested Woodpecker (*see* p.364, species 4).

5   MAGELLANIC WOODPECKER *Campephilus magellanicus*   43cm
The largest of the genus in S America. Bill black. Head and neck red. Crest tips forward. Rest black but for white tertial flight feathers, underwing and axillaries. ♀: black head with crimson at the base of the bill. Long, floppy, forward-curling crest. Call nasal *pisssaaah*. S beech woods and forest in S Andes.

RODRIGUEZ MATA

GLOSSARY

Araucaria – Primitive southern hemisphere pines with sharp scale-like 'needles' sheathing the branches, also known as Monkey-puzzles. Open woods of these species at elevations in S Brazil and NE Argentina.

Atlantic forest – Forest in SE Brazil, on coastal mountains and uplands, elevation descending westwards to NE Argentina and E Paraguay.

Caatinga – The sub-arid NE shoulder of Brazil, extending SW, mostly plateaus with a 7–8-month dry season, dominated by thorny vegetation, becoming green and grassy with the rains.

Cecropia – A small pioneer tree with huge palmate leaves and drooping, finger-like fruit much sought by birds and mammals.

Cerrado – Transition between Caatinga and Amazonia – savannah-like with many trees and palms.

Chaco – Region in NC Argentina, W Paraguay and E Bolivia dominated by thorny hardwood woodland, humid in the eastern reaches, dry in the west; summer rains.

Edge – The interface between two habitats as of woods or forest bordering on grassland or marsh. Transition areas where one gradually turns into another would be 'ecotone'.

Elphin woods – Composed of stunted and dwarf trees in wetter areas at the tree line.

Gallery forest – Dense tree vegetation in ribbon formation along watercourses and fringing lagoons, in grassland or forest (hard to identify in the last case), due to increased availability of water.

Heliconia – Plant of the banana family, with hanging flowering stems in a zig-zag distribution.

Lamellae – Filtering structures along the edge of bills of ducks and flamingos, composed of small parallel platelets.

Llanos – Seasonally flooded grasslands E of Andes in S Venezuela.

Neotropics – One of the natural regions of the world, with faunal characteristics unlike any other, corresponding to all S and C America as far as Mexico.

Pampas – A wide belt of humid grassland in EC Argentina.

Paramo – Wet Andean grasslands extending from tree line to upper limit of vegetation.

Patagonia – The region at the S tip of S America from about 40°S to Cape Horn. The E part is steppe, while woods and cool temperate forest cloak the mountains to the W.

Polylepis – Small tree growing in patches in sheltered nooks of high Andes.

Precocial – Said of chicks that leave the nest on hatching, such as ducklings or chickens.

Podocarp – Genus of short-leafed pines in upper cloud-forest and uplands.

Puna – Elevated Andean inter-montane desert plateaus of Peru, Bolivia and N Argentina.

Puya – A huge and strange bromeliad up to 10m tall in the dry Andes with a gigantic conical flowering head.

Tepuis – Isolated and scattered cliff-sided mesas or flat-topped mountains emerging from surrounding lowland forest to elevations of over 1,500m (5,000ft), forming 'islands' of speciation. SE Venezuela and Guianas.

Terra firme – Amazonian rainforest which is never flooded.

Varzea – Seasonally flooded Amazonian rainforest.

Xerophytic – Vegetation type found in dry areas; often thorny, from brushland to woods.

FURTHER READING

GENERAL

De La Peña, M.R. & Rumboll, M. (1998) *Birds of Southern South America and Antarctica.*
Collins Illustrated Checklist, Harper Collins, London.

Del Hoyo, J. *et al.* (1992 to 2004) *Handbook of the Birds of the World*, Vols I to IX.
Lynx Editions, Barcelona.

De Schauensee, R.M. (1966) *The Species of Birds of South America and Their Distribution.*
Livingston Publishing Company, Wynnwood, Pennsylvania.

De Schauensee, R.M. (1970) *A Guide to the Birds of South America.*
Academy of Sciences of Philadelphia, Philadelphia, Pennsylvania.

Dickinson, E.C. (ed.) (2003) *The Howard & Moore Checklist of the Birds of the World*, 3rd
edition. Princeton University Press, Princeton, New Jersey.

Dunning, J.S. (1982) *South American Land Birds.*
Harrowood Books, Pennsylvania.

Enticott, J. & Tipling, D. (2002) *Photographic Handbook of the Seabirds of the World.*
New Holland, London.

Fjeldsa, J. & Krabbe, N. (1990) *Birds of the High Andes.*
Apollo, Svendborg, Denmark.

Harrison, P. (1983) *Seabirds: an Identification Guide.*
Croom Helm, Beckenham, Kent.

Olrog, C.C. (1968) *Las Aves Sudamericanas, una Guía de Campo*, Tomo I.
Univ. Nac. de Tucumán, Instituto Miguel Lillo, Tucumán.

Ridgely, R. & Tudor, G. (1989–1994) *The Birds of South America*, Vols I & II – *Oscine
passerines and Sub-oscine passerines.*
University of Texas Press, Austin.

Wheatley, N. (2005) *Where to Watch Birds in South America*,
2nd edn. Christopher Helm, London.

REGIONAL

Arribas, M.A. *et al.* (1995) *Lista de las Aves de Bolivia.*
Asoc. Armonia, S.C.de la Sierra, Bolivia.

Aspiroz, A.B. (2001) *Aves del Uruguay.*
Aves Uruguay, Montevideo.

Canevari, M. *et al.* (1991) *Nueva Guía de las Aves Argentinas*, Vols I & II.
Fundación Acindar, Buenos Aires.

Clements, J.F. & Shany, N. (2001) *A Field Guide to the Birds of Peru.*
Lynx Editions, Barcelona.

Couve, E. & Vidal, C. (2003) *Birds of Patagonia, Tierra del Fuego, and Antarctic Peninsula*.
Fantastico Sur, Punta Arenas.

Dalgas Frisch, J. (1981) *Aves Brasileiras*.
Dalgas-Ecoltec Ecologia Tecnica e Comercio, Sao Paolo.

Fitter, J. *et al.* (2000) *Wildlife of the Galapagos: Safari Guide*.
Harper Collins Publishers, London.

Gore, M.E.J. & Gepp, A.R.M. (1978) *Las Aves del Uruguay*.
Mosca Hnos, Montevideo.

Harris, G. (1998) *A Guide to the Birds and Mammals of Coastal Patagonia*.
Princeton University Press, NJ.

Harris, M. (1974) *A Field Guide to the Birds of Galapagos*.
Collins, London.

Haverschmidt, F. (1968) *Birds of Surinam*.
Oliver & Boyd, Edinburgh and London.

Hayes, F.E. (1995) *Status, Distribution and Biogeography of the Birds of Paraguay*.
American Birding Association.

Hilty, S.L. (2000) *Field Guide to the Birds of Venezuela*.
Christopher Helm.

Hilty, S.L. & Brown, W.L. (1986) *A Guide to the Birds of Colombia*.
Princeton University Press, NJ.

Jaramillo, A. (2003) *Field Guide to the Birds of Chile*.
Christopher Helm & Princeton University Press, London and Princeton.

Mercado, N.K. (1985) *Aves de Bolivia*.
Edn. Gisbert & Cia., La Paz.

Narosky, T. & Izurieta, D. (2003) *Birds of Argentina and Uruguay*, 15th edn.
Vazquez Mazzini Editores, Buenos Aires.

Phelps, W.H. & De Schauensee, R.M. (1978) *A Guide to the Birds of Venezuela*.
Princeton University Press, NJ.

Ridgely, R. & Greenfield, P. (2001) *The Birds of Ecuador*, Vols I & II.
Comstock Publishing Associates, Ithaca, NY.

Shirihai, H. (2002) *A Complete Guide to Antarctic Wildlife*.
Alula Press & Princeton University Press, Finland & NJ.

Sick, H. (1985) *Ornitologia Brasileira, uma Introduçao*, Vols I & II.
Editora Universidade do Brasilia, Brasilia.

Swash, A. & Still, R. (2000) *Birds, Mammals and Reptiles of the Galapagos Islands*.
Pica Press & Wild Guides, East Sussex and Hampshire, UK.

INDEX